The Essential Humanities Reader
ᘓᙠ

The Essential Humanities Reader

☙❧

Edited by
Gerard P. NeCastro
Professor of English & Fine Arts
University of Maine at Machias

The Primavera Press
2013

DEDICATION

To the thousands of students
who have through their enthusiasm
inspired me to present for these many years
the finest works of art and literature
in the history of ideas known as
Introduction to Humanities.

With great appreciation to my family,
whose care and support has allowed me
to complete this collection.

With Special Thanks to Michael Hinden,
Professor of English and Integrated Liberal Studies,
University of Wisconsin,
whose Literature & the Arts Class
changed the course of my life.

For Julia

TABLE OF CONTENTS

INTRODUCTION AND APOLOGY

The study of the Humanities is the study of what makes us human, which is a seemingly infinite and infinitely difficult subject. Most definitions of what make us human seem to break down or melt into definitions of other living beings. One thing that does seem to distinguish humans from other species is our attempt both to discuss the human condition and to record that discussion for future generations. The best of these recordings, which take various forms in arts and letters, help us to understand the world around us and to give it meaning. For this reason, people seeking answers to difficult questions tend to return century after century to these same readings.

The pages of this volume include many of these recordings. As you can see, there are readings from the Bible, Homer, Dante, Shakespeare, and dozens of other great works. It also includes some lesser-known works, such as "*Stabat Mater*," "Love Armed," and *Love Intrigued*, which are included because they speak to parts of the human experience that are often neglected in volumes such as this. Everything included in this volume is among the very best writings we as humans have created.

This volume, however, does not include many important recordings. Many of them are far too long to put in this anthology. It would be wonderful to include essential readings such as Shakespeare's *A Midsummer Night's Dream*, Voltaire's *Candide,* or Shelley's *Frankenstein* here, but these works are easily found in other well-edited volumes. In some cases I have included selections from longer works, in part, so that you will be enticed to read the entire works. It would also be wonderful to include newer works such as those of Marquez, Borges, Calvino, and Morrison; these works, however, are not only too long for inclusion, but legal arrangements prohibit inclusion. Fortunately, the works of these and many other great modern writers are also readily available. This book is also missing many important works from other cultures, as it focuses largely on the traditional texts of the "Western Tradition." Thus there is no inclusion of such essential longer texts as The Koran, *The Tale of Gengi, Monkey*, the Dhammapada or even shorter works from cultures beyond Europe and North America.

For all of these omissions, I apologize. I hope, nonetheless, that, whether you are using this book for a class or enjoying it on your own, you will read, and continue to read, as many of the great works of the world as you can.

Gerard P. NeCastro
Machias, Maine
May 15, 2013

The Bible
Passages from the Old Testament

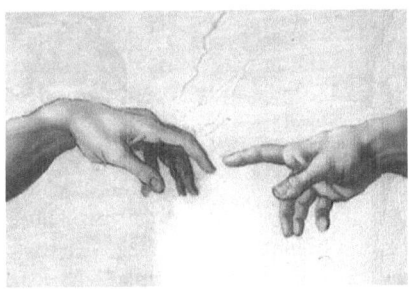

The Bible is a collection of writings that follow the history of the Hebrew people from their beginnings to the coming of the Savior, Jesus Christ, the life of Jesus Christ, and the writings of the early followers of Christ. It is considered the holy book of Christianity, inspired by God and containing the central truths of life. There are two major parts of the Bible, the Old Testament and the New Testament. The Old Testament contains not only the history of the Hebrew people, but also books of law, prophecy, wisdom, and poetry. The New Testament contains the four Gospels, the narratives of the life of Jesus Christ, and the writings of early Christians, most notably Saint Paul.

The passages included here recount the creation of the world, the accounts of the earliest humans (Adam and Eve, and Cain and Abel), and major events in the lives of two early heroic figures (David and Judith). The first three readings are from Genesis, the opening book of the Old Testament; the third is from Samuel, one of the historical chronicles; and the last is from Judith, a biographical book.

There are many translations of the Bible. The passages below are drawn from the King James Version, but somewhat modernized.

ೞಀ

The Creation
Genesis, Chapters 1 – 2
Traditionally Ascribed to Moses, c. 1400 BC

In the beginning God created the heaven and the earth. And the earth was without form, and void; and darkness was upon the face of the deep. And the Spirit of God moved upon the face of the waters. And God said, "Let there be light": and there was light. And God saw the light, that it was good: and God divided the light from the darkness. And God called the light Day, and the darkness he called Night. And the evening and the morning were the first day.

And God said, "Let there be a firmament in the midst of the waters, and let it divide the waters from the waters." And God made the firmament, and divided the waters which were under the firmament from the waters which were above the firmament: and it was so. And God called the firmament Heaven. And the evening and the morning were the second day.

And God said, "Let the waters under the heaven be gathered together into one place, and let the dry land appear": and it was so. And God called the dry land Earth; and the gathering together of the waters called the Seas: and God saw that it was good. And God said, "Let the earth bring forth grass, the herb-yielding seed, and the fruit tree yielding fruit after his kind, whose seed is in itself, upon the earth": and it was so. And the earth brought forth grass, and herb-yielding seed after his kind, and the tree yielding fruit, whose seed was in itself, after his kind: and God saw that it was good. And the evening and the morning were the third day.

And God said, "Let there be lights in the firmament of the heaven to divide the day from the night; and let them be for signs, and for seasons, and for days, and years: and let them be for lights in the firmament of the heaven to give light upon the earth": and it was so. And God made two great lights; the greater light to rule the day, and the lesser light to rule the night: he made the stars also. And God set them in the firmament of the heaven to give light upon the earth, and to rule over the day and over the night, and to divide the light from the darkness: and God saw that it was good. And the evening and the morning were the fourth day.

And God said, "Let the waters bring forth abundantly the moving creature that has life, and fowl that may fly above the earth in the open firmament of heaven." And God created great whales and every living creature that moves, which the waters brought forth abundantly, after their kind, and every winged fowl after his kind: and God saw that it was good. And God blessed them, saying, "Be fruitful, and multiply, and fill the waters in the seas, and let fowl multiply in the earth." And the evening and the morning were the fifth day.

And God said, "Let the earth bring forth the living creature after his kind, cattle, and creeping thing, and beast of the earth after his kind": and it was so. And God made the beast of the earth after his kind, and cattle after their kind, and every thing that creeps upon the earth after his kind: and God saw that it was good. And God said, "Let us make man in our image, after our likeness: and let them have dominion over the fish of the sea, and over the fowl of the air, and over the cattle, and over all the earth, and over every creeping thing that creeps upon the earth." So God created man in his own image, in the image of God created he him; male and female created he them. And God blessed them, and God said to them, "Be fruitful, and multiply, and replenish the earth, and subdue it: and have dominion over the fish of the sea, and over the fowl of the air, and over every living thing that moves upon the earth." And God said, "Behold, I have given you every herb bearing seed, which is upon the face of all the earth, and every tree, in which is the fruit of a tree yielding seed; to you it shall be for meat. And to every beast of the earth, and to every fowl of the air, and to every thing that creeps upon the earth, wherein there is life, I have given every green herb for meat": and it was so. And God saw every thing that he had made, and, behold, it was very good. And the evening and the morning were the sixth day.

Thus the heavens and the earth were finished, and all the host of them. And on the seventh day God ended his work which he had made; and he rested on the seventh day from all his work which he had made. And God blessed the seventh day, and sanctified it: because that in it he had rested from all his work which God created and made.

CႽ੬౭

Creation of Adam and Eve, and Their Fall from Grace
Genesis, Chapters 2 and 3
Traditionally Ascribed to Moses, c. 1400 BC

[T]he Lord God had not caused it to rain upon the earth, and there was not a man to till the ground. But there went up a mist from the earth, and watered the whole face of the ground. And the Lord God formed man of the dust of the ground, and breathed into his nostrils the breath of life; and man became a living soul. And the Lord God planted a garden eastward in Eden; and there he put the man whom he had formed. And out of the ground made the Lord God to grow every tree that is pleasant to the sight, and good for food; the tree of life also in the midst of the garden, and the tree of knowledge of good and evil....

And the Lord God took the man, and put him into the Garden of Eden to dress it and to keep it. And the Lord God commanded the man, saying, "Of every tree of the garden you may freely eat: but of the tree of the knowledge of good and evil, you shall not eat of it: for in the day that you eat of it you shall surely die." And the Lord God said, "It is not good that the man should be alone; I will make a help mate for him." And out of the ground the Lord God formed every beast of the field and every fowl of the air, and brought them to Adam to see what he would call them: and whatever Adam called every living creature, that was its name. And Adam gave names to all cattle, to the fowl of the air, and to every beast of the field; but for Adam there was not found a help mate.

And the Lord God caused a deep sleep to fall upon Adam, and he slept: and he took one of his ribs, and closed up his flesh instead; and the rib, which the Lord God had taken from man, he made a woman and brought her to the man. And Adam said, "This is now bone of my bones and flesh of my flesh: she shall be called Woman, because she was taken out of Man." Therefore shall a man leave his father and his mother, and shall cleave to his wife: and they shall be one flesh. And they were both naked, the man and his wife, and were not ashamed.

Now the serpent was more subtle than any beast of the field which the Lord God had made. And he said to the woman, "Yea, God has said, 'You shall not eat of every tree of the garden?'" And the woman said to the serpent, "We may eat of the fruit of the trees of the garden: But of the fruit of the tree which is in the midst of the garden, God has said, 'You shall not eat of it, nor shall you touch it, or you shall die.'" And the serpent said to the woman, "You shall not surely die: for God knows that in the day you eat of it, then your eyes shall be opened, and you shall be as gods, knowing good and evil." And when the woman saw that the tree was good for food, and that it was pleasant to the eyes, and a tree to be desired to make one wise, she took of the fruit of it and did eat, and gave also to her husband with her; and he did eat. And the eyes of them both

3

were opened, and they knew that they were naked; and they sewed fig leaves together, and made themselves aprons.

And they heard the voice of the Lord God walking in the garden in the cool of the day: and Adam and his wife hid themselves from the presence of the Lord God amongst the trees of the garden. And the Lord God called to Adam, and said to him, "Where are you?"

And he said, "I heard your voice in the garden, and I was afraid, because I was naked; and I hid myself."

And he said, "Who told you that you were naked? Have you eaten of the tree, whereof I commanded you that you should not eat?"

And the man said, "The woman whom you gave to be with me, she gave me of the tree, and I did eat."

And the Lord God said to the woman, "What is this that you have done?"

And the woman said, "The serpent beguiled me, and I did eat."

And the Lord God said to the serpent, "Because you have done this, you are cursed above all cattle, and above every beast of the field; upon your belly shall you go, and dust shall you eat all the days of your life: and I will put enmity between you and the woman, and between your seed and her seed; it shall bruise your head, and you shall bruise its heel."

To the woman he said, "I will greatly multiply your sorrow and your conception; in sorrow you shall bring forth children; and your desire shall be to your husband, and he shall rule over you."

And to Adam he said, "Because you have listened to the voice of your wife, and have eaten of the tree, of which I commanded you, saying, 'You shall not eat of it': cursed is the ground for your sake; in sorrow shall you eat of it all the days of your life. Thorns and thistles shall it bring forth to you; and you shall eat the herb of the field. In the sweat of your face shall you eat bread, until you return to the ground; for from it were you taken: for dust you are, and to dust shall you return."

And Adam called his wife's name Eve, because she was the mother of all living. To Adam also and to his wife did the Lord God make coats of skins, and clothed them.

And the Lord God said, "Behold, the man has become as one of us, to know good and evil: and now, lest he put forth his hand, and take also of the tree of life, and eat, and live for ever." Therefore the Lord God sent him forth from the garden of Eden to till the ground from whence he was taken. So he drove out the man, and he placed at the east of the garden of Eden Cherubims, and a flaming sword which turned every way, to protect the tree of life.

C03&O

Cain and Abel
Genesis, Chapter 4
Traditionally Ascribed to Moses, c. 1400 BC

And Adam knew Eve his wife; and she conceived, and bore Cain, and said, "I have gotten a man from the Lord." And she again bore his brother Abel. And Abel was a keeper of sheep, but Cain was a tiller of the ground. And in process of time it came to pass that Cain brought of the fruit of the ground an offering to the Lord. And Abel, he also brought of the firstlings of his flock and of the best of them. And the Lord had favored Abel and his offering, but he did not favor Cain and his offering. And Cain was very angry, and his countenance fell.

And the Lord said to Cain, "Why are you angry? And why is your countenance fallen? If you do well, shall you not be accepted? And if you do not well, sin lies at the door. And to you shall be his desire, and you shall rule over him."

And Cain talked with his brother Abel: and when they were in the field, Cain rose up against Abel his brother, and slew him.

And the Lord said to Cain, "Where is Abel your brother?"

And he said, "I know not: Am I my brother's keeper?"

And he said, "What have you done? The voice of your brother's blood cries to me from the ground. And now are you cursed from the earth, which has opened her mouth to receive your brother's blood from your hand; when you till the ground, it shall not henceforth yield to you her strength; a fugitive and a vagabond shall you be on the earth."

And Cain said to the Lord, "My punishment is greater than I can bear. Behold, you have driven me out this day from the face of the earth; and from your face shall I be hid; and I shall be a fugitive and a vagabond in the earth; and it shall come to pass, that every one that finds me shall slay me."

And the Lord said to him, "Therefore whosoever slays Cain, vengeance shall be taken on him sevenfold. And the Lord set a mark upon Cain, lest any finding him should kill him."

And Cain went out from the presence of the Lord, and dwelt in the land of Nod, east of Eden.

ᘓᘔ

David and Goliath
1 Samuel, Chapter 17
Traditionally Ascribed to Samuel, c. 1100 BC

Now the Philistines gathered together their armies to battle, and were gathered together at Shochoh, which belongs to Judah, and pitched between Shochoh and Azekah, in Ephesdammim. And Saul and the men of Israel were gathered together, pitched by the valley of Elah, and set the battle in array against the Philistines. And the Philistines stood on a mountain on the one side, and Israel stood on a mountain on the other side: and there was a valley between them.

And there went out a champion out of the camp of the Philistines, named Goliath, of Gath, whose height was six cubits and a span. And he had a helmet of brass upon his head, and he was armed with a coat of mail; and the weight of the coat was five thousand shekels of brass. And he had greaves of brass upon his legs and a target of brass between his shoulders. And the staff of his spear was like a weaver's beam; and his spear's head weighed six hundred shekels of iron: and one bearing a shield went before him.

And he stood and cried to the armies of Israel, and said to them, "Why have you come out to set your battle in array? Am not I a Philistine, and you servants to Saul? Choose you a man for you, and let him come down to me. If he be able to fight with me, and to kill me, then will we be your servants: but if I prevail against him, and kill him, then shall you be our servants, and serve us." And the Philistine said, "I defy the armies of Israel this day; give me a man, so that we may fight together." When Saul and all Israel heard those words of the Philistine, they were dismayed, and greatly afraid.

Now David was the son of that Ephrathite of Bethlehemjudah, whose name was Jesse; and he had eight sons: and the man went among men for an old man in the days of Saul. And the three eldest sons of Jesse went and followed Saul to the battle: and the names of his three sons that went to the battle were Eliab the firstborn, and next to him Abinadab, and the third Shammah. And David was the youngest: and the three eldest followed Saul. But David went and returned from Saul to feed his father's sheep at Bethlehem.

And the Philistine drew near morning and evening, and presented himself forty days. And Jesse said to David his son, "Take now for your brethren an ephah of this parched corn, and these ten loaves, and run to the camp of your brethren; and carry these ten cheeses to the captain of their thousand, and observe how your brethren fare, and take their pledge." Now Saul, and they, and all the men of Israel, were in the valley of Elah, fighting with the Philistines. And David rose up early in the morning, and left the sheep with a keeper, and took, and went, as Jesse had commanded him; and he came to the trench, as the host was going forth to the fight, and shouted for the battle. For Israel and the Philistines had put the battle in array, army against army.

And David left his carriage in the hand of the keeper of the carriage, and ran into the army, and came and saluted his brethren. And as he talked with them, behold, there came up the champion, the Philistine of Gath, Goliath by name, out of the armies of the Philistines, and spoke according to the same words: and David heard them. And all the men of Israel, when they saw the man, fled from him, and were sorely afraid.

And the men of Israel said, "Have you seen this man that has come up? Surely to defy Israel has he come up: and it shall be that the man who kills him, the king will enrich him with great riches, and will give him his daughter, and make his father's house free in Israel."

And David spoke to the men that stood by him, saying, "What shall be done to the man that kills this Philistine, and takes away the reproach from Israel? For who is this uncircumcised Philistine, that he should defy the armies of the living God?" And the people answered him in this manner, saying, "So shall it be done to the man that kills him."[1]

And Eliab his eldest brother heard when he spoke to the men; and Eliab's anger was kindled against David, and he said, "Why did you come down here? And with whom have you left those few sheep in the wilderness? I know your pride and the naughtiness of your heart; for you have come down that you might see the battle."

---

[1] So shall it be done...kills him. I.e., he will be rewarded with great riches and the daughter of the king. David may be trying to get the attention of the king, Saul.

And David said, "What have I now done? Is there not a cause?" And he turned from him toward another and spoke in the same manner: and the people answered him again as they had earlier. When David's words were heard, they repeated them to Saul: and he sent for him.

And David said to Saul, "Let no man's heart fail because of him; your servant will go and fight with this Philistine."

And Saul said to David, "You are not able to go against this Philistine to fight with him: for you are but a youth, and he a man of war from his youth."

And David said to Saul, "Your servant kept his father's sheep, and there came a lion, and a bear, and took a lamb out of the flock: And I went out after him, and smote him, and delivered it out of his mouth: and when he arose against me, I caught him by his beard, and smote him, and slew him. Your servant slew both the lion and the bear: and this uncircumcised Philistine shall be like one of them, seeing that he has defied the armies of the living God." David said moreover, "The Lord that delivered me out of the paw of the lion, and out of the paw of the bear, he will deliver me out of the hand of this Philistine."

And Saul said to David, "Go, and may the Lord be with you." And Saul armed David with his armor, and he put a helmet of brass upon his head; also he armed him with a coat of mail. And David girded his sword upon his armor, and he assayed to go; for he had not proved it.

And David said to Saul, "I cannot go with these; for I have not tested them." And David put them off him. And he took his staff in his hand, and he chose five smooth stones out of the brook, and put them in a shepherd's bag which he had, in his wallet; and his sling was in his hand: and he drew near to the Philistine.

And the Philistine came on and drew near to David; and the man that bore the shield went before him. And when the Philistine looked about, and saw David, he disdained him: for he was but a youth, and ruddy, and of a fair countenance.

And the Philistine said to David, "Am I a dog, that you come to me with staves?" And the Philistine cursed David by his gods. And the Philistine said to David, "Come to me, and I will give your flesh to the fowls of the air, and to the beasts of the field."

Then said David to the Philistine, "You come to me with a sword, and with a spear, and with a shield: but I come to you in the name of the Lord of hosts, the God of the armies of Israel, whom you have defied. This day will the Lord deliver you into my hand; and I will smite you, and take your head from you; and I will give the carcasses of the host of the Philistines this day to the fowls of the air, and to the wild beasts of the earth; that all the earth may know that there is a God in Israel. And all this assembly shall know that the Lord saves not with sword and spear: for the battle is the Lord's, and he will give you into our hands."

And it came to pass, when the Philistine arose, and came, and drew near to meet David, that David hastened and ran toward the army to meet the Philistine.

And David put his hand in his bag, and took from it a stone, and slung it, and smote the Philistine in his forehead, so that the stone sank into his forehead; and he fell upon his face to the earth.

So David prevailed over the Philistine with a sling and with a stone, and smote the Philistine, and slew him; but there was no sword in the hand of David. Therefore David ran, and stood upon the Philistine, and took his sword, and drew it out of the sheath, and slew him, and cut off his head therewith.

And when the Philistines saw their champion was dead, they fled. And the men of Israel and of Judah arose, and shouted, and pursued the Philistines, until they came to the valley, and to the gates of Ekron. And the wounded of the Philistines fell down by the way to Shaaraim, even to Gath, and to Ekron. And the children of Israel returned from chasing after the Philistines, and they spoiled their tents. And David took the head of the Philistine, and brought it to Jerusalem; but he put his armor in his tent.

ᘓᘔᘖᘒ

Judith and Holofernes
Judith, Chapters 10 – 13
Author Unknown, Written c. 100 BC, Based on Events c. 630 BC

And [Judith] said to them, "Command the gates of the city to be opened to me, so that I may go forth to accomplish the things whereof you have spoken with me." So they commanded the young men to open the gates to her, as she had spoken. And when they had done so, Judith went out, she, and her maid with her; and the men of the city looked after her, until she was gone down the mountain, and until she had passed the valley, and could see her no more.

Thus they went straight forth in the valley: and the first watch of the Assyrians met her, and took her, and asked her, "Of what people are you? And whence come you? And whither go you?"

And she said, "I am a woman of the Hebrews, and am fled from them: for they shall be given you to be consumed: And I am coming before Holofernes the chief captain of your army, to declare words of truth; and I will show him a way, whereby he shall go, and win all the hill country, without losing the body or life of any one of his men."

Now when the men heard her words and beheld her countenance, they wondered greatly at her beauty, and said to her, "You have saved your life, in that you have hastened to come down to the presence of our lord: now therefore come to his tent, and some of us shall conduct you, until they have delivered you to his hands. And when you stand before him, be not afraid in your heart, but show this to him according to your word; and he will entreat you well."

Then they chose out of them a hundred men to accompany her and her maid; and they brought her to the tent of Holofernes. Then was there a concourse throughout all the camp: for her coming was discussed among the tents, and they came about her, as she stood outside the tent of Holofernes, until they told him of her. And they wondered at her beauty and admired the children of Israel because of her, and every one said to his neighbor, "Who would despise this people, that have among them such women? Surely it is not good that one

8

man of them be left who being let go might deceive the whole earth."

And they that lay near Holofernes went out, and all his servants and they brought her into the tent. Now Holofernes rested upon his bed under a canopy, which was woven with purple, and gold, and emeralds, and precious stones. So they showed him of her; and he came out before his tent with silver lamps going before him. And when Judith was come before him and his servants they all marveled at the beauty of her countenance; and she fell down upon her face, and paid reverence to him: and his servants took her up.

Then said Holofernes to her, "Woman, be of good comfort, fear not in your heart: for I never hurt any that was willing to serve Nebuchadnezzar, the king of all the earth. Now therefore, if your people that dwell in the mountains had not set light by me, I would not have lifted up my spear against them: but they have done these things to themselves. But now tell me why you have fled from them, and have come to us: for you have come for safeguard; be of good comfort, you shall live this night, and hereafter: For none shall hurt you, but entreat you well, as they do the servants of king Nebuchadnezzar my lord."

Then Judith said to him, "Receive the words of your servant, and allow your handmaid to speak in your presence, and I will declare no lie to my lord this night. And if you will follow the words of your handmaid, God will bring the thing perfectly to pass by you; and my lord shall not fail of his purposes. As Nebuchadnezzar king of all the earth lives, and as his power lives, who has sent you for the upholding of every living thing: for not only men shall serve him by you, but also the beasts of the field, and the cattle, and the fowls of the air, shall live by your power under Nebuchadnezzar and all his house.

"For we have heard of your wisdom and your policies, and it is reported in all the earth, that you only are excellent in all the kingdom, and mighty in knowledge, and wonderful in feats of war. Now as concerning the matter, which Achior did speak in your council, we have heard his words; for the men of Bethulia saved him, and he declared to them all that he had spoken to you. Therefore, O lord and governor, reject not his word; but lay it up in your heart, for it is true: for our nation shall not be punished, neither can sword prevail against them, unless they sin against their God....

"And I will lead you through the midst of Judea, until you come before Jerusalem; and I will set your throne in the midst of them; and you shall drive them as sheep that have no shepherd, and a dog shall not so much as open his mouth at you: for these things were told me according to my foreknowledge, and they were declared to me, and I am sent to tell you."

Then her words pleased Holofernes and all his servants; and they marveled at her wisdom, and said, "There is not such a woman from one end of the earth to the other, both for beauty of face, and wisdom of words. Likewise Holofernes said to her, "God has done well to send you before the people, that strength might be in our hands and destruction upon them that lightly regard my lord. And now you are both beautiful in your countenance and witty in your words: surely if you do as you have spoken your God shall be my God, and you shall dwell in the house of king Nebuchadnezzar, and shall be renowned through the whole earth."

Then he commanded to bring her in where his plate was set; and bade that they should prepare for her of his own meats, and that she should drink of his own wine. And Judith said, "I will not eat this, lest there be an offence: but provision shall be made for me of the things that I have brought."

Then Holofernes said to her, "If your provision should fail, how should we give you the like? For there is none with us of your nation."

Then said Judith to him, "As your soul lives, my lord, your handmaid shall not spend those things that I have, before the Lord work by my hand the things that he has determined." Then the servants of Holofernes brought her into the tent, and she slept until midnight, and she arose when it was toward the morning watch, and sent to Holofernes, saving, "Let my lord now command that your handmaid may go forth to prayer."

Then Holofernes commanded his guard that they should not stay her: thus she remained in the camp three days, and went out in the night into the valley of Bethulia, and washed herself in a fountain of water by the camp. And when she came out, she prayed to the Lord God of Israel to direct her way to the raising up of the children of her people. So she came in clean, and remained in the tent, until she did eat her meat at evening.

And in the fourth day Holofernes made a feast to his own servants only, and called none of the officers to the banquet. Then said he to Bagoas the eunuch, who had charge over all that he had, "Go now, and persuade this Hebrew woman who is with you, that she will come to us, and eat and drink with us. For, lo, it will be a shame for our person, if we shall let such a woman go, not having had her company; for if we draw her not to us, she will laugh us to scorn."

Then went Bagoas from the presence of Holofernes, and came to her, and he said, "Let not this fair damsel fear to come to my lord, and to be honored in his presence, and drink wine, and be merry with us and be made this day as one of the daughters of the Assyrians, which serve in the house of Nebuchadnezzar."

Then said Judith to him, "Who am I now, that I should contradict my lord? Surely whatever pleases him I will do speedily, and it shall be my joy until the day of my death." So she arose and decked herself with her apparel and all her woman's attire, and her maid went and laid soft skins on the ground for her over against Holofernes, which she had received of Bagoas for her daily use, so that she might sit and eat upon them.

Now when Judith came in and sat down, the heart of Holofernes was ravished with her, and his mind was moved, and he desired greatly her company; for he waited a time to deceive her, from the day that he had seen her. Then Holofernes said to her, "Drink now, and be merry with us."

So Judith said, "I will drink now, my lord, because my life is magnified in me this day more than all the days since I was born." Then she took and ate and drank before him what her maid had prepared. And Holofernes took great delight in her, and drank more wine than he had drunk at any time in one day since he was born.

Now when the evening had come, his servants made haste to depart, and Bagoas shut his tent outside, and dismissed the waiters from the presence of his lord; and they went to their beds: for they were all weary, because the feast had been long. And Judith was left alone in the tent, and Holofernes lying along upon his bed: for he was filled with wine. Now Judith had commanded her maid to stand outside of her bedchamber and to wait for her coming forth, as she did daily: for she said she would go forth to her prayers, and she spoke to Bagoas according to the same purpose. So all went forth and none was left in the bedchamber, neither little nor great.

Then Judith, standing by his bed, said in her heart, "O Lord God of all power, look now upon the works of my hands for the exaltation of Jerusalem. For now is the time to help your inheritance, and to execute your enterprises to the destruction of the enemies which are risen against us. Then she came to the pillar of the bed, which was at Holofernes' head, and took down his sword from there and approached his bed, and took hold of the hair of his head, and said, "Strengthen me, O Lord God of Israel, this day." And she smote twice upon his neck with all her might, and she took away his head from him. And tumbled his body down from the bed, and pulled down the canopy from the pillars; and quickly she went forth and gave Holofernes' head to her maid; And she put it in her bag of meat: so the two of them went together according to their custom to prayer: and when they left the camp, they crossed the valley and went up the mountain of Bethulia, and came to the gates there.

Then Judith said from a distance to the watchmen at the gate, "Open, open now the gate: God, our very God, is with us, to show his power yet in Jerusalem, and his forces against the enemy, as he has done this very day."

Now when the men of her city heard her voice, they made haste to go down to the gate of their city, and they called the elders of the city. And then they ran all together, both small and great, for it was strange to them that she had come: so they opened the gate, and received them, and made a fire for a light, and stood around them. Then she said to them with a loud voice, "Praise, praise God, praise God, I say, for he has not taken away his mercy from the house of Israel, but has destroyed our enemies by my hands this night." So she took the head out of the bag, and showed it, and said to them, "behold the head of Holofernes, the chief captain of the army of Assur, and behold the canopy, wherein he did lie in his drunkenness; and the Lord has smitten him by the hand of a woman. As the Lord lives, who has upheld me in my way as I went, my countenance has deceived [this captain] to his destruction, and yet has he not committed sin with me, to defile and shame me."

Then all the people were wonderfully astonished, and bowed themselves and worshipped God, and said with one accord, "Blessed be you, O our God, who has this day brought to nothing the enemies of your people."

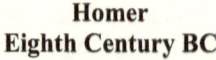

Homer
Eighth Century BC

Homer is often used as the starting point for the world of literature. Though there are certainly works of other authors before him, his two major works, *The Iliad* and *The Odyssey*, are the paradigms of what follows in the history of literature. His work still lives on in translations into virtually every language and in countless retellings and adaptations.

Little is known about Homer's life, though most believe that he was a blind poet of ancient Greece. Even these facts, however, are disputed; some believe that Homer is simply a name given to the collected stories of the Trojan War and its aftermath and that the possibility of his blindness is simply a pun in Greek on his name. There is a growing consensus that he would have sung his epic poems in much the same way that the blind poet Demodocus sings in the Phaeacian court in *The Odyssey*.

The first reading from Homer below is from the last book of *The Iliad*, the story of the Trojan War, which seems to have taken place in the thirteenth century BC. In the mythical retelling of Homer and other early poets, Troy (in modern-day Turkey) is attacked by the Greeks (or Achaeans) after Paris, a prince of Troy, seduces Helen, the wife of the powerful Spartan king named Menelaus, and takes her back to Troy. Paris had been promised the most beautiful woman in the world if he would chose Aphrodite, above Hera and Athena, as the rightful owner of a golden apple inscribed "to the fairest". As a large number of Greek kings who had been suitors to Helen made a pact promising that they would defend the honor of the man who won her hand in marriage, all of these kings and their armies joined Menelaus in battle against the powerful Trojan nation. The Greeks were led by the Atrides (the sons of Atreus), Agamemnon and his brother of Menelaus, while the Trojans were led by Hector, son of the reigning King Priam and Queen Hecuba.

The Iliad depicts a series of battles that follow the withdrawal of Achilles from the war, because he has been offended by Agamemnon's taking for himself Achilles' concubine Chryseïs. Achilles remains brooding in his ship until his closest friend Patroclus, dressed in Achilles' armor, is slain by the Trojan leader Hector. Achilles' mother Thetis, a goddess of water, commissions Hephaestus, the smith of the gods, to forge a new set of armor, and Achilles finally returns to the war. He calls out Hector into a one-to-one battle, slays him, ties the fallen warrior to his chariot, drags him around the city three times, and leaves his body unburied outside of his ship in the Greek camp. In the first passage below, Priam, the aged king of the Trojans, goes to the ship of the Greek champion to beg for the body of his beloved son.

In the second passage below, which is drawn from Homer's *Odyssey*, we encounter Odysseus, the crafty king of Ithaca, Greece, the tactician who made the plan for the Trojan Horse that ended the Trojan War. The Greeks, after ten years of war against the Trojans, with over 1000 ships moored on the shore, pretended to leave for home. As they made their fictitious departure, they wheeled a huge wooden horse up to the gate of the walled city of Troy and pretended to leave, though they only sailed to the nearest island until dark. Though some of the Trojans were wary of the peace offering from the Greeks and argued that they should not wheel it into the city, they eventually opened the gates to the horse and began their celebration. They did not realize, however, that the horse was filled with the best of the Greek warriors, who, once night had fallen and the Trojans were completely off guard in the midst of their celebration, climbed out of the horse and, joined by all of their compatriots who had now returned from the nearby island, attacked the Trojans and set the city on fire.

After the sack of Troy, the Greeks headed for home. Odysseus, however, has a great deal of trouble getting back to Ithaca. Partly because of his bad fortune and partly because of his penchant for alienating the wrong people, he is unable to return to his ever-faithful Penelope and dutiful son Telemachus, as he and his men are forced to wander around the Mediterranean for ten years, sometimes as guests and sometimes as captives. By the end of the journey, all of Odysseus' men have been lost at sea, and only his son Telemachus and his loyal swineherd Eumaeus assist him in his battle against the many suitors of Penelope to reclaim his kingdom and wife.

The second passage below is from Book 9 of *The Odyssey*, in which the homesick hero recounts to King Alcinous and the generous Phaeacians his encounter with the huge one-eyed Cyclops named Polyphemus.

ඥ๛

Priam and Achilles
***From* The Iliad**
Homer, Eighth Century BC
TRANSLATED BY SAMUEL BUTLER

The assembly now broke up and the people went their ways, each to his own ship. There they made ready their supper, and then thought of the blessed gift of sleep; but Achilles still wept for thinking of his dear comrade, and sleep, before whom all things bow, could take no hold upon him. This way and that did he turn as he thought about the might and manfulness of Patroclus; he thought of all they had done together, and all they had gone through both on the field of battle and on the waves of the weary sea. As he dwelt on these things he wept bitterly and lay now on his side, now on his back, and now face downwards, until at last

13

he rose and went out as one distraught to wander upon the seashore. Then, when he saw dawn breaking over beach and sea, he yoked his horses to his chariot, and bound the body of Hector behind it that he might drag it about. Thrice did he drag it round the tomb of the son of Menoetius, and then went back into his tent, leaving the body on the ground full length and with its face downwards. But Apollo would not suffer it to be disfigured, for he pitied the man, dead though he now was; therefore he shielded him with his golden aegis continually, that he might take no hurt while Achilles was dragging him.

Thus shamefully did Achilles in his fury dishonor Hector; but the blessed gods looked down in pity from heaven, and urged Mercury, slayer of Argus, to steal the body. All were of this mind save only Juno, Neptune, and Jove's grey-eyed daughter, who persisted in the hate which they had ever borne towards Ilius with Priam and his people; for they forgave not the wrong done them by Alexandrus in disdaining the goddesses who came to him when he was in his sheep-yards, and preferring her who had offered him a wanton to his ruin.

When, therefore, the morning of the twelfth day had now come, Phoebus Apollo spoke among the immortals saying, "You gods ought to be ashamed of yourselves; you are cruel and hard-hearted. Did not Hector burn you thigh-bones of heifers and of unblemished goats? And now dare you not rescue even his dead body, for his wife to look upon, with his mother and child, his father Priam, and his people, who would forthwith commit him to the flames, and give him his due funeral rites? So, then, you would all be on the side of mad Achilles, who knows neither right nor ruth? He is like some savage lion that in the pride of his great strength and daring springs upon men's flocks and gorges on them. Even so has Achilles flung aside all pity, and all that conscience which at once so greatly banes yet greatly boons him that will heed it. man may lose one far dearer than Achilles has lost – a son, it may be, or a brother born from his own mother's womb; yet when he has mourned him and wept over him he will let him bide, for it takes much sorrow to kill a man; whereas Achilles, now that he has slain noble Hector, drags him behind his chariot round the tomb of his comrade. It would be better of him, and for him, that he should not do so, for, brave though he may be, we gods may take it ill that he should vent his fury upon dead clay."

Juno spoke up in a rage. "This were well," she cried, "O lord of the silver bow, if you would give like honor to Hector and to Achilles; but Hector was mortal and suckled at a woman's breast, whereas Achilles is the offspring of a goddess whom I myself reared and brought up. I married her to Peleus, who is above measure dear to the immortals; you gods came to her wedding; you feasted with them yourself and brought your lyre – false, and fond of low company, that you have ever been."

Then said Jove, "Juno, be not so bitter. Their honor shall not be equal, but of all that dwell in Ilius, Hector was dearest to the gods, as also to myself, for his offerings never failed me. Never was my altar stinted of its dues, nor of the drink-offerings and savor of sacrifice which we claim of right. I shall therefore permit the body of mighty Hector to be stolen; and yet this may hardly be without Achilles coming to know it, for his mother keeps night and day beside him.

Let some one of you, therefore, send Thetis to me, and I will impart my counsel to her, namely that Achilles is to accept a ransom from Priam, and give up the body."

On this Iris fleet as the wind went forth to carry his message. Down she plunged into the dark sea midway between Samos and rocky Imbrus; the waters hissed as they closed over her, and she sank into the bottom as the lead at the end of an ox-horn, that is sped to carry death to fishes. She found Thetis sitting in a great cave with the other sea-goddesses gathered round her; there she sat in the midst of them weeping for her noble son who was to fall far from his own land, on the rich plains of Troy. Iris went up to her and said, "Rise Thetis; Jove, whose counsels fail not, bids you come to him." And Thetis answered, "Why does the mighty god so bid me? I am in great grief, and shrink from going in and out among the immortals. Still, I will go, and the word that he may speak shall not be spoken in vain."

The goddess took her dark veil, than which there can be no robe more somber, and went forth with fleet Iris leading the way before her. The waves of the sea opened them a path, and when they reached the shore they flew up into the heavens, where they found the all-seeing son of Saturn with the blessed gods that live for ever assembled near him. Minerva gave up her seat to her, and she sat down by the side of father Jove. Juno then placed a fair golden cup in her hand, and spoke to her in words of comfort, whereon Thetis drank and gave her back the cup; and the sire of gods and men was the first to speak.

"So, goddess," said he, "for all your sorrow, and the grief that I well know reigns ever in your heart, you have come hither to Olympus, and I will tell you why I have sent for you. These past nine days the immortals have been quarrelling about Achilles waster of cities and the body of Hector. The gods would have Mercury, slayer of Argus, steal the body, but in furtherance of our peace and amity henceforward, I will concede such honor to your son as I will now tell you. Go, then, to the host and lay these commands upon him; say that the gods are angry with him, and that I am myself more angry than them all, in that he keeps Hector at the ships and will not give him up. He may thus fear me and let the body go. At the same time I will send Iris to great Priam to bid him go to the ships of the Achaeans, and ransom his son, taking with him such gifts for Achilles as may give him satisfaction."

Silver-footed Thetis did as the god had told her, and forthwith down she darted from the topmost summits of Olympus. She went to her son's tents where she found him grieving bitterly, while his trusty comrades round him were busy preparing their morning meal, for which they had killed a great woolly sheep. His mother sat down beside him and caressed him with her hand saying, "My son, how long will you keep on thus grieving and making moan? You are gnawing at your own heart, and think neither of food nor of woman's embraces; and yet these too were well, for you have no long time to live, and death with the strong hand of fate are already close beside you. Now, therefore, heed what I say, for I come as a messenger from Jove; he says that the gods are angry with you, and himself more angry than them all, in that you keep Hector at the ships

15

and will not give him up. Therefore let him go, and accept a ransom for his body."

And Achilles answered, "So be it. If Olympian Jove of his own motion thus commands me, let him that brings the ransom bear the body away."

Thus did mother and son talk together at the ships in long discourse with one another. Meanwhile the son of Saturn sent Iris to the strong city of Ilius. "Go," said he, "fleet Iris, from the mansions of Olympus, and tell King Priam in Ilius, that he is to go to the ships of the Achaeans and free the body of his dear son. He is to take such gifts with him as shall give satisfaction to Achilles, and he is to go alone, with no other Trojan, save only some honored servant who may drive his mules and wagon, and bring back the body of him whom noble Achilles has slain. Let him have no thought nor fear of death in his heart, for we will send Mercury, the slayer of Argus, to escort him, and bring him within the tent of Achilles. Achilles will not kill him nor let another do so, for he will take heed to his ways and sin not, and he will entreat a suppliant with all honorable courtesy."

On this Iris, fleet as the wind, sped forth to deliver her message. She went to Priam's house, and found weeping and lamentation therein. His sons were seated round their father in the outer courtyard, and their raiment was wet with tears: the old man sat in the midst of them with his mantle wrapped close about his body, and his head and neck all covered with the filth which he had clutched as he lay groveling in the mire. His daughters and his sons' wives went wailing about the house, as they thought of the many and brave men who lay dead, slain by the Argives. The messenger of Jove stood by Priam and spoke softly to him, but fear fell upon him as she did so. "Take heart," she said, "Priam, offspring of Dardanus, take heart and fear not. I bring no evil tidings, but am minded well towards you. I come as a messenger from Jove, who though he is not near, takes thought for you and pities you. The lord of Olympus bids you go and ransom noble Hector, and take with you such gifts as shall give satisfaction to Achilles. You are to go alone, with no Trojan, save only some honored servant who may drive your mules and wagon, and bring back to the city the body of him whom noble Achilles has slain. You are to have no thought, nor fear of death, for Jove will send the slayer of Argus to escort you. When he has brought you within Achilles' tent, Achilles will not kill you nor let another do so, for he will take heed to his ways and sin not, and he will entreat a suppliant with all honorable courtesy."

Iris went her way when she had thus spoken, and Priam told his sons to get a mule-wagon ready, and to make the body of the wagon fast upon the top of its bed. Then he went down into his fragrant store-room, high-vaulted, and made of cedar-wood, where his many treasures were kept, and he called Hecuba his wife. "Wife," said he, "a messenger has come to me from Olympus, and has told me to go to the ships of the Achaeans to ransom my dear son, taking with me such gifts as shall give satisfaction to Achilles. What think you of this matter? For my own part, I am greatly moved to pass through the camps of the Achaeans and go to their ships."

His wife cried aloud as she heard him, and said, "Alas, what has become of that judgment for which you have been ever famous both among strangers and your own people? How can you venture alone to the ships of the Achaeans, and look into the face of him who has slain so many of your brave sons? You must have iron courage, for if the cruel savage sees you and lays hold on you, he will know neither respect nor pity. Let us then weep Hector from afar here in our own house, for when I gave him birth the threads of overruling fate were spun for him that dogs should eat his flesh far from his parents, in the house of that terrible man on whose liver I would fain fasten and devour it. Thus would I avenge my son, who showed no cowardice when Achilles slew him, and thought neither of Right nor of avoiding battle as he stood in defense of Trojan men and Trojan women."

Then Priam said, "I would go, do not therefore stay me nor be as a bird of ill omen in my house, for you will not move me. Had it been some mortal man who had sent me some prophet or priest who divines from sacrifice – I should have deemed him false and have given him no heed; but now I have heard the goddess and seen her face to face, therefore I will go and her saying shall not be in vain. If it be my fate to die at the ships of the Achaeans even so would I have it; let Achilles slay me, if I may but first have taken my son in my arms and mourned him to my heart's comforting."

So saying, he lifted the lids of his chests, and took out twelve goodly vestments. He took also twelve cloaks of single fold, twelve rugs, twelve fair mantles, and an equal number of shirts. He weighed out ten talents of gold, and brought moreover two burnished tripods, four cauldrons, and a very beautiful cup which the Thracians had given him when he had gone to them on an embassy; it was very precious, but he grudged not even this, so eager was he to ransom the body of his son. Then he chased all the Trojans from the court and rebuked them with words of anger. "Out," he cried, "shame and disgrace to me that you are. Have you no grief in your own homes that you are come to plague me here? Is it a small thing, think you, that the son of Saturn has sent this sorrow upon me, to lose the bravest of my sons? Nay, you shall prove it in person, for now he is gone the Achaeans will have easier work in killing you. As for me, let me go down within the house of Hades, before my eyes behold the sacking and wasting of the city."

He drove the men away with his staff, and they went forth as the old man sped them. Then he called to his sons, upbraiding Helenus, Paris, noble Agathon, Pammon, Antiphonus, Polites of the loud battle-cry, Deiphobus, Hippothous, and Dius. These nine did the old man call near him. "Come to me at once," he cried, "worthless sons who do me shame; would that you had all been killed at the ships rather than Hector. Miserable man that I am, I have had the bravest sons in all Troy – noble Nestor, Troilus the dauntless charioteer, and Hector who was a god among men, so that one would have thought he was son to an immortal – yet there is not one of them left. Mars has slain them and those of whom I am ashamed are alone left me. Liars, and light of foot, heroes of the dance, robbers of lambs and kids from your own people, why do you not get a wagon ready for me at once, and put all these things upon it that I may set out on my way?"

Thus did he speak, and they feared the rebuke of their father. They brought out a strong mule-wagon, newly made, and set the body of the wagon fast on its bed. They took from the peg on which it hung a mule- yoke of boxwood with a knob on the top of it and rings for the reins to go through. Then they brought a yoke-band eleven cubits long, to bind the yoke to the pole; they bound it on at the far end of the pole, and put the ring over the upright pin making it fast with three turns of the band on either side the knob, and bending the thong of the yoke beneath it. This done, they brought from the store-chamber the rich ransom that was to purchase the body of Hector, and they set it all orderly on the wagon; then they yoked the strong harness-mules which the Mysians had on a time given as a goodly present to Priam; but for Priam himself they yoked horses which the old king had bred, and kept for own use.

Thus heedfully did Priam and his servant see to the yoking of their cars at the palace. Then Hecuba came to them all sorrowful, with a golden goblet of wine in her right hand, that they might make a drink-offering before they set out. She stood in front of the horses and said, "Take this, make a drink-offering to father Jove, and since you are minded to go to the ships in spite of me, pray that you may come safely back from the hands of your enemies. Pray to the son of Saturn lord of the whirlwind, who sits on Ida and looks down over all Troy, pray him to send his swift messenger on your right hand, the bird of omen which is strongest and most dear to him of all birds, that you may see it with your own eyes and trust it as you go forth to the ships of the Danaans. If all-seeing Jove will not send you this messenger, however set upon it you may be, I would not have you go to the ships of the Argives."

And Priam answered, "Wife, I will do as you desire me; it is well to lift hands in prayer to Jove, if so be he may have mercy upon me."

With this the old man bade the serving-woman pour pure water over his hands, and the woman came, bearing the water in a bowl. He washed his hands and took the cup from his wife; then he made the drink-offering and prayed, standing in the middle of the courtyard and turning his eyes to heaven. "Father Jove," he said, "who rules from Ida, most glorious and most great, grant that I may be received kindly and compassionately in the tents of Achilles; and send your swift messenger upon my right hand, the bird of omen which is strongest and most dear to you of all birds, that I may see it with my own eyes and trust it as I go forth to the ships of the Danaans."

So did he pray, and Jove the lord of counsel heard his prayer. Forthwith he sent an eagle, the most unerring portent of all birds that fly, the dusky hunter that men also call the Black Eagle. His wings were spread abroad on either side as wide as the well-made and well-bolted door of a rich man's chamber. He came to them flying over the city upon their right hands, and when they saw him they were glad and their hearts took comfort within them. The old man made haste to mount his chariot, and drove out through the inner gateway and under the echoing gatehouse of the outer court. Before him went the mules drawing the four-wheeled wagon, and driven by wise Idaeus; behind these were the horses, which the old man lashed with his whip and drove swiftly through the city, while his friends followed after, wailing and lamenting for him as though he were on his road to death. As soon as they had come down from the city and had reached the plain, his sons and sons-in-law who had followed him went back to Ilius.

But Priam and Idaeus as they showed out upon the plain did not escape the ken of all-seeing Jove, who looked down upon the old man and pitied him; then he spoke to his son Mercury and said, "Mercury, for it is you who are the most disposed to escort men on their way, and to hear those whom you will hear, go, and so conduct Priam to the ships of the Achaeans that no other of the Danaans shall see him nor take note of him until he reach the son of Peleus."

Thus he spoke, and Mercury, guide and guardian, slayer of Argus, did as he was told. Forthwith he bound on his glittering golden sandals with which he could fly like the wind over land and sea; he took the wand with which he seals men's eyes in sleep, or wakes them just as he pleases, and flew holding it in his hand until he came to Troy and to the Hellespont. To look at, he was like a young man of noble birth in the hey-day of his youth and beauty with the down just coming upon his face.

Now when Priam and Idaeus had driven past the great tomb of Ilius, they stayed their mules and horses that they might drink in the river, for the shades of night were falling, when, therefore, Idaeus saw Mercury standing near them he said to Priam, "Take heed, descendant of Dardanus; here is matter which demands consideration. I see a man who I think will presently fall upon us; let us fly with our horses, or at least embrace his knees and implore him to take compassion upon us?

When he heard this the old man's heart failed him, and he was in great fear; he stayed where he was as one dazed, and the hair stood on end over his whole body; but the bringer of good luck came up to him and took him by the hand, saying, "Whither, father, are you thus driving your mules and horses in the dead of night when other men are asleep? Are you not afraid of the fierce Achaeans who are hard by you, so cruel and relentless? Should some one of them see you bearing so much treasure through the darkness of the flying night, what would not your state then be? You are no longer young, and he who is with you is too old to protect you from those who would attack you. For myself, I will do you no harm, and I will defend you from any one else, for you remind me of my own father."

And Priam answered, "It is indeed as you say, my dear son; nevertheless some god has held his hand over me, in that he has sent such a wayfarer as yourself to meet me so opportunely; you are so comely in mien and figure, and your judgment is so excellent that you must come of blessed parents."

Then said the slayer of Argus, guide and guardian, "Sir, all that you have said is right; but tell me and tell me true, are you taking this rich treasure to send it to a foreign people where it may be safe, or are you all leaving strong Ilius in dismay now that your son has fallen who was the bravest man among you and was never lacking in battle with the Achaeans?"

And Priam said, "Who are you, my friend, and who are your parents, that you speak so truly about the fate of my unhappy son?"

Mercury, the slayer of Argus, guide and guardian, answered him, "Sir, you would prove me, that you question me about noble Hector. Many a time have I set eyes upon him in battle when he was driving the Argives to their ships and putting them to the sword. We stood still and marveled, for Achilles in his anger with the son of Atreus suffered us not to fight. I am his squire, and came with him in the same ship. I am a Myrmidon, and my father's name is Polyctor: he is a rich man and about as old as you are; he has six sons besides myself, and I am the seventh. We cast lots, and it fell upon me to sail hither with Achilles. I am now come from the ships on to the plain, for with daybreak the Achaeans will set battle in array about the city. They chafe at doing nothing, and are so eager that their princes cannot hold them back."

Then answered Priam, "If you are indeed the squire of Achilles son of Peleus, tell me now the whole truth. Is my son still at the ships, or has Achilles hewn him limb from limb, and given him to his hounds?"

"Sir," replied Mercury, slayer of Argus, guide and guardian, "neither hounds nor vultures have yet devoured him; he is still just lying at the tents by the ship of Achilles, and though it is now twelve days that he has lain there, his flesh is not wasted nor have the worms eaten him although they feed on warriors. At daybreak Achilles drags him cruelly round the sepulcher of his dear comrade, but it does him no hurt. You should come yourself and see how he lies fresh as dew, with the blood all washed away, and his wounds every one of them closed though many pierced him with their spears. Such care have the blessed gods taken of your brave son, for he was dear to them beyond all measure."

The old man was comforted as he heard him and said, "My son, see what a good thing it is to have made due offerings to the immortals; for as sure as that he was born my son never forgot the gods that hold Olympus, and now they requite it to him even in death. Accept therefore at my hands this goodly chalice; guard me and with heaven's help guide me until I come to the tent of the son of Peleus."

Then answered the slayer of Argus, guide and guardian, "Sir, you are tempting me and playing upon my youth, but you shall not move me, for you are offering me presents without the knowledge of Achilles whom I fear and hold it great guiltless to defraud, lest some evil presently befall me; but as your guide I would go with you even to Argos itself, and would guard you so carefully whether by sea or land, that no one should attack you through making light of him who was with you."

The bringer of good luck then sprang on to the chariot, and seizing the whip and reins he breathed fresh spirit into the mules and horses. When they reached the trench and the wall that was before the ships, those who were on guard had just been getting their suppers, and Mercury, the slayer of Argus, threw them all into a deep sleep. Then he drew back the bolts to open the gates, and took Priam inside with the treasure he had upon his wagon. Before long they came to the lofty dwelling of the son of Peleus for which the Myrmidons had cut pine and which they had built for their king; when they had built it they thatched it with coarse tussock-grass which they had mown out on the plain, and all round it they made a large courtyard, which was fenced with stakes set close together. The gate was barred with a single bolt of pine which it took three men to force into its place, and three to draw back so as to open the gate, but Achilles could draw it by himself. Mercury opened the gate for the old man, and brought in the treasure that he was taking with him for the son of Peleus. Then he sprang from the chariot on to the ground and said, "Sir, it is I, immortal Mercury, that am come with you, for my father sent me to escort you. I will now leave you, and will not enter into the presence of Achilles, for it might anger him that a god should befriend mortal men thus openly. Go you within, and embrace the knees of the son of Peleus: beseech him by his father, his lovely mother, and his son; thus you may move him."

With these words Mercury went back to high Olympus. Priam sprang from his chariot to the ground, leaving Idaeus where he was, in charge of the mules and horses. The old man went straight into the house where Achilles, loved of the gods, was sitting. There he found him with his men seated at a distance from him: only two, the hero Automedon, and Alcimus of the race of Mars, were busy in attendance about his person, for he had but just done eating and drinking, and the table was still there. King Priam entered without their seeing him, and going right up to Achilles he clasped his knees and kissed the dread murderous hands that had slain so many of his sons.

As when some cruel spite has befallen a man that he should have killed some one in his own country, and must fly to a great man's protection in a land of strangers, and all marvel who see him, even so did Achilles marvel as he beheld Priam. The others looked one to another and marveled also, but Priam besought Achilles saying, "Think of your father, O Achilles, so like the gods, who is such even as I am, on the sad threshold of old age. It may be that those who dwell near him harass him, and there is none to keep war and ruin from him. Yet when he hears of you being still alive, he is glad, and his days are full of hope that he shall see his dear son come home to him from Troy; but I, wretched man that I am, had the bravest in all Troy for my sons, and there is not one of them left. I had fifty sons when the Achaeans came here; nineteen of them were from a single womb, and the others were borne to me by the women of my household. The greater part of them has fierce Mars laid low, and Hector, him who was alone left, him who was the guardian of the city and ourselves, him have you lately slain; therefore I have now come to the ships of the Achaeans to ransom his body from you with a great ransom. Fear, O Achilles, the wrath of heaven; think on your own father and have compassion upon me, who am the more pitiable, for I have steeled myself as no man yet has ever steeled himself before me, and have raised to my lips the hand of him who slew my son."

Thus spoke Priam, and the heart of Achilles yearned as he bethought him of his father. He took the old man's hand and moved him gently away. The two wept bitterly – Priam, as he lay at Achilles' feet, weeping for Hector, and Achilles now for his father and now for Patroclus, until the house was filled with their lamentation. But when Achilles was now sated with grief and had unburdened the bitterness of his sorrow, he left his seat and raised the old man by the hand, in pity for his white hair and beard; then he said, "Unhappy man, you have indeed been greatly daring; how could you venture to come alone to the ships of the Achaeans, and enter the presence of him who has slain so many of your brave sons? You must have iron courage: sit now upon this seat, and for all our grief we will hide our sorrows in our hearts, for weeping will not avail us. The immortals know no care, yet the lot they spin for man is full of sorrow; on the floor of Jove's palace there stand two urns, the one filled with evil gifts, and the other with good ones. He for whom Jove the lord of thunder mixes the gifts he sends, will meet now with good and now with evil fortune; but he to whom Jove sends none but evil gifts will be pointed at by the finger of scorn, the hand of famine will pursue him to the ends of the world, and he will go up and down the face of the earth, respected neither by gods nor men. Even so did it befall Peleus; the gods endowed him with all good things from his birth upwards, for he reigned over the Myrmidons excelling all men in prosperity and wealth, and mortal though he was they gave him a goddess for his bride. But even on him too did heaven send misfortune, for there is no race of royal children born to him in his house, save one son who is doomed to die all untimely; nor may I take care of him now that he is growing old, for I must stay here at Troy to be the bane of you and your children. And you too, O Priam, I have heard that you were aforetime happy. They say that in wealth and plenitude of offspring you surpassed all that is in Lesbos, the realm of Makar to the northward, Phrygia that is more inland, and those that dwell upon the great Hellespont; but from the day when the dwellers in heaven sent this evil upon you, war and slaughter have been about your city continually. Bear up against it, and let there be some intervals in your sorrow. Mourn as you may for your brave son, you will take nothing by it. You cannot raise him from the dead, before you do so yet another sorrow shall befall you."

And Priam answered, "O king, bid me not be seated, while Hector is still lying uncared for in your tents, but accept the great ransom which I have brought you, and give him to me at once that I may look upon him. May you prosper with the ransom and reach your own land in safety, seeing that you have suffered me to live and to look upon the light of the sun."

Achilles looked at him sternly and said, "Vex me, sir, no longer; I am of myself minded to give up the body of Hector. My mother, daughter of the old man of the sea, came to me from Jove to bid me deliver it to you. Moreover I know well, O Priam, and you cannot hide it, that some god has brought you to the ships of the Achaeans, for else, no man however strong and in his prime would dare to come to our host; he could neither pass our guard unseen, nor draw the bolt of my gates thus easily; therefore, provoke me no further, lest I sin against the word of Jove, and suffer you not, suppliant though you are, within my tents."

The old man feared him and obeyed. Then the son of Peleus sprang like a lion through the door of his house, not alone, but with him went his two squires Automedon and Alcimus who were closer to him than any others of his comrades now that Patroclus was no more. These unyoked the horses and mules, and bade Priam's herald and attendant be seated within the house. They lifted the ransom for Hector's body from the wagon, but they left two mantles and a goodly shirt, that Achilles might wrap the body in them when he gave it to be taken home. Then he called to his servants and ordered them to wash the body and anoint it, but he first took it to a place where Priam should not see it, lest if he did so, he should break out in the bitterness of his grief, and enrage Achilles, who might then kill him and sin against the word of Jove. When the servants had washed the body and anointed it, and had wrapped it in a fair shirt and mantle, Achilles himself lifted it on to a bier, and he and his men then laid it on the wagon. He cried aloud as he did so and called on the name of his dear comrade, "Be not angry with me, Patroclus," he said, "if you hear even in the house of Hades that I have given Hector to his father for a ransom. It has been no unworthy one, and I will share it equitably with you."

Achilles then went back into the tent and took his place on the richly inlaid seat from which he had risen, by the wall that was at right angles to the one against which Priam was sitting. "Sir," he said, "your son is now laid upon his bier and is ransomed according to desire; you shall look upon him when you him away at daybreak; for the present let us prepare our supper. Even lovely Niobe had to think about eating, though her twelve children – six daughters and six lusty sons – had been all slain in her house. Apollo killed the sons with arrows from his silver bow, to punish Niobe, and Diana slew the daughters, because Niobe had vaunted herself against Leto; she said Leto had borne two children only, whereas she had herself borne many – whereon the two killed the many. Nine days did they lie weltering, and there was none to bury them, for the son of Saturn turned the people into stone; but on the tenth day the gods in heaven themselves buried them, and Niobe then took food, being worn out with weeping. They say that somewhere among the rocks on the mountain pastures of Sipylus, where the nymphs live that haunt the river Achelous, there, they say, she lives in stone and still nurses the sorrows sent upon her by the hand of heaven. Therefore, noble sir, let us two now take food; you can weep for your dear son hereafter as you are bearing him back to Ilius – and many a tear will he cost you."

With this Achilles sprang from his seat and killed a sheep of silvery whiteness, which his followers skinned and made ready all in due order. They cut the meat carefully up into smaller pieces, spitted them, and drew them off again when they were well roasted. Automedon brought bread in fair baskets and served it round the table, while Achilles dealt out the meat, and they laid their hands on the good things that were before them. As soon as they had had enough to eat and drink, Priam, descendant of Dardanus, marveled at the strength and beauty of Achilles for he was as a god to see, and Achilles marveled at Priam as he listened to him and looked upon his noble presence. When they had gazed their fill, Priam spoke first. "And now, O king," he said, "take me to my couch that we may lie down and enjoy the blessed boon of sleep. Never once have my eyes been closed from the day your hands took the life of my son; I have groveled without ceasing in the mire of my stable-yard, making moan and brooding over my countless sorrows. Now, moreover, I have eaten bread and drunk wine; hitherto I have tasted nothing."

As he spoke Achilles told his men and the women-servants to set beds in the room that was in the gatehouse, and make them with good red rugs, and spread coverlets on the top of them with woolen cloaks for Priam and Idaeus to wear. So the maids went out carrying a torch and got the two beds ready in all haste. Then Achilles said laughingly to Priam, "Dear sir, you shall lie outside, lest some counselor of those who in due course keep coming to advise with me should see you here in the darkness of the flying night, and tell it to Agamemnon. This might cause delay in the delivery of the body. And now tell me and tell me true, for how many days would you celebrate the funeral rites of noble Hector? Tell me, that I may hold aloof from war and restrain the host."

And Priam answered, "Since, then, you suffer me to bury my noble son with all due rites, do thus, Achilles, and I shall be grateful. You know how we are pent up within our city; it is far for us to fetch wood from the mountain, and the people live in fear. Nine days, therefore, will we mourn Hector in my house; on the tenth day we will bury him and there shall be a public feast in his honor; on the eleventh we will build a mound over his ashes, and on the twelfth, if there be need, we will fight."

And Achilles answered, "All, King Priam, shall be as you have said. I will stay our fighting for as long a time as you have named."

As he spoke he laid his hand on the old man's right wrist, in token that he should have no fear; thus then did Priam and his attendant sleep there in the forecourt, full of thought, while Achilles lay in an inner room of the house, with fair Briseis by his side.

And now both gods and mortals were fast asleep through the livelong night, but upon Mercury alone, the bringer of good luck, sleep could take no hold for he was thinking all the time how to get King Priam away from the ships without his being seen by the strong force of sentinels. He hovered therefore over Priam's head and said, "Sir, now that Achilles has spared your life, you seem to have no fear about sleeping in the thick of your foes. You have paid a great ransom, and have received the body of your son; were you still alive and a prisoner the sons whom you have left at home would have to give three times as much to free you; and so it would be if Agamemnon and the other Achaeans were to know of your being here."

When he heard this the old man was afraid and roused his servant. Mercury then yoked their horses and mules, and drove them quickly through the host so that no man perceived them. When they came to the ford of eddying Xanthus, begotten of immortal Jove, Mercury went back to high Olympus, and dawn in robe of saffron began to break over all the land. Priam and Idaeus then drove on toward the city lamenting and making moan, and the mules drew the body of Hector. No one neither man nor woman saw them, until Cassandra, fair as golden Venus standing on Pergamus, caught sight of her dear father in his chariot, and his servant that was the city's herald with him. Then she saw him that was lying upon the bier, drawn by the mules, and with a loud cry she went about the city saying, "Come hither Trojans, men and women, and look on Hector; if ever you rejoiced to see him coming from battle when he was alive, look now on him that was the glory of our city and all our people."

At this there was not man nor woman left in the city, so great a sorrow had possessed them. Hard by the gates they met Priam as he was bringing in the body. Hector's wife and his mother were the first to mourn him: they flew towards the wagon and laid their hands upon his head, while the crowd stood weeping round them. They would have stayed before the gates, weeping and lamenting the livelong day to the going down of the sun, had not Priam spoken to them from the chariot and said, "Make way for the mules to pass you. Afterwards when I have taken the body home you shall have your fill of weeping."

On this the people stood asunder, and made a way for the wagon. When they had borne the body within the house they laid it upon a bed and seated minstrels round it to lead the dirge, whereon the women joined in the sad music of their lament. Foremost among them all Andromache led their wailing as she clasped the head of mighty Hector in her embrace. "Husband," she cried, "you have died young, and leave me in your house a widow; he of whom we are the ill-starred parents is still a mere child, and I fear he may not reach manhood. Before he can do so our city will be razed and overthrown, for you who watched over it are no more – you who were its savior, the guardian of our wives and children. Our women will be carried away captives to the ships, and I among them; while you, my child, who will be with me will be put to some unseemly tasks, working for a cruel master. Or, may be, some Achaean will hurl you (O miserable death) from our walls, to avenge some brother, son, or father whom Hector slew; many of them have indeed bitten the dust at his hands, for your father's hand in battle was no light one. Therefore do the people mourn him. You have left, O Hector, sorrow unutterable to your parents, and my own grief is greatest of all, for you did not stretch forth your arms and embrace me as you lay dying, nor say to me any words that might have lived with me in my tears night and day for evermore."

She wept bitterly, and the women joined in her lament. Hecuba in her turn took up the strains of woe. "Hector," she cried, "dearest to me of all my children. As long as you were alive the gods loved you well, and even in death they have been mindful of you; for when Achilles took any other of my sons, he would sell him beyond the seas, to Samos Imbrus or rugged Lemnos; and when he had slain you too with his sword, many times he dragged you around his comrade's sepulcher – though this could not give him life – yet here you lie all fresh as dew, and comely as one whom Apollo has slain with his painless shafts."

Thus did she too speak through her tears with bitter moan, and then Helen for a third time took up the strain of lamentation. "Hector," said she, "dearest of all my brothers-in-law-for I am wife to Alexandrus who brought me hither to Troy – would that I had died before he did so – twenty years are come and gone since I left my home and came from over the sea, but I have never heard one word of insult or unkindness from you. When another would chide with me, as it might be one of your brothers or sisters or of your brothers' wives, or my mother-in-law – for Priam was as kind to me as though he were my own father – you would rebuke and check them with words of gentleness and goodwill. Therefore my tears flow both for you and for my unhappy self, for there is no one else in Troy who is kind to me, but all shrink and shudder as they go by me."

She wept as she spoke and the vast crowd that was gathered round her joined in her lament. Then King Priam spoke to them saying, "Bring wood, O Trojans, to the city, and fear no cunning ambush of the Argives, for Achilles when he dismissed me from the ships gave me his word that they should not attack us until the morning of the twelfth day."

Forthwith they yoked their oxen and mules and gathered together before the city. Nine days long did they bring in great heaps wood, and on the morning of the tenth day with many tears they took Hector forth, laid his dead body upon the summit of the pile, and set the fire thereto. Then when the child of morning rosy-fingered dawn appeared on the eleventh day, the people again assembled, round the pyre of mighty Hector. When they were got together, they first quenched the fire with wine wherever it was burning, and then his brothers and comrades with many a bitter tear gathered his white bones, wrapped them in soft robes of purple, and laid them in a golden urn, which they placed in a grave and covered over with large stones set close together. Then they built a barrow hurriedly over it keeping guard on every side lest the Achaeans should attack them before they had finished. When they had heaped up the barrow they went back again into the city, and being well assembled they held high feast in the house of Priam their king.

Thus, then, did they celebrate the funeral of Hector tamer of horses.

CBEO

Odysseus and Polyphemus
From The Iliad
Homer, Eighth Century BC
TRANSLATED BY SAMUEL BUTLER

For a brief introduction to this reading, please see the end of the introduction to Homer before the reading from The Odyssey *above. Please note that Odysseus here is speaking to the Phaeacian court, where, after ten years of the war at Troy and ten more years of misadventures at sea, he, a complete stranger, has been given – in complete contrast to the story he is about to tell – great hospitality.*

"We sailed from there, always in much distress, until we came to the land of the lawless and inhuman Cyclopes. Now the Cyclopes neither plant nor plough, but trust in providence, and live on such wheat, barley, and grapes as grow wild without any kind of tillage, and their wild grapes yield them wine as the sun and the rain may grow them. They have no laws nor assemblies of the people, but live in caves on the tops of high mountains; each is lord and master in his family, and they take no account of their neighbors.

"Now off their harbor there lies a wooded and fertile island not quite close to the land of the Cyclopes, but still not far. It is overrun with wild goats, that breed there in great numbers and are never disturbed by foot of man; for sportsmen – who as a rule will suffer so much hardship in forest or among mountain precipices – do not go there, nor yet again is it ever ploughed or fed down, but it lies a wilderness untilled and unsown from year to year, and has no living thing upon it but only goats. For the Cyclopes have no ships, nor yet shipwrights who could make ships for them; they cannot therefore go from city to city, or sail over the sea to one another's country as people who have ships can do; if they had had these they would have colonized the island, for it is a very good one, and would yield everything in due season. There are meadows that in some places come right down to the sea shore, well watered and full of luscious grass; grapes would do there excellently; there is level land for ploughing, and it would always yield heavily at harvest time, for the soil is deep. There is a good harbor where no cables are wanted, nor yet anchors, nor need a ship be moored, but all one has to do is to beach one's vessel and stay there until the wind becomes fair for putting out to sea again. At the head of the harbor there is a spring of clear water coming out of a cave, and there are poplars growing all round it.

"Here we entered, but so dark was the night that some god must have brought us in, for there was nothing whatever to be seen. A thick mist hung all round our ships; the moon was hidden behind a mass of clouds so that no one could have seen the island if he had looked for it, nor were there any breakers to tell us we were close in shore before we found ourselves upon the land itself; when, however, we had beached the ships, we took down the sails, went ashore and camped upon the beach until daybreak.

"When the child of morning, rosy-fingered Dawn, appeared, we admired the island and wandered all over it, while the nymphs Jove's daughters roused the wild goats that we might get some meat for our dinner. On this we fetched our spears and bows and arrows from the ships, and dividing ourselves into three bands began to shoot the goats. Heaven sent us excellent sport; I had twelve ships with me, and each ship got nine goats, while my own ship had ten; thus through the livelong day to the going down of the sun we ate and drank our fill, – and we had plenty of wine left, for each one of us had taken many jars full when we sacked the city of the Cicons, and this had not yet run out. While we were feasting we kept turning our eyes towards the land of the Cyclopes, which was hard by, and saw the smoke of their stubble fires. We could almost fancy we heard their voices and the bleating of their sheep and goats, but when the sun went down and it came on dark, we camped down upon the beach, and next morning I called a council.

"'Stay here, my brave fellows,' said I, 'all the rest of you, while I go with my ship and exploit these people myself: I want to see if they are uncivilized savages, or a hospitable and humane race.'

"I went on board, bidding my men to do so also and loose the hawsers; so they took their places and smote the grey sea with their oars. When we got to the land, which was not far, there, on the face of a cliff near the sea, we saw a great cave overhung with laurels. It was a station for a great many sheep and goats, and outside there was a large yard, with a high wall round it made of stones built into the ground and of trees both pine and oak. This was the abode of a huge monster who was then away from home shepherding his flocks. He would have nothing to do with other people, but led the life of an outlaw. He was a horrid creature, not like a human being at all, but resembling rather some crag that stands out boldly against the sky on the top of a high mountain.

"I told my men to draw the ship ashore, and stay where they were, all but the twelve best among them, who were to go along with myself. I also took a goatskin of sweet black wine which had been given me by Maron, Apollo son of Euanthes, who was priest of Apollo the patron god of Ismarus, and lived within the wooded precincts of the temple. When we were sacking the city we respected him, and spared his life, as also his wife and child; so he made me some presents of great value – seven talents of fine gold, and a bowl of silver, with twelve jars of sweet wine, unblended, and of the most exquisite flavor. Not a man nor maid in the house knew about it, but only himself, his wife, and one housekeeper: when he drank it he mixed twenty parts of water to one of wine, and yet the fragrance from the mixing-bowl was so exquisite that it was impossible to refrain from drinking. I filled a large skin with this wine, and took a wallet full of provisions with me, for my mind misgave me that I might have to deal with some savage who would be of great strength, and would respect neither right nor law.

"We soon reached his cave, but he was out shepherding, so we went inside and took stock of all that we could see. His cheese-racks were loaded with cheeses, and he had more lambs and kids than his pens could hold. They were kept in separate flocks; first there were the hoggets, then the oldest of the younger lambs and lastly the very young ones all kept apart from one another; as for his dairy, all the vessels, bowls, and milk pails into which he milked, were swimming with whey. When they saw all this, my men begged me to let them first steal some cheeses, and make off with them to the ship; they would then return, drive down the lambs and kids, put them on board and sail away with them. It would have been indeed better if we had done so but I would not listen to them, for I wanted to see the owner himself, in the hope that he might give me a present. When, however, we saw him my poor men found him ill to deal with.

"We lit a fire, offered some of the cheeses in sacrifice, ate others of them, and then sat waiting until the Cyclops should come in with his sheep. When he came, he brought in with him a huge load of dry firewood to light the fire for his supper, and this he flung with such a noise on to the floor of his cave that we hid ourselves for fear at the far end of the cavern. Meanwhile he drove all the ewes inside, as well as the she-goats that he was going to milk, leaving the males, both rams and he-goats, outside in the yards. Then he rolled a huge stone to the mouth of the cave – so huge that two and twenty strong four-wheeled wagons would not be enough to draw it from its place against the doorway. When he had so done he sat down and milked his ewes and goats, all in due course, and then let each of them have her own young. He curdled half the milk and set it aside in wicker strainers, but the other half he poured into bowls that he might drink it for his supper. When he had got through with all his work, he lit the fire, and then caught sight of us, whereon he said:

"'Strangers, who are you? Where do sail from? Are you traders, or do you sail the sea as rovers, with your hands against every man, and every man's hand against you?'

"We were frightened out of our senses by his loud voice and monstrous form, but I managed to say, 'We are Achaeans on our way home from Troy, but

28

by the will of Jove, and stress of weather, we have been driven far out of our course. We are the people of Agamemnon, son of Atreus, who has won infinite renown throughout the whole world, by sacking so great a city and killing so many people. We therefore humbly pray you to show us some hospitality, and otherwise make us such presents as visitors may reasonably expect. May your excellency fear the wrath of heaven, for we are your suppliants, and Jove takes all respectable travelers under his protection, for he is the avenger of all suppliants and foreigners in distress.'

"To this he gave me but a pitiless answer, 'Stranger,' said he, 'you are a fool, or else you know nothing of this country. Talk to me, indeed, about fearing the gods or shunning their anger? We Cyclopes do not care about Jove or any of your blessed gods, for we are ever so much stronger than they. I shall not spare either yourself or your companions out of any regard for Jove, unless I am in the humor for doing so. And now tell me where you made your ship fast when you came on shore. Was it round the point, or is she lying straight off the land?'

"He said this to draw me out, but I was too cunning to be caught in that way, so I answered with a lie; 'Neptune,' said I, 'sent my ship on to the rocks at the far end of your country, and wrecked it. We were driven on to them from the open sea, but I and those who are with me escaped the jaws of death.'

"The cruel wretch vouchsafed me not one word of answer, but with a sudden clutch he gripped up two of my men at once and dashed them down upon the ground as though they had been puppies. Their brains were shed upon the ground, and the earth was wet with their blood. Then he tore them limb from limb and supped upon them. He gobbled them up like a lion in the wilderness, flesh, bones, marrow, and entrails, without leaving anything uneaten. As for us, we wept and lifted up our hands to heaven on seeing such a horrid sight, for we did not know what else to do; but when the Cyclops had filled his huge paunch, and had washed down his meal of human flesh with a drink of neat milk, he stretched himself full length upon the ground among his sheep, and went to sleep. I was at first inclined to seize my sword, draw it, and drive it into his vitals, but I reflected that if I did we should all certainly be lost, for we should never be able to shift the stone which the monster had put in front of the door. So we stayed sobbing and sighing where we were until morning came.

"When the child of morning, rosy-fingered Dawn, appeared, he again lit his fire, milked his goats and ewes, all quite rightly, and then let each have her own young one; as soon as he had got through with all his work, he clutched up two more of my men, and began eating them for his morning's meal. Presently, with the utmost ease, he rolled the stone away from the door and drove out his sheep, but he at once put it back again – as easily as though he were merely clapping the lid on to a quiver full of arrows. As soon as he had done so he shouted, and cried 'Shoo, shoo,' after his sheep to drive them on to the mountain; so I was left to scheme some way of taking my revenge and covering myself with glory.

"In the end I deemed it would be the best plan to do as follows. The Cyclops had a great club which was lying near one of the sheep pens; it was of green olive wood, and he had cut it intending to use it for a staff as soon as it should be dry. It was so huge that we could only compare it to the mast of a twenty-oared merchant vessel of large burden, and able to venture out into open sea. I went up to this club and cut off about six feet of it; I then gave this piece to the men and told them to fine it evenly off at one end, which they proceeded to do, and lastly I brought it to a point myself, charring the end in the fire to make it harder. When I had done this I hid it under dung, which was lying about all over the cave, and told the men to cast lots which of them should venture along with myself to lift it and bore it into the monster's eye while he was asleep. The lot fell upon the very four whom I should have chosen, and I myself made five. In the evening the wretch came back from shepherding, and drove his flocks into the cave – this time driving them all inside, and not leaving any in the yards; I suppose some fancy must have taken him, or a god must have prompted him to do so. As soon as he had put the stone back to its place against the door, he sat down, milked his ewes and his goats all quite rightly, and then let each have her own young one; when he had got through with all this work, he gripped up two more of my men, and made his supper off them. So I went up to him with an ivy-wood bowl of black wine in my hands:

"'Look here, Cyclops,' said I, you have been eating a great deal of man's flesh, so take this and drink some wine, that you may see what kind of liquor we had on board my ship. I was bringing it to you as a drink-offering, in the hope that you would take compassion upon me and further me on my way home, whereas all you do is to go on ramping and raving most intolerably. You ought to be ashamed yourself; how can you expect people to come see you any more if you treat them in this way?'

"He then took the cup and drank. He was so delighted with the taste of the wine that he begged me for another bowl full. 'Be so kind,' he said, 'as to give me some more, and tell me your name at once. I want to make you a present that you will be glad to have. We have wine even in this country, for our soil grows grapes and the sun ripens them, but this drinks like nectar and ambrosia all in one.'

"I then gave him some more; three times did I fill the bowl for him, and three times did he drain it without thought or heed; then, when I saw that the wine had got into his head, I said to him as plausibly as I could: 'Cyclops, you ask my name and I will tell it you; give me, therefore, the present you promised me; my name is Noman; this is what my father and mother and my friends have always called me.'

"But the cruel wretch said, 'Then I will eat all Noman's comrades before Noman himself, and will keep Noman for the last. This is the present that I will make him.'

As he spoke he reeled, and fell sprawling face upwards on the ground. His great neck hung heavily backwards and a deep sleep took hold upon him. Presently he turned sick, and threw up both wine and the gobbets of human flesh on which he had been gorging, for he was very drunk. Then I thrust the beam of wood far into the embers to heat it, and encouraged my men lest any of them should turn faint-hearted. When the wood, green though it was, was about to blaze, I drew it out of the fire glowing with heat, and my men gathered round me, for heaven had filled their hearts with courage. We drove the sharp end of the beam into the monster's eye, and bearing upon it with all my weight I kept turning it round and round as though I were boring a hole in a ship's plank with an auger, which two men with a wheel and strap can keep on turning as long as they choose. Even thus did we bore the red hot beam into his eye, until the boiling blood bubbled all over it as we worked it round and round, so that the steam from the burning eyeball scalded his eyelids and eyebrows, and the roots of the eye sputtered in the fire. As a blacksmith plunges an axe or hatchet into cold water to temper it – for it is this that gives strength to the iron – and it makes a great hiss as he does so, even thus did the Cyclops' eye hiss round the beam of olive wood, and his hideous yells made the cave ring again. We ran away in a fright, but he plucked the beam all besmirched with gore from his eye, and hurled it from him in a frenzy of rage and pain, shouting as he did so to the other Cyclopes who lived on the bleak headlands near him; so they gathered from all quarters round his cave when they heard him crying, and asked what was the matter with him.

"'What ails you, Polyphemus,' said they, 'that you make such a noise, breaking the stillness of the night, and preventing us from being able to sleep? Surely no man is carrying off your sheep? Surely no man is trying to kill you either by fraud or by force?

"But Polyphemus shouted to them from inside the cave, 'Noman is killing me by fraud! Noman is killing me by force!'

"'Then,' said they, 'if no man is attacking you, you must be ill; when Jove makes people ill, there is no help for it, and you had better pray to your father Neptune.'

"Then they went away, and I laughed inwardly at the success of my clever stratagem, but the Cyclops, groaning and in an agony of pain, felt about with his hands until he found the stone and took it from the door; then he sat in the doorway and stretched his hands in front of it to catch anyone going out with the sheep, for he thought I might be foolish enough to attempt this.

"As for myself I kept on puzzling to think how I could best save my own life and those of my companions; I schemed and schemed, as one who knows that his life depends upon it, for the danger was very great. In the end I deemed that this plan would be the best. The male sheep were well grown, and carried a heavy black fleece, so I bound them noiselessly in threes together, with some of the withies on which the wicked monster used to sleep. There was to be a man under the middle sheep, and the two on either side were to cover him, so that there were three sheep to each man. As for myself there was a ram finer than any of the others, so I caught hold of him by the back, ensconced myself in the thick wool under his belly, and flung on patiently to his fleece, face upwards, keeping a firm hold on it all the time.

"Thus, then, did we wait in great fear of mind until morning came, but when the child of morning, rosy-fingered Dawn, appeared, the male sheep hurried out to feed, while the ewes remained bleating about the pens waiting to be milked, for their udders were full to bursting; but their master in spite of all his pain felt the backs of all the sheep as they stood upright, without being sharp enough to find out that the men were underneath their bellies. As the ram was going out, last of all, heavy with its fleece and with the weight of my crafty self; Polyphemus laid hold of it and said:

"'My good ram, what is it that makes you the last to leave my cave this morning? You are not wont to let the ewes go before you, but lead the mob with a run whether to flowery mead or bubbling fountain, and are the first to come home again at night; but now you lag last of all. Is it because you know your master has lost his eye, and are sorry because that wicked Noman and his horrid crew have got him down in his drink and blinded him? But I will have his life yet. If you could understand and talk, you would tell me where the wretch is hiding, and I would dash his brains upon the ground until they flew all over the cave. I should thus have some satisfaction for the harm that this no-good Noman has done me.'

"As spoke he drove the ram outside, but when we were a little way out from the cave and yards, I first got from under the ram's belly, and then freed my comrades; as for the sheep, which were very fat, by constantly heading them in the right direction we managed to drive them down to the ship. The crew rejoiced greatly at seeing those of us who had escaped death, but wept for the others whom the Cyclops had killed. However, I made signs to them by nodding and frowning that they were to hush their crying, and told them to get all the sheep on board at once and put out to sea; so they went aboard, took their places, and smote the grey sea with their oars. Then, when I had got as far out as my voice would reach, I began to jeer at the Cyclops.

"'Cyclops,' said I, 'you should have taken better measure of your man before eating up his comrades in your cave. You wretch, eat up your visitors in your own house? You might have known that your sin would find you out, and now Jove and the other gods have punished you.'

"He got more and more furious as he heard me, so he tore the top from off a high mountain, and flung it just in front of my ship so that it was within a little of hitting the end of the rudder. The sea quaked as the rock fell into it, and the wash of the wave it raised carried us back towards the mainland, and forced us towards the shore. But I snatched up a long pole and kept the ship off, making signs to my men by nodding my head that they must row for their lives, whereon they laid out with a will. When we had got twice as far as we were before, I was for jeering at the Cyclops again, but the men begged and prayed of me to hold my tongue.

"'Do not,' they exclaimed, 'be mad enough to provoke this savage creature further; he has thrown one rock at us already which drove us back again to the mainland, and we made sure it had been the death of us; if he had then heard any further sound of voices he would have pounded our heads and our ship's timbers into a jelly with the rugged rocks he would have heaved at us, for he can throw them a long way.'

"But I would not listen to them, and shouted out to him in my rage, 'Cyclops, if any one asks you who it was that put your eye out and spoiled your beauty, say it was the valiant warrior Ulysses, son of Laertes, who lives in Ithaca.'

"On this he groaned, and cried out, 'Alas, alas, then the old prophecy about me is coming true. There was a prophet here, at one time, a man both brave and of great stature, Telemus son of Eurymus, who was an excellent seer, and did all the prophesying for the Cyclopes until he grew old; he told me that all this would happen to me some day, and said I should lose my sight by the hand of Ulysses. I have been all along expecting some one of imposing presence and superhuman strength, whereas he turns out to be a little insignificant weakling, who has managed to blind my eye by taking advantage of me in my drink; come here, then, Ulysses, that I may make you presents to show my hospitality, and urge Neptune to help you forward on your journey – for Neptune and I are father and son. He, if he so will, shall heal me, which no one else neither god nor man can do.'

"Then I said, 'I wish I could be as sure of killing you outright and sending you down to the house of Hades, as I am that it will take more than Neptune to cure that eye of yours.'

"On this he lifted up his hands to the firmament of heaven and prayed, saying, 'Hear me, great Neptune; if I am indeed your own true-begotten son, grant that Ulysses may never reach his home alive; or if he must get back to his friends at last, let him do so late and in sore plight after losing all his men let him reach his home in another man's ship and find trouble in his house.'

"Thus did he pray, and Neptune heard his prayer. Then he picked up a rock much larger than the first, swung it aloft and hurled it with prodigious force. It fell just short of the ship, but was within a little of hitting the end of the rudder. The sea quaked as the rock fell into it, and the wash of the wave it raised drove us onwards on our way towards the shore of the island.

"When at last we got to the island where we had left the rest of our ships, we found our comrades lamenting us, and anxiously awaiting our return. We ran our vessel upon the sands and got out of her on to the sea shore; we also landed the Cyclops' sheep, and divided them equitably amongst us so that none might have reason to complain. As for the ram, my companions agreed that I should have it as an extra share; so I sacrificed it on the sea shore, and burned its thigh bones to Jove, who is the lord of all. But he heeded not my sacrifice, and only thought how he might destroy my ships and my comrades."

Pericles
c. 495 – 429 BC
Thucydides
c. 460 – c. 395 BC

Pericles, the brilliant and charismatic Greek politician and general, perished in the plague that devastated Athens the year after he gave his famous funeral oration for the deceased Athenian soldiers.

Well known as the "father of scientific history" for its careful use of evidence, Thucydides was a Greek historian and Athenian general, whose *History of the Peloponnesian War* relates the war between Sparta and Athens to the year 411 BC.

Pericles delivered this speech at the end of the first year of the Peloponnesian War (431 – 404 BC) as a part of the annual public funeral for the war dead.

છ૪૦

Pericles' Funeral Oration
Pericles, 431 BC; Thucydides, 431 – 395 BC
TRANSLATED BY BENJAMIN JOWETT

Most of those who have spoken here before me have commended the lawgiver who added this oration to our other funeral customs. It seemed to them a worthy thing that such an honor should be given at their burial to the dead who have fallen on the field of battle. But I should have preferred that, when men's deeds have been brave, they should be honored in deed only, and with such an honor as this public funeral, which you are now witnessing. Then the reputation of many would not have been imperiled on the eloquence or want of eloquence of one, and their virtues believed or not as he spoke well or ill. For it is difficult to say neither too little nor too much; and even moderation is apt not to give the impression of truthfulness. The friend of the dead who knows the facts is likely to think that the words of the speaker fall short of his knowledge and of his wishes; another who is not so well informed, when he hears of anything which surpasses his own powers, will be envious and will suspect exaggeration. Mankind are tolerant of the praises of others so long as each hearer thinks that he can do as well or nearly as well himself, but, when the speaker rises above him, jealousy is aroused and he begins to be incredulous. However, since our ancestors have set the seal of their approval upon the practice, I must obey, and to the utmost of my power shall endeavor to satisfy the wishes and beliefs of all who hear me.

I will speak first of our ancestors, for it is right and seemly that now, when we are lamenting the dead, a tribute should be paid to their memory. There has never been a time when they did not inhabit this land, which by their valor they will have handed down from generation to generation, and we have received from them a free state. But if they were worthy of praise, still more were our fathers, who added to their inheritance, and after many a struggle transmitted to us their sons this great empire. And we ourselves assembled here today, who are still most of us in the vigor of life, have carried the work of improvement further, and have richly endowed our city with all things, so that she is sufficient for herself both in peace and war. Of the military exploits by which our various possessions were acquired, or of the energy with which we or our fathers drove back the tide of war, Hellenic or Barbarian, I will not speak; for the tale would be long and is familiar to you. But before I praise the dead, I should like to point out by what principles of action we rose to power, and under what institutions and through what manner of life our empire became great. For I conceive that such thoughts are not unsuited to the occasion, and that this numerous assembly of citizens and strangers may profitably listen to them.

Our form of government does not enter into rivalry with the institutions of others. Our government does not copy our neighbors', but is an example to them. It is true that we are called a democracy, for the administration is in the hands of the many and not of the few. But while there exists equal justice to all and alike in their private disputes, the claim of excellence is also recognized; and when a citizen is in any way distinguished, he is preferred to the public service, not as a matter of privilege, but as the reward of merit. Neither is poverty an obstacle, but a man may benefit his country whatever the obscurity of his condition. There is no exclusiveness in our public life, and in our private business we are not suspicious of one another, nor angry with our neighbor if he does what he likes; we do not put on sour looks at him which, though harmless, are not pleasant. While we are thus unconstrained in our private business, a spirit of reverence pervades our public acts; we are prevented from doing wrong by respect for the authorities and for the laws, having a particular regard to those which are ordained for the protection of the injured as well as those unwritten laws which bring upon the transgressor of them the reprobation of the general sentiment.

And we have not forgotten to provide for our weary spirits many relaxations from toil; we have regular games and sacrifices throughout the year; our homes are beautiful and elegant; and the delight which we daily feel in all these things helps to banish sorrow. Because of the greatness of our city the fruits of the whole earth flow in upon us; so that we enjoy the goods of other countries as freely as our own.

Then, again, our military training is in many respects superior to that of our adversaries. Our city is thrown open to the world, though, and we never expel a foreigner and prevent him from seeing or learning anything of which the secret if revealed to an enemy might profit him. We rely not upon management or trickery, but upon our own hearts and hands. In the matter of education, whereas they from early youth are always undergoing laborious exercises which are to make them brave, we live at ease, and yet are equally ready to face the perils which they face. Here is the proof: the Lacedaemonians come into Athenian territory not by themselves, but with their whole confederacy; we go alone into a neighbor's country; and although our opponents are fighting for their homes and we on a foreign soil, we have seldom any difficulty in overcoming them. Our enemies have never felt our united strength, the care of a navy divides our attention, and on land we are obliged to send our own citizens everywhere. But they, if they meet and defeat a part of our army, are as proud as if they had routed us all, and when defeated they pretend to have been vanquished by us all.

If then we prefer to meet danger with a light heart but without laborious training, and with a courage which is gained by habit and not enforced by law, are we not greatly the better for it? Since we do not anticipate the pain, although, when the hour comes, we can be as brave as those who never allow themselves to rest; thus our city is equally admirable in peace and in war. For we are lovers of the beautiful in our tastes and our strength lies, in our opinion, not in deliberation and discussion, but that knowledge which is gained by discussion preparatory to action. For we have a peculiar power of thinking before we act, and of acting, too, whereas other men are courageous from ignorance but hesitate upon reflection. And they are surely to be esteemed the bravest spirits who, having the clearest sense both of the pains and pleasures of life, do not on that account shrink from danger. In doing good, again, we are unlike others; we make our friends by conferring, not by receiving favors. Now he who confers a favor is the firmer friend, because he would rather by kindness keep alive the memory of an obligation; but the recipient is colder in his feelings, because he knows that in requiting another's generosity he will not be winning gratitude but only paying a debt. We alone do good to our neighbors not upon a calculation of interest, but in the confidence of freedom and in a frank and fearless spirit. To sum up: I say that Athens is the school of Hellas, and that the individual Athenian in his own person seems to have the power of adapting himself to the most varied forms of action with the utmost versatility and grace. This is no passing and idle word, but truth and fact; and the assertion is verified by the position to which these qualities have raised the state. For in the hour of trial Athens alone among her contemporaries is superior to the report of her. No enemy who comes against her is indignant at the reverses which he sustains at the hands of such a city; no subject complains that his masters are unworthy of him. And we shall assuredly not be without witnesses; there are mighty monuments of our power which will make us the wonder of this and of succeeding ages; we shall not need the praises of Homer or of any other panegyrist whose poetry may please for the moment, although his representation of the facts will not bear the light of day. For we have compelled every land and every sea to open a path for our valor, and have everywhere planted eternal memorials of our friendship and of our enmity. Such is the city for whose sake these men nobly fought and died; they could not bear the thought that she might be taken from them; and every one of us who survive should gladly toil on her behalf.

I have dwelt upon the greatness of Athens because I want to show you that we are contending for a higher prize than those who enjoy none of these privileges, and to establish by manifest proof the merit of these men whom I am now commemorating. Their loftiest praise has been already spoken. For in magnifying the city I have magnified them, and men like them whose virtues made her glorious. And of how few Hellenes[1] can it be said as of them, that their deeds when weighed in the balance have been found equal to their fame! I believe that a death such as theirs has been the true measure of a man's worth; it may be the first revelation of his virtues, but is at any rate their final seal. For even those who come short in other ways may justly plead the valor with which they have fought for their country; they have blotted out the evil with the good, and have benefited the state more by their public services than they have injured her by their private actions. None of these men were enervated by wealth or hesitated to resign the pleasures of life; none of them put off the evil day in the hope, natural to poverty, that a man, though poor, may one day become rich. But, deeming that the punishment of their enemies was sweeter than any of these things, and that they could fall in no nobler cause, they determined at the hazard of their lives to be honorably avenged, and to leave the rest. They resigned to hope their unknown chance of happiness; but in the face of death they resolved to rely upon themselves alone. And when the moment came they were minded to resist and suffer, rather than to fly and save their lives; they ran away from the word of dishonor, but on the battlefield their feet stood fast, and in an instant, at the height of their fortune, they passed away from the scene, not of their fear, but of their glory.

Such was the end of these men; they were worthy of Athens, and the living need not desire to have a more heroic spirit, although they may pray for a less fatal issue. The value of such a spirit is not to be expressed in words. Any one can discourse to you for ever about the advantages of a brave defense, which you know already. But instead of listening to him I would have you day by day fix your eyes upon the greatness of Athens, until you become filled with the love of her; and when you are impressed by the spectacle of her glory, reflect that this empire has been acquired by men who knew their duty and had the courage to do it, who in the hour of conflict had the fear of dishonor always present to them, and who, if ever they failed in an enterprise, would not allow their virtues to be lost to their country, but freely gave their lives to her as the fairest offering which they could present at her feast. The sacrifice which they collectively made was individually repaid to them; for they received again each one for himself a praise which grows not old, and the noblest of all tombs, I speak not of that in which their remains are laid, but of that in which their glory survives, and is proclaimed always and on every fitting occasion both in word and deed. For the whole earth is the tomb of famous men; not only are they commemorated by columns and inscriptions in their own country, but in foreign lands there dwells

[1] Hellenes. Greeks.

also an unwritten memorial of them, graven not on stone but in the hearts of men. Make them your examples, and, esteeming courage to be freedom and freedom to be happiness, do not weigh too nicely the perils of war. The unfortunate who has no hope of a change for the better has less reason to throw away his life than the prosperous who, if he survive, is always liable to a change for the worse, and to whom any accidental fall makes the most serious difference. To a man of spirit, cowardice and disaster coming together are far more bitter than death striking him unperceived at a time when he is full of courage and animated by the general hope.

Wherefore I do not now pity the parents of the dead who stand here; I would rather comfort them. You know that your dead have passed away amid manifold vicissitudes; and that they may be deemed fortunate who have gained their utmost honor, whether an honorable death like theirs, or an honorable sorrow like yours, and whose share of happiness has been so ordered that the term of their happiness is likewise the term of their life. I know how hard it is to make you feel this, when the good fortune of others will too often remind you of the gladness which once lightened your hearts. And sorrow is felt at the want of those blessings, not which a man never knew, but which were a part of his life before they were taken from him. Some of you are of an age at which they may hope to have other children, and they ought to bear their sorrow better; not only will the children who may hereafter be born make them forget their own lost ones, but the city will be doubly a gainer. She will not be left desolate, and she will be safer. For a man's counsel cannot have equal weight or worth, when he alone has no children to risk in the general danger. To those of you who have passed their prime, I say: Congratulate yourselves that you have been happy during the greater part of your days; remember that your life of sorrow will not last long, and be comforted by the glory of those who are gone. For the love of honor alone is ever young, and not riches, as some say, but honor is the delight of men when they are old and useless.

To you who are the sons and brothers of the departed, I see that the struggle to emulate them will be an arduous one. For all men praise the dead, and, however preeminent your virtue may be, I do not say even to approach them, and avoid living their rivals and detractors, but when a man is out of the way, the honor and goodwill which he receives is unalloyed. And, if I am to speak of womanly virtues to those of you who will henceforth be widows, let me sum them up in one short admonition: For a woman not to show more weakness than is natural to her sex is a great glory, and not to be talked about for good or for evil among men.

I have paid the required tribute, in obedience to the law, making use of such fitting words as I had. The tribute of deeds has been paid in part; for the dead have them in deeds, and it remains only that their children should be maintained at the public charge until they are grown up: this is the solid prize with which, as with a garland, Athens crowns her sons living and dead, after a struggle like theirs. For where the rewards of virtue are greatest, there the noblest citizens are enlisted in the service of the state. And now, when you have duly lamented, every one his own dead, you may depart.

Plato
423 – 347 BC

Plato is often used as the starting point of Western philosophy, though there were many philosophers who preceded him, including his own teacher Socrates. Plato was the founder of the Academy in Athens, in a sense the first school of advanced learning in Europe.

Many have said that the world of philosophy can be divided into two schools, that of Plato and that of Aristotle, his student and the teacher of Alexander the Great. Plato insisted that the things of this world are only reflections of the paradigms, or original models, in the heavens, and we must therefore contemplate these paradigms. In contrast, Aristotle argued that the truth can be found in our close observation of the things of this world.

Plato's work is vast, covering most every aspect of human existence, and his ideas are still discussed in many fields from Philosophy and Ethics to Political Science and Literary Studies.

In the selection below, generally known as "The Allegory of the Cave," Plato, using the form of a dialogue between Socrates and his disciple Glaucon (Plato's older brother), attempts to explain the nature of reality and its relationship to human perception by offering an allegory (a story used to explain some deeper meaning) in which people are chained to the wall of a cave watching shadows that are produced by fire that is behind them.

Major Works
The Republic
The Symposium
Laws

ᚠ
Allegory of the Cave
From The Republic
Plato, c. 380 BC
TRANSLATED BY BENJAMIN JOWETT

Socrates. And now, I said, let me show in a figure how far our nature is enlightened or unenlightened: – Behold! Human beings living in an underground cave, which has a mouth open towards the light and reaching all along the cave; here they have been from their childhood, and have their legs and necks chained so that they cannot move, and can only see before them, being prevented by the chains from turning round their heads. Above and behind them a fire is blazing at a distance, and between the fire and the prisoners there is a raised way; and you will see, if you look, a low wall built along the way, like the screen which marionette players have in front of them, over which they show the puppets.

Glaucon. I see.

Socrates. And do you see, I said, men passing along the wall carrying all sorts of vessels, and statues and figures of animals made of wood and stone and various materials, which appear over the wall? Some of them are talking, others silent.

Glaucon. You have shown me a strange image, and they are strange prisoners.

Socrates. Like ourselves, I replied; and they see only their own shadows, or the shadows of one another, which the fire throws on the opposite wall of the cave?

Glaucon. True, he said; how could they see anything but the shadows if they were never allowed to move their heads?

Socrates. And of the objects which are being carried in like manner they would only see the shadows?

Glaucon. Yes.

Socrates. And if they were able to converse with one another, would they not suppose that they were naming what was actually before them?

Glaucon. Very true.

Socrates. And suppose further that the prison had an echo which came from the other side, would they not be sure to fancy when one of the passers-by spoke that the voice which they heard came from the passing shadow?

Glaucon. No question, he replied.

Socrates. To them, I said, the truth would be literally nothing but the shadows of the images.

Glaucon. That is certain.

Socrates. And now look again, and see what will naturally follow if the prisoners are released and disabused of their error. At first, when any of them is liberated and compelled suddenly to stand up and turn his neck round and walk and look towards the light, he will suffer sharp pains; the glare will distress him, and he will be unable to see the realities of which in his former state he had seen the shadows; and then conceive some one saying to him, that what he saw before was an illusion, but that now, when he is approaching nearer to being and his eye is turned towards more real existence, he has a clearer vision: what will be his reply? And you may further imagine that his instructor is pointing to the objects as they pass and requiring him to name them: will he not be perplexed? Will he not fancy that the shadows which he formerly saw are truer than the objects which are now shown to him?

Glaucon. Far truer.

Socrates. And if he is compelled to look straight at the light, will he not have a pain in his eyes which will make him turn away to take and take in the objects of vision which he can see, and which he will conceive to be in reality clearer than the things which are now being shown to him?

Glaucon. True, he now.

Socrates. And suppose once more, that he is reluctantly dragged up a steep and rugged ascent, and held fast until he is forced into the presence of the sun himself, is he not likely to be pained and irritated? When he approaches the light his eyes will be dazzled, and he will not be able to see anything at all of what are now called realities.

Glaucon. Not all in a moment, he said.

Socrates. He will be required to grow accustomed to the sight of the upper world. And first he will see the shadows best, next the reflections of men and other objects in the water, and then the objects themselves; then he will gaze upon the light of the moon and the stars and the spangled heaven; and he will see the sky and the stars by night better than the sun or the light of the sun by day?

Glaucon. Certainly.

Socrates. Last of he will be able to see the sun, and not mere reflections of him in the water, but he will see him in his own proper place, and not in another; and he will contemplate him as he is.

Glaucon. Certainly.

Socrates. He will then proceed to argue that this is he who gives the season and the years, and is the guardian of all that is in the visible world, and in a certain way the cause of all things which he and his fellows have been accustomed to behold?

Glaucon. Clearly, he said, he would first see the sun and then reason about him.

Socrates. And when he remembered his old habitation, and the wisdom of the cave and his fellow-prisoners, do you not suppose that he would felicitate himself on the change, and pity them?

Glaucon. Certainly, he would.

Socrates. And if they were in the habit of conferring honors among themselves on those who were quickest to observe the passing shadows and to remark which of them went before, and which followed after, and which were together; and who were therefore best able to draw conclusions as to the future, do you think that he would care for such honors and glories, or envy the possessors of them? Would he not say with Homer, "Better to be the poor servant of a poor master," and to endure anything, rather than think as they do and live after their manner?

Glaucon. Yes, he said, I think that he would rather suffer anything than entertain these false notions and live in this miserable manner.

Socrates. Imagine once more, I said, such a one coming suddenly out of the sun to be replaced in his old situation; would he not be certain to have his eyes full of darkness?

Glaucon. To be sure.

Socrates. And if there were a contest, and he had to compete in measuring the shadows with the prisoners who had never moved out of the cave, while his sight was still weak, and before his eyes had become steady (and the time which would be needed to acquire this new habit of sight might be very considerable) would he not be ridiculous? Men would say of him that up he went and down he came without his eyes; and that it was better not even to think of ascending; and if any one tried to loose another and lead him up to the light, let them only catch the offender, and they would put him to death.

Glaucon. No question.

Socrates. This entire allegory, I said, you may now append, dear Glaucon, to the previous argument; the prison-house is the world of sight, the light of the fire is the sun, and you will not misapprehend me if you interpret the journey upwards to be the ascent of the soul into the intellectual world according to my poor belief, which, at your desire, I have expressed whether rightly or wrongly God knows. But, whether true or false, my opinion is that in the world of knowledge the idea of good appears last of all, and is seen only with an effort; and, when seen, is also inferred to be the universal author of all things beautiful and right, parent of light and of the lord of light in this visible world, and the immediate source of reason and truth in the intellectual; and that this is the power upon which he who would act rationally, either in public or private life must have his eye fixed.

Glaucon. I agree, he said, as far as I am able to understand you.

Socrates. Moreover, I said, you must not wonder that those who attain to this beatific vision are unwilling to descend to human affairs; for their souls are ever hastening into the upper world where they desire to dwell; which desire of theirs is very natural, if our allegory may be trusted.

Glaucon. Yes, very natural.

Socrates. And is there anything surprising in one who passes from divine contemplations to the evil state of man, misbehaving himself in a ridiculous manner; if, while his eyes are blinking and before he has become accustomed to the surrounding darkness, he is compelled to fight in courts of law, or in other places, about the images or the shadows of images of justice, and is endeavoring to meet the conceptions of those who have never yet seen absolute justice?

Glaucon. Anything but surprising, he replied.

Socrates. Any one who has common sense will remember that the bewilderments of the eyes are of two kinds, and arise from two causes, either from coming out of the light or from going into the light, which is true of the mind's eye, quite as much as of the bodily eye; and he who remembers this when he sees any one whose vision is perplexed and weak, will not be too ready to laugh; he will first ask whether that soul of man has come out of the brighter light, and is unable to see because unaccustomed to the dark, or having turned from darkness to the day is dazzled by excess of light. And he will count the one happy in his condition and state of being, and he will pity the other; or, if he have a mind to laugh at the soul which comes from below into the light, there will be more reason in this than in the laugh which greets him who returns from above out of the light into the cave.

Glaucon. That, he said, is a very just distinction.

Socrates. But then, if I am right, certain professors of education must be wrong when they say that they can put a knowledge into the soul which was not there before, like sight into blind eyes.

Glaucon. They undoubtedly say this.

Socrates. Whereas our argument shows that the capacity of learning exists in the soul already; and that just as the eye was unable to turn from darkness to light without the whole body, so too the instrument of knowledge can only by the movement of the whole soul be turned from the world of becoming into that of being, and learn by degrees to endure the sight of being, and of the best of being, or of the good.

Glaucon. Very true.

Socrates. And must there not be some art which will effect conversion in the easiest and quickest manner; not implanting the faculty of sight, for that exists already, but has been turned in the wrong direction, and is looking away from the truth?

Glaucon. Yes, such an art may be presumed.

Socrates. And whereas the other so-called virtues of the soul seem to be akin to bodily qualities, for even when they are not originally innate they can be implanted later by habit and exercise, the of wisdom more than anything else contains a divine element which always remains, and by this conversion is rendered useful and profitable; or, on the other hand, hurtful and useless. Did you never observe the narrow intelligence flashing from the keen eye of a clever rogue – how eager he is, how clearly his paltry soul sees the way to his end; he is the reverse of blind, but his keen eyesight is forced into the service of evil, and he is mischievous in proportion to his cleverness.

Glaucon. Very true.

Vergil
(Publius Vergilius Maro)
70 – 19 BC

Before Vergil wrote *The Aeneid*, the national epic of Rome, for which is most remembered, he had already established himself as one of the great Roman poets with his *Eclogues* and *Georgics*. *The Eclogues* was a collection of ten extended poems on herdsmen whose lives and loves were mythological parallels for Roman politics. The fourth of these poems, which predicted the coming of a child to lead the nation, was often misinterpreted in Christian culture as Vergil's prophecy of the coming of Jesus Christ, though he was likely imagining a unifying emperor. *The Georgics*, which also purports to describe the agricultural life, is more of a commentary on the conditions of the contemporary Roman world.

The *Aeneid* was well received by the Emperor Augustus, whose hopes of unifying the empire and legitimating his own rule were solidified in this national epic glorifying Rome. Vergil, who wrote three lines a day between 29 and 19 BC, set out to describe the journey of Aeneas, a prince of Troy, after fleeing from the burning city when it was sacked by the Greeks. The poem then follows Aeneas to Italy, where he does battle with the Italian prince Turnus and eventually founds a city that would eventually be Rome.

The Aeneid is modeled on Homer's *Iliad* and *Odyssey*, the first six books of Vergil's poem following the wanderings of Aeneas (as *The Odyssey* followed the wanderings of Odysseus), and the last six following the battles of the soon-to-be Romans (as *The Iliad* followed the Trojan War). Throughout the work, Vergil contrasts the virtuous band of Trojans with the error-prone Greeks in order to show the superiority of the Roman nation.

The selection below is from Book VI of *The Aeneid*. It follows Aeneas to Cumae (in southern Italy, near Naples), where, in order to ensure his safe passage to the underworld, he must retrieve the "golden bough," a branch of a tree that sprouts again after he plucks it. He presents this bough to the Cumaean Sibyl, who conducts him to the River Styx and through the Underworld, where Aeneas sees many of the famous personalities of the ancient world and meets the dead Anchises, his father, who reveals Rome's destiny to his son.

44

Cঠ৪০
From **The Aeneid (Book 6)**
Vergil (Publius Vergilius Maro), 19 BC
TRANSLATED BY JOHN DRYDEN AND GERARD P. NECASTRO

He said, and wept; then spread his sails before the winds, and reached at length the Cumaean shore: their anchors dropped, his crew the vessels moored. They turn their heads to sea, their sterns to land, and greet with greedy joy the Italian strand. Some make fire from clashing flints; some gather sticks, the kindled flames to feed, or search the open woods, and fell the woods, or trace through valleys the streams they have found.

Thus, while their several charges they fulfilled, the pious prince ascended the sacred hill where Phoebus is adored; and sought the shade which hid from sight his venerable maid. Deep in a cave the Sibyl made abode; to there, full of knowledge of fate and of the god, she returned. Through Trivia's grove they walked; and now behold, and now enter, the temple roofed with gold.

When Daedalus, the first who sailed in air, flew from the Cretan shore, his heavy limbs on jointed pinions bore, as it is sung by Fame, to the Cumaean coast at length he came, and here alighting, built this costly frame. It is said of Phoebus that here he hung on high the steerage of his wings, which cut the sky: then over the lofty gate his art embossed Androgeos' death, and offerings to his spirit. Here also seven youths from Athens were sent yearly to meet the fate appointed by revengeful Crete.[1]

And next to those the dreadful urn was placed, in which the destined names by lots were cast: the mournful parents stand around in tears, and rising Crete against their shore appears. There too, in living sculpture, might be seen the mad affection of the Cretan queen; then how she cheats her bellowing lover's eye; the rushing leap, the doubtful progeny, the lower part a beast, a man above, the monument of their polluted love.

Not far from there he designed the wondrous maze, a thousand doors, a thousand winding ways: here dwells the monster, hid from human view, not to be found, but by the faithful ball of string; until the kind artist, moved with pious grief, lent to the loving maid this last relief, and all those wandering paths described so well that Theseus conquered and the monster fell. Here hapless Icarus[2] had found his part, had not the father's grief restrained his art. He twice attempted to cast his son in gold; twice from his hands he dropped the forming mold.

All this with wondering eyes Aeneas viewed; each varying object his delight renewed: eager to read the rest. Achates came, and by his side the mad divining woman, the priestess of Apollo, the Cuamaean Sybil, Deiphobe. "Time suffers not," she said, "to feed your eyes with empty pleasures; haste the

---

[1] Here also…revengeful Crete. This is the story of the creation of the Minotaur of Crete, the Athenian youths sacrificed to it in the labyrinth, and its destruction by Theseus, who was aided by Ariadne, the king's daughter, with the aid of a ball of string.
[2] Icarus, whose father Daedalus crafted wings, fell to earth when he drew too close to the sun.

sacrifice. Seven bullocks, yet unyoked, for Phoebus choose, and for Diana seven unspotted ewes." This said, the servants urge the sacred rites, while to the temple she the prince invites. A spacious cave, within its farthest part, was hewed and fashioned by laborious art through the hill's hollow sides: before the place, a hundred doors grace a hundred entries; as many voices issue, and the sound of Sybil's words as many times echo. Now to the mouth they come.

Aloud the Sybil cried, "This is the time; enquire your destinies. He comes; behold the god!" Thus while she spoke (and shivering at the sacred entry stayed), her color changed; her face was not the same, and hollow groans from her deep spirit came. Her hair stood up. Convulsive rage possessed her trembling limbs, and heaved her laboring breast. Greater than humankind she seemed to look, and with an accent more than mortal spoke. Her staring eyes with sparkling fury roll, when the divine presence came rushing on her soul.

Swiftly the Sybil turned, and, foaming as she said, "Why this delay?" she cried, "Invoke the powers! Your prayers alone can open this abode; otherwise vain are my demands, and the god is silent."

She said no more. The trembling Trojans hear, overspread with a damp sweat and holy fear. Aeneas, possessed with awful dread, addressed his vows to great Apollo: "Indulgent god, propitious power to Troy, swift to relieve, unwilling to destroy, directed by whose hand the Trojan Paris' arrow pierced the proud Achilles' only mortal part: thus far, by fate's decrees and your commands, through ambient seas and through devouring sands, our exiled crew has sought the Italian ground; and now, at length, the flying coast is found. Thus far the fate of Troy, from place to place, with fury has pursued her wandering race. Here cease, ye powers, and let your vengeance end: Troy is no more, and can no more offend.

"And you, O sacred maid, inspired to see the event of things in dark futurity, give me what the heavens have promised to my fate: to conquer and command the Latian state; to fix my wandering gods, and find a place for the long exiles of the Trojan race. Then shall my grateful hands a temple rear to the twin gods, with vows and solemn prayer; and annual rites, and festivals, and games, shall be performed to their auspicious names. Nor shall you lack your honors in my land; for there your faithful oracles shall stand, preserved in shrines; and every sacred lay, which, by your mouth, Apollo shall convey: all shall be treasured by a chosen train of holy priests, and ever shall remain. But, O, commit not your prophetic mind to flitting leaves, the sport of every wind, lest they disperse in air our empty fate; write not, but tell what the powers ordain."

Struggling in vain, impatient of her load, and laboring underneath the ponderous god, the more she strove to shake him from her breast, the more Apollo pressed; he commanded his entrance and usurped her organs and inspired her soul. Now, with a furious blast, the hundred doors opened by themselves; a rushing whirlwind roare within the cave, and Sibyl's voice was restored: "Escaped the dangers of the watery reign, yet more and greater ills by land remain. The coast, so long desired (nor doubt the event), your troops shall reach, but, having reached, repent. Wars, horrid wars, I view – a field of blood, and Tiber rolling with a purple flood. Neither Simois nor Xanthus shall be wanting there:

a new Achilles shall in arms appear, and he, too, goddess-born. Fierce Juno's hate, added to hostile force, shall urge your fate. To what strange nations shall not you resort, driven to solicit aid at every court! The cause is the same which Ilium once oppressed: a foreign mistress and a foreign guest. But you, secure of soul, unbent with woes, the more your fortune frowns, the more oppose. The dawnings of your safety shall be shown from whence you least shall hope, a Grecian town."

Thus, from the dark recess, the Sibyl spoke, and thunder broke the resisting air; the cave resounded, and the temple shook. The ambiguous god, who ruled her laboring breast, expressed his mind in these mysterious words and some truths revealed. At length her fury fell, her foaming ceased, and, ebbing in her soul, the god decreased.

Then Aeneas said, "No terror to my view, no frightful face of danger can be new. Inured to suffer, and resolved to dare, the Fates, without my power, shall be without my care. This let me crave, since near your grove the road To hell lies open, and the dark abode Which Acheron surrounds, the unnavigable flood; conduct me through the regions void of light, and lead me longing to my father's sight. For him, a thousand dangers I have sought, and, rushing where the thickest Grecians fought, safe on my back the sacred burden brought. He, for my sake, the raging ocean tried, and wrath of the heavens, my still auspicious guide, and bore beyond the strength decrepit age supplied. Oft, since he breathed his last, in dead of night his reverend image stood before my sight; enjoined to seek, below, his holy shade; conducted there by your unerring aid.

"But you, if pious minds by prayers are won, oblige the father and protect the son. Yours is the power; Proserpine has not in vain made you priestess of her nightly reign. If Orpheus,[1] armed with his enchanting lyre, the ruthless king with pity could inspire, and from the shades below redeem his wife; if Pollux, offering his alternate life, could free his brother, and can daily go both above and below. Why should I name Theseus or Hercules, who trod the downward path, and upward could ascend? Not less than theirs from Jove my lineage came; my mother greater, my descent the same." So prayed Aeneas, and, while he prayed, his hand upon the holy altar laid.

Then the prophetess said, "O goddess-born of great Anchises' line, the gates of hell are open night and day; smooth the descent, and easy is the way: but to return, and view the cheerful skies, in this the task and mighty labor lies. Great Jupiter imparts this grace to few people, those of shining worth and heavenly race. Between those regions and our upper light, deep forests and impenetrable night possess the middle space, surrounded by the wailing river of Cocytus. But if so dire a love invades your soul, as twice below to view the trembling shades; if you so hard a toil will undertake, as twice to pass Tarturus, receive now my counsel.

"In the neighboring grove there stands hidden in a dark tree a golden bough, golden in leaves and pliant stem, sacred to Proserpine, queen of the underworld. Proserpine commands that only one who can take the golden fruit

---

[1] Orpheus sang to Hades and freed his wife Eurydice temporarily from the underworld.

from it may enter earth's hidden places. When one fruit is blucked a second fruit of gold always appears. Look round the wood, with lifted eyes, to see the lurking gold on the fatal tree: tear it off, as holy rites command; the willing metal will obey your hand, following with ease, if favored by your fate, you are ordained to view the Stygian state: if not, no labor can the tree constrain; and strength of stubborn arms and steel are vain. Besides, you know not, while you here attend, the unworthy fate of your unhappy friend: breathless he lies; and his unburied spirit, deprived of funeral rites, pollutes your host. Pay first his pious dues; and, for the dead, lead two sable sheep around his hearse; then, living turfs upon his body lay: this done, securely take the destined way, to find the regions destitute of day."

Thus she said, and held her peace. Aeneas went sad from the cave, and full of discontent, unknowing whom the sacred Sibyl meant. Achates, his close companion, grieved by his side, oppressed with equal cares. Walking, they talked, and fruitlessly divined what friend the priestess by those words designed. But soon they found an object to deplore: Misenus lay on the shore; son of the God of Winds: none are so renowned as he to sound the trumpet to call the warrior in the field and to kindle with his breath fierce alarms to rouse soldiers to dare the fate in honorable arms. He served great Hector, and was ever near, not with his trumpet only, but his spear as well. But by Pelides' arms when Hector fell, he chose Aeneas; and he chose as well. Swollen with applause, and aiming still at more, he now provoked the sea gods from the shore; with envy Triton heard the martial sound, and drowned the bold Misenus, for his challenge and cast his mangled carcass on the strand. The gazing crowd stood around the body.

All wept, but Aeneas mostly mourned his fate and hastened to perform the funeral rite. At the altar, a stately beam they raised up; the foundation broad below and the top advanced in air. An ancient wood, fit for the work designed (the shady covert of the salvage kind), the Trojans found: the sounding ax was plied; firs, pines, and pitch trees, and the towering pride of forest ashes, felt the fatal stroke, and piercing wedges cleaved the stubborn oak. Huge trunks of trees, felled from the steep crown of the bare mountains, rolled with ruin down. Armed like the rest the Trojan prince appeared, and by his pious labor urged theirs.

Thus while he worked, revolving in his mind the ways to complete what his wish designed, he cast his eyes upon the gloomy grove, and then with vows implored his mother Venus: "O may your power, favorable still to me, conduct my steps to find the fatal tree in this deep forest; since the Sibyl's breath foretold, alas, too true, Misenus' death."

Scarce had he said, when, full before his sight, two doves, descending from their airy flight, secure upon the grassy plain alighted. He knew his mother's birds; and thus he prayed: "Please be my guides, with your auspicious aid, and lead my footsteps, until the branch may be found, whose glittering shadow gilds the sacred ground. And you, great parent, with celestial care, in this distress please hear my prayer!"

Thus having said, he stopped with watchful sight, observing still the motions of their flight, what course they took, what happy signs they show. They fed, and, fluttering, by degrees withdrew still farther from the place, but still in view: hopping and flying, thus they led him on to the slow lake, whose baleful stench to shun they winged their flight aloft. They glided low and perched on the double tree that bears the golden bough. Through the green leafs the glittering shadows glow; as, on the sacred oak, the wintry mistletoe, where the proud mother viewed her precious brood, and happier branches, which she never sowed. Such was the glittering; such the ruddy rind, and dancing leaves, that flitted in the wind. He seized the shining bough with a firm hold, plucked the lingering gold with ease, and bore it to the Sibyl's palace.

Meanwhile the Trojan troops, with weeping eyes, to dead Misenus paid his obsequies. First, from the ground a lofty pyre they build, of pitch trees, oaks, and pines, and unctuous fir: the fabric's front with cypress twigs they strew, and stick the sides with boughs of baleful yew. The topmost part his glittering arms adorn; then warm waters, borne in brazen caldrons, were poured to wash his body, joint by joint, and fragrant oils the stiffened limbs anointed. With groans and cries they lay the breathless body of Misenus on a bier, covered with purple, and lit the pyre and looked away.

Such reverend rites their fathers used to pay. Pure oil and incense they cast on the fire, and the fat of victims, which his friends bestowed. These gifts the greedy flames devoured to dust; then on the living coals they pour red wine; and, last, the relics by themselves set down, which in a brazen urn the priests enclosed. Old Corynaeus three times rounded his fellow warrriors and dipped an olive branch in holy dew; which three times he sprinkled about and three times aloud invoked the dead, and then dismissed the crowd. But good Aeneas ordered on the shore a stately tomb, which bore the soldier's trumpet, sword, and oar. Thus was his friend interred beneath the lofty mountain which bears his name Misenus, through the ages.

These rites performed, the prince, without delay, hastened to the nether world to carry out the Sybil's instructions. Deep was the cave; and, downward as it went from the wide mouth, a rocky and rough descent; and here the access defended a gloomy grove, and there the unnavigable lake extended, over whose unhappy waters, void of light, no bird presumed to steer its airy flight. Deadly stenches from the depths arose, and steaming sulfur, that infected the skies. From this place the Grecian bards made their legends and gave the name Avernus to the lake. Four sable bullocks, bound in the yoke, for sacrifice the pious hero brought. The priestess poured the wine between their horns; then cut the curling hair as a first offering, invoking Hecate to come, a powerful name in hell and upper air. Others with ready knives bereaved the beasts of life, and in full bowls received the streaming blood. Aeneas offered to Night, mother of the Furies, and Earth, her sister, a lamb of sable wool without a streak of white; and to Proserpine a barren heifer. Then on Pluto's altar he sacrificed seven brawny bulls, killed with his own hand, and poured fine oil over the broiling entrails, which the raging flame devoured. Late did the nocturnal sacrifice begin and did not end until the next returning sun. Then earth began to bellow, trees to dance, and dogs to howl in the glimmering light as the goddess Hecate advanced.

"Keep your distance, souls profane!" the Sibyl cried, "and remove yourselves from this grove! Now, Aeneas, be on your way; take courage, and unsheathe your sword." Thus she said and descended into the cave, and Aeneas pursued her steps with equal pace.

You realms yet unrevealed to human sight, you gods who rule the regions of the night, and you gliding shadows, permit me to relate the mystic wonders of your silent state!

In darkness they went through dreary shades that led along the waste dominions of the dead. Thus by night the travelers wandered in the woods, by the moon's doubtful and malignant light, when Jove moves the skies in dusky clouds, and the faint crescent shoots dby fits before their eyes.

Just in the gate and in the jaws of Hell, revengeful Cares and sullen Sorrows dwell, and pale Diseases, and repining Age, want, fear, and Famine's unstoppable rage; here Toils, and Death, and Sleep, Death's half-brother, forms terrible to view, their sentry keep; with anxious Pleasures of a guilty mind, deep Frauds before, and open Force in the rear; the Furies' iron beds; and Strife, that shakes her hissing tresses and unfolds her snakes. In the midst of this infernal road, an elm displayed her dusky arms abroad: the God of Sleep there hid his heavy head, and empty dreams on every leaf were spread. Various and countless forms of specters, centaurs, and double shapes, besieged the door. Before the passage, horrid Hydra lurks, and Briareus with all his hundred hands; gorgons, Geryon with his triple frame; and vain Chimaera vomited empty flame. The chief unsheathed his shining steel, prepared, though seized with sudden fear, to force the guard, offering his brandished weapon at their face. Had not the Sibyl stopped his eager pace and told him what those empty phantoms were (forms without bodies, and impassive air), he would have attacked them in vain.

From there they took their way to deep Acheron, whose troubled eddies, thick with ooze and clay, were whirled aloft, and lost in Cocytus. There Charon stood, who rules the dreary coast, a sordid god. Down from his hoary chin a length of beard descended, uncombed, unclean; his eyes, like hollow furnaces on fire; a sash, foul with grease, bound his obscene attire. He spread his canvas and steered with his pole; his dark ferry bore the freight of flitting spirits. He had many years; yet in his years were seen a youthful vigor and autumnal green. An airy crowd came rushing where he stood, which filled the shore of the fatal waters: husbands and wives, boys and unmarried maidens, and the dead bodies of mighty heroes, and youths, entombed before their fathers' eyes, with hollow groans, and shrieks, and feeble cries. Thick as the leaves in autumn strewn in the woods, or birds that in winter forsake the waters and wing their hasty flight to sunnier lands; in this way they stood shivering and pressed for passage with extended hands. Now these, now those, the surly boatman bore: the rest he drove away from the shore. The hero, who beheld with wondering eyes the tumult mixed with shrieks, lamented and cried, and asked of his guide, what the rude concourse meant; why the thronging people bent to the shore; what forms of law were in place among the spirits; why some were ferried over, and some refused.

"Aeneas, Son of Anchises, offspring of the gods," The Sibyl said, "you see the River Styx, the sacred stream which the imperial state of the heavens attests in oaths and fears to violate. The rejected spirits are the unhappy crew deprived of sepulchers and proper funerals. The boatman, Charon; ferries the buried spirits over to the farther coast, and his vessel dares not cross the waves with those whose bones are not composed in graves. A hundred years they wander on the shore; at length, their penance done, they are wafted over."

The Trojan chief Aeneas halted in his forward pace, revolving anxious thoughts within his breast, he saw his friends, who, overwhelmed beneath the waves, their funeral honors claimed, and pitied their sad fate. The lost Leucaspis in the crowd he knew, and the brave leader of the Lycian crew, whom, on the Tyrrhene seas, the tempests met; which engulfed both ship and crew with waves.

Amid the spirits, his helmsman Palinurus pressed, yet fresh from life, a newly admitted guest, who, while viewing the stars and bearing his course from Africa to the Latian shore, fell headlong into the waves. Aeneas fixed his view and scarcely recognized the sullen shadow through the gloom. Then thus the prince said, "What envious power, O dear friend Palinurus, brought your dear life to this disastrous end? For Phoebus, ever true in all he said, has in your fate alone my faith betrayed. The god foretold you should not die before you reached, secure from seas, the Italian shore. Is this the way he shows truth?"

The spirit Palinurus replied, "Phoebus neither failed nor lied; and no envious gods have sent me to the deep: but, while the stars and course of the heavens I kept, my wearied eyes were seized with fatal sleep. I fell; and, with my weight, the helm was torn away and drawn along, though I still retained my grip. Now by the winds and raging waves I swear, your safety, more than mine, was then my care; lest, with your guide taken from you, the rudder lost, your ship should run against the rocky coast. Three blustering nights, borne by the southern blast, I floated, and discovered land at last: high on a mounting wave my head I bore, forcing my strength, and gathering to the shore. Panting, but past the danger, now I seized the craggy cliffs and eased my tired limbs. While, encumbered by my soaked clothes, I lay, the cruel people, seeking a prey, stained with my blood the inhospitable coast; and now my lifeless limbs are tossed by winds and waves, and, by the sweet light of the heavens, I have been lost to this eternal night! Or, if by dearer ties you may be won, by your dead father, and by your living son, redeem from this evil my wandering spirit; or with your navy seek the coast of Velia,[1] and set my corpse in a peaceful grave. Or, if your mother, without whose aid you would not dare to undertake this frightful passage over the Stygian lake, shows you a more direct way, lend to this wretch your hand, and waft him over to the sweet banks of that forbidden shore."

Scarce had he said this than the prophetess began: "What hopes delude you, miserable man? Do you intend, thus unentombed, to cross the floods, to view the Furies and infernal gods and visit, without leave, the dark abodes of

---

[1] Velia. Ancient southern Italian town, near the Tyrrhenian Sea, twenty-five miles south of Salerno,

Cocytus? Note the practice of many years; fate and the dooming gods are deaf to tears. Take this comfort of your dire misfortune: the wrath of the heavens, inflicted for your sake, with vengeance shall pursue the inhuman coast, until they appease your offended spirit and raise a tomb with vows and solemn prayer; and the place shall bear Palinurus' name." This calmed his cares; soothed with his future fame, and pleased to hear his propagated name.

Now nearer to the Stygian lake they drew, whom the surly boatman saw from the shore. He observed their passage through the shady wood, and marked their near approaches to the flood. Then thus he called aloud, inflamed with wrath: "Mortal, who this forbidden path in arms you presume to tread, I charge you, stand, and tell your name, and business in the land. Know this, the realm of night, the Stygian shore: my boat conveys no living bodies over; nor was I pleased great Theseus once to bear, who forced a passage with his pointed spear, nor strong Hercules either, both men of mighty fame, and from the immortal gods their lineage came. In fetters one tied the barking porter Cerberus and took him trembling from his sovereign's side: both Theseus and Hercules sought by force to seize Proserpina, his beauteous bride."

To him the Sibyl thus said: "Compose your mind: no such fraud has been planned here, nor force designed. Still may you giant watch-dog constrain the wandering troops of airy spirits, and terrify the guilty train; and with her grisly lord Pluto his lovely queen Proserpine may remain. The Trojan chief, Aeneas, whose lineage is from Jove, much famed for arms, and more for filial love, is sent to seek his father in your Elysian grove. If neither piety nor the command of the heavens can gain his passage to the Stygian shore, this fatal present shall prevail at least."

Then she made visible the shining bough, which had been concealed within her robes. No more was needed: for the gloomy boatman stood mute with awe, to see the golden rod; admired the destined offering to his queen, a venerable gift, so rarely seen. His fury thus appeased, he pulls his skiff to the shore; the spirits already aboard forsook their seats at his command. The deck cleared, he received the mighty Aeneas; the leaky vessel groans beneath the weight. Slowly she sailed, and scarcely stemmed the tides; the pressing water poured within her sides. His passengers, the hero and the prophetess, at length were carried safely across, landing in the muddy weeds upon the blue-grey shore.

No sooner landed, in his den they found the triple-necked porter of the, grim Cerberus, who soon began to howl and arouse the snakes about his neck. The prudent Sibyl had before prepared a sop, steeped in honey, to charm the guard dog; which, mixed with powerful drugs, she cast before his greedy grinning jaws, opened wide and roaring. With three enormous mouths he seized her offering and, with hunger pressed, devoured the pleasing bait. Long draughts of sleep enslaved his monstrous limbs; he reeled, and, falling, filled the spacious cave. The gate-keeper charmed, the chief without delay passed on, and took the way with no return. Before the gates, the cries of babes new born, whom fate had from their tender mothers torn, assaulted his ears: then did those, whom laws condemned to die, when traitors judged their cause: these are not judged without a trial. Minos, the strict inquisitor, appears, convenes the court, shakes the urn, hears the lives and crimes, and pronounces judgment. The next, in place and punishment, were they who died by their own hand, throwing their souls away. Now, with late repentance, they would retrieve the bodies they forsook, and wished to live; their former pains and poverty they wished to bear, in order to view the light of the heavens and breathe the vital air. Fate forbid it, however, and the waters of Styx opposed it, and enclosed with circling streams the captive souls.

Not far from there, the Fields of Mourning appeared, so called from lovers that inhabited there. The souls whom that unhappy flame invaded, in secret solitude and myrtle shades made endless moans, and, pining with desire, lamented too late their unextinguished fire. Here Aeneas found Phaedra, Procris, and Eriphyle, baring her breast, bleeding with the wound made by her son, Evadne. He saw also Pasiphae, Laodamia, and Caeneus (a woman once, and once a man, but ending in the sex she first began), all moving unhappily along, but loyal in their loves. Not far from these, stood, fresh from her wound, her bosom bathed in blood, the Phoenician Dido, whom the Trojan hero could hardly recognize, obscure in shades, and with a doubtful view, like one who sees through dusky night, or thinks he sees, the moon's uncertain light.

With tears he first approached the sullen shade; and, as his love inspired him, he said, "Unhappy queen, is the news of reported death by your own blade true, and am I, alas, the cause? By the heavens, I vow, and all the powers that rule the realms below, unwillingly I forsook your friendly state, commanded by the gods, and forced by fate. Those gods, that fate, through their endless might sent me to these regions void of light, through the vast empire of eternal night. I dared not to presume, that, pressed with grief, my flight should bring you to such grief. Stay, and do not leave my sight. Stop your footsteps, and listen to my vows: this will be the last speech that fate allows!" In vain he thus attempted to move her mind with tears and prayers and late-repenting love.

Disdainfully she looked; but turning around and fixed her eyes unmoved upon the ground, and she regards what he says and swears no more than the sea cliffs, when the loud billows roar. She whirled away, to shun his hateful sight, hid in the forest and the shades of night; then sought Sichaeus, her husband, through the shady grove, who answered all her cares, and equaled all her love.

Some pious tears the pitying Aeneas paid, and followed with his eyes the flitting Dido, then pushed forward way, by fate ordained, and, with his guide, the farther fields attained, where, severed from the rest, the warrior souls remained. Here he met Tydeus and Parthenopaeus, the pride of armies, and grace of soldiers, and pale Adrastus with his ghastly face. He viewed a numerous train of Trojan chiefs, all much lamented, all in battle slain; Glaucus and Medon, high above the rest, Antenor's sons; Polyboetes, Ceres' sacred priest; and proud Idaeus, Priam's charioteer, who shook his empty reins, and aims his airy spear. The gladsome spirits, beholding their friend with unwearied eyes and delighting to remain near him, circled around him and longed to know what business brought him to the realms below. But the Greek princes and Agamemnon's retinue, when Aeneas' gleaming weapons flashed through the shady plain, fled with cries from his well-known face, with well-known fear, as when his thundering sword and pointed spear drove them headlong to their ships. They raised a feeble cry, with trembling notes; but the weak voice deceived their gasping throats.

Here he found Priam's son, Deiphobus, through whose face and limbs was one continued wound: mutilated, with his arms chopped off, the youth appears, his face deformed, his nose hacked off, and his ears gone. Aeneas scarcely knew Deiphobus, who strove to hide his blotted form and blushed to be known. Aeneas began, "O noble blood of Teucer, who dares your faultless figure thus to deface? What heart could wish, what hand inflict, this dire disgrace? It is told that in our last and fatal night your single prowess long sustained the fight, until, wearied by the killing.of numberless Greeks, you fell upon a heap of slaughtered foes. But, in remembrance of so brave a deed, I established a tomb and funeral honors for you; thrice called on your spirit on the Trojan plains, which now retain your armor and your name. Your body too I sought, and, had I found it, would have buried it in your native ground."

The shadow replied, "Your piety has carried out all the rites necessary to rest my wandering shade; but cruel fate, and that crueler Spartan woman,[1] drowned me in sorrows and betrayed memories of me. These are the monuments of Helen's love: the shame I bear below, the marks I bore above. You know in what deluding joys we passed the night that was by the heavens decreed our last: for, when the fatal Trojan Horse, pregnant with arms, overwhelmed the unhappy town, she left my bed, and, mixed with Trojan women, led them in feigned Bacchic dances. Then, waving high her torch, she made the signal, which roused the Greeks to ambush the city. Worn down with watching, with cares oppressed, I unhappily had laid me down to rest, and heavy sleep overtook my weary limbs. In the mean time my illustrious wife removed from our house our arms, including my very sword from beneath my head. With the door unlatched and repeated calls, she invited her former husband within my walls. Thus she believed that in her new crime she would redeem her old treason. What more need I say? Into the room they ran and ruthlessly murdered a defenseless man. Ulysses, basely born, first led the way. Avenging powers, with justice I pray that my fortune may be their own another day! But answer now, and in your turn relate, what brought you, still living, to the region of Styx. Were you driven by the winds and wanderings of the sea, or did you obey the superior judgment of the heavens? Or tell what other fortune conducts your way, to view with mortal eyes our dark retreats, tumults and torments of the infernal seats."

While they spoke, Aurora, the goddess of the dawn, and her rosy chariot passed the zenith of her daily path, and the warriors had spent in words and tears all the time the heavens had allowed. Thus the Sibyl warned Aeneas, her companion: "Night approaches and drives out the day: we waste the hours in tears.

---

[1] Crueler Spartan woman. Helen of Troy, who was the wife of Menelaus, king of Sparta, seduced by Paris, son of King Priam of Troy, was later taken as "wife" (perhaps by force) by Deiphobus after the death of Paris but betrayed him by signaling Menelaus to Deiphobus' bedroom where the Spartan hacked the newer husband to pieces.

The route divides itself here into two paths, the right goes to Pluto's golden palace; the left to that unhappy region that descends to the depth of Tartarus, the seat of profound night and punished fiends."

Then thus Deiphobus said, "O sacred maid, do not be angry with us, and your will shall be obeyed! Lo, to the secret shadows I retire, to pay my penance until my years expire. Go, glorious prince, and enjoy a better fate than I have found." So he said; and, as he spoke, turned his steps to secret shadows, and in silence he mourned.

The hero, looking on the left, saw a lofty tower, strong on every side with triple walls, which the Phlegethon of Tartarus surrounded, whose fiery flood bound the burning empire; and, pressed between the rocks, the bellowing noise resounded. Wide is the front gate, and, raised on high with steel columns, raised to the sky. Vain was the force of humans and the heavens to topple the pillars by war. Here and iron tower rises, and before it sat the dire Fury, Tisiphone, as a guard, dressed in her sanguine gown, by night and day, observant of the souls that pass downward. From here were heard the groans of spirits, the pains of sounding lashes and of dragging chains. Aeneas stood astonished at their cries and loud laments that rent the liquid air. He asked his guide from what place those yells arise; and what the crimes, and what the tortures were.

She thus replied, "The chaste and the holy ones are all forbidden from this polluted place. But when Hecate appointed me gave to rule the woods of Avernus, she led me trembling through these dire abodes and taught me the tortures of the avenging gods. These are the realms of unrelenting fate; and awful Rhadamanthus of Crete rules the state. He hears and judges each committed crime, gathers confessions, and doles out punishments. The wretches must reveal all their acts (though they are loath to confess and unable to conceal them), from the first moment of their vital breaths to their last hour of unrepenting death. Straight, over the guilty spirit, the Fury Tisiphone shakes the sounding whip and brandishes her snakes, and the pale sinner, with her sisters, takes.

"Then, by itself, the eternal door unfolds, and with dreadful sounds the brazen hinges roar. You see before the gate, what stalking spirit commands the guard, what sentries keep the post. The more formidable Hydra stands within, whose jaws with iron teeth severely grin. The gaping gulf lies low to the center and twice as deep as earth is distant from the skies. The rivals of the gods, the Titan race, here, singed with lightning, roll within the measureless space. Here lie the twin sons of Aloeus – I saw them both – enormous bodies, of gigantic growth, who dared to defy the Thunderer in fight, to destroy his heavens and force him from the sky. I found Salmoneus as well, suffering cruel pains for emulating Jove's thunder and lightning: through Elis and the Grecian towns the fool rode triumphantly, with four fiery horse drawing him: he waved a torch aloft and, madly vain, sought godlike worship from the people. Ambitious fool, the hoofs passed over hollow arches of resounding brass, attempting to rival thunder in its rapid course, But he, the King of the heavens bared his red arm, and, launching from the sky his lightning bolt (not shaking empty smoke) down to the deep abyss the flaming felon struck.

"There Tityus is also, who took his birth from the heavens, his nursing from the bountiful earth. Here his gigantic limbs, with large embrace, enfold nine acres of infernal space. A ravenous vulture with her crooked beak and cruel talons feeds from his opened side. Forever the growing liver supplies the vulture's feast.

"Shall I tell of Ixion and Perithous of the Lapiths, over whose heads a moldering rock is placed high, one that promises a fall and shakes at every blast. They lie below, on golden beds; and great feasts with regal pomp are set forth. The Queen of the Furies by their sides is set, and snatches from their mouths their food, at which her hissing snakes she rears, brandishing her torch and thundering in their ears.

"Then there are brothers who hated their own brothers, who struck out at their parents and usurped the throne; There are those who defrauded their clients, and, sold to sordid money, sat brooding on unprofitable gold; who dared not give, and even refused, to lend to their poor kindred or a needful friend. Vast is the throng of these shadows; nor is the train of lustful youths, slain for foul adultery, any smaller. And hosts of deserters, who sold their honor and basely broke their faith for bribes of gold.

"All these within the dungeon's depth remain, despairing pardon and waiting pain. Ask not what pains; nor farther seek to know their process, or the forms of law below. Some roll a weighty stone; some are spread out, bound with burning wires, on spokes of wheels, and hung miserably.

"Theseus, doomed forever there, is fixed by fate on his eternal chair; and wretched Phlegyas warns the world (as if warning could make the world more just or wise): 'Learn righteousness, and dread the avenging deities.' To tyrants others have their country sold, imposing foreign lords, for foreign gold; some have old laws repealed and new statutes created, not as the people pleased, but as they paid; with incest some their daughters' bed profaned: all dared the worst of ills, and attained what they dared. Had I a hundred mouths, a hundred tongues, and throats of brass, inspired with iron lungs, I could not half those horrid crimes repeat, nor half the punishments those crimes have met. But let us haste our voyage to pursue: the walls of Pluto's palace are in view; the gate, and iron arch above it, stands on anvils labored by the Cyclops' hands. Before our farther way the Fates allow, here must we fix on high the golden bough."

When she had said this, they passed through the gloomy shades and chose the middle path. Having arrived at last, Aeneas sprinkled living water over his limbs and body, approached the door, and on the front above he fixed the fatal bough on the threshold. These holy rites performed, they took their way where long extended plains of pleasure lay: the verdant field, the Elysian Fields and the abodes of the fortunate and the blessed. Stars of their own, and suns as well, they know; they wrestle on the yellow sands and compete in other sports. Some sing songs and others dance. Orpheus accompanies on his harp the voices of the singers, playing with his fingers or the ivory quill, strikes seven distinguished notes. Here they also found Teucer's ancient heroic race, born in happier years; Assaracus and Ilus here enjoy perpetual fame, along with Dardanus, who founded Troy. Aeneas beheld their chariots from afar, their shining arms, and horses trained for war: their lances fixed in earth, their steeds, free from their harness, graze the flowery ground. The love of horses and care of chariots while they lived, after death survive.

Some cheerful souls were feasting on the plain; some sing a joyful song in chorus beneath a laurel shade, where the mighty Po flows through the woods above. Here patriots lived, who, for their country's good, suffered wounds in the fields of battle; priests of unblemished lives make their homes here, and true poets worthy of Apollo; and thinkers who improved the world in the Arts and Sciences, and those whose achievements earned the memories of others. The heads of these were bound with holy ribbons, and all their temples were with garlands crowned.

To these the Sibyl thus her speech addressed, and first to him surrounded by and towering above the rest: "Please tell us, happy souls, divine Musaeus, where Anchises lives. For him we have come here, crossing the bitter waters to seek the dark abodes."

To this the sacred poet replied, "In no fixed place the happy souls reside. In groves we live, and lie on mossy beds, by crystal streams, that murmur through the meads: but, if you wish, climb over this ridge and from there descend; the path conducts you to your journey's end." This said, he led them along and, leaving the hills behind, showed them all the shining fields below.

But old Anchises, in a green valley, reviewed his own people enclosed there, happy spirits, which, ordained by fate, for future beings and new bodies wait. With studious thought he observed the illustrious throng: their names, their fates, their conduct, and their care. When he saw Aeneas coming toward him on the plain, he met his son with open arms and falling tears.

"Welcome," he said, "O, how long I have waited. Once more it is given me to behold your face! Your love and pious duty have surpassed the perils of so hard a way. It is true, as I calculate the time, I now believed the happy day approached; and my hopes are not deceived. What length of lands, what oceans have you crossed? What storms and troubles have cast you about? How have I feared your fate, but feared it most, when love assailed you, on the Libyan coast."

To this, the dutiful son replied, "Your sacred spirit before my sleeping eyes appeared and often urged me to come here. My ships have long been tossed on the Tyrrhenian Sea. But reach out your hand, dear father, and do not shun the embraces of your longing son!" Thus he said; and tears soaked his face. Three times he tries to throw his arms around his father's neck, and three times the flitting shadow slipped through his hands, like the breeze, or dreams that fly away.

Now, in a receding valley, Aeneas saw a secluded grove, where the wind whispered through the trees and the river of Lethe glided past. About the boughs a robust nation hovered, thick as the humming bees that on a bright summer's day, working the many flowers and the sweet lilies, fill the meadows with their humming. Aeneas stood in wonder, and, not knowing, asked what river he saw in the distance and who all who were all those crowding near it.

Then his father Anchises said, "The souls that throng the river are those to whom, by fate, are other bodies owed. In Lethe's stream they taste the happy waters and a long oblivion, forgetful of the past. Long has my soul desired to set before your sight your glorious race, so that this presaging joy may fire your mind to seek the shores by destiny designed."

"O father, can it be, that spirits return to visit our terrestrial clime above, and return to lazy limbs and mortal breath?"

Anchises then began to clear those wonders one at a time. "Know, first," he said, "that one common soul inspires and feeds and animates the heavens, the earth's compacted frame, the flowing waters, the starry flame, and both the radiant lights. This active mind, infused through all the space, unites and mingles with the mighty mass. From this humans and animals obtain the breath of life, and birds of air, and the creatures of the sea. The ethereal power is the same in all, divine in origin, and every soul is filled with an equal flame; so long as earthy limbs, and mortal bodies, subject to decay, do not impede the beams of the heavens. From this coarse mixture of terrestrial parts, desire and fear by turns possess their hearts, and grief, and joy; nor can the groveling mind, confined in the dark dungeon of the limbs, rise to the native skies, or own its heavenly kind: nor can death itself wholly wash their stains; but long-contracted filth even in the soul remains. They wear the relics of long-lived vice, and spots of obscene sin in every face appear. For this are various penances enjoined, and some are hung to bleach upon the wind; some plunged in waters, others purged in fires, until all the dregs are drained and all the rust expires. All have their spirits, and all bear those spirits: the few, so cleansed, to these abodes come, and breathe, in ample fields, the soft Elysian air. Then are they happy, when by length of time the stain is worn away of each committed crime; no speck is left of their habitual stains, but the pure ether of the soul remains. But, when a thousand rolling years have passed (as long as their punishments and penance last), whole multitudes of minds are, by the gods, compelled to drink the deep Lethaean flood, in large forgetful draughts to steep the cares of their past labors and their irksome years, so that, forgetful of its former pain, these souls may return to the world above and to their mortal flesh again."

Having said this, the spirit of Anchises led his son Aeneas and the Cumaean Sybil through swarms of spirit-shades, and chose a hill from which to see the long procession of his progeny. "Come," said the father, "and I will explain to you the glory of these children of Dardanus, the descendents of the Italian race, great ones, whose fate will join with ours. Observe the youth who first appears in sight, and holds the nearest station to the light, leaning forward on a shining spear: he is Silvius, an Alban name, your last-born son, but first in order sent to fill your place. He will be born in a shady wood to Lavinia, your surviving wife, in your old age. In Alba Longa he shall fix his royal seat, and, being born a king, he will begin a race of kings. Then Procas, honor of the Trojan name, Capys, and Numitor, of endless fame. A second Silvius after these appears, Silvius Aeneas, for he will bear your name; for he will also be like you, excelling in virtue and arms, and will restore the Alban rule. How wondrous they look! How vigorously they wield their weighty lances and sustain their shields! But they, who appear crowned with oaken wreaths, shall Gabian walls and strong Fidena rear; Nomentum, Bola, with Pometia, found; and raise Collatian towers on rocky ground. All these shall then be towns of mighty fame, though now they lie obscure, lands without a name.

"See Romulus the great, born to restore the crown that once his injured grandfather wore. This prince a priestess of your blood shall bear, and like his father in arms he shall appear. Two rising crests adorn his royal head; born from a god, himself to godhead born: his father already signs him for the skies, and marks the seat amid the deities. Auspicious chief, Aeneas, your race, in times to come, shall spread the conquests of imperial Rome – Rome, whose ascending towers shall invade the heavens, setting earth and ocean in her shade; high as the Mother of the Gods in place, and proud, like her, of an immortal race. Then, when in pomp she makes the Phrygian round, with golden turrets on her temples crowned; a hundred gods supply her sweeping train; her offspring all, and all command the sky.

"Now fix your sight, and stand intent, to see Your Roman race and your Julian progeny. The mighty Caesar waits his vital hour, impatient for the world, and grasps his promised power. But next behold the youth of form divine, Caesar himself, exalted in his line; Augustus, promised often, and long foretold, sent to the realm that Saturn once ruled; born to restore a better age of gold. Africa and India shall obey his power; he shall extend his broad sway beyond the solar year, without the starry way, where Atlas turns the rolling heavens around, and his broad shoulders are crowned with their lights. At his foreseen approach Maeotia and the Caspian kingdoms already quake: their prophets behold his coming, and the restless seven mouths of the Nile are fearful. Hercules knew no more lands or labors, even though the brazen-footed hind he slew, freed Erymanthus from the foaming boar, and dipped his arrows in Lernaean gore; nor Bacchus, turning from his Indian war, by tigers drawn triumphant in his car, from Nisus' top descending on the plains, with curling vines around his purple reins. And yet should we hesitate through dangers to pursue the paths of honor, and should fear prevent us from settling the Italian realm?

Anchises continues to recount the long line of Aeneas' descendents and eventually concludes.

"Seek not to know," the spirit replied with tears, "the sorrows of your sons in future years. This youth (the blissful vision of a day) shall just be shown on earth, and snatched away. The gods too high had raised the Roman state, were but their gifts as permanent as great. What groans of men shall fill the Martian field! How fierce a blaze his flaming pile shall yield! What funeral pomp shall the floating Tiber see, when, rising from his bed, he views the sad solemnity! No youth shall equal hopes of glory give, no youth afford so great a cause to grieve; the Trojan honor, and the Roman boast, admired when living, and adored when lost! Mirror of ancient faith in early youth! Undaunted worth, inviolable truth! No foe, unpunished, in the fighting field shall dare you, foot to foot, with sword and shield; much less in arms oppose your matchless force, when your sharp spurs shall urge your foaming horse. Ah, if you could break through fate's severe decree, a new Marcellus shall arise in you! Full canisters of fragrant lilies bring, mixed with the purple roses of the spring; let me with funeral flowers his body strew; this gift which parents to their children owe, this unavailing gift, at least, I may bestow!"

Having said this, he led the hero round the confines of the blest Elysian ground. When Anchises had shown this to his son and fired his mind to mount the promised throne, he spoke of future wars, ordained by fate; the strength and customs of the Latian state; the prince, and people; and forearmed his care with rules, to push his fortune, or to bear it.

The silent house of Sleep stood, adorned by two gates, one of polished ivory, the other of transparent horn: true visions through transparent horn arise; through polished ivory pass deluding lies. Anchises bent his steps there at last, discussing various things as he passed. At last, through the gate of ivory he dismissed his valiant offspring and divining guest. Straight to the ships Aeneas took his way, embarked his men, and skimmed along the sea, still coasting, until he gained Cajeta's bay. At length on oozy ground his galleys moored; their heads were turned to sea, their sterns to shore.

Horace (Quintus Horatius Flaccus)
65 – 8 BC

Horace was the premiere lyric poet of his day. Born to a poor working-class family, he rose to fame as a poet after a career in the military (he was among the officers of the Republic in their loss in the Battle of Philippi in 42 BC) and in state service. He was befriended in this work by the Emperor Augustus' advisor Maecenas, who later gave Horace an estate on which the poet retired and wrote.

Along with his poetry, Horace is credited with three well-known concepts. Scholars of literature know that in his *Ars Poetica* (*The Art of Poetry*), he said that literature should "instruct and delight": "By once delighting and instructing the reader, the poet who mixes the sweet with the useful has everyone's approval." Scholars of history know his phrase "*dulce et decorum est*," (it is sweet and honorable to die for one's country), though not all agree with it. (This poem is included below.) Most everyone knows the phrase "*carpe diem*" (seize the day), which has become a part of our everyday language and was coined by Horace in the following passage in his Ode 1.11:

> Do not ask, you may not know, what end the gods have granted to me or you, Leuconoe, and do not play with Babylonian numbers. How much better it is to endure whatever will be, whether Jupiter has allotted to you many more winters or only this last one, which even now wears out the Tyrrhenian Sea on the opposing rocks. Be wise, strain the wines, and scale back your long hopes to a shorter period of time. While we speak, envious time is already fleeing: *seize this day*, trusting as little as possible in the next.[1]

Major Works
Ars poetica
Odes and Epodes
The Necessity for Reform
Satires

---

[1] Translation into prose by the editor. The original is in verse.

 CʒꙨↃ

Snow Is Gone (*Diffugere Nives*)
Horace
TRANSLATED BY JOHN CONINGTON

The snow is fled: the trees their leaves put on,
    The fields their green:
Earth owns the change, and rivers lessening run.
    Their banks between.
5 Naked the Nymphs and Graces in the meads
    The dance essay:
"No 'scaping death" proclaims the year, that speeds
    This sweet spring day.
Frosts yield to zephyrs; Summer drives out Spring,
10   To vanish, when
Rich Autumn sheds his fruits; round wheels the ring, –
    Winter again!
Yet the swift moons repair Heaven's detriment:
    We, soon as thrust
15 Where good Aeneas, Tullus, Ancus went,
    What are we? dust.
Can Hope assure you one more day to live
    From powers above?
You rescue from your heir whate'er you give
20   The self you love.
When life is o'er, and Minos has rehearsed
    The grand last doom,
Not birth, nor eloquence, nor worth, shall burst
    Torquatus' tomb.
25 Not Dian's self can chaste Hippolytus
    To life recall,
Nor Theseus free his loved Pirithous
    From Lethe's thrall.

CʒꙨↃ

Dulce et Decorum Est
Horace
TRANSLATED BY JOHN CONINGTON

To suffer hardness with good cheer,
    In sternest school of warfare bred,
Our youth should learn; let steed and spear
    Make him one day the Parthian's dread;
5 Cold skies, keen perils, brace his life.
    Methinks I see from rampired town
Some battling tyrant's matron wife,
    Some maiden, look in terror down, –
"Ah, my dear lord, untrain'd in war!

62

10   O tempt not the infuriate mood
    Of that fell lion I see! from far
        He plunges through a tide of blood!"
    What joy, for fatherland to die!
        Death's darts e'en flying feet o'ertake,
15 Nor spare a recreant chivalry,
        A back that cowers, or loins that quake.
    True Virtue never knows defeat:
        Her robes she keeps unsullied still,
    Nor takes, nor quits, her curule seat
20   To please a people's veering will.
    True Virtue opens heaven to worth:
        She makes the way she does not find:
    The vulgar crowd, the humid earth,
        Her soaring pinion leaves behind.
25 Seal'd lips have blessings sure to come:
        Who drags Eleusis' rite today,
    That man shall never share my home,
        Or join my voyage: roofs give way
    And boats are wreck'd: true men and thieves
30   Neglected Justice oft confounds:
    Though Vengeance halt, she seldom leaves
        The wretch whose flying steps she hounds.

Ovid (43 B.C. – 18 A.D.)
Publius Ovidius Naso

Ovid is best known for his collection of Roman mythology known as *The Metamorphoses*. Included in this volume are most of the Greco-Roman myths that we find in modern books, stories, poems, and movies.

The selection included here is the tale of two star-crossed lovers, Pyramus and Thisbe, whose families are at odds but whose hearts are drawn together. The tale has been retold many times in all forms of storytelling and is most delightfully represented in Act V of Shakespeare's *A Midsummer Night's Dream*.

Major Works
Heroides (*The Heroines*)
Amores (*The Loves*)
Ars Amatoria (*The Art of Love*)
Remedia Amoris (*The Cure for Love*)
Metamorphoses (*Transformations*)
Fasti (*The Festivals*)
Tristia (*Sorrows*)

CBBO

The Story of Pyramus and Thisbe
From The Metamorphoses
Ovid, 8 AD

TRANSLATED BY ARTHUR GOLDING, 1565 – 1567

In Babylon, where first her queen, for state
Rais'd walls of brick magnificently great,
Liv'd Pyramus, and Thisbe, lovely pair!
He found no eastern youth his equal there,
5   And she beyond the fairest nymph was fair.
A closer neighbourhood was never known,
Tho' two the houses, yet the roof was one.
Acquaintance grew, th' acquaintance they improve
To friendship, friendship ripen'd into love:
10 Love had been crown'd, but impotently mad,
What parents could not hinder, they forbad.

For with fierce flames young Pyramus still burn'd,
And grateful Thisbe flames as fierce return'd.
Aloud in words their thoughts they dare not break,
15 But silent stand; and silent looks can speak.
The fire of love the more it is supprest,
The more it glows, and rages in the breast.
When the division-wall was built, a chink
Was left, the cement unobserv'd to shrink.
20 So slight the cranny, that it still had been
For centuries unclos'd, because unseen.
But oh! what thing so small, so secret lies,
Which scapes, if form'd for love, a lover's eyes?
Ev'n in this narrow chink they quickly found
25 A friendly passage for a trackless sound.
Safely they told their sorrows, and their joys,
In whisper'd murmurs, and a dying noise,
By turns to catch each other's breath they strove,
And suck'd in all the balmy breeze of love.
30 Oft as on diff'rent sides they stood, they cry'd,
"Malicious wall, thus lovers to divide!
Suppose, thou should'st a-while to us give place
To lock, and fasten in a close embrace:
But if too much to grant so sweet a bliss,
35 Indulge at least the pleasure of a kiss.
We scorn ingratitude: to thee, we know,
This safe conveyance of our minds we owe."
Thus they their vain petition did renew
'Til night, and then they softly sigh'd adieu.
40 But first they strove to kiss, and that was all;
Their kisses dy'd untasted on the wall.
Soon as the morn had o'er the stars prevail'd,
And warm'd by Phoebus, flow'rs their dews exhal'd,
The lovers to their well-known place return,
45 Alike they suffer, and alike they mourn.
At last their parents they resolve to cheat
(If to deceive in love be call'd deceit),
To steal by night from home, and thence unknown
To seek the fields, and quit th' unfaithful town.
50 But, to prevent their wand'ring in the dark,
They both agree to fix upon a mark;
A mark, that could not their designs expose:
The tomb of Ninus was the mark they chose.
There they might rest secure beneath the shade,
55 Which boughs, with snowy fruit encumber'd, made:
A wide-spread mulberry its rise had took
Just on the margin of a gurgling brook.

Impatient for the friendly dusk they stay;
And chide the slowness of departing day;
60 In western seas down sunk at last the light,
From western seas up-rose the shades of night.
The loving Thisbe ev'n prevents the hour,
With cautious silence she unlocks the door,
And veils her face, and marching thro' the gloom
65 Swiftly arrives at th' assignation-tomb.
For still the fearful sex can fearless prove;
Boldly they act, if spirited by love.
When lo! a lioness rush'd o'er the plain,
Grimly besmear'd with blood of oxen slain:
70 And what to the dire sight new horrors brought,
To slake her thirst the neighb'ring spring she sought.
Which, by the moon, when trembling Thisbe spies,
Wing'd with her fear, swift, as the wind, she lies;
And in a cave recovers from her fright,
75 But drop'd her veil, confounded in her flight.
When sated with repeated draughts, again
The queen of beasts scour'd back along the plain,
She found the veil, and mouthing it all o'er,
With bloody jaws the lifeless prey she tore.
80 The youth, who could not cheat his guards so soon,
Late came, and noted by the glimm'ring moon
Some savage feet, new printed on the ground,
His cheeks turn'd pale, his limbs no vigour found;
But when, advancing on, the veil he spied
85 Distain'd with blood, and ghastly torn, he cried,
"One night shall death to two young lovers give,
But she deserv'd unnumber'd years to live!
'Tis I am guilty, I have thee betray'd,
Who came not early, as my charming maid.
90 Whatever slew thee, I the cause remain,
I nam'd, and fix'd the place where thou wast slain.
Ye lions from your neighb'ring dens repair,
Pity the wretch, this impious body tear!
But cowards thus for death can idly cry;
95 The brave still have it in their pow'r to die."
Then to th' appointed tree he hastes away,
The veil first gather'd, tho' all rent it lay:
The veil all rent yet still it self endears,
He kist, and kissing, wash'd it with his tears.
100 Tho' rich (he cry'd) with many a precious stain,
Still from my blood a deeper tincture gain.
Then in his breast his shining sword he drown'd,
And fell supine, extended on the ground.

As out again the blade lie dying drew,
105 Out spun the blood, and streaming upwards flew.
So if a conduit-pipe e'er burst you saw,
Swift spring the gushing waters thro' the flaw:
Then spouting in a bow, they rise on high,
And a new fountain plays amid the sky.
110 The berries, stain'd with blood, began to show
A dark complexion, and forgot their snow;
While fatten'd with the flowing gore, the root
Was doom'd for ever to a purple fruit.
Mean-time poor Thisbe fear'd, so long she stay'd,
115 Her lover might suspect a perjur'd maid.
Her fright scarce o'er, she strove the youth to find
With ardent eyes, which spoke an ardent mind.
Already in his arms, she hears him sigh
At her destruction, which was once so nigh.
120 The tomb, the tree, but not the fruit she knew,
The fruit she doubted for its alter'd hue.
Still as she doubts, her eyes a body found
Quiv'ring in death, and gasping on the ground.
She started back, the red her cheeks forsook,
125 And ev'ry nerve with thrilling horrors shook.
So trembles the smooth surface of the seas,
If brush'd o'er gently with a rising breeze.
But when her view her bleeding love confest,
She shriek'd, she tore her hair, she beat her breast.
130 She rais'd the body, and embrac'd it round,
And bath'd with tears unfeign'd the gaping wound.
Then her warm lips to the cold face apply'd,
"And is it thus, ah! thus we meet, she cry'd!
My Pyramus! whence sprung thy cruel fate?
135 My Pyramus! – ah! speak, ere 'tis too late.
I, thy own Thisbe, but one word implore,
One word thy Thisbe never ask'd before."
At Thisbe's name, awak'd, he open'd wide
His dying eyes; with dying eyes he try'd
140 On her to dwell, but clos'd them slow, and dy'd.
The fatal cause was now at last explor'd,
Her veil she knew, and saw his sheathless sword:
"From thy own hand thy ruin thou hast found,"
She said, "but love first taught that hand to wound,
145 Ev'n I for thee as bold a hand can show,
And love, which shall as true direct the blow.
I will against the woman's weakness strive,
And never thee, lamented youth, survive.
The world may say, I caus'd, alas! thy death,

150 But saw thee breathless, and resign'd my breath.
    Fate, tho' it conquers, shall no triumph gain,
    Fate, that divides us, still divides in vain.
    Now, both our cruel parents, hear my pray'r;
    My pray'r to offer for us both I dare;
155 Oh! see our ashes in one urn confin'd,
    Whom love at first, and fate at last has join'd.
    The bliss, you envy'd, is not our request;
    Lovers, when dead, may sure together rest.
    Thou, tree, where now one lifeless lump is laid,
160 Ere-long o'er two shalt cast a friendly shade.
    Still let our loves from thee be understood,
    Still witness in thy purple fruit our blood."
    She spoke, and in her bosom plung'd the sword,
    All warm and reeking from its slaughter'd lord.
165 The pray'r, which dying Thisbe had preferr'd,
    Both Gods, and parents, with compassion heard.
    The whiteness of the mulberry soon fled,
    And rip'ning, sadden'd in a dusky red:
    While both their parents their lost children mourn,
170 And mix their ashes in one golden urn.

The Bible
Selections from the New Testament

The New Testament of the Bible contains the writings about the life of Jesus Christ and his followers. Jesus Christ was the Jewish theologian, teacher, miracle-worker, and savior, around whose life and teaching Christianity, the world's most widespread religion, is built.

The first four books of the New Testament, Matthew, Mark, Luke, and John (known as the Four Gospels), recount the life of Christ. These are followed by the Acts of the Apostles, the story of his followers after Christ ascends into Heaven, and then a series of letters from leaders in the Christian community (Paul, James, Peter, John, and Jude) to various groups of believers. The last book of the New Testament is known as Revelation (or The Apocalypse), and it tells of the predicted end of the world.

The selections included here are from the Book of Matthew, one of the four Gospels (gospel means "Good News"). It retells the passion (suffering) and death of Jesus. There are many translations of the Bible: the selections here are taken from the Revised Standard Version from the early twentieth century.

⊂⊃⥽⊃

The Passion of Christ
From The Gospel of Mark

Judas Arranges to Hand Jesus Over
Then Judas Iscariot, who was one of the twelve, went to the chief priests in order to betray him to them. And when they heard it they were glad, and promised to give him money. And he sought an opportunity to betray him.

Preparation for the Passover
And on the first day of Unleavened Bread, when they sacrificed the Passover lamb, his disciples said to him, "Where will you have us go and prepare for you to eat the Passover?" And he sent two of his disciples, and said to them, "Go into the city, and a man carrying a jar of water will meet you; follow him, and wherever he enters, say to the householder, 'The Teacher says, "Where is my guest room, where I am to eat the Passover with my disciples?"'" And he will

69

show you a large upper room furnished and ready; there prepare for us." And the disciples set out and went to the city, and found it as he had told them; and they prepared the Passover.

The One Who Hands Jesus Over
And when it was evening he came with the twelve. And as they were at table eating, Jesus said, "Truly, I say to you, one of you will betray me, one who is eating with me." They began to be sorrowful, and to say to him one after another, "Is it I?" He said to them, "It is one of the twelve, one who is dipping bread into the dish with me. For the Son of man goes as it is written of him, but woe to that man by whom the Son of man is betrayed! It would have been better for that man if he had not been born."

The Memorial Meal
And as they were eating, he took bread, and blessed, and broke it, and gave it to them, and said, "Take; this is my body." And he took a cup, and when he had given thanks he gave it to them, and they all drank of it. And he said to them, "This is my blood of the covenant, which is poured out for many. Truly, I say to you, I shall not drink again of the fruit of the vine until that day when I drink it new in the kingdom of God."

Simon Peter's Denial Predicted
And when they had sung a hymn, they went out to the Mount of Olives. And Jesus said to them, "You will all fall away; for it is written, 'I will strike the shepherd, and the sheep will be scattered.' But after I am raised up, I will go before you to Galilee." Peter said to him, "Even though they all fall away, I will not." And Jesus said to him, "Truly, I say to you, this very night, before the cock crows twice, you will deny me three times." But he said vehemently, "If I must die with you, I will not deny you." And they all said the same.

Jesus in Gethsemane
And they went to a place which was called Gethsemane; and he said to his disciples, "Sit here, while I pray." And he took with him Peter and James and John, and began to be greatly distressed and troubled. And he said to them, "My soul is very sorrowful, even to death; remain here, and watch." And going a little farther, he fell on the ground and prayed that, if it were possible, the hour might pass from him. And he said, "Abba, Father, all things are possible to thee; remove this cup from me; yet not what I will, but what thou wilt." And he came and found them sleeping, and he said to Peter, "Simon, are you asleep? Could you not watch one hour? Watch and pray that you may not enter into temptation; the spirit indeed is willing, but the flesh is weak." And again he went away and prayed, saying the same words. And again he came and found them sleeping, for their eyes were very heavy; and they did not know what to answer him. And he came the third time, and said to them, "Are you still sleeping and taking your rest? It is enough; the hour has come; the Son of man is betrayed into the hands of sinners. Rise, let us be going; see, my betrayer is at hand."

The Arrest of Jesus
And immediately, while he was still speaking, Judas came, one of the twelve,

and with him a crowd with swords and clubs, from the chief priests and the scribes and the elders. Now the betrayer had given them a sign, saying, "The one I shall kiss is the man; seize him and lead him away under guard." And when he came, he went up to him at once, and said, "Master!" And he kissed him. And they laid hands on him and seized him. But one of those who stood by drew his sword, and struck the slave of the high priest and cut off his ear. And Jesus said to them, "Have you come out as against a robber, with swords and clubs to capture me? Day after day I was with you in the temple teaching, and you did not seize me. But let the scriptures be fulfilled." And they all forsook him, and fled. And a young man followed him, with nothing but a linen cloth about his body; and they seized him, but he left the linen cloth and ran away naked.

Jesus before the Sanhedrin. Peter's Denial
And they led Jesus to the high priest; and all the chief priests and the elders and the scribes were assembled. And Peter had followed him at a distance, right into the courtyard of the high priest; and he was sitting with the guards, and warming himself at the fire. Now the chief priests and the whole council sought testimony against Jesus to put him to death; but they found none. For many bore false witness against him, and their witness did not agree. And some stood up and bore false witness against him, saying, "We heard him say, 'I will destroy this temple that is made with hands, and in three days I will build another, not made with hands.'" Yet not even so did their testimony agree. And the high priest stood up in the midst, and asked Jesus, "Have you no answer to make? What is it that these men testify against you?" But he was silent and made no answer. Again the high priest asked him, "Are you the Christ, the Son of the Blessed?" And Jesus said, "I am; and you will see the Son of man seated at the right hand of Power, and coming with the clouds of heaven." And the high priest tore his garments, and said, "Why do we still need witnesses? You have heard his blasphemy. What is your decision?" And they all condemned him as deserving death. And some began to spit on him, and to cover his face, and to strike him, saying to him, "Prophesy!" And the guards received him with blows. And as Peter was below in the courtyard, one of the maids of the high priest came; and seeing Peter warming himself, she looked at him, and said, "You also were with the Nazarene, Jesus." But he denied it, saying, "I neither know nor understand what you mean." And he went out into the gateway. And the maid saw him, and began again to say to the bystanders, "This man is one of them." But again he denied it. And after a little while again the bystanders said to Peter, "Certainly you are one of them; for you are a Galilean." But he began to invoke a curse on himself and to swear, "I do not know this man of whom you speak." And immediately the cock crowed a second time. And Peter remembered how Jesus had said to him, "Before the cock crows twice, you will deny me three times." And he broke down and wept.

Jesus Delivered to Pilate
And as soon as it was morning the chief priests, with the elders and scribes, and the whole council held a consultation; and they bound Jesus and led him away and delivered him to Pilate.

The Trial before Pilate

And Pilate asked him, "Are you the King of the Jews?" And he answered him, "You have said so." And the chief priests accused him of many things. And Pilate again asked him, "Have you no answer to make? See how many charges they bring against you." But Jesus made no further answer, so that Pilate wondered.

The Sentence of Death

Now at the feast he used to release for them one prisoner for whom they asked. And among the rebels in prison, who had committed murder in the insurrection, there was a man called Barabbas. And the crowd came up and began to ask Pilate to do as he was wont to do for them. And he answered them, "Do you want me to release for you the King of the Jews?" For he perceived that it was out of envy that the chief priests had delivered him up. But the chief priests stirred up the crowd to have him release for them Barabbas instead. And Pilate again said to them, "Then what shall I do with the man whom you call the King of the Jews?" And they cried out again, "Crucify him." And Pilate said to them, "Why, what evil has he done?" But they shouted all the more, "Crucify him." So Pilate, wishing to satisfy the crowd, released for them Barabbas; and having scourged Jesus, he delivered him to be crucified.

The Mocking by Soldiers

And the soldiers led him away inside the palace (that is, the praetorium); and they called together the whole battalion. And they clothed him in a purple cloak, and plaiting a crown of thorns they put it on him. And they began to salute him, "Hail, King of the Jews!" And they struck his head with a reed, and spat upon him, and they knelt down in homage to him. And when they had mocked him, they stripped him of the purple cloak, and put his own clothes on him. And they led him out to crucify him.

The Road to Golgotha

And they compelled a passer-by, Simon of Cyrene, who was coming in from the country, the father of Alexander and Rufus, to carry his cross.

The Crucifixion

And they brought him to the place called Golgotha (which means the place of a skull). And they offered him wine mingled with myrrh; but he did not take it. And they crucified him, and divided his garments among them, casting lots for them, to decide what each should take. And it was the third hour, when they crucified him. And the inscription of the charge against him read, "The King of the Jews." And with him they crucified two robbers, one on his right and one on his left. And those who passed by derided him, wagging their heads, and saying, "Aha! You who would destroy the temple and build it in three days, save yourself, and come down from the cross!" So also the chief priests mocked him to one another with the scribes, saying, "He saved others; he cannot save himself. Let the Christ, the King of Israel, come down now from the cross, that we may see and believe." Those who were crucified with him also reviled him.

Jesus' Death

And when the sixth hour had come, there was darkness over the whole land until the ninth hour. And at the ninth hour Jesus cried with a loud voice, "Elo-i, Elo-i, lama sabach-thani?" which means, "My God, my God, why hast thou forsaken me?" And some of the bystanders hearing it said, "Behold, he is calling Elijah." And one ran and, filling a sponge full of vinegar, put it on a reed and gave it to him to drink, saying, "Wait, let us see whether Elijah will come to take him down." And Jesus uttered a loud cry, and breathed his last. And the curtain of the temple was torn in two, from top to bottom. And when the centurion, who stood facing him, saw that he thus breathed his last, he said, "Truly this man was the Son of God!" There were also women looking on from afar, among whom were Mary Magdalene, and Mary the mother of James the younger and of Joses, and Salome, who, when he was in Galilee, followed him, and ministered to him; and also many other women who came up with him to Jerusalem.

The Burial of Jesus

And when evening had come, since it was the day of Preparation, that is, the day before the Sabbath, Joseph of Arimathea, a respected member of the council, who was also himself looking for the kingdom of God, took courage and went to Pilate, and asked for the body of Jesus. And Pilate wondered if he were already dead; and summoning the centurion, he asked him whether he was already dead. And when he learned from the centurion that he was dead, he granted the body to Joseph. And he bought a linen shroud, and taking him down, wrapped him in the linen shroud, and laid him in a tomb which had been hewn out of the rock; and he rolled a stone against the door of the tomb. Mary Magdalene and Mary the mother of Joses saw where he was laid.

The Women at the Tomb

And when the Sabbath was past, Mary Magdalene, and Mary the mother of James, and Salome, bought spices, so that they might go and anoint him. And very early on the first day of the week they went to the tomb when the sun had risen. And they were saying to one another, "Who will roll away the stone for us from the door of the tomb?" And looking up, they saw that the stone was rolled back, which was very large. And entering the tomb, they saw a young man sitting on the right side, dressed in a white robe; and they were amazed. And he said to them, "Do not be amazed; you seek Jesus of Nazareth, who was crucified. He has risen, he is not here; see the place where they laid him. But go, tell his disciples and Peter that he is going before you to Galilee; there you will see him, as he told you." And they went out and fled from the tomb; for trembling and astonishment had come upon them; and they said nothing to any one, for they were afraid.

Dies Irae (Day of Wrath)
Thomas à Celano, 13ᵗʰ Century
TRANSLATED BY WILLIAM JOSIAH IRONS

In the Christian world of the Middle Ages, believers understood that they would be judged on the last day, Judgment Day. On this day, God would gather the good souls, the sheep, on his right hand, and the bad souls, the goats, on his left. The good would remain in heaven eternally, while the bad would be damned to hell. Those who had not been perfect, but who were penitent for their deeds, would be saved through the intercession of Mary or Christ. Though little is known about the author, "*Dies Irae*," which paints a vivid picture of the "Day of Wrath," was one of the most popular songs in the European Middle Ages.

಼ಜಿ

Day of wrath, that day whose knelling[1]
Gives to flame this earthly dwelling;
Psalm and Sybil thus foretelling.[2]

Oh, what agony of trembling,
5   When the judge,[3] mankind assembling,
Probeth all, beyond dissembling.[4]

Pealing[5] wondrous through the regions,
Shall the trumpet force obedience,
And the graves yield up their legions.[6]

10 Startled Death and Nature sicken,

---

[1] Knelling. Tolling, as of a bell.

[2] Psalm...foretelling. The end of the world was foretold both by prophets in Bible literature and by sybils, mysterious wise women, in classical literature.

[3] Judge. This, of course, is God, often depicted as God the Father, as opposed to God the Son, Jesus Christ.

[4] Dissembling. Dissembling, or deceiving, God is impossible, as God sees the truth in all.

[5] Pealing, Ringing, resounding. The trumpet blast announces Judgment Day.

[6] Graves...yield legions. The dead rise from the grave (the "resurrection of the body").

Thus to see the creatures quicken,[1]
Waiting judgment terror-stricken.

Open, then, with all recorded,
Stands the book from whence awarded
15 Doom shall pass with deed accorded.[2]

When the judge is throned in session,[3]
All things hid shall find confession,
Unavenged be no transgression.

Wretch, what then shall be my pleading?
20 Who my patron interceding?
Scarce the just securely speeding.

Thou, O king of awful splendor,
Saving grace dost freely render;
Save me, fount of pity tender.[4]

25 Think, 'twas I, my lost condition,
Caused, O pitying Lord, thy mission;
Spare my soul that day's perdition.

Seeking me, thy footstep hasted;[5]
Me to save, the cross was tasted,
30 Be not toil so mighty wasted.

Righteous judge of retribution,
Grant the gift of absolution[6]
Ere[7] the day of restitution.

Me my culprit heart accuses;
35 Inmost guilt my face suffuses;
Heal, O Lord, thy suppliant's[8] bruises.

Thou who Mary's sin hast shriven,[9]
Thou who brought'st the thief to heaven,
Hope to me hast also given.

40 Nothing worth is mine endeavor,

---

[1] Startled Death…quicken. Nature and, ironically, Death, will sicken when they witness people quicken, or come back to life.
[2] Dooms shall…accorded. The names and judgments (or dooms) of all are written in the book of judgment.
[3] Session. God is enthroned as a judge in a court session.
[4] Save me…tender. He appeals to Christ's mercy, as opposed to justice.
[5] Hasted. Hastened.
[6] Absolution. Forgiveness for sins.
[7] Ere. Before.
[8] Suppliant. One who pleads. His heart accuses him and his guilt shows in his face.
[9] Shriven. Heard the confession of.

Yet, in ruth, my soul deliver
From the flame that burns forever.

With thy sheep, thy chosen, place me,
Severed from the goats, embrace me;
45 On thy right hand, ransomed, place me.

When the reprobate confounded
Lie with wrathful fire surrounded,
May my call to bliss be sounded.

Crushed to dust and prostrate bending,
50 All my heart contrition rending;
I implore thee, guard my ending.

Oh, that awful day of mourning,
When, from earthly dust returning,

Guilty man shall bide his sentence;
55 Spare him, God, for his repentance.

Jesus, Lord, thy mercy lending,
Grant them rest, thy rest unending.

Stabat Mater (The Mother Stands)
Jacobus de Benedictis, 13th Century
TRANSLATED BY D. F. MACCARTHY

"*Stabat Mater*" is perhaps one of the most representative poems of the Christian
Middle Ages, as it shows the intense devotion to Mary, the mother of Jesus
Christ, at the most central moment in Christian history. It also shows how the
speaker, a representative Christian, wishes both to join Mary in her sorrow over
the death of her son and to become part of Christ's own pain.

ℭℬ

By the cross, on which suspended,
With his bleeding hands extended,
    Hung that Son she so adored,
Stood the mournful Mother weeping,
5   She whose heart, its silence keeping,
    Grief had cleft as with a sword.

Oh, that mother's sad affliction –
Mother of all benediction –
    Of the sole-begotten One;[1]
10 Oh, the grieving, sense bereaving,
Of her heaving breast, perceiving
    The dread sufferings of her Son.

What man is there so unfeeling,
Who, his heart to pity steeling,[2]
15   Could behold that sight unmoved?
Could Christ's Mother see there weeping,
See the pious Mother keeping
    Vigil by the Son she loved?

---

[1] One. Christ is the only son of God.
[2] Steeling. Becoming like steel.

For his people's sins atoning,
20 She saw Jesus writhing, groaning,
        'Neath[1] the scourge wherewith he bled;
Saw her loved one, her consoler,
Dying in his dreadful dolor,[2]
        'Til at length his spirit fled.

25 O thou Mother of election,
Fountain of all pure affection,
        Make thy grief, thy pain, my own;
Make my heart to God returning,
In the love of Jesus burning,
30   Feel the fire that thine has known.

Blessed mother of prediction,
Stamp the marks of crucifixion
        Deeply on my stony heart,
Ever leading where thy bleeding
35 Son is pleading for my needing,
        Let me in his wounds take part.

Make me truly, each day newly
While life lasts, O mother, duly[3]
        Weep with him, the Crucified.
40 Let me, 'tis my sole demanding,
Near the cross, where thou art standing,
        Stand in sorrow at thy side.

Queen of virgins, best and dearest,
Grant, oh, grant, the prayer thou hearest,
45   Let me ever mourn with thee;
Let compassion me so fashion
That Christ's wounds, his death and passion,
        Be each day renewed in me.

Oh, those wounds do not deny me;
50 On that cross, oh, crucify me;
        Let me drink his blood I pray:
Then on fire, enkindled, daring,
I may stand without despairing
        On that dreadful judgment day.

55 May that cross be my salvation;
Make Christ's death my preservation;
        May his grace my heart make wise;
And when death my body taketh,

---

[1] 'Neath. Beneath.
[2] Dolor. Pain, suffering.
[3] Duly. As is appropriate or due.

May my soul when it awaketh
60   Ope[1] in heaven its raptured[2] eyes.

---

[1] Ope. Open.
[2] Raptured. Ecstatic.

Gaudeamus Igitur (Let Us Be Joyful Then)
Anonymous, 13th Century
TRANSLATED BY JOHN ADDINGTON SYMONDS

Goliardic poetry, written by medieval students and wandering scholars and sung at social gathering, was typically irreverent of the "official" viewpoints of the church, the university, and the state. "*Gaudeamus Igitur*" is perhaps the most famous of these songs.

∝◊∞

Let us live, then, and be glad
      While young life is still with us!
After youthful pastime had,
After old age, hard and sad,
5   Earth will slumber over us.

Where are they who in this world
      Ere we kept, were keeping?[1]
Go ye to the gods above,
Go to hell; inquire thereof;
10   They are not; they are sleeping.

Brief is life, and brevity
      Briefly shall be ended;
Death comes like a whirlwind strong,
Bears us with his blast along;
15   None shall be defended.

Live this university,
      Those that learning nourish;
Live each member of the same,
Live long all that bear its name,
20   Let them ever flourish!

Live the commonwealth also,
      And the men that guide it!

---

[1] Ere we kept, were keeping. Before (ere) we lived (and enjoyed), were living.

Live our town in strength and health,
Founders, patrons, by whose wealth
25   We are here provided!

Live all gods! All health to you.
      Melting maids and beauteous;
Live the wives and women too,
Gentle, loving, tender, true,
30   Good, industrious, duteous!

Perish cares that pule and pine!
      Perish envious blamers!
Die the Devil, thine and mine!
Die the starch-neck Philistine![1]
35   Scoffers and defamers.

---

[1] Philistines. "Know-it-alls." University professors wore starched collars.

Dante Alighieri
1265 – 1321

Dante Alighieri was born in Florence, Italy, in 1265 of a noble but unwealthy family. Little is known of Dante's early life or formal education, but he was likely trained by one of the religious orders. In his youth, though some of his time was admittedly misspent, he became friends with the poet Guido Cavalcanti and the learned scholar Brunetto Latini, as well as numerous other poets, musicians, and artists of his day, the makers of the *dolce stil nuova* (the sweet new style).

At about the age of twenty he married Gemma Donati, and they had three children. He produced *La Vita Nuova* in the early 1290s and began his best-known work, the *Commedia* (*The Divine Comedy*) shortly afterward.

As a young man in the midst of the Guelph – Ghibelline conflict (Dante was a Guelph, siding with the Pope), Dante served in the army and fought victoriously in the battle of Campaldino in 1289. In 1295 Dante entered Florentine politics and in 1300 became one of the six Priors of Florence. In 1301, after the Guelphs had split into White and Black factions (the Whites advocating limited papal control in temporal matters), the Black Guelphs took control and destroyed much of Florence while Dante was in Rome visiting the Pope. At this point, Dante and other members of the White Guelph party were forced into exile, and Dante never again returned to his beloved city.

For the rest of his life he wandered throughout Italy and perhaps beyond, relying on the generosity of various nobles. During these years he served as a diplomat, but spent much of his time discussing and writing about his controversial ideas. Throughout all of this, Dante continued to work on *The Divine Comedy*. Late in life he took asylum in Ravenna where he completed the *Commedia* and died, much honored, in 1321.

Major Works
La Vita Nuova (The New Life)
De Vulgaria Eloquentia (On the Common Language)
De Monarchia (On the Monarchy)
Il Convivio (The Banquet)

Commedia (The Divine Comedy)
  Inferno (Hell)
  Purgatorio (Purgatory)
  Paradiso (Paradise)

ଔ୫ଠ
The Inferno
From **The Divine Comedy**
Dante Alighieri, 1321
TRANSLATED BY CHARLES ELIOT NORTON. ADAPTED BY GERARD P. NECASTRO

The selections below are from The Inferno *of Dante. The italicized pasages are summaries of the action between the selections.*

Dante spends a pivotal night, the eve of Good Friday 1300, in a forest. The date is important because it makes Dante's journey through Hell parallel with Christ's decent into Hell after his death on the cross. Dante tries to climb a mountain but is obstructed by a lion, a wolf, and a leopard. At that critical moment, the spirit of the great Latin poet Vergil appears and offers to take him by another path to the top of the mountain. The way will lead through Hell and Purgatory, and end in Paradise. Despite his doubts and fears, he agrees to join Vergil.

CANTO I. *Dante, astray in a wood, reaches the foot of a hill which he begins to ascend; he is hindered by three beasts; he turns back and is met by Vergil, who proposes to guide him into the eternal world.*
Midway upon the road of our life I found myself within a dark wood, for the right way had been missed. Ah, how hard a thing it is to tell what this wild and rough and dense wood was, which in thought renews the fear! So bitter is it that death is little more. But in order to treat of the good that there I found, I will tell of the other things that I have seen there. I cannot well recount how I entered it, so full was I of slumber at that point where I abandoned the true way. But after I had arrived at the foot of a hill, where that valley ended which had pierced my heart with fear, I looked on high, and saw its shoulders clothed already with the rays of the planet[1] that leads men aright along every path. Then was the fear a little quieted which in the lake of my heart had lasted through the night that I passed so piteously. And even as one who with spent breath, issued out of the sea upon the shore, turns to the perilous water and gazes, so did my soul, which still was flying, turn back to look again upon the pass which never had a living person left.

After I had rested a little my weary body I took my way again along the desert slope, so that the firm foot was always the lower. And ho, almost at the beginning of the steep a she-leopard, light and very nimble, which was covered with a spotted coat. And she did not move from before my face, nay, rather hindered so my road that to return I oftentimes had turned.

~~The time was at the beginning~~ of the morning, and the Sun was mounting

[1] The planet. The sun, a planet according to the Ptolemaic system.

upward with those stars that were with him when Love Divine first set in motion those beautiful things;[1] so that the hour of the time and the sweet season were occasion of good hope to me concerning that wild beast with the dappled skin. But not so that the sight which appeared to me of a lion did not give me fear. He seemed to be coming against me, with head high and with ravening hunger, so that it seemed that the air was affrighted at him. And a she-wolf,[2] who with all cravings seemed laden in her meagerness, and already had made many folk to live forlorn: she caused me so much heaviness, with the fear that came from sight of her, that I lost hope of the height And such as he is who gains willingly, and the time arrives that makes him lose, who in all his thoughts weeps and is sad: such made me the beast without repose that, coming on against me, little by little was pushing me back to where the Sun is silent.

While I was falling back to the low place, before my eyes appeared one who through long silence seemed hoarse. When I saw him in the great desert, "Have pity on me!" I cried to him, "Whatever you are, either shade or real man."

He answered me: "Not man; man once I was, and my parents were Lombards and Mantuans[3] by country both. I was born *sub Julio*,[4] though late, and I lived at Rome under the good Augustus,[5] in the time of the false and lying gods. Poet was I, and sang of that just son of Anchises who came from Troy after proud Ilion had been burned.[6] But you, why do you return to such a great annoyance? Why do you not ascend the delectable mountain which is the source and cause of every joy?"

"Are you then that Vergil and that fount which pours forth so large a stream of speech?" replied I to him with bashful front: "O honor and light of the other poets, whose work may I long avail myself, and the great love, which have made me search your volume! You are my master and my author; you alone are he from whom I took the fair style that has done me honor. Behold the beast because of which I turned; help me against her, famous sage, for she makes my veins and pulses tremble."

"You must go along another path," he replied, when he saw me weeping, "If you wish to escape from this savage place; for this beast, because of which you cry out, lets not any one pass along her way, but so hinders each one so that she kills him! And she has a nature so malign and evil that she never sates her greedy will, and after food is hungrier than before. Many are the animals with which she wives, and there shall be more yet, until the hound[7] shall come that

---

[1] When love...things. According to old tradition the spring was the season of the creation.
[2] She-wolf. These three beasts correspond to the triple division of sins into those of incontinence, of violence, and of fraud.
[3] Lombards and Mantuans. People of two regions in northern Italy.
[4] *Sub-Julio.* Under Julius Caesar.
[5] Augustus. Augustus Caesar.
[6] Poet was...burned. Dante is speaking to Vergil, the author of the great Roman epic poem *The Aeneid*, a selection of which appears earlier in this volume.
[7] Hound. Of whom the hound is the symbol, and to whom Dante looked for the deliverance of Italy from the discord that made her wretched, is still uncertain. Likewise, the reference to "Feltro and Feltro" is unclear.

will make her die of grief. He shall not feed on land or goods, but wisdom and love and valor, and his birthplace shall be between Feltro and Feltro. Of that humble[1] Italy shall he be the salvation, for which the virgin Camilla died, and Euryalus, Turnus and Nisus of their wounds. He shall hunt her through every town until he shall have set her back in hell, there whence envy first sent her forth.[2]

"For this reason I think and deem it for your best that you follow me, and I will be your guide, and will lead you from here through the eternal place where you shall hear the despairing shrieks, shall see the ancient spirits woeful who each proclaim the second death.[3] And then you shall see those who are contented in the fire, because they hope to come, whenever it may be, to the blessed folk;[4] to whom, if you will thereafter ascend, a certain one shall be a soul more worthy than I for that.[5] With her[6] I will leave you at my departure; for that Emperor who reigns them above, because I was rebellious to His law, wills not that into His city any one should come through me. In all parts He governs and them He reigns: there in His city and His lofty seat. O happy he whom thereto He elects!" And I to him, "Poet, I beseech you by that God whom you did not know, in order that I may escape this ill and worse, that you lead me there whom you now have said, so that I may see the gate of St. Peter, and those whom you make so afflicted."

Then he moved on, and I behind him kept.

CANTO II. *Dante, doubtful of his own powers, is discouraged. – Vergil cheers him by telling him that he has been sent to his aid by a blessed Spirit from Heaven. – Dante casts off fear; the poets proceed.*

The day was going, and the dusky air was taking the living things that are on earth from their fatigues, and I alone was preparing to sustain the war alike of the road, and of the woe which the mind that errs not shall retrace. O Muses, O lofty genius, now assist me! O mind that didst inscribe that which I saw, here shall your nobility appear! I began: – "Poet, that guide me, consider my virtue, if it is sufficient, before to the deep pass you trust me. You say that the parent of Silvius while still corruptible went to the immortal world and was there in the body. For this reason if the Adversary of every ill was then courteous, thinking on the high effect that should proceed from him, and on the Who and the What,[7] it seems not unmeet to the man of understanding; for in the empyreal heaven he had been chosen for father of revered Rome and of her empire; both which (to say truth indeed) were ordained for the holy place where the successor of the

---

[1] Humble. Fallen, humiliated.
[2] Sent her forth. All persons mentioned in the Aeneas; all died in the battles leading to Aeneas eventual success in forming the nation that was eventually to become Rome.
[3] Second death. Through Hell (Inferno).
[4] Blessed folk. Through Purgatory (Purgatorio).
[5] For that. Through Heaven (Paradiso).
[6] Her. We later dicover that he means Beatrice, the love of whom Dante had chronicled in *La Vita Nuova*.
[7] Who…What. Who he was, and what should result.

greater Peter[1] has his seat. Through this going, for which you give him a boast, he learned things which were the cause of his victory and of the papal mantle. Afterward the Chosen Vessel went thither to bring from there comfort to that faith which is the beginning of the way of salvation. But I, why do I go to that place? Or who concedes it? I am not Aeneas, I am not Paul;[2] neither I nor others think me worthy of this; therefore if I give myself up to go, I fear lest the going may be mad. You are wise, you understand better than I speak."

And as is he who unwills what he willed, and because of new thoughts changes his design, so that he quite withdraws from beginning, such I became on that dark hillside: therefore in my thought I abandoned the enterprise which had been so hasty in the beginning.

"If I have rightly understood your speech," replied that shade of the magnanimous one, "thy soul is hurt by cowardice, which oftentimes encumbers a man so that it turns him back from honorable enterprise, as false seeing does a beast when it is startled. In order that you loose you from this fear I will tell you why I have come, and what I heard at the first moment that I grieved for you. I was among those who are suspended,[3] and a Lady called me, so blessed and beautiful that I besought her to command. Her eyes were more lucent than the star, and she began to speak to me sweet and low, with angelic voice, in her own tongue: 'O courteous Mantuan soul, of whom the fame yet lasts in the world, and shall last so long as the world endures! A friend of mine and not of fortune upon the desert hillside is so hindered on his road that he has turned for fear, and I am afraid, through that which I have heard of him in heaven, lest already he be so astray that I may have risen late to his succor. Now do you move, and with your speech ornate, and with whatever is needful for his deliverance, assist him so that I may be consoled for him. I am Beatrice who bids you to go. I come from a place from which I desire to return. Love moved me, and makes me speak. When I shall be before my Lord, I will commend you often to Him.'

"Then she was silent, and on that I began: 'O Lady of Virtue, you alone through whom the human race surpasses all contained within that heaven which has the smallest circles![4] so pleasing to me is your command that to obey it, were it already done, were slow to me. You have no need further to reveal to me your will; but tell me the cause why you guard not yourself from descending down here into this center, from the ample place whither you burn to return.' 'Since you wish to know so inwardly, I will tell you briefly,' she replied to me, 'because I fear not to come here within. One ought to fear those things only that have power of doing harm, the others not, for they are not dreadful. I am made by God, thanks be to Him, such that your misery touches me not, nor doth the flame of this burning assail me. A gentle Lady[5] is in heaven who has pity for

---

[1]Peter. The apostle of Christ and the first Pope.

[2] I am not...Paul. Both Aeneas and Paul made journeys to the underworld. Likewise, the Chosen Vessel, Jesus Christ, descended into Hell to free all the worthy souls. This is known as "the harrowing of hell."

[3] Those who are suspended. In Limbo, neither in Hell nor Heaven.

[4] Heaven...circles. The heaven of the moon, nearest to the earth.

[5] Gentle Lady. The Virgin Mary, the mother of Jesus Christ.

this hindrance in the place I send you, so that stern judgment there above she breaks. She summoned Lucia in her request, and said, "Thy faithful one now has need of you, and to you I commend him." Lucia, the foe of every cruel one, rose and came to the place where I was, seated with the ancient Rachel. She said, "Beatrice, true praise of God, why you do not succor him who so loved you that for you he came forth from the vulgar throng? Do you not hear the pity of his plaint? Do you not see the death that combats him beside the stream whereof the sea has no vaunt?" In the world never were persons swift to seek their good, and to fly their harm, as I, after these words were uttered, came here below, from my blessed seat, putting my trust in your upright speech, which honors you and them who have heard it.'

"After she had said this to me, weeping she turned her lucent eyes, whereby she made me more speedy in coming. And I came to you as she willed. You have I delivered from that wild beast that took from you the short ascent of the beautiful mountain. What is it then? Why, why do you hold back? Why do you harbor such cowardice in your heart? Why do you not have daring and boldness, since three blessed Ladies care for you in the court of Heaven, and my speech pledges you such good?"

As flowerets, bent and closed by the chill of night, after the sun shines on them straighten themselves all open on their stem, so I became with my weak virtue, and such good daring hastened to my heart that I began like one enfranchised: "Oh compassionate woman who succored me, and courteous one who did speedily obey the true words that she addressed to you! You by your words have so disposed my heart with desire of going, that I have returned to my first intent. Go on now, for one sole will is in us both: Leader, Lord, and Master." Thus I said to him; and when he had moved on, I entered along the deep and savage road.

As they approach the entrance to Hell, Vergil and Dante see a crowd of people blank flag and being continually stung by wasps. Vergil tells Dante these are people who never took a position in life, so they now must take up a position that is no position at all. They are ferried across the river by Charon and meet the noble non-Christians in a castle on the first ring of Hell, which is a sort of inverted mountain deep in the earth. There is no punishment for these noble souls, except that they may never enter Paradise. Among the residents of this castle are Homer, Plato, Hector, Aeneas, and Vergil himself.

CANTO III. The gate of Hell. – Vergil lends Dante in. – The punishment of the neither good nor bad. – Acheron, and the sinners on its bank. – Charon. – Earthquake. – Dante swoons.

"Through me is the way into the woeful city; through me is the way into eternal woe; through me is the way among the lost people. Justice moved my lofty maker: the divine Power, the supreme Wisdom and the primal Love made me. Before me were no things created, unless eternal, and I eternal last. Leave every hope, ye who enter!"

These words of color obscure I saw written at the top of a gate; at this I said, "Master, their meaning is dire to me."

And he to me, like one who knew, "Here it is necessary to leave every fear; it is necessary that all cowardice should here be dead. We have come to the place where I have told you that you shall see the woeful people, who have lost the good of the understanding."

And when he had put his hand on mine, with a glad countenance, wherefrom I took courage, he brought me within the secret things. Here sighs, laments, and deep wailings were resounding though the starless air; for this reason at first I wept at this. Strange tongues, horrible cries, words of woe, accents of anger, voices high and hoarse, and sounds of hands with them, were making a tumult which whirls forever in that air dark without change, like the sand when the whirlwind breathes.

And I, who had my head girt with horror, said, "Master, what is it that I hear? And what people are they who seem in woe so vanquished?"

And he to me, "This miserable measure the wretched souls maintain of those who lived without infamy and without praise. Mingled are they with that despicably mean choir of the angels, who were not rebels, nor were faithful to God, but were for themselves. The heavens chased them out in order to be not less beautiful, nor doth the depth of Hell receive them, because the damned would have some glory from them."

And I asked, "Master, what is so grievous to them, that makes them lament so bitterly?"

He answered, "I will tell you very briefly. These have no hope of death; and their blind life is so debased, that they are envious of every other lot. Fame of them the world permits not to be; mercy and justice disdain them. Let us not speak of them, but look and pass on."

And I, who was gazing, saw a banner, that whirling ran so swiftly that it seemed to me to scorn all repose, and behind it came so long a train of folk, that I could never have believed death had undone so many. After I had distinguished some among them, I saw and knew the shade of him who made, through cowardice, the great refusal.[1] At once I understood and was certain, that this was the sect of the caitiffs displeasing to God, and to his enemies. These wretches, who never were alive, were naked, and much stung by gad-flies and by wasps that were there. These streaked their faces with blood, which, mingled with tears, was harvested at their feet by loathsome worms.

And when I gave myself to looking onward, I saw people on the bank of a great river; therefore I said, "Master, now grant to me that I may know who these are, and what rule makes them appear so ready to pass over, as I discern through the faint light."

And he replied to me, "The things will be clear to you, when we shall set our steps on the sad shore of Acheron." Then with eyes bashful and cast down, fearing lest my speech had been irksome to him, far as to the river I refrained from speaking.

---

[1] Great refusal. Though it is not entirely certain, it seems that this refers to Pope Celestine V, who gave up the position of Pope after only five months to Boniface VIII, an enemy of Dante.

And lo, coming toward us in a boat, an old man, white with ancient hair, crying, "Woe to you, wicked souls! Hope not ever to see Heaven! I come to carry you to the other bank, into eternal darkness, to heat and frost. And you who are there, living soul, depart from these that are dead." But when he saw that I did not depart, he said, "By another way, by other ports you shall come to the shore, not here, for passage; it is necessary that a lighter bark bear you."[1]

And my Leader to him, "Charon, vex not yourself: it is thus willed there where is power to do that which is willed; and ask not further." Then the fleecy cheeks were quiet of the pilot of the livid marsh, who round about his eyes had wheels of flame.

But those souls, who were weary and naked, changed color, and gnashed their teeth soon as they heard his cruel words. They blasphemed God and their parents, the human race, the place, the time and the seed of their sowing and of their birth. Then, bitterly weeping, they drew back all of them together to the evil bank, that waits for every man who fears not God. Charon the demon, with eyes of glowing coal, beckoning them, collects them all; he beats with his oar whoever lingers.

As in autumn the leaves fall off one after the other, until the bough sees all its spoils upon the earth, in like wise the evil seed of Adam throw themselves from that shore one by one at signals, as the bird at his call. Thus they go over the dusky wave, and before they have landed on the farther side, already on this a new throng is gathered.

"My son," said the courteous Master, "those who die in the wrath of God, all meet together here from every land. And they are eager to pass over the stream, for the divine justice spurs them, so that fear is turned to desire. This way a good soul never passes; and therefore if Charon snarls at you, you now may well know what his speech signifies." This ended, the dark plain trembled so mightily, that the memory of the terror even now bathes me with sweat. The tearful land gave forth a wind that flashed a vermilion light which vanquished every sense of mine, and I fell as a man whom slumber seizes.

CANTO IV. *The further side of Acheron. – Vergil leads Dante into Limbo, the First Circle of Hell, containing the spirits of those who lived virtuously but without Christianity. – Greeting of Vergil by his fellow poets. – They enter a castle, where are the shades of ancient worthies. – Vergil and Dante proceed.*

A heavy thunder broke the deep sleep in my head, so that I started up like a person who by force is wakened. And risen erect, I moved my rested eye round about, and looked fixedly to distinguish the place where I was. True it is that I found myself on the verge of the valley of the woeful abyss that gathers in thunder of infinite wailings. Dark, profound it was, and cloudy, so that though I fixed my sight on the bottom I did not discern anything there.

"Now we descend down here into the blind world," began the Poet all deadly pale, "I will be first, and you shall be second."

And I, who had observed his color, said, "How shall I come, if you fear,

---

[1] Bear you. The boat that bears the souls to Purgatory. Charon recognizes that Dante, because he has weight, is not among the damned.

who are accustomed to be a comfort to my doubting?"

And he to replied me, "The anguish of the folk who are down here depicts upon my face that pity which you take for fear. Let us go on, for the long way urges us."

So he set forth, and so he made me enter within the first circle that girds the abyss. Here, so far as could be heard, there was no plaint but that of sighs which made the eternal air to tremble: this came of the woe without torments felt by the crowds, which were many and great, of infants and of women and of men.

The good Master to me, "You do not ask what spirits are these that you see. Now I would have you know, before you go farther, that they sinned not; and if they have merits it suffices not, because they had not baptism, which is part of the faith that you believe; and if they were before Christianity, they did not duly worship God: and of such as these am I myself. Through such defects, and not through other guilt, are we lost, and only so far harmed that without hope we live in desire."

Great woe seized me at my heart when I heard him, because I knew that people of much worth were suspended in that limbo. "Tell me, my Master, tell me, Lord," I began, with wish to be assured of that faith which vanquishes every error,[1] "did ever any one who afterwards was blessed go out from here, either by his own or by another's merit?"

And he, who understood my covert speech, answered, "I was new in this state when I saw a Mighty One come hither crowned with sign of victory. He drew out hence the shade of the first parent, of Abel his son, and that of Noah, of Moses the law-giver and obedient, Abraham the patriarch, and David the King, Israel with his father, and with his offspring, and with Rachel, for whom he did so much, and others many; and He made them blessed: and I would have you know that before these, human spirits were not saved."

We ceased not going on because he spoke, but all the while were passing through the wood, the wood I mean of crowded spirits. Nor yet had our way been long from where I slept, when I saw a fire, which conquered a hemisphere of darkness. We were still a little distant from it, yet not so far that I could not partially discern that honorable folk possessed that place. "O you that honor both science and are, these, who are they, that have such honor that from the condition of the others it sets them apart?"

And he answered, "The honorable fame of them which resounds above in your life wins grace in heaven that so advances them."

At this a voice was heard by me, "Honor the loftiest Poet! His shade returns that was departed." When the voice had ceased and was quiet, I saw four great shades coming to us: they had a semblance neither sad nor glad.

The good Master began to say, "Look at him with that sword in hand who comes before the three, even as lord. He is Homer, the sovereign poet; the next who comes is Horace, the satirist; Ovid is the third, and the last is Lucan. Since

---

[1] With wish...error. Wishing especially to be assured in regard to the descent of Christ into Hell.

each shares with me the name that the single voice sounded, they do me honor, and in that do well"

Thus I saw assembled the fair school of that Lord of the loftiest song which above the others as an eagle flies. After they had discoursed somewhat together, they turned to me with sign of salutation; and my Master smiled at that. And far more of honor yet they did me, for they made me of their band, so that I was the sixth amid so much wit. Thus we went on as far as the light, speaking things concerning which silence is becoming, even as was speech there where I was.

We came to the foot of a noble castle, seven times circled by high walls, defended round about by a fair streamlet. This we passed as if hard ground; through seven gates I entered with these sages; we came to a meadow of fresh verdure. People were there with eyes slow and grave, of great authority in their looks; they seldom spoke, and with soft voices. Thus we drew apart, on one side, into a place open, luminous, and high, so that they all could be seen. There opposite upon the green enamel were shown to me the great spirits, whom to have seen I inwardly exalt myself.

I saw Electra[1] with many companions, among whom I knew both Hector and Aeneas, Caesar in armor, with his gerfalcon[2] eyes; I saw Camilla and Penthesilea on the other side, and I saw the King Latinus, who was seated with Lavinia his daughter. I saw that Brutus who drove out Tarquin; Lucretia, Julia, Marcia, and Cornelia; and alone, apart, I saw the Saladin. When I raised my brow a little more, I saw the Master of those who know, seated amid the philosophic family; all regard him, all do him honor. Here I saw both Socrates and Plato, who before the others stand nearest to him; Democritus, who ascribes the world to chance; Diogenes, Anaxagoras, and Thales, Empedocles, Heraclitus, and Zeno; and I saw the good collector of the qualities, Dioscorides, I mean; and I saw Orpheus, Tully, and Linus, and moral Seneca, Euclid the geometer, and Ptolemy, Hippocrates, Avicenna, Galen, and Averroes, who made the great comment. I cannot report of all in full, because the long theme so drives me that many times speech comes short of fact.

The company of six is reduced to two. By another way the wise guide leads me, out from the quiet, into the air that trembles, and I come into a region where there is nothing that can give light.

The Second Circle is guarded by powerful judge Minos, who wraps his tail around the sinners and slings them into the pit below. There are four rings in which souls are punished for the excessive indulgence of their natural desires. In the Second Circle, the souls of the lustful are blown about haphazardly by the never-ending winds, a reminder of how they were moved in life by their passion.

CANTO V. *The Second Circle, that of Carnal Sinners. – Minos. – Shades renowned of old. – Francesca da Rimini.*
Thus I descended from the first circle down into the second, which girdles less

---

[1] Electra. The list of souls that follows is, in a sense, the underworld hall of fame of the Greco-Roman world.
[2] Gerfalcon. The largest of the falcon species.

space, and so much more woe that it goads to wailing. There awaits Minos horribly, and snarls; he examines the sins at the entrance; he judges, and he sends according as he entwines himself. I mean, that, when the miscreant spirit comes there before him, it confesses itself wholly, and that discerner of sins sees what place of Hell is for it; he girdles himself with his tail so many times as the degrees he wills it should be sent down. Always before him stand many of them. They go, in turn, each to the judgment; they speak, and hear, and then are whirled below.

"O you that come to the woeful inn," said Minos to me, when he saw me, leaving the act of so great an office, "beware how you enter, and to whom you trust yourself; let not the amplitude of the entrance deceive you." And my Leader to him, "Why then do you cry out? Hinder not his fated going; thus is it willed there where is power to do that which is willed; and ask you no more."

Now the woeful notes begin to make themselves heard; now am I come where much lamentation smites me. I had come into a place mute of all light, that bellows as the sea does in a tempest, if it be combated by opposing winds. The infernal hurricane that never rests carries along the spirits in its rapine; whirling and smiting it molests them. When they arrive before its rushing blast, here are shrieks, and bewailing, and lamenting; here they blaspheme the power divine. I understood that to such torment are condemned the carnal sinners who subject reason to appetite. And as their wings bear along the starlings in the cold season in a troop large and full, so that blast the evil spirits; here, there, down, up it carries them; no hope ever comforts them, not of repose, but even of less pain.

And as the cranes go singing their lays, making in air a long line of themselves, so saw I come, uttering wails, shades borne along by the aforesaid strife. Therefore I said, "Master, who are those folk whom the black air so castigates?"

"The first of these of whom you wish to have knowledge," he said to me then, "was empress of many tongues. To the vice of luxury was she so abandoned that lust she made licit in her law, to take away the blame she had incurred. She is Semiramis, of whom it is read that she succeeded Ninus and had been his spouse; she held the land which the Soldan rules. That other is she who, for love, killed herself, and broke faith to the ashes of Sichaeus. Next is Cleopatra, the luxurious. See Helen, for whom so long a time of ill revolved; and see the great Achilles, who at the end fought with love. See Paris, Tristan – " and more than a thousand shades he showed me with his finger, and named them, whom love had parted from our life.

After I had heard my Teacher name the ladies of olden days and the cavaliers, pity overcame me, and I was very nearly bewildered. I began, "Poet, willingly would I speak with those two that go together, and seem to be so light upon the wind."

And he answered to me, "You shall see when they shall be nearer to us, and do you then pray them by that love which leads them, and they will come."

Soon as the wind sways them toward us I lifted my voice, "O weary souls, come speak to us, if One forbid it not."

As doves, called by desire, with wings open and steady, fly through the air to their sweet nest, borne by their will, these issued from the troop where Dido is, coming to us through the malign air, so strong was the compassionate cry.

"O living creature, gracious and benign, who does go through the lurid air visiting us who stained the world blood-red – if the King of the universe were a friend we would pray Him for your peace, since you have pity on our perverse ill. Of what it pleases you to hear, and what to speak, we will hear and we will speak to you, while the wind, as now, is hushed for us. The city where I was born sits upon the sea-shore, where the Po, with its followers, descends to have peace. Love, that on gentle heart quickly lays hold, seized him for the fair person that was taken from me, and the mode still hurts me. Love, which absolves no loved one from loving, seized me for the pleasing of him so strongly that, as you see, it does not even now abandon me. Love brought us to one death. Caina awaits him who quenched our life." These words were borne to us from them.

Soon as I had heard those injured souls I bowed my face, and held it down, until the Poet said to me, "What are you thinking?"

When I replied, I began, "Alas! How many sweet thoughts, how great desire, led these to the woeful pass." Then I turned me again to them, and I spoke, and began, "Francesca, your torments make me sad and piteous to weeping. But tell me, at the time of the sweet sighs by what and how did love concede to you to know the dubious desires?"

And she replied to me, "There is no greater woe than in misery to remember the happy time, and that your Teacher knows. But if to know the first root of our love you have so great a longing, I will do like one who weeps and tells.

"We were reading one day, for delight, of Lancelot, how love constrained him. We were alone and without any suspicion. Many times that reading made us lift our eyes, and took the color from our faces, but only one point was that which overcame us. When we read of the longed-for smile being kissed by such a lover, this one, who never from me shall be divided, kissed my mouth all trembling. Galahaut was the book, and he who wrote it. That day we read in it no farther."[1]

While one spirit said this the other was weeping so that through pity I swooned, as if I had been dying, and fell as a dead body falls.

In the Third Circle, the Dante and Vergil meet the Gluttonous, who are soaked by heavy rain and clawed by the three-headed dog Cerberus. They encounter Ciacco, a soul from Dante's home of Florence, who predicts that one of the two warring factions in that city will conquer the other. As they continue downwards, they meet Pluto, the Greek god of wealth, at the entrance to the Fourth Circle, where both the Squanderers of wealth and the Hoarders. These souls are condemned to push heavy stones back and forth with their chests for eternity. The Fifth Circle also holds two types of sinners: the Wrathful, who battle one another on the surface of the muddy marsh of the Styx, and the Sullen,

---

[1] Galahaut...no farther. In the Romance, it was Galahaut that prevailed on Guinevere to give a kiss to Lancelot.

who, completely covered in the mud, gurgle beneath the surface. Dante and Vergil are then ferried across the Fifth Circle to the entrance of the imposing walled City of Dis, but a band of fallen angels deny them entry. A messenger from heaven arrives, however, and opens the door for them, even though the Furies have threatened to turn Dante into stone with the head of Medusa, and rebukes the foes of Dante. Within the walls of Dis is a plain filled with flaming tombs in which Dante can see the souls of heretics, Christians who denied the teachings of the Church. Dante converses with the soul of a political rival of his family, Farinata, and is disturbed by his prediction that Dante will be exiled from Florence, but Vergil reassures him that he shall hear his entire future when he reaches the Paradiso.

Dante and Vergil pause at the cliff that divides the Sixth Circle from the others below, and Vergil gives an overview of the various classes of sinners held in the three circles below. The Seventh Circle is reserved for the violent and divided into three parts: the Violent toward God, towards one's self, and towards one's neighbor. The Eighth Circle contains ten bolgias (or pockets): Panderers and Seducers; Flatterers; Simoniacs (those who profited from their Church positions); Sorcerers and False Prophets; Corrupt Politicians; Hypocrites, Thieves, False Counselors; Sowers of Discord; and a variety of Falsifiers. The Ninth Circle of the City of Dis holds Traitors.

After Vergil's introduction, they enter the Seventh Circle. Passing the Minotaur, they view the Phlegethon, a river of boiling blood in which men, who committed acts of violence towards their fellow humans, are sunk to varying depths according to their sins. Centaurs, under the lead of Chiron and armed with arrows, guard them; one of the Centaurs guides the poets to a ford in the river. They cross and find themselves in a mystical wood. Here men who committed suicide are transformed into trees and tormented by Harpies who tear their leaves. At the edge of the wood lies a great plain of fiery sand. Blasphemers, Sodomites, and Usurers are punished here by the scorching heat. The poets meet Geryon, a reptilian monster with a human face, who guards the Usurers; they ride upon its back down a watery vortex to reach the Eighth Circle that holds the Fraudulent.

The Eighth Circle, Malebolge (evil pouches), is divided into ten rounds, which are like ten fortified trenches of a citadel. The poets pass through the circle along footpaths that bridge the chasms. In the First Bolgia, former Seducers are lashed as they march. In the Second Bolgia, Flatterers covered in excrement and enveloped in vile vapors gasp for air and beat themselves. The Third Bolgia holds those who sold spiritual things, the Simoniacs. Here Dante meets Pope Nicholas III, imprisoned upside-down in a stone cylinder with flames licking the soles of his feet. The Fourth Bolgia holds Sorcerers who attempted to see the future. They weep and march backwards because their heads have been twisted around backwards. The Fifth Bolgia holds those who used their public office or authority to make money. They boil in pitch and are attacked by hook-wielding demons when they rise above the surface of the black substance. One of the demons informs Vergil that the next bridge is in ruins and outfits the pilgrims-poets with an escort of unruly demons to take them to the next bridge further along the bolgia wall. Along the way the demons are distracted by a wily soul and end up fighting among themselves while the poets move along. As they are easily angered, the demons pursue the poets, who plunge into the Sixth Bolgia rather than await the fiery escorts. There they see the Hypocrites trudging along in leaden cloaks gilded on the outside. Climbing out of the bolgia they reach the Seventh Bolgia, which holds Thieves. The Thieves are enveloped by snakes and lizards, and some are transformed into reptiles and back again. The Eighth Bolgia holds evil counselors, including Ulysses, who are each enveloped in flames.

CANTO XXVI. *Eighth Circle: eighth pit fraudulent counselors. – Ulysses and Diomed.*

Rejoice, Florence, since you are so great that over sea and land you beat your wings, and your name is spread through Hell. Among the thieves I found five such, your citizens, from which shame comes to me, and you to great honor rise not by that. But, if near the morning one dreams the truth, you shall feel within little time what Prato, as well as others, craves for you.[1] And if now it were, it would not be too soon. Would that it were so! Since surely it must be; for the more it will weigh on me the more I age.

We departed from there, and up along the stairs that the bourns[2] had made for our descent before, my Leader remounted and dragged me. And pursuing the solitary way mid the splinters and rocks of the crag, the foot without the hand sped not. Then I grieved, and now I grieve again when I direct my mind to what I saw; and I curb my genius more than I am accustomed to, that it may not run unless virtue guide it; so that if a good star, or better thing, has given me of good, I may not grudge it to myself.

As the rustic who rests him on the hill in the season when he that brightens the world keeps his face least hidden from us, that time the fly yields to the gnat,[3] sees many fireflies down in the valley, perhaps there where he makes his vintage and ploughs – with as many flames all the eighth pit was resplendent, as I perceived soon as I was there where the bottom became apparent. And as he[4] who was avenged by the bears saw the chariot of Elijah at its departure, when the horses rose erect to heaven, and could not so follow it with his eyes as to see aught save the flame alone, even as a little cloud, mounting upward: thus each [of these flames] was moving through the gulley of the ditch, for not one shows its theft, and every flame steals away a sinner.[5]

I was standing on the bridge, risen up to look, so that if I had not taken hold of a rock I should have fallen below without being pushed. And the Leader, who saw me thus leaning over, said, "Within these fires are the spirits; each is swathed by that wherewith he is enkindled."

"My Master," I replied, "by hearing you am I more certain, but already I

---

[1] Craves for you. If that which I foresee is not a vain dream, the calamities which your enemies crave for you will soon be felt.
[2] Bourns. The projections of the rocky wall.
[3] That time...gnat. That is, in the summer twilight.
[4] He. Elisha. See 2 Kings 2. 9-24.
[5] Steals awaya sinner. Within each flame a sinner was concealed.

deemed that it was so, and already I wished to say to you, Who is in that fire that comes so divided at its top that it seems to rise from the pyre on which Eteocles was put with his brother?"[1]

He answered me, "There within are tormented Ulysses and Diomed, and thus together they go in punishment, as of old in wrath.[2] And within their flame they groan for the ambush of the horse that made the gate, whence the gentle seed of the Romans issued forth. Within it they lament for the artifice whereby the dead Deidamia still mourns for Achilles, and there for the Palladium they bear the penalty."

"If they can speak within those sparkles," I said, "Master, much I pray you, and pray again that the prayer is helpful to a thousand, that you make not to me denial of waiting until the horned flame come hither; you see that with desire I bend me toward it."

And he said to me, "Thy prayer is worthy of much praise, and therefore I accept it, but take heed that your tongue restrain itself. Leave speech to me, for I have conceived what you wish, for, because they are Greeks, they would be shy, perchance, of your words."[3]

When the flame had come there where it seemed to my Leader time and place, in this form I heard him speak to it: "O ye who are two within one fire, if I deserved of you while I lived, if I deserved of you much or little, when in the world I wrote the lofty verses, move not, but let one of you tell us, where, having lost himself, he went away to die."

The greater horn of the ancient flame began to waver, murmuring, even as a flame that the wind wearies. Then moving its tip hither and thither, as it had been the tongue that would speak, it cast forth a voice, and said, "When I departed from Circe, who had retained me more than a year there near to Gaeta, before Aeneas had so named it, neither fondness for my son, nor piety for my old father, nor the due love that should have made Penelope glad, could overcome within me the ardor that I had to gain experience of the world, and of the vices of men, and of their valor. But I put forth on the deep, open sea, with one vessel only, and with that little company by which I had not been deserted. One shore and the other[4] I saw as far as Spain, far as Morocco and the island of Sardinia, and the rest which that sea bathes round about. I and my companions were old and slow when we came to that narrow strait where Hercules set up his

---

[1] Eteocles...brother. Eteocles and Polynices, sons of Oedipus and Jocaste, who, contending at the siege of Thebes, slew each other. Such was their mutual hate that, when their bodies were burned on the same funeral pile, the flames divided in two.
[2] Ulysses and Diomed...wrath. Against the Trojans. It was through the stratagem of the wooden horse that Troy was destroyed, and Aeneas thus compelled to lead forth his followers who became the seed of the Romans. Deidamia was the wife of Achilles, who slew herself for grief at his desertion and departure for Troy, which had been brought about by the deceit of Ulysses and Diomed. The Palladium was the statue of Athena, on which the safety of Troy depended, stolen by the two heroes.
[3] Your words. The ancient heroes might be averse to talking with a man of the strange modern world.
[4] Other. Of the Mediterranean.

bounds, to the end that man may not put out beyond. On the right hand I left Seville, on the other already I had left Ceuta. 'O brothers,' I said, 'who through a hundred thousand perils have reached the West, to this so little vigil of your senses that remains be ye unwilling to deny, the experience, following the sun, of the world that has no people. Consider your origin; ye were not made to live as brutes, but for pursuit of virtue and of knowledge.' With this little speech I made my companions so eager for the road that hardly afterwards could I have held them back. And turning our stern to the morning, with our oars we made wings for the mad flight, always gaining on the left hand side. The night saw now all the stars of the other pole, and ours so low that it rose not forth from the ocean floor. Five times rekindled and as many quenched was the light beneath the moon, since we had entered on the deep pass, when there appeared to us a mountain dim through the distance, and it appeared to me so high as I had not seen any. We rejoiced at that, and soon it turned to lamentation, for from the strange land a whirlwind rose, and struck the fore part of the vessel. Three times it made her whirl with all the waters, the fourth it made her stern lift up, and the prow go down, as pleased Another, until the sea had closed over us."

CANTO XXVII. *Eighth Circle: eighth pit fraudulent counselors. – Guido da Montefeltro.*
Now was the flame erect and quiet, through not speaking more, and now was going from us, with the permission of the sweet poet, when another that was coming behind it made us turn our eyes to its tip, by a confused sound that is-sued forth from that place. As the Sicilian bull[1] – that bellowed first with the plaint of him (and that was right) who had shaped it with his file – was accus-tomed to bellow with the voice of the sufferer, so that, although it was of brass, yet it appeared transfixed with pain, thus, through not at first having way or outlet from the fire, the disconsolate words were converted into its language. But when they had taken their course up through the point, giving it that vibration which the tongue had given in their passage, we heard say, "O you, to whom I direct my voice, you who was just speaking Lombard,[2] saying, 'Now go your way, no more I urge you,' although I may have arrived perchance somewhat late, let it not irk you to stop to speak with me, behold, it irks not me, and I am burning. If you but now into this blind world are fallen from that sweet Italian land whence I bring all my sin, tell me if the Romagnuoli have peace or war; for I was from the mountains there between Urbino and the chain from which Tiber is unlocked."[3]

I was still downward looking down and leaning over when my Leader touched me on the side, saying, "Speak you, this is an Italian." And I, who even

---

[1] Sicilian bull. The brazen bull of Phalaris, tyrant of Agrigentum, made to hold criminals to be burned within it. Perillus, its inventor, was the first to suffer. So these sinners are wrapped in the flames which their fraudulent counsels had prepared for them.
[2] Lombard. Because the words were those of Vergil, whose "parents were Lombards," and in speaking he had used a form peculiar to the Lombard dialect.
[3] If you...unlocked. It is the spirit of the Ghibelline count, Guido da Montefeltro, a famous freebooting captain, who speaks.

now had my answer ready, without delay began to speak, "O soul, that are hidden there below, your Romagna is not, and never was, without war in the hearts of her tyrants, but open war none have I left there now. Ravenna is as it has been for many years; the eagle of Polenta[1] is brooding there, so that he covers Cervia with his wings. The city[2] that made in days past the long struggle, and of the French a bloody heap, finds itself again beneath the green paws. And the old mastiff and the new of Verrucchio,[3] who made the ill disposal of Montagna, make an anger of their teeth there where they are accustomed to. The little lion of the white lair[4] governs the city of Lamone and of Santerno, and changes side from summer to winter. And she[5] whose flank the Savio bathes, even as she sits between the plain and the mountain, lives between tyranny and a free state. Now who you are, I pray you that you tell us; be not harder than another has been,[6] so may your name in the world hold front."

After the fire had somewhat roared according to its fashion, the sharp point moved this way and that, and then gave forth this breath: "If I could believe that my answer might be to a person who should ever return to the world, this flame would stand without more quivering; but inasmuch as, if I hear truth, never from this depth did any living man return, without fear of infamy I answer you.

"I was a man of arms, and then became a cordelier, trusting, thus girt, to make amends; and surely my trust had been fulfilled except for the Great Priest[7] – may ill-fortune come to him – who set me back into my first sins; and how and why, I would like you to hear from me. While I was that form of bone and flesh that my mother gave me, my works were not leonine, but of the fox. The wily practices, and the covert ways, I knew them all, and I so plied their art that to the earth's end the sound went forth. When I saw me arrived at that part of my age where every one ought to strike the sails and to coil up the ropes, what formerly was pleasing to me then gave me pain, and I yielded me repentant and confessed. Alas, wretched me! And it would have availed. The Prince of the new Pharisees having war near the Lateran[8] – and not with Saracens nor with Jews, for every enemy of his was Christian, and none of them had been to conquer Acre,[9] nor a trafficker in the land of the Soldan – regarded in himself neither his

---

[1] Eagle of Polenta. Guido Novello da Polenta had been lord of Ravenna since 1275. He was father of Francesca da Rimini (see Canto V), and a friend of Dante.
[2] The city. Forli, where in 1282 Guido da Montefeltro had defeated, with great slaughter, a troop, largely of French soldiers, sent against him by Pope Martin III.
[3] Verrucchio. Malatesta, father and son, rulers of Rimini; father and brother of the husband and of the lover of Francesca da Rimim. They had cruelly put to death Montagna di Parcitade, the head of the Ghibellines of Rimini; and they ruled as tyrants, sucking the blood of their subjects.
[4] Little lion…white lair. This is Maghinardo da Susinana, who bore a lion azure (blue) on a field argent (silver).
[5] She. The city of Cesena.
[6] Be not harder…been. Refuse not to answer me as I have answered thee.
[7] Great Priest. Pope Boniface VIII.
[8] Lateran. With the Colonna family, whose stronghold was Palestrina.
[9] Acre. Not one had been a renegade, to help the Saracens at the siege of Acre in 1291.

supreme office, nor the holy orders, nor in me that cord which is accustomed to make those girt with it more lean; but as Constantine besought Sylvester within Soracte to cure his leprosy,[1] so this one besought me as master to cure his proud fever. He asked counsel of me, and I kept silence, because his words seemed drunken. And then he said to me, 'Let not your heart mistrust; from now I absolve you, and please teach me to act so that I may throw Palestrina to the ground. Heaven can I lock and unlock, as you know; for two are the keys that my predecessor held not dear.' Then his grave arguments pushed me to where silence seemed to me the worst, and I said, 'Father, since you wash me of that sin wherein I now must fall, long promise with short keeping will make you triumph on the High Seat.' Francis[2] came for me afterwards, when I was dead, but one of the Black Cherubim said to him, 'Bear him not away; do me not wrong; he must come down among my drudges because he gave the fraudulent counsel, since which until now I have been at his hair; for he who repents not cannot be absolved, nor can repentance and will exist together, because of the contradiction that allows it not.' O woeful me! How I shuddered when he took me, saying to me, 'Perhaps you did not think that I was a logician.' To Minos he bore me; and he twined his tail eight times round his hard back, and, after he had bitten it in great rage, he said, 'This is one of the sinners of the thievish fire.' Therefore I, where you see, am lost, and going thus robed I rankle." When he had thus completed his speech the flame, sorrowing, departed, twisting and flapping its sharp horn.

We passed onward, I and my Leader, along the crag, far as upon the next arch that covers the ditch in which the fee is paid by those who, sowing discord, win their burden.

The Ninth Bolgia holds those who willingly created division among other people, the Sowers of Discord, including Muhammad and Bertran de Born, who carries his head as if it were a lantern. They are mutilated in various ways symbolic of their particular sins. The Tenth Bolgia of the Eighth Circle holds the Falsifiers, who are afflicted by various diseases.

The Ninth Circle of Hell is a well surrounded by giants embedded to the waist in its wall. Nimrod, who led the building of the tower of Babel, is the first they encounter. The mythical giant Antæus lifts the two poets and sets them down in the frozen marsh at the center of the well. The circle of the traitors is divided into four rounds: Betrayers of Family, Betrayers of Country, Betrayers of Guests, and Betrayers of Lords or Benefactors. All are frozen into the marsh. They meet various infamous Italians, most of whom Dante treats mercilessly.

CANTO XXXII. *Ninth Circle: traitors. First ring: Caina. – Counts of Mangona. – Camicion de' Pazzi. – Second ring: Antenora. – Bocca degli Abati. – Buoso da Duera. – Count Ugolino.*

---

[1] Constantine...leprosy. It was for this service that Constantine was supposed to have made Sylvester "the first rich Father." His predecessor, Celestine V, had renounced the papacy.
[2] Francis. St. Francis came for his soul, as Montefeltro had been a Franciscan friar.

If I had rhymes both harsh and raucous, such as would befit the dismal hole on which all the other rocks rest their weight, I would press out the juice of my conception more fully; but since I have them not, not without fear I bring myself to speak; for to describe the bottom of the whole universe is no enterprise to take up in jest, nor a tongue that cries mamma or babbo. But may those Dames aid my verse who aided Amphion to close in Thebes; so that from the fact the speech may be not diverse.

O populace miscreant above all, that are in the place whereof to speak is hard, better had ye been here [on earth] or sheep or goats!

When we were down in the dark abyss beneath the feet of the giant, but far lower, and I was gazing still at the high wall, I heard say to me, "Beware how you step; take heed you trample not with your soles the heads of the wretched weary brethren." At this I turned, and saw before me, and under my feet, a lake which through frost had semblance of glass and not of water.

The Danube in Austria makes not for its current so thick a veil in winter, nor the Don yonder under the cold sky, as there was here; for if Tambernich[1] had fallen thereupon, or Pietrapana,[2] it would not even at the edge have given a creak. And as to croak the frog lies with muzzle out of the water, in the time[3] when often the peasant girl dreams of gleaning, so, livid up to where shame appears [up to the face], were the woeful shades within the ice, setting their teeth to the note of the stork.[4] Every one held his face turned downward; from the mouth the cold, and from the eyes the sad heart compels witness of itself among them.

When I had looked round awhile, I turned to my feet, and saw two so close that they had the hair of their heads mixed together. "Tell me, ye who so press tight your breasts," I said, "who are ye?" And they bent their necks, and after they had raised their faces to rue, their eyes, which before were moist only within, gushed up through the lids, and the frost bound the tears between them, and locked them up again. Clamp never girt board to board so strongly; and so they like two he goats butted together, such anger overcame them.

And one who had lost both his ears through the cold, still with his face downward, said to me, "Why do you so mirror yourself on us? If you wouldst know who are these two, the valley whence the Bisenzio descends belonged to their father Albert, and to them.[5] From one body they issued, and all Caina[6] you may search, and you will not find shade more worthy to be fixed in ice; not he whose breast and shadow were broken by one and the same blow by the hand of Arthur;[7] not Focaccia;[8] not he who encumbers me with his head, so that I cannot

---

[1] Tambernich. A mountain, the locality of which is uncertain.
[2] Pietrapana. One of the Toscan Apennines
[3] Time. In summer.
[4] Note…stork. Chattering with cold.
[5] Sisenzio…Albert. They were of the Alberti, counts of Mangona, in Tuscany, and had killed each other.
[6] Caina. The first division of this ninth and lowest circle of Hell.
[7] Not he…Arthur. Mordred, the traitorous son of Arthur.
[8] Foccaccia. From the crimes of Focaccia, a member of the great Cancellieri family of

THE ESSENTIAL HUMANITIES READER

see beyond, and was named Sassol Mascheroni:[1] if you are Tuscan, well you know now who he was. And that you may not put me to more speech, know that I was Camicion de' Pazzi,[2] and I await Carlino that he may exonerate me."

Then I saw a thousand faces made currish by the cold, whence shuddering comes to me, and will always come, at frozen pools.

And while we were going toward the center[3] to which tends every weight, and I was trembling in the eternal shade, whether it was will or destiny, or fortune I know not, but, walking among the heads, I struck my foot hard in the face of one. Wailing he cried out to me, "Why do you trample me? If you come not to increase the vengeance of Mont' Aperti, why do you molest me?"

And I said, "My Master, now wait here for me, so that I may free me from a doubt by means of this one, then you shall make me hasten as much as you will." The Leader stopped, and I said to that shade who was bitterly blaspheming still, "Who are you that thus rails at another?"

"Now you, who are you, that goes through the Antenora,"[4] he answered, "smiting the cheeks of others, so that if you were alive, it would be too much?"

"Alive I am, and it may be dear to you," was my reply, "if you demand fame, that I should set your name amid the other notes."

And he said to me, "For the contrary do I long; take yourself hence, and give me no more trouble, for ill you know to flatter on this plain."

Then I took him by the hair of the crown, and said, "It will be necessary that you name yourself, or that not a hair remain upon you here."

Then he said to me, "Though you strip me of hair, I will not tell you who I am, nor will I show it to you if a thousand times you fall on my head."

I already had his hair twisted in my hand, and had pulled out more than one shock, he barking, with his eyes kept close down, when another cried out, "What ails you, Bocca?[5] Is it not enough for you to make music with your jaws, but you must bark? What devil has hold of you?"

"Now," I said, "I would not have you speak, accursed traitor, for to your shame will I carry true news of you."

"Begone," he answered, "and relate what you will, but be not silent, if from here within you go forth, of him who now had his tongue so ready. He weeps

---

Pistoia, began the feud of the Black and the White factions, which long raged in Pistoia and in Florence.

[1] Mascheroni. A Florentine who murdered his nephew for an inheritance.

[2] Camicion de' Pazzi. A murderer of one of his kinsmen, whose crime was surpassed by that of Carlino de' Pazzi, who, in 1302, betrayed a band of the Florentine exiles who had taken refuge in a stronghold of his in Valdarno.

[3] Center. I.e., of the earth.

[4] Antenora. The second division of the Ninth Circle; so named after the Trojan who, though of good repute in Homer, was charged by a later tradition with having betrayed Troy.

[5] Bocca. Bocca degli Abati, the most noted of Florentine traitors, who in the heat of the battle of Mont' Aperti, in 1260, cut off the hand of the standard-bearer of the cavalry, so that the standard fell, and the Guelphs of Florence, disheartened thereby, were put to rout with frightful slaughter.

here the money of the French; I saw, you can say, him of Duera,[1] there where the sinners stand cooling. Should you be asked who else was there, you have at your side that Beccheria[2] whose gorget[3] Florence cut. Gianni del Soldanier[4] I think is farther on with Ganellon[5] and Tribaldello,[6] who opened Faenza when it was sleeping."

We had now parted from him when I saw two frozen in one hole, so that the head of one was a hood for the other. And as bread is devoured in hunger, so the uppermost one set his teeth upon the other where the brain joins with the nape. Not otherwise Tydeus gnawed for spite the temples of Menalippus than this one did the skull and the other parts. "O you that by so bestial a sign show hatred against him whom you do eat, tell me the reason,"

I said, "with this compact, that if you rightfully give your account of him, I, knowing who you are, and his sin, may yet recompense you for it in the world above, if that with which I speak be not dried up."

Finally they arrive in the presence of Satan, who is a massive three-faced, winged monster frozen breast-deep in the center of Hell. In each of his three terrible mouths he chews an archetypal betrayer, either of Church or State. Judas, Brutus, and Cassius hold these places of dishonor in Hell. After a brief pause, Vergil takes Dante in his arms and climbs down Satan's back emerging on the other side of the center of the earth, which marks their exit from Hell. It is now the dawn of Holy Saturday. To reach the surface of the earth and the foot of the mountain of Purgatory, the two poets follow the path of the river Lethe, which at the end offers a view of the beauties of the stars.

CANTO XXXIII. *Ninth Circle: traitors. Second ring: Antenora. – Count Ugolino. – Third ring Ptolomaea. – Brother Alberigo. Branca d' Oria.*

From his savage repast that sinner raised his mouth, wiping it with the hair of the head that he had spoiled behind: then he began, "You wish that I renew a desperate grief that oppresses my heart already only in thinking before I speak of it. But, if my words are to be seed that may bear fruit of infamy for the traitor whom I gnaw, you shall see me speak and weep at once. I know not who you are, nor by what mode you are come down hither, but Florentine you seem to me truly when I hear you. You have to know that I was the Count Ugolino and he

---

[1] Duera. Buoso da Duera of Cremona, who, for a bribe, let pass near Parma, without resistance, the cavalry of Charles of Anjou, led by Gui de Montfort to the conquest of Naples in 1265.

[2] Beccheria. Tesauro de' Beccheria, Abbot of Vallombrosa, and Papal Legato, beheaded by the Florentines in 1258, because of his treacherous dealings with the exiled Ghibellines.

[3] Gorget. An ornament usually worn over the chest or neck which may be either suspended on a cord or attached directly to clothing.

[4] Soldanier. A Ghibelline leader, who, after the defeat of Manfred in 1266, plotted against his own party.

[5] Ganellon. The traitor who brought about the defeat by the Moors of Roland, the most trusted general of Charlemagne, at Roncesvalles.

[6] Tribaldello. He betrayed Faenza to the French, in 1282.

the Archbishop Ruggieri.[1] Now will I tell you why I am such a neighbor. That by the effect of his evil thoughts, I, trusting to him, was taken and then put to death, there is no need to tell. But that which you can not have heard, namely, how cruel was my death, you shall hear, and shall know if he has wronged me.

"A narrow slit in the mew, which from me has the name of Famine, and in which others yet must be shut up, had already shown me through its opening many moons, when I had the bad dream that rent for me the veil of the future. "This one appeared to me master and lord, chasing the wolf and his whelps upon the mountain[2] for which the Pisans cannot see Lucca. With lean, eager, and trained hounds, Gualandi with Sismondi and with Lanfranchi[3] he had put before him at the front. After short course, the father and his sons seemed to me weary, and it seemed to me I saw their flanks torn by the sharp fangs.

"When I awoke before the morrow, I heard my sons, who were with me, wailing in their sleep, and asking for bread. Truly you are cruel if already you do not grieve, thinking on what my heart foretold; and if you do not weep, at what are you accustomed to weep? Now they were awake, and the hour drew near when food was accustomed to be brought to us, and because of his dream each one was apprehensive. And I heard the door below of the horrible tower locking up; at this I looked on the faces of my sons without saying a word. I wept not, I was so turned to stone within. They wept; and my poor little Anselm said, 'You look so, father, what troubles you?' Yet I did not weep; nor did I answer all that day, nor the night after, until the next sun came out upon the world. When a little ray entered the woeful prison, and I discerned by their four faces my own very aspect, both my hands I bit for woe; and they, thinking I did it through desire of eating, of a sudden rose, and said, 'Father, it will be far less pain to us if you eat of us; you did clothe us with this wretched flesh, and now you may strip it off.' I quieted me then, not to make them more sad: that day and the next we all stayed dumb. Ah, you hard earth, why did you not open? After we had come to the fourth day, Gaddo threw himself stretched out at my feet, saying, 'My father, why do you not help me?' Here he died: and, even as you see me, I saw the three fall one by one between the fifth day and the sixth; then I betook me, already blind, to groping over each, and two days I called them after they were dead: then fasting had more power than grief."

---

[1] Count Ugolino...Archbishop Ruggieri. In July, 1288, Ugolino della Gherardesca, Count of Donoratico, head of a faction of the Guelphs in Pisa, in order to deprive Nino of Gallura, head of the opposing faction, of the lordship of the city, treacherously joined forces with the Archbishop Ruggieri degli Ubaldini, head of the Ghibellines, and drove Nino and his followers from the city. The archbishop thereupon took advantage of the weakening of the Guelphs and excited the populace against Ugolino, charging him with having for a bribe restored to Florence and Lucca some of their towns of which the Pisans had made themselves masters. He, with his followers, attacked Count Ugolino in his house, took him prisoner, with two of his sons and two of his grandsons, and shut them up in the Tower of the Gualandi, where in the following March, on the arrival of Count Guido da Montefeltro, as Captain of Pisa, they were starved to death.

[2] Mountain. Monte San Giuliano.

[3] Gualandi...Lanfranchi Three powerful Ghibelline families of Pisa.

When he had said this, with his eyes distorted, he seized again the wretched skull with his teeth, which were strong as a dog's upon the bone.

Ah Pisa! reproach of the people of the fair country where the *si* doth sound,[1] since your neighbors are slow to punish you, let Caprara and Gorgona[2] move and make a hedge for Arno at its mouth, so that it drown every person in you; for if Count Ugolino had repute of having betrayed you in your towns, you ought not to have set his sons on such a cross. Their young age, you modern Thebes, made Uguccione and the Brigata innocent, and the other two that the song names above!

We passed onward to where the ice roughly enswathes another folk, not turned downward, but all upon their backs. Their very weeping lets them not weep, and the pain that finds a barrier on the eyes turns inward to increase the anguish; for the first tears form a block, and like a visor of crystal fill all the cup beneath the eyebrow.

And although, because of the cold, as from a callus, all feeling had left its abode in my face, it now seemed to me I felt some wind, for which reason I said, "My Master, who moves this? Is not every vapor[3] quenched here below?"

To this he replied to me, "Speedily shall you be where your eye shall make answer to you of this, beholding the cause that rains down the blast."

And one of the wretches of the cold crust cried out to us, "O souls so cruel that the last station is given to you, lift from my eyes the hard veils, so that I may vent the grief that swells my heart, a little before the weeping re-congeal!"

And so I said to him, "If you will that I relieve you, tell me who you are, and if I rid you not, may it be mine to go to the bottom of the ice."

He replied then, "I am friar Alberigo;[4] I am he of the fruits of the bad garden, and here I receive a date for a fig."[5]

"Oh!" I said to him; "are you now already dead?"

And he replied to me, "How it may go with my body in the world above I bear no knowledge. Such vantage has this Ptolomaea[6] that oftentimes the soul falls here before Atropos has given motion to it.[7] And that you may the more willingly scrape the glassy tears from my face, know that soon as the soul be-

---

[1] Si...sound. Italy, whose language Dante calls *il volgare di ci* (the common language of yes).

[2] Caprara and Gorgona. Two little islands not far from the mouth of the Arno, on whose banks Pisa lies.

[3] Vapor. Wind being supposed to be caused by the action of the sun on the vapors of the atmosphere.

[4] Alberigo. Alberigo de' Manfredi, of Faenza; one of the Jovial Friars. Having received a blow from one of his kinsmen, he pretended to forgive it, and invited him and his son to a feast. Toward the end of the meal he gave a prearranged signal by calling out, "Bring the fruit," upon which his emissaries rushed in and killed the two guests. The "fruit of Brother Alberigo" became a proverb.

[5] Fig. A fig is the cheapest of Tuscan fruits; the imported date is more costly.

[6] Ptolomaea. The third ring of ice, named for that Ptolemy of Jericho who slew his father-in-law, the high-priest Simon, and his sons (1 Maccabees 16.11-16).

[7] Before Atropos...it. That is, before its life on earth is ended.

trays, as I did, its body is taken from it by a demon, who thereafter governs it until its time be all revolved. The soul falls headlong into this cistern, and perchance the body of the shade that here behind me winters still appears above; you ought to know him if you come down but now. He is Ser Branca d' Oria,[1] and many years have passed since he was thus shut up."

"I think," I said to him, "that you deceive me, for Branca d' Oria is not yet dead, and he eats, and drinks, and sleeps, and puts on clothes."

"In the ditch of the Malebranche above," he said, "there where the tenacious pitch is boiling, Michel Zanche had not yet arrived when this one left in his own stead a devil in his body, and in that of one of his near kin, who committed the treachery together with him. But now stretch out hither your hand; open my eyes for me." And I opened them not for him, and to be rude to him was courtesy.

Ah Genoese! Men strange to all morality and full of all corruption, why are ye not scattered from the world? For with the worst spirit of Romagna I found one of you such that for his deeds in soul he is bathed in Cocytus, and in body he seems still alive on earth.

CANTO XXXIV. *Ninth Circle: traitors. Fourth ring: Judecca. – Lucifer. – Judas, Brutus, and Cassius. – Center of the universe. – Passage from Hell. – Ascent to surface of the Southern Hemisphere.*
"*Vexilla regis prodeunt inferni,*[2] toward us; therefore look in front," said my Master; "if you discern him." As a mill that the wind turns seems from afar when a thick fog breathes, or when our hemisphere grows dark with night, such a structure then it seemed to me I saw.

Then, because of the wind, I drew me behind my Leader; for there was no other shelter. I was now, and with fear I put it in verse, there[3] where the shades were wholly covered, and showed through like a straw in glass. Some are lying; some stand erect, this on his head, and that on his soles; another like a bow inverts his face to his feet.

When we had gone so far forward that it pleased my Master to show me the creature that had the fair semblance, from before me he took himself and made me stop, saying, "Behold Dis, and behold the place where it is needful that with fortitude you arm yourself." How I became then chilled and hoarse, ask it not, Reader, for I write it not, because all speech would be little. I did not die, and I did not remain alive. Think now for yourself, if you have grain of wit, what I became, deprived of one and the other.

The emperor of the woeful realm from his midbreast issued forth from the ice; and I match better with a giant, than the giants do with his arms. See now

---

[1] Ser Branca d' Oria. Murderer, in 1275, of his father-in-law, Michel Zanche. Already heard of in the fifth pit.
[2] "*Vexilla Regis prodeunt Inferni.*" The banners of the King of Hell advance. *Vexilla Regis prodeunt* are the first words of a hymn in honor of the Cross, sung at vespers on the Feast of the Exaltation of the Holy Cross and on Monday of Holy Week. Here at the low point of Hell, the image has been perverted to honor, or dishonor, Lucifer.
[3] There. In the fourth, innermost ring of ice of the ninth circle, the Judecca.

how great must be that whole which corresponds to such parts. If he was as fair as he now is foul, and against his Maker lifted up his brow, surely may all tribulation proceed from him. Oh how great a marvel it seemed to me, when I saw three faces on his head! One in front, and that was red; the others were two that were joined to this above the very middle of each shoulder, and they were joined together at the place of the crest; and the right seemed between white and yellow, the left was such to sight as those who come from where the Nile flows valleyward. Beneath each came forth two great wings, of size befitting so huge a bird. Sails of the sea never saw I such. They had no feathers, but their fashion was of a bat; and he was flapping them so that three winds went forth from him, whereby Cocytus was all congealed. With six eyes he was weeping, and over three chins trickled the tears and bloody drivel. With each mouth he was crushing a sinner with his teeth, in manner of a brake, so that he thus was making three of them woeful. To the one in front the biting was nothing to the clawing, so that sometimes his spine remained all stripped of skin.

"That soul up there which has the greatest punishment," said the Master, "is Judas Iscariot, who has his head within, and plies his legs outside. Of the other two who have their heads down, he who hangs from the black muzzle is Brutus; see how he writhes and says no word; and the other is Cassius, who seems so large-limbed. But the night is rising again, and now we must depart, for we have seen the whole."

As was his pleasure, I clasped his neck, and he took opportunity of time and place, and when the wings were opened wide he caught hold on the shaggy flanks; from shag to shag he then descended between the bushy hair and the frozen crusts. When we were just where the thigh turns on the thick of the haunch, my Leader, with effort and stress of breath, turned his head where he had his shanks, and clambered by the hair as a man that ascends, so that I thought to return again to hell.

"Cling fast hold," said the Master, panting like one weary, "for by such stairs it is necessary to depart from so much evil." Then he came forth through the opening of a rock, and placed me upon its edge to sit; then stretched toward me his cautious step.

I raised my eyes, and thought to see Lucifer as I had left him, and I saw him holding his legs upward. And if I then became perplexed, let the dull folk think it that see not what that point is that I had passed.[1]

"Rise up," said the Master, "on your feet; the way is long and the road is difficult, and already the sun to mid-tierce[2] returns."

---

[1] What that point...passed. This point is the center of the universe; when Vergil had turned upon the haunch of Lucifer, the passage had been made from one hemisphere of the earth – the inhabited and known hemisphere – to the other where no living men dwell, and where the only land is the mountain of Purgatory. In changing one hemisphere for the other there is a change of time of twelve hours. A second Saturday morning begins for the poets, and they pass nearly as long a time as they have been in Hell, that is, twenty-four hours, in traversing the long and hard way that leads through the new hemisphere on which they have just entered.

[2] Tierce. The church office sung at the third hour of the day, and the name is given to the

THE ESSENTIAL HUMANITIES READER

It was no hallway of a palace where we were, but a natural dungeon that had a bad floor, and lack of light. "Before I tear me from the abyss," I said when I had risen up, "my Master, speak a little to me to draw me out of error. Where is the ice? And this one, how is he fixed thus upside down? And how in such short while has the sun from eve to morn made transit?"

And he said to me, "You imagine that you still are on the other side of the center where I laid hold on the hair of the guilty Worm that pierces the world. On that side were you so long as I descended; when I turned you did pass the point to which from all parts whatever has weight is drawn; and you are now arrived beneath the hemisphere opposite to that which the great dry land covers, and beneath whose zenith the Man was slain who was born and lived without sin. You have your feet upon the little sphere which forms the other face of the Judecca. Here it is morning when there it is evening; and he who made for us a stairway with his hair is still fixed even as he was before. Upon this side he fell down from heaven, and the earth, which before was spread out here, through fear of him made of the sea a veil, and came to your hemisphere; and perchance to flee from him that land[1] which on this side appears left here this empty space and upward ran back."

A place is there below, stretching as far from Beelzebub as his tomb extends,[2] which not by sight is known, but by the sound of a rivulet that here descends along the hollow of a rock that it has gnawed with its course that winds and little falls. My Leader and I entered through that hidden way, to return to the bright world. And without care, to have any repose, we mounted up, he first and I second, until through a round opening I saw of those beauteous things which heaven bears, and at that place we came forth to see again the stars.

---

first three hours after sunrise. Midtierce consequently here means about half-past seven o'clock. In Hell Dante never mentions the sun to mark division of time, but now, having issued from Hell, Vergil marks the hour by a reference to the sun.

[1] That land. The Mount of Purgatory.

[2] His tomb extends. Hell is his tomb; this vacant dark passage through the opposite hemisphere is, of course, of the same depth as Hell from surface to center.

107

Dante Alighieri
La Vita Nuova **(The New Life)**
TRANSLATED BY DANTE GABRIEL ROSSETTI

Though Dante is best known for *The Divine Comedy*, it was with *La Vita Nuova* that he established himself as a writer. *La Vita Nuova* is often taken to be the literal story of Dante's love for Beatrice Portinari, but it is more likely that he is using this idealized portrait of young love as a way to discuss the nature of love and its relationship to more spiritual matters.

On the one hand, it is easy to see in Dante's story the sort of love that the twelfth-century writer Andreas Cappelanus described in *The Art of Courly Love*: "Love is an inborn suffering proceeding from the sight and immoderate thought upon the beauty of the other sex, for which cause above all other things one wishes to embrace the other and, by common assent, in this embrace to fulfill the commandments of love."[1] On the other hand, we know not only that Dante began a very long commentary on *La Vita Nuova* that focused on spiritual growth, but he also seems to have written *The Divine Comedy* as a way of expressing more completely what he had begun in this earlier work. More directly we can see that his love is more than earthly love in the fine details of his precise language. Still, the work is a beautiful portrait of love as it builds to fruition.

The text presented below is roughly one third of the work; as many passages have been removed, especially thirty-one poems and Dante's commentary on them. (In the image above, Beatrice is depicted in white.)

---

[1] Andreas Capellanus. *The Art Of Courtly Love*. Translated by John Jay Parry. New York: Columbia University Press, 1941.

ය8න

La Vita Nuova
Dante Alighieri, 1295
TRANSLATED BY DANTE G. ROSSETTI. ADAPTED BY GERARD P. NECASTRO

1. In that part of the book of my memory before which is little that can be read, there is a rubric, saying, *Incipit Vita Nuova.*[1] Under such rubric I find written many things; and among them the words which I propose to copy into this little book; if not all of them, at least their substance.

2. Nine times already since my birth had the heaven of light returned to the self-same point almost, as concerns its own revolution,[2] when first the glorious Lady of my mind was made manifest to my eyes; even when she who was called Beatrice by many who knew not why.[3] She had already been in this life for not so long as that, within her time, the starry heaven had moved towards its Eastern quarter one of the twelve parts of a degree; so that she appeared to me at the beginning of her ninth year almost, and I saw her almost at the end of my ninth year. Her dress, on that day, was of a most noble color, a subdued and delicate crimson, girdled and adorned in such sort as best suited with her very tender age.

At that moment, I say most truly that the spirit of life, which has its dwelling in the most secret chamber of her heart, began to tremble so violently that the least pulses of my body shook. In trembling it said these words: *Ecce deus fortier me, qui veniens dominabitur mihi.*[4] At that moment the animate spirit, which dwells in the lofty chamber where all the senses carry their perceptions, was filled with wonder, and said these words: *Apparuit jam beatitudo vestra.*[5] At that moment the natural spirit, which dwells where our nourishment is administered, began to weep, and in weeping said these words: *Heu miser! quia frequenter impeditus ero deinceps.*[6]

I say that, from that time forward, Love fully governed my soul; which was immediately espoused to him, and with so safe and undisputed a lordship (by virtue of strong imagination), that I had nothing left for it but to do all his bidding continually. He sometimes commanded me to seek, if I could, this youngest of the Angels. Thus I in my boyhood often went in search of her and found her

---

[1] *Incipit Vita Nuova.* Here begins the new life. Rubrics are reading directions, usually written in red.

[2] Nine times...revolution. In other words, he was nine years old. Note that Dante must both be precise and explain everything in certain terms, usually celestial or numerological. Beatrice was eight, going on nine.

[3] Beatrice...why. In reference to the meaning of the name of Beatrice, "She who confers blessing." Note how often the word beatitude (heavenly joy or blessedness) is used. We learn also from Boccaccio that this first meeting took place at a May Feast, given in the year 1274 by Folco Portinari, father of Beatrice, who ranked among the principal citizens of Florence: to which feast Dante accompanied his father, Alighiero Alighieri.

[4] *Ecce deus fortier me, qui veniens dominabitur mihi.* Here is a deity stronger than I; who, coming, shall rule over me.

[5] *Apparuit jam beatitudo vestra.* Your beatitude has now appeared to you.

[6] *Heu miser! quia frequenter impeditus ero deinceps.* Alas! how often shall I be disturbed from this time forth!

so noble and praiseworthy that one might have said of her those words of Homer, "She seemed not to be the daughter of a mortal man, but of God."[1]

And albeit her image, which was with me always, was an exultation of Love to subdue me, it was yet of so perfect a quality that it never allowed me to be overruled by Love without the faithful counsel of reason, whenever such counsel was useful to be heard. But seeing that, were I to dwell overmuch on the passions and doings of such early youth, my words might be counted something fabulous, I will therefore put them aside; and passing over many things that may be conceived by the pattern of these, I will come to such as are written in my memory more distinctly.

At the end of almost every chapter, Dante resolves to make a point of writing a poem about the event that has just occurred. He also explains the structure of the poem.

3. After the lapse of so many days that nine years exactly were completed since the above-written appearance of this most gracious being, on the last of those days it happened that the same wonderful lady appeared to me dressed all in pure white, between two gentle ladies elder than she. And passing through a street, she turned her eyes to where I stood sorely abashed: and by her unspeakable courtesy, which is now rewarded in the Great Cycle, she saluted me with so virtuous a bearing that I seemed then and there to behold the very limits of blessedness.

The hour of her most sweet salutation was certainly the ninth of that day; and because it was the first time that any words from her reached my ears, I came into such sweetness that I parted from that place as one intoxicated. And taking myself to the loneliness of my own room, I began thinking of this most courteous lady, thinking of whom I was overtaken by a pleasant slumber, in which a marvelous vision was presented to me. For there appeared to me in my room a mist of the color of fire, within which I discerned the figure of a lord of terrible aspect to any who should gaze upon him, but who seemed to rejoice inwardly in such a way that it was a marvel to see.

Speaking to me, he said many things, among which I could understand but few; and of these, this: *Ego dominus tuus.*[2] In his arms it seemed to me that a person was sleeping, covered only with a blood-colored cloth; upon whom looking very attentively, I knew that it was the lady of the salutation who had deigned the day before to salute me. And he who held her held also in his hand a thing that was burning in flames; and he said to me, *Vide cor tuum.*[3] But when he had remained with me a little while, I thought that he set himself to awaken her who slept; after which he made her to eat that thing which flamed in his hand; and she ate as one fearing.

Then, having waited again a while, all his joy was turned into most bitter weeping; and as he wept he gathered the lady into his arms, and it seemed to me

---

[1] She seemed...god. This is a description of Helen of Troy from Homer's *Iliad*.

[2] *Ego dominus tuus*. I am your master.

[3] *Vide cor tuum*. Behold your heart.

that he went with her up towards heaven; whereby such a great anguish came upon me that my light slumber could not endure through it, but was suddenly broken. And immediately having considered the event, I knew that the hour in which this vision had been made manifest to me was the fourth hour (which is to say, the first of the nine last hours) of the night.

Dante discovers that he can be in the company of Beatrice without tarnishing her reputation in any way by pretending that he is interested in another woman, whom he refers to as the "Screen Lady." Even when this lady moves away from Florence, he finds another such lady.

10. On my return, I set myself to seek out that lady whom my master had named to me while I journeyed sighing. And because I would be brief, I will now narrate that in a short while I made her my security, in such sort that the matter was spoken of by many in terms scarcely courteous; through which I had often many troublesome hours. And by this it happened (that is, by this false and evil rumor which seemed to disrepute me in vice) that she who was the destroyer of all evil and the queen of all good,[1] coming where I was, denied me her most sweet salutation, in the which alone was my blessedness.

11. And here it is fitting for me to depart a little from this present matter, that it may be rightly understood of what surpassing virtue her salutation was to me. To this end I say that when she appeared in any place, it seemed to me, by the hope of her excellent salutation, that there was no one my enemy any longer. And such warmth of charity came upon me that most certainly in that moment I would have pardoned whosoever had done me an injury. . . . By this it is made manifest that in her salutation alone was there any beatitude for me, which then very often went beyond my endurance.

12. . . . After this I began to speak with Love concerning her salutation, which she had denied me. And when I had questioned him about the cause, he said these words: "Our Beatrice has heard from certain persons, that the lady whom I named to you while you journeyed full of sighs, is sorely disquieted by your solicitations. And therefore this most gracious creature, who is the enemy of all disquiet, being fearful of such disquiet, refused to salute you. Albeit, in very truth, your secret must have become known to her by familiar observation.

After this, Love bids Dante to explore the importance of love in his poetry. The next ten chapters are filled with such explorations.

14. After this battling with many thoughts, it chanced on a day that my most gracious lady was with a gathering of ladies in a certain place. I was conducted to this place by a friend of mine, he thinking to do me a great pleasure by showing me the beauty of so many women. Then I, hardly knowing where he conducted me, but trusting in him (who yet was leading his friend to the last verge of life), asked him, "For what purpose have we come among these ladies?" and he answered: "For the purpose that they may be worthily served."

---

[1] Destroyer of all evil and the queen of all good. I.e., Beatrice

And they were assembled around a gentlewoman who was given in marriage on that day, the custom of the city being that these should bear her company when she sat down for the first time at table in the house of her husband. Therefore I, as was my friend's pleasure, resolved to stay with him and do honor to those ladies.

As soon as I had thus resolved, I began to feel a faintness and a throbbing at my left side, which soon took possession of my whole body. I remember that I covertly leaned my back onto a painting that ran round the walls of that house; and being fearful lest my trembling should be discerned by them, I lifted my eyes to look on those ladies, and then first perceived among them the excellent Beatrice. When I perceived her, all my senses were overpowered by the great Lordship that Love obtained, finding himself so near to that most gracious being, until nothing but the spirits of sight remained to me. And even these spirits remained driven out of their own instruments because Love entered in that honored place of theirs, so that he might behold her better. Although I was other than this at first, I grieved for the spirits so expelled which kept up a sore lament, saying: "If he had not in this way thrust us forth, we also should behold the marvel of this lady."

By this, many of her friends, having discerned my confusion, began to wonder; and together with herself, kept whispering about me and mocking me. Whereupon my friend, who knew not what to conceive, took me by the hands, and drawing me forth from among them, asked what ailed me. Then, having first held me at quiet for a space until my perceptions were come back to me, I answered to my friend: "Surely I have now set my feet on that point of life, beyond which he must not pass who would return."[1]

Afterwards, leaving him, I went back to the room where I had wept before; and again weeping and ashamed, said: "If this lady only knew of my condition I do not think that she would thus mock me; nay, I am sure that she must feel some pity."

22. Not many days after this (it being the will of the most High God, who also from Himself put not away death), the father of wonderful Beatrice, going out of this life, passed certainly into glory. Thereby it happened that this lady was truly made full of the bitterness of grief: seeing that such a parting is very grievous to those friends who are left, and that no other friendship is like to that between a good parent and a good child; and furthermore considering that this lady was good in the supreme degree, and her father (as by many it has been truly verified) of exceeding goodness.

And because it is the usage of that city that men meet with men in such grief, and women with women, certain ladies of her companionship gathered

---

[1] Return. It is not clear who is the bride in this scene. It is true that in her twenty-first year Beatrice was wedded to Simone de' Bardi. Many critics make too much of the possibility that this could be Beatrice's wedding, which it is likely not to be. We must be careful, though, not to equate the historical Beatrice with the fictional one. Though there are clear similarities, we must allow Dante some room for creating a fiction that works on its own terms.

themselves around Beatrice, where she kept alone in her weeping. And as they passed in and out, I could hear them speak concerning her, how she wept. At length two of them went by me, who said: "Certainly she grieves in such sort that one might die for pity, beholding her." Then, feeling the tears upon my face, I put up my hands to hide them. And had it not been that I hoped to hear more concerning her (seeing that where I sat, her friends passed continually in and out), I should assuredly have gone from there to be alone, when I felt the tears come.

But as I still sat in that place, certain ladies again passed near me, who were saying among themselves: "Which of us shall be joyful any more, who have listened to this lady in her piteous sorrow?" And there were others who said as they went by me: "He that sits here could not weep more if he had beheld her as we beheld her;" and again: "He is so altered that he seems not as himself." And still as the ladies passed to and from, I could hear them speak after this fashion of her and of me.

23. A few days after this, my body became afflicted with a painful infirmity, whereby I suffered bitter anguish for many days, which at last brought me to such weakness that I could no longer move. And I remember that on the ninth day, being overcome with intolerable pain, a thought came into my mind concerning my lady. But when it had a little nourished this thought, my mind returned to its brooding over my enfeebled body. And then perceiving how frail a thing life is, even though health keep with it, the matter seemed to me so pitiful that I could not choose but weep; and weeping I said within myself: "Certainly it must sometime come to pass that the very gentle Beatrice will die." Then, feeling bewildered, I closed my eyes; and my brain began to become overworked, as the brain of one frantic, and to have such imaginings as here follow.

At first, it seemed to me that I saw certain faces of women with their hair loosened, who called out to me, "You shall surely die;" after which, other terrible and unknown appearances said to me, "You are dead." At length, as my imagination kept to its wanderings, I came to be I knew not where, and to behold a throng of disheveled ladies sad beyond all description, who kept going here and there weeping. Then the sun went out, so that the stars showed themselves, and they were of such a color that I knew they must be weeping; and it seemed to me that the birds fell out of the sky, and that there were great earthquakes.

With that, while I wondered in my trance, and was filled with a grievous fear, I conceived that a certain friend came to me and said: "Have you not heard? She that was your excellent lady has been taken out of life." Then I began to weep very piteously; and not only in my imagination, but also with my eyes, which were wet with tears. And I seemed to look towards Heaven, and to behold a multitude of angels who were returning upwards, having before them an exceedingly white cloud. And these angels were singing together gloriously, and the words of their song were these; "*Osanna in excelsis:*"[1] and there was no

---

[1] *Osanna in excelsis.* Hosanna in the Highest; usual words of praise for God.

more that I heard.

Then my heart that was so filled with Love, who said to me: "It is true that our lady lies dead:" and it seemed to me that I went to look upon the body in which that blessed and most noble spirit had had its abiding-place. And so strong was this idle imagining that it made me behold my lady in death; whose head certain ladies seemed to be covering with a white veil. And she was so humble in her aspect that it was as though she had said, "I have attained to look on the beginning of peace."

And with that I came to such humility by the sight of her, that I cried out upon Death, saying: "Now come to me, and be not bitter against me any longer: surely, there where you have been, you have learned gentleness.[1] So come now to me who greatly desires you: see you not that I wear your color already?" And when I had seen all those offices performed that are fitting to be done with respect to the dead, it seemed to me that I went back into my own chamber and looked up towards heaven. And so strong was my imagination that I wept again in very truth, and said with my true voice: "O excellent soul! How blessed is he who now looks upon you!"

And as I said these words with a painful anguish of sobbing and another prayer to Death, a young and gentle lady, who had been standing beside me where I lay, conceiving that I wept and cried out because of the pain of my infirmity, was taken with trembling and began to shed tears. Other ladies, who were about the room, becoming aware of my discomfort by reason of the moan that she made (who indeed was of my very near kindred), led her away from where I was, and then set themselves to awaken me, thinking that I dreamed, and saying: "Sleep no longer, and be not disquieted."

Then, by their words, this strong vision was brought suddenly to an end, at the moment I was about to say, "O Beatrice! Peace be with you." And already I had said, "O Beatrice!" when, being aroused, I opened my eyes, and knew that it had been a deception. But albeit I had indeed uttered her name, yet my voice was so broken with sobs, that it was not understood by these ladies; so that in spite of the sore shame that I felt, I turned towards them by Love's counseling. And when they beheld me, they began to say, "He seems as one dead," and to whisper among themselves, "Let us strive to comfort him." Whereupon they spoke to me many soothing words, and questioned me moreover concerning the cause of my fear.

24. . . . A short while after these words that my heart spoke to me with the tongue of Love, I saw coming towards me a certain lady who was very famous for her beauty, and of whom my friend (whom I have already called the first among my friends) had long been enamored. This lady's right name was Joan; but because of her comeliness (or at least it was so imagined) she was called by many *Primavera* (Spring), and went by that name among them. Then looking again, I perceived that the most noble Beatrice followed after her.

And when both of these ladies had passed by me, it seemed to me that

---

[1] You have learned gentleness. I.e.., by being in the presence of Beatrice.

Love spoke again in my heart, saying: "She that came first was called Spring, only because of that which was to happen on this day. And it was I myself who caused that name to be given her; seeing that as the Spring comes first in the year, so should she come first on this day,[1] when Beatrice was to show herself after the vision of her servant. And even if you go about to consider her right name, it is also as one should say, "She shall come first;" inasmuch as her name, Joan, is taken from John who went before the True Light, saying "*Ego vox clamantis in deserto: Parate viam Domini.*[2] And it also seemed to me that he added other words, namely: "He who should inquire delicately about this matter, could not but call Beatrice by my own name, which is to say, Love; beholding her so much like me."

28. I was still occupied with this poem (having composed only the above-written stanza of it), when the Lord God of justice called my most gracious lady to Himself, that she might be glorious under the banner of that blessed Queen Mary, whose name had always a deep reverence in the words of holy Beatrice. And because, by chance, it might be found good that I should say somewhat concerning her departure, I will here declare the reasons that I shall not do so.

And the reasons are three. First, such matter belongs not rightly to the present argument, if one consider the opening of this little book. Second even though the present argument required it, my pen does not suffice to write in a fit manner of this thing. Third, were it both possible and of absolute necessity, it would still be unseemly for me to speak about it, seeing that by this it is necessary for me to speak also my own praises: a thing that it is worthy of blame, whoever does it. For these reasons, I will leave this matter to be treated by someone other than myself.

Nevertheless, as the number nine, which has often been mentioned above (and not, as it might appear, without reason), seems also to have borne a part in the manner of her death. It is therefore right that I should say somewhat about that. And for this cause, having first told the part it played to this point, I will afterwards point out a reason that this number was so closely allied to my lady.

29. I say, then, that according to the division of time in Italy, her most noble spirit departed from among us in the first hour of the ninth day of the month; and according to the division of time in Syria, in the ninth month of the year: seeing that Tismim, which with us is October, is there the first month. Also she was taken from among us in that year of our reckoning (namely, of the years of our Lord) in which the perfect number was nine times multiplied within that century wherein she was born into the world: which is to say, the thirteenth century of Christians.[3]

---

[1] Spring…this day. There is a play in the original upon the words *Primavera* (Spring) and *prima verrà* (she shall come first).

[2] *Parate viam Domini.* John the Baptist, cousin of Christ, predicted the Savior's coming: "I am the voice of one crying in the wilderness: '*Prepare ye the way of the Lord.*'"

[3] Also she…Christians. According to the information offered here, Beatrice Portinari died during the first hour of the ninth of June, 1290. And from what Dante says at the opening of this work, it may also be gathered that she was, at the time of her death, twnty-four

A lot more is said about the number nine here. Dante's mourning continues, and he writes a series of poems about his loss.

35. Then, having sat for some space sorely in thought because of the time that was now past, I was so filled with grievous imaginings that it became outwardly manifest in my altered countenance. Thus, feeling this and being in dread lest any should have seen me, I lifted my eyes to look; and then perceived a young and very beautiful lady, who was gazing upon me from a window with a gaze full of pity, so that the very sum of pity appeared gathered together in her. And seeing that unhappy persons, when they beget compassion in others, are then most moved to weeping, as though they also felt pity for themselves, it came to pass that my eyes began to be inclined to tears. For this reason, becoming fearful lest I should make manifest my abject condition, I rose up, and went where I could not be seen of that lady; saying afterwards within myself: "Certainly with her also must abide most noble Love."

36. It happened after this that whenever I was seen by this lady, she became pale and of a piteous countenance, as though it had been with love; whereby she remembered me many times of my own most noble lady, who was usually of a like paleness. And I know that often, when I could not weep nor in any way give ease to my anguish, I went to look upon this lady, who seemed to bring the tears into my eyes by the mere sight of her.

37. At length, by the constant sight of this lady, my eyes began to be gladdened overmuch with her company; through which thing many times I had much unrest, and rebuked myself as a base person: also many times I cursed the unsteadiness of my eyes, and said to them inwardly: "Was not your grievous condition of weeping wont one while to make others weep? And will you now forget this thing because a lady looks upon you, you who so looks merely in compassion of the grief you then showed for your own blessed lady? But what you can, that do you, accursed eyes! Many a time will I make you remember it! For never, until death dry you up, should you make an end of your weeping." And when I had spoken thus to my eyes, I was taken again with extreme and grievous sighing.

38. The sight of this lady brought me into such an unaccustomed condition that I often thought of her as one too dear to me; and I began to consider her thus: "This lady is young, beautiful, gentle, and wise: perchance it was Love himself who set her in my path, that so my life might find peace." And there were times when I thought yet more fondly, until my heart consented to its reasoning. But when it had so consented, my thought would often turn round upon me, as moved by reason, and cause me to say within myself: "What hope is this which would console me after so base a fashion and which has taken the place of all other imagining?"

Also there was another voice within me that said: "And will you, having

years and three months old. The "perfect number" mentioned here is the number ten.

suffered so much tribulation through Love, not escape while yet you may from so much bitterness? You must surely know that this thought carries with it the desire of Love, and drew its life from the gentle eyes of that lady who vouchsafed you so much pity."

39. But against this adversary of reason, there rose up in me on a certain day, about the ninth hour, a strong visible vision, in which I seemed to behold the most gracious Beatrice, clothed in that crimson garment which she had worn when I had first beheld her. She also appeared to me of the same tender age as then. Whereupon I fell into a deep thought of her: and my memory ran back according to the order of time, to all those matters in which she had borne a part; and my heart began painfully to repent of the desire by which it had so basely let itself be possessed during so many days, contrary to the constancy of reason.

And then, this evil desire being quite gone from me, all my thoughts turned again to their excellent Beatrice. And I say most truly that from that hour I thought constantly of her with the whole humbled and ashamed heart; which became often manifest in sighs, that had among them the name of that most gracious creature, and how she departed from us. Also it would come to pass very often, through the bitter anguish of some one thought, that I forgot it, myself, and where I was.

By this increase of sighs, my weeping, which before had been somewhat lessened, increased in like manner; so that my eyes seemed to long only for tears and to cherish them. My eyes came at last to be circled about with red as though they had suffered martyrdom; neither were they able to look again upon the beauty of any face that might again bring them to shame and evil. From these things it will appear that they were fitly repaid for their weakness.

42. After writing this sonnet, it was given to me to behold a very wonderful vision;[1] in which I saw things that convinced me that I would say nothing further of this most blessed one, until such time as I could discourse more worthily concerning her. And to this end I labor all I can; as she well knows. Thus, if it be His pleasure through whom is the life of all things that my life continue with me a few years, it is my hope that I shall write about her what has not before been written of any woman. After this, may it seem good to Him who is the Master of Grace, that my spirit should go from here to behold the glory of its lady: namely, of that blessed Beatrice who now gazes continually on His countenance *qui est per omnia saecula benedictus. Laus Deo.*[2]

---

[1] Wonderful vision. This likely refers to the *Divina Commedia*. The Latin words ending the *Vita Nuova* are almost identical with those at the close of the letter in which Dante, on concluding the *Commedia*, and accomplishing the hope here expressed, dedicates his great work to Can Grande della Scala.

[2] *Qui est per omnia saecula benedictus. Laus Deo.* Who is blessed throughout all ages. Praise be to God.

Petrarch (Francesco Petrarca)
1304 – 1374

Francesco Petrarch, the Italian poet and Humanist, was the son of a notary who was a member of the White Guelph party of Florence and was expelled from his beloved city (in the same year as Dante) by the Black Guelphs. They moved to Avignon in 1312, where Petrarch later (in 1327) saw the woman who inspired his love-poetry. The woman who has come to be known as Laura ("L'aura" means "the light" in Italian) may have been Laura de Noves, a married woman who seems to have refused his love. This did not prevent him, however, from writing no less than 365 poems in her honor.

Petrarch was much celebrated as a poet in his time and in 1341 was crowned Poet Laureate in Rome, the most memorable event of his life. He spent most of his life traveling throughout Italy, especially enjoying the generosity of patrons in Milan, Padua, Venice, Pavia, and finally Arquà.

∞

SONNET XVII
Son animali al mondo di si altera.
Petrarch, c. 1336 – 1374
TRANSLATED BY CHARLES MACGREGOR

Creatures there are in life of such keen sight
That no defense they need from noonday sun,
And others dazzled by excess of light
Who issue not abroad till day is done,
5   And, with weak fondness, some because 'tis bright.
Who in the death flame for enjoyment run,
Thus proving theirs a different virtue quite–
Alas! of this last kind myself am one;
For, of this fair the splendor to regard,
10   I am but weak and ill–against late hours
And darkness gath'ring round–myself to ward.

Wherefore, with tearful eyes of failing powers,
My destiny condemns me still to turn
Where following faster I but fiercer burn.

࿂

SONNET XIX
Mille fiate, o dolce mia guerrera.
Petrarch, c. 1336 – 1374
TRANSLATED BY CHARLES MACGREGOR

A THOUSAND times, sweet warrior, have I tried,
Proffering my heart to thee, some peace to gain
From those bright eyes, but still, alas! in vain,
To such low level stoops not thy chaste pride.
5 If others seek the love thus thrown aside,
Vain were their hopes and labors to obtain;
The heart thou spurnest I alike disdain,
To thee displeasing, 'tis by me denied.
But if, discarded thus, it find not thee
10 Its joyless exile willing to befriend,
Alone, untaught at others' will to wend,
Soon from life's weary burden will it flee.
How heavy then the guilt to both, but more
To thee, for thee it did the most adore.

࿂

SONNET LXXXIV
Non veggio ove scampar mi possa omai.
Petrarch, c. 1336 – 1374
TRANSLATED BY CHARLES MACGREGOR

No hope of respite, of escape no way,
Her bright eyes wage such constant havoc here;
Alas! excess of tyranny, I fear,
My doting heart, which ne'er has truce, will slay:
5 Fain would I flee, but ah! their amorous ray,
Which day and night on memory rises clear,
Shines with such power, in this the fifteenth year,
They dazzle more than in love's early day.
So wide and far their images are spread
10 That whereso'er I turn I always see
Her, or some sister-light on hers that fed.
Springs such a wood from one fair laurel tree,
That my old foe, with admirable skill,
Amid its boughs misleads me at his will.

Geoffrey Chaucer
c. 1340 – 1400

Geoffrey Chaucer, often referred to as the father of English Poetry, was born between 1340 and 1343 to a middle-class merchant family, whose father and grandfather were wine merchants. Most of his life was given in service to the state, beginning his career first as a page at court and then as a soldier. He was captured in 1360 at the Siege of Rheims (in the Hundred Years War) and was ransomed by King Edward, but not before he lost his thumb and forefinger, the typical punishment for archers. In 1366 he was married to Philippa de Roet, a lady-in-waiting to Philippa of Hainault, Queen Consort to Edward III, and to-gether the Chaucers had four children.

During the early years of their marriage, Chaucer seems to have studied law at the Inns of Court and traveled on several diplomatic missions to France and Italy. Through the 1380s he served as Controller of the Customs House in London, as a Commissioner of Peace in Kent, and Clerk of the King's Works under King Richard II. After Richard's deposition and murder in 1399, records of Chaucer's life practically disappear. He died in 1400 and was buried at West-minster Abbey, the first person buried in Poets' Corner.

Though Chaucer is best known for *The Canterbury Tales,* he wrote many other works and translated several others. Beginning in his own day and con-tinuing for several centuries, many works not written by Chaucer came to be collected in volumes of his own work. These spurious works are now referred to as the Chaucerian Apocrypha.

The first selection below is the opening of *The Canterbury Tales*, which is a collection of stories told by a group of pilgrims on their way to Canterbury. The tales reflect the tellers and are often used to criticize others on the pilgrimage, which adds a compelling dimension to the collection. The short passage included here begins like hundreds of other medieval poems that describe the coming of Spring, but is transformed into something else.

The second selection below, Chaucer's *Book of the Duchess*, is his first major work. It is thought to be a poem commemorating the death of Blanche, the Duchess of Lancaster and the wife of John of Gaunt, the most powerful man in England. Gaunt, the brother of Edward III and uncle of Richard II, granted

Chaucer for his efforts a "tun" (or cask) of wine each year for the rest of his life. The poem, written shortly after the death of Blanche, was perhaps presented again to Gaunt at the eighth anniversary of her death, when a monument to her was also dedicated.

Major Works
Book of the Duchess
Parliament of Fowls
House of Fame
Troilus and Criseyde
Legend of Good Women
Romance of the Rose (Translation)
The Consolation of Philosophy (*Boece*; Translation)

ↂↈ

From The Canterbury Tales (*Beginning of the* General Prologue)
Geoffrey Chaucer, 1390s

Whan that Aprill with his shoures soote
The droghte of March hath perced to the roote,
And bathed every veyne in swich licour
Of which vertu engendred is the flour;
5   Whan Zephirus eek with his sweete breeth
Inspired hath in every holt and heeth
The tendre croppes, and the yonge sonne
Hath in the Ram his half cours yronne,
And smale foweles maken melodye,
10   That slepen al the nyght with open ye
(So priketh hem Nature in hir corages),
Thanne longen folk to goon on pilgrimages,
And palmeres for to seken straunge strondes,
To ferne halwes, kowthe in sondry londes;
15   And specially from every shires ende
Of Engelond to Caunterbury they wende,
The hooly blisful martir for to seke,
That hem hath holpen whan that they were seeke.
Bifil that in that seson on a day,
20   In Southwerk at the Tabard as I lay
Redy to wenden on my pilgrymage
To Caunterbury with ful devout corage,
At nyght was come into that hostelrye
Wel nyne and twenty in a compaignye
25   Of sondry folk, by aventure yfalle
In felaweshipe, and pilgrimes were they alle,
That toward Caunterbury wolden ryde.
The chambres and the stables weren wyde,
And wel we weren esed atte beste.
30   And shortly, whan the sonne was to reste,

121

So hadde I spoken with hem everichon
That I was of hir felaweshipe anon,
And made forward erly for to ryse,
To take oure wey ther as I yow devyse.
35   But nathelees, whil I have tyme and space,
Er that I ferther in this tale pace,
Me thynketh it acordaunt to resoun
To telle yow al the condicioun
Of ech of hem, so as it semed me,
40   And whiche they weren, and of what degree,
And eek in what array that they were inne;
And at a knyght than wol I first bigynne.

CR80

Beginning of the General Prologue
TRANSLATED BY GERARD P. NeCASTRO

When the sweet showers of April have pierced to the root the dryness of March, and bathed every vein in moisture by which strength are the flowers brought forth; when Zephyr also with his sweet breath has given breath to the tender new shoots in the grove and field, and the young sun has run half his course through Aries the Ram, and little birds make melody and sleep all night with an open eye, so nature pricks them in their hearts: then people long to go on pilgrimages to renowned shrines in various distant lands, and palmers to seek foreign shores.

And especially from every shire's end in England they go their way to Canterbury, to seek the holy blessed martyr who helped them when they were sick.

One day in that season, as I was waiting at the Tabard Inn at Southwark, about to make my pilgrimage with devout heart to Canterbury, it happened that there came at night to that inn a company of twenty-nine various people, who by chance had fallen into fellowship. All were pilgrims, riding to Canterbury.

The chambers and the stables were spacious, and we were lodged well. But in brief, when the sun had gone to rest, I had spoken with every one of them and was soon of their company, and agreed to rise early to take our way to where I have told you.

Nevertheless, while I have time and space, before this tale goes further, I think it is reasonable to tell you all the qualities of each of them, as they appeared to me, what sort of people they were, of what station and how they were fashioned. I will begin with a knight.

ᑳᔥ

The Book of the Duchess
Geoffrey Chaucer, 1372, 1376
TRANSLATED BY GERARD P. NECASTRO

I wonder and wonder, by the light of the moon, how I stay alive, for I can hardly sleep at all, day or night. I have so many idle thoughts, all for lack of sleep, that, I swear, I care about nothing at all – whether anything comes or goes. There is nothing dear nor despised for me – it's all alike to me – joy or sorrow, it doesn't matter. For I feel nothing about anything, as if I am some sort of dazed thing, always on the brink of falling over; for sorrowful visions and images are always and everywhere fully in my mind.

And well you should know, it is against nature to live this way, for nature would not allow any earthly creature to endure for such a long time to be without sleep and in sorrow. And as I can not sleep, neither by night nor morning, I am melancholy and afraid that I shall die. Lack of sleep and heaviness[1] have slain my spirit of liveliness, so that I have lost all joy and vigor. My head is so full of fantasies that I don't know what's best to do.

But one might ask me why I can not sleep and what is wrong with me. But nonetheless, whoever asks this truly wastes his question. I, myself, can not tell why. But surely, the truth is that I maintain it is a sickness, I suppose, that I have suffered these eight years; and yet my remedy is never the nearer, for there is but one physician who can heal me – but enough about that. Let's pass over this until later. (What will not come about must be left behind.) It's best to return to our first subject.

So, recently, the other night, when I saw that I could not sleep, I sat up in my bed and bid someone to bring me a book,[2] a romance. And he brought it to me to read and drive the night away; for it seemed to me a better activity than playing either at chess or backgammon. And in this book were written fables that clerks and other poets had in old times (when people loved the law of nature) put into rhyme to be read and remembered. This book spoke primarily of queen's lives and king's lives, and many other smaller matters.

Among all this I found a tale that seemed to me an amazing thing. This was the tale. There was a king named Ceyx, and he had a wife, the best who ever lived, and this queen was named Alcyone. So it happened soon thereafter, this king would venture over the sea. To tell it shortly, when he was thus at sea, such a tempest rose up that their mast was broken and it toppled. It cleft their ship in two and drowned them all. They were never found, as the book says, ship nor man nor nothing else. In this way this King Ceyx lost his life.

Now, to speak of Alcyone, his wife: this lady, who was left at home, wondered why the king didn't come home, for it was a long time. Soon her heart began to grieve, as she believed more and more that he did not fare well. She so longed for the king that it is a pitiful thing to tell the exceedingly sorrowful life that she, this noble wife, had, for, alas, she loved him best of all.

---

[1] Heaviness. Spiritual heaviness (melancholy).
[2] Book. Probably Ovid's *Metamorphoses*.

Soon she sent messengers to seek him both east and west, but they found nothing. "Alas!" she said, "that I was created! If only I could know whether or not my lord, my love, is dead. Surely, I will never eat one crumb of bread, I make a vow to my god here, unless I might hear of my lord!" Such sorrow this lady took to herself that, truly, I, the person who wrote this book, had such pity and such sorrow to read of her sorrow that, I swear, I fared all the worse the entire morning afterwards to think about her sorrow.

So when this lady received no word and as no man had found her lord, very often she swooned and cried "Alas!" When she was nearly out of her mind for sorrow, she could think of only one plan of action; she set down on her knees and wept so tenderly that it was a pity to hear. "O, mercy, sweet lady dear!" she said to Juno,[1] her goddess, "Help me out of this distress, and give me grace to see my lord soon, or to know where he may be, or how he fares, or in what manner, and I shall make you a sacrifice and become wholly yours, with good will, body, heart, and all. And, if you would, lady sweet, please send me grace to sleep, and dream in my sleep a clear vision whereby I may know for certain whether my lord is alive or dead."

With that word she hung down her head and fell a-swoon, as cold as stone. Her women caught her up quickly, undressed her, and brought her to bed, and she, exhausted from weeping and lack of sleep, was so weary that a dead sleep fell on her before she noticed, thanks to Juno, who had heard her prayer and made her fall straight asleep. For as Alcyone prayed, just so was the deed done; for Juno immediately called her messenger[2] to do her errand, and he came without hesitation.

When he had come, she instructed him thus: "Go quickly," said Juno, "to Morpheus – you know him well, the god of sleep. Now listen carefully and remember well! Say this on my behalf: that he must go fast into the Great Sea,[3] and bid him that, above all, he take up Ceyx, the king's, body, which lies so pale and lacking all color. Bid him creep into that body and make it go to Alcyone the queen, where she lies alone, and show it to her briefly, so that there is no denying how he was drowned days ago. And make the body speak just as it used to do when it was alive. Go now quickly, and hurry!"

This messenger took leave, went upon his way, and never stopped until he came to the dark valley that stood between two rocks where there never grew wheat nor grass nor trees nor nothing that was anything. There was no beast, man, or anything else,, but there were, running down from the cliffs, a few springs which made a lifeless, sleeping sound. And the waters ran down next to a cave that was carved under a rock amidst the deep valley. There these gods, Morpheus and Eclympasteyr (the god of sleep's son), who sleep and do no other work, lie and sleep. This cave was also as dark as the pit of hell all around. They had the fine leisure to snore away, as if to contend over who could sleep best. Some hung their chin upon their breast and slept upright, their head hidden, and some lay undressed

---

[1] Juno. The goddess of women and the wife of Jupiter. Also known as Hera.
[2] Messenger. Probably Iris, as mentioned in Chaucer's sources.
[3] Great Sea. The Mediterranean.

in their bed and slept all day long.

This messenger came flying fast and cried, "Awake! Awake now!" It was no use: none heard him there. "Awake!" he said, "who is lying there?" And he blew his horn right in their ears, and cried "Awake!" extremely loud. This god of sleep looked up with his one eye and asked, "Who calls there?"

"It is I," said this messenger. "Juno instructed that you should go." And he told him what he should do (as I have told you before – there is no need to rehearse it again) and went his way when he had said this. Immediately this god of sleep jumped out of his slumber and started to go, and did as he had been bidden to do: he took up the drowned body and bore it forth to Alcyone, his wife the queen, where she lay, exactly three hours before dawn, and stood at the foot of her bed. And he called her by her very name and said, "My sweet wife, Awake! Leave your sorrowful life, for in your sorrow there lies no remedy; for, surely, sweet, I am surely dead. You shall never see me alive. But, good sweet heart, see that you bury my body, for at a certain time you can find it beside the sea. Farewell, sweet, my world's bliss! I pray to God to lessen your sorrow. Our bliss lasts for so short a time!"

With that she cast up her eyes and saw nothing. "Alas!" she said for sorrow, and died within the third morning. But what else she said in that anguish I may not tell you now – it would be too long to dwell on it.

I will return you to my original subject, the reason why I have told this story of Alcyone and Ceyx the king, for I dare say this much: I would have been entirely buried and dead, because of lack of sleep, if I had not read and heeded this tale. And I will tell you why: for I could not, for comfort or suffering, sleep before I had read this tale of this drowned Ceyx the king and of the gods of sleeping. When I had read this tale well and looked over every bit of, it seemed amazing to me that it would be so, for I had never heard mention before then of any gods that could make people sleep, nor to wake, for I had known only one god.

And in my amusement I said then (and yet I had little desire to play) rather than I should so die through lack of sleep, I would give this Morpheus, or his goddess, Lady Juno, or some other creature, I care not who – "Make me sleep and have some rest, and I will give him, or her, the best gift anyone ever hoped to receive. And into his possession, immediately, if he will make me sleep a little, I will give him a feather-bed of down of pure white doves, arrayed with gold and finely covered in fine black satin from abroad, and many pillows, and every pillowcase of linen from Reynes,[1] to sleep softly – he will not need to toss and turn so often. And I will give him everything that belongs to a bedchamber, and all his rooms I will have painted with pure gold and arrayed with many matching tapestries. All this shall he have (if only I knew where his cave is) if he can make me sleep soon, as he did for the goddess, queen Alcyone. And thus this same god, Morpheus, may gain from me more rewards than he ever won; and to Juno, who is his goddess, I shall so do, I believe, whatever will please her."

I had hardly said that word, exactly as I have told it to you, that suddenly, I know not how, such a desire overtook me to sleep that I fell asleep right on my

---

[1] Reynes. In France. Famous for its textiles.

book, and then I dreamed so inwardly sweet a dream, so wonderful a dream that I believe that no one has ever had the insight to interpret my dream correctly. No, not Joseph of Egypt,[1] without a doubt, who interpreted the Pharaoh's dream – no more than could the least of us; no, not even Macrobius[2] (who wrote all of the vision that he dreamed, about King Scipio the African, the noble man, of such marvels that happened then), could even interpret my dreams, I believe. Lo, thus it was; this was my dream.

It seemed this way to me: that it was May, and in the dawning of day I lay (I dreamed this) in my bed all undressed and looked about, for I was waked by a great heap of small birds that had startled me out of my sleep through the sound and sweetness of their song. And, as I dreamed, they sat together upon my chamber roof outside, upon the tiles, all over, and sang, each one in its own manner, the most solemn service, in harmony, that ever a person, I believe, has heard, for some of them sang low, some high, and all of one accord. In short, in a word, there was never heard so sweet a voice unless it had been a creation of heaven – so merry a sound, so sweet the tunes, that surely I would not have believed it for all the town of Tunis[3] unless I had heard them sing. For all of my chamber began to ring through the singing of their harmony. There was nowhere to be heard a sound half so sweet in instrument or voice, nor half as agreeable. For none of them pretended to sing, as each of them made great pains to find merry and skillful notes. They spared not their throats.

And the truth be told, my chamber was carefully decorated with pictures, and with glass were all the windows brightly glazed, not a flaw in any of them, so that to behold them it was a great joy. For the entire story of Troy[4] was wrought in the glasswork thus: of Hector and of King Priam, of Achilles and of King Laomedon, and also of Medea and of Jason, of Paris, Helen, and of Lavinia. And on all the walls were painted with fine colors the entire Romance of the Rose,[5] both text and

---

[1] Joseph of Egypt. Interpreted the Pharaoh of Egypt's dreams. See Genesis 41.

[2] Macrobius. *The Dream of Scipio*, the African King, was originally written by the Roman Cicero and later expanded via lengthy commentary by Macrobius. In the dream Scipio, visited by the spirit of his grandfather, is shown a vision of the universe. The topic of the work the discordant and limited nature of human existence in a world which is otherwise harmonious.

[3] Tunis. He is punning. Tunis, tunes, towns. Tunis is in northern Africa.

[4] Troy. Of the Trojan War. The ancient war between the Greeks (or Achaeans) and the Trojans, fought over Helen, wife of Menelaus, the King of Sparta, whose wife was seduced and taken by the Trojan Paris back to Troy. The story is best-known from its telling in Homer's *Iliad* and *Odyssey* and Vergil's *Aeneid*. Hector was the military champion of Troy and son to Priam, king of Troy, who was the son of Laomedon. Achilles was the military champion of the Greeks. Aeneas was the Trojan prince, nephew of Priam, who, upon the fall and destruction of Troy, sailed to Italy and founded what eventually became the Roman Empire. There he married Lavinia. Medea, magician and princess of Colchis, who married Jason, leader of the Argonauts who sought and won the Golden Fleece (with Medea's help), but later, after they were married and had two children, he deserted her. Eventually she kills Jason, his lover, and her own two children by Jason.

[5] *Romance of the Rose*. The most famous medieval French poem (which Chaucer translated). In this poem is contained "all things related to love".

gloss.[1] My windows were all shut, and through the glass the sun shone upon my bed with bright beams, with many pleasant golden streams. And the sky was so fair, blue and bright, the air was clear and truly temperate, for it was neither too hot nor too cold, and there was not a cloud in the sky.

And as I lay thus, I thought I heard a hunter attempt to blow his horn tremendously loud to tell if the horn were clear or hoarse in its sound. And I heard men, horses, hounds, and other things going up and down, and all the men speaking of hunting – how they would slay the hart with their strength, and how the hart would at length become exhausted from the hunt – I don't remember what else.

As soon as I heard that, how they would go a-hunting, I was rather glad, and right away I took my horse and went forth out of my chamber. I never stopped until I came to the field outside. There I overtook a great company of hunters and foresters, with many chasing hounds and tracking hounds. They rushed to the forest, and I, with them. So finally I asked one of them who led a tracking dog: "Say, fellow, who shall hunt here?" I said, and he answered, "Sir, the Emperor Octavian,"[2] he said, "and he is near here."

"In God's name, in good time!" I said, "Let's go quickly!" and began to ride. When we came to the edge of the forest, every man right away went about doing what hunters are supposed to do. The master-hunter then, without delay, blew three notes with a great horn at the release of his hounds. Within a while the hart is sought, halooed after, and pursued for a great time; and so, at last, this hart deceived them and stole away from all the hounds a secret way. The hounds had overshot him completely and were defeated because of the lack of a scent. And so, at last, the hunter quickly blew his horn.

I walked away from my assigned tree,[3] and as I went, there came near me a whelp, that fawned on me as I stood there. It had followed me and did not know what to do. It came and crept toward me humbly, just as if it had known me. He held down his head and put back his ears and laid his hair down all smooth. I wanted to catch it, but quickly it fled from me and was gone. And I followed him, and it went forth down by a flowery green path, soft under my feet, thick with grass, soft and sweet, with many flowers, and rarely tread upon. So it seemed, for both Flora and Zephirus[4] – the two who make flowers grow, had made their dwelling there, I believe; for it was, to behold it, as though the earth would contend to be more ornate than the heavens, as it had more flowers, seven times as many, as there are stars in the sky. It had forgotten the poverty that Winter, through his cold mornings, had made it suffer, and the sorrows he brought; all was forgotten, and that was visible, for all the woods had grown green; the sweetness

---

[1] Gloss. A footnote or commentary on the text.

[2] Octavian. Augustus Caesar. Founder of the Roman Empire, which he ruled from 27 BC until his death in 14 AD.

[3] Tree. He was posted, for the purpose of the hunt, at a tree, towards which, supposedly, the hart would be driven.

[4] Flora and Zephirus. Emblems of the beginning of Spring. When Flora is ravished by Zephirus, the West Wind, the flowers return.

of the dew had made it grow.

There is no need to ask me if there were many green branches or thickets of trees full of leaves; every tree stood by itself, ten to twelve feet from the next. Such great trees, such immense strength; of forty or fifty fathoms high, neatly maintained, without a stray bough or twig, with crowns equally broad and thick – they were not an inch apart, so that it was entirely shady underneath. And many harts and hinds[1] were both before me and behind. The wood was full of fawns, sorrels, bucks, and does, as were there many roes, and many squirrels that sat high upon the trees and ate, making many feasts in their own fashion. In short, it was so full of beasts that, even if Algus, the noble mathematician,[2] were to sit in his counting house and calculate with his ten numerals – for by those numerals all may learn, if they are sharp enough, to count and calculate – he would still fail to calculate correctly the wonders I dreamed in my dream.

But I roamed very quickly through the wood, until at last I became aware of a man in black, who had turned his back to a huge oak tree and sat. "Lord," thought I, "who may that be? What ails him to sit here so?" Quickly I drew up close to him; then I found him sitting upright, a striking, attractive knight – so was my impression of him – well-proportioned, and moreover rather young, twenty-four years old, with little hair in his beard, and he was clothed all in black.

I stalked directly behind him and I stood there as still as possible, so that, to tell the truth, he didn't see me; so he hung his head down, and with a deadly sorrowful sound he made a complaint[3] of ten or twelve rhymed verses to himself, the most pitiful, the most doleful, I ever heard; for, I swear, it is a great wonder that Nature might allow any creature to have such sorrow and not be dead. So piteously pale and lacking any ruddiness, he spoke his lay, a kind of tune, without music, without song; and this was it, for I can repeat it word for word – it began like this:

> "I am by sorrow so much undone
> That I get joy forever none,
> Now that I see my lady bright,
> Whom I have loved with all my might,
> Is from me dead and is gone.
>
> "Alas, death, what so ails thee,
> That thou wouldn't have taken me,
> When thou took my lady dear,
> That was so fair, so fresh, so free,[4]
> So good that all may well see
> Of all good folk she had no peer!"

When he had thus made his complaint, his sorrowful heart quickly became faint and his spirits grew dead; his blood had fled, for pure dread, down to his heart, to make him warm – for well it felt the heart had grief – to learn also why

---

[1] Hart and Hind. Male and female deer.

[2] Algus. The inventor of Arabic numerals.

[3] Complaint. A type of poetry which expresses some type of sorrow or hardship.

[4] Free. Noble.

it was terrified, by nature, and to make it glad again, for it is the principal organ of the body. And this rush of blood made his entire hue change and grow green and pale, for there was no blood to be seen in any of his limbs.

As soon as I saw this – he fared so poorly, as he sat there – I went and stood right at his feet and greeted him; he spoke nothing, but argued with his own thoughts, and in his mind disputed firmly why and how his life might continue, as his sorrows seemed to him so painful and lay so coldly on his heart. So, his sorrow and gloomy thoughts made him so that he did not hear me – for he had pretty nearly lost his mind; even Pan,[1] whom we call the god of nature, was never so disturbed for his sorrows.

But at last, to tell the absolute truth, he became aware of me, as I stood before him and took off my hood, and had greeted him courteously and humbly, as best I knew how. He said, "I pray you, be not upset. I heard you not, to tell the truth, nor did I see you, sir, truly."

"Ah, good sir, it does not matter," I said, "I am quite sorry if I have at all disturbed you from your thought. Forgive me, if I have made a mistake."

"Yes, but it is easy to make amends," he said, "for no offense has been taken; nothing wrong has been said or done."

Lo, how well this knight spoke, as if it had been another person; he presented himself as neither blunt nor strange. As I noticed this, I began to acquaint myself with him, and he seemed to me, for all his suffering, so agreeable, so very knowledgeable and reasonable. Straightaway I began to search, to look where I might, for a worthy subject for discussion, so that I could get to know him better.

"Sir," I said, "this game is done. I maintain that this hart is gone; these hunters can find him nowhere."

"I do not care about that," he said; "my thoughts are not the least bit on that."

"By our Lord," I said, "I believe you well; that seems plain to me in your face. But, sir, will you listen to one thing? It seems to me I see you in great sorrow; but surely, sir, if you would reveal to me your woe, I would remedy it, if I can or may. You can test it by trying; for, by my word, to make you whole and well, I will give it all of my power. Please tell me of your painful sorrows; by chance it may ease your heart, which seems so sick within."

With that he looked on me askance, as one who says, "No, that will not be."

"Grant mercy, good friend," he said, "I thank you for wishing it so, but it may not be done so soon. No one may lighten my sorrow, which makes my hue to lessen and fade, and which has made me to lose my understanding, so that I am woeful that I was ever born! Nothing can make my sorrows slide away, not all the remedies of Ovid,[2] nor Orpheus,[3] the god of music, nor Daedalus with his

---

[1] Pan. Lost his beloved Syrinx when she was turned into the reeds. He then created a musical instrument (the pan-flute) by twining together seven reeds.

[2] Ovid. Author of the *Remedies of Love*, more famous for his *Metamorphoses*.

[3] Orpheus. Well-known for his love of Eurydice, who, bitten by a snake, is taken to the underworld, Hades, where she is rescued by Orpheus, whose beautiful lyre music pleases (or puts to sleep) the god of the underworld. As they exit the underworld, Orpheus looks back at his wife, and she must return to Hades, where Orpheus later joins her after his own death. In the medieval version of *Sir Orfeo*, she was snatched by the fairy king, and,

ingenious inventions;[1] no physician may heal me, not Hippocrates nor Galen.[2] Woe is me that I should live even another twelve hours! But whoever wishes to try his hand to see if his heart can have pity for my sorrow, let him see me. I am a wretch whom death has stripped naked of all the bliss that ever was made and made lowest of all creatures, so much so that I hate all my days and my nights!

"All my pleasures, indeed, my whole life, are loathsome to me, for myself and my welfare are at odds. Death itself is so surely my foe that if I would say I want to die, he would say no; for when I pursue him, he flees; I wish to have him, but he will not have me. This is my pain without comfort, always dying and not dead, and so much so that not even Sisyphus,[3] who lies in hell, has no more sorrow to tell. And whosoever might come to know all my sorrow, I swear, unless he should sympathize and take pity on my painful sorrows, that man has a fiendish heart. For whosoever sees me tomorrow may say he has met with Sorrow, for I am Sorrow, and Sorrow is I.

"Alas! And I will tell you why: why my song is turned to lament, my laughter to weeping, my glad thoughts to sad ones; why all my work is also my idleness and my rest; why my wellness is woe, my good is harm; and why my joyful pastimes are turned into wrath, my delight into sorrow. So too my good health is turned into sickness, my security into dread, all my light to dark; my wit is folly, my day is night, my love is hate, my sleep waking, my mirth and meals are fasting; my self-confidence is turned to foolishness and I am entirely disconcerted, wherever I may be; my peace is turned into lawsuits and war.

"Alas, how would I ever fare in war? My boldness is turned to shame, for false Fortune has played a game of chess with me. Alas, the time it happened! The traitoress, false and full of guile, she who promises everything and delivers nothing, who walks upright and still limps, who squints so foully and still looks lovely, the disdainful and gracious one, who scorns so many creatures! She is an idol of false self-portraiture, for she would gladly deceive; she is the monster's head pleasantly disguised, like a dung-heap over-strewn with flowers. Her most innate and representative quality is her lying, for that is her nature; she is false – without sincerity, lawfulness, or moderation, as she is ever laughing with one eye, and weeping with the other. Whatever rises, she knocks down. I liken her to the scorpion, a false, flattering beast, for with his head he makes merry, but as he is flattering you, he will sting and envenom you. Fortune is the hostile charity, who is always false and seems true. So she turns her false wheel around, for it never remains stationary – at one moment you are being served at the table, at another you are a servant standing by the fire. She has blinded many: she is an enchantress, who seems to be one thing and is another.

---

after the descent to the underworld, Orfeo and Heurodis live happily ever after.

[1] Daedalus. Mythical inventor (whose name means "cunning inventor"). Invented wings with which his son Icarus could fly. But Icarus flew too close to the sun, the wax on them melted, and he plunged to his death.

[2] Hippocrates, Galen. Famous Greek and Roman physicians. (Thus the Hippocratic Oath.)

[3] Sisyphus. For his misdeeds on earth, he was condemned to eternal punishment in Hades, where he rolled to the top of a hill a large stone, which when it reached the summit rolled down again.

"The false thief! What has she done? What do you suppose? By our Lord I will tell you: she began to play with me at chess; and with her various little cheating moves, she tricked me and stole away my queen. And when I saw my queen had been taken away, alas, I could not figure out how to continue playing, but said, 'Farewell, sweet, surely, and farewell everything, now and forever!'

"At that moment Fortune said, 'Check her!' And check-mated me, with an errant pawn, in the mid-point of the checker board! Alas, craftier at play was she than Attalus,[1] so was his name, who invented the game of chess. But I wish to God that I could have understood, just once or twice, the chess problems the way that the Greek Pythagoras[2] might have. I should have played better at chess and thereby kept my queen better. But what does it matter? For truly, I say that wish isn't worth a straw! It would have turned out no better for me, for Fortune knows so many tricks that there are few who can beguile her; and she is also the less to blame; myself, I would have done the same, as God is my witness, had I been her; she ought, I suppose, to be more excused than me. For I must say a bit more about this: had I been God and might have done as I wished when she captured my queen, I would have made the same move. For, as surely as God may give me rest, I dare well swear she took the best. But through that move I have lost my bliss; alas, that I was born!

"Forevermore, I truly believe, in spite of all my wishes, my joy is entirely reversed; but yet, what can I do? By our Lord, the only option seems to be to die soon. For I care nothing about anything, but live and die right in this thought; for there is no planet in the firmament, nor in the air nor in the earth or elements, that does not give me a gift of weeping when I am alone. For when I consider everything, how there is nothing owing to me in matters of sorrow, and how there exists no merriment that may relieve me of my distress, and how I have lost all my contentment, and how for all that I have no delight, then may I say I have absolutely nothing. And when all this comes into my mind, alas, then I am overcome! For whatever is done can not be changed. I have more sorrow than Tantalus."[3]

And when I heard him tell this tale so pitifully, as I have told you, hardly could I remain there longer, as it gave my heart so much woe. "A, good sir," I said, "do not say so! Have some pity on your Nature that formed you as a creature. Remember Socrates,[4] for he considered anything that Fortune could do to be worth three straws."

"No," he said, "I don't think so."

"Why so, good sir? Yes, by God!" I said; "do not say so, for truly, even if you had lost twelve queens, and you murdered yourself for sorrow, you should be

---

[1] Attalus. Attalus Philometer, king of Cappadocia

[2] Pythagoras. Greek philosopher and ruler who greatly advanced fields of mathematics and geometry.

[3] Tantalus. For stealing the nectar of the gods and for revealing their secrets, he was punished by being placed, hungry and thirsty, in Hades, under fruit trees which moved when he tried to pick them and in a river which receded when he tried to drink it.

[4] Socrates. Greek philosopher who argued that self-control, not Fortune, brought us pleasure.

damned in this case, as was Medea, who slew her children on account of Jason;[1] and Phyllis, who was so desperate that she hung herself for Demophoun, for he had broken his appointed day to come to her. Another such rage had Dido, the queen of Carthage, who, because Aeneas was false to her slew herself – for which she was a fool![2] And Echo died because Narcissus would not love her,[3] and likewise have many others done such folly; and Samson, who slew himself with a pillar, died for Dalilah.[4] But there is no man alive today who would undergo such woe for a queen!"

"Why so?" he said, "it is not so. You know full little what you mean by your words; I have lost more than you think."

"Lo, tell me how that may be?" I said; "Good sir, tell me entirely, how, why, by what cause, and in what ways you have thus lost your bliss."

"Gladly," he said; "come sit down! I'll tell you upon the condition that you shall wholly, with all your wit, carry out your intention to listen carefully to it."

"Yes, sir."

"Swear your promise to do so."

"Gladly."

"Then you better keep your word!"

"I shall, with great joy, God save me, wholly, with all the wit I have, listen to you as well as I can."

"In God's name!" he said, and began. "Sir," he said, "ever since I first could in my youth by learning or natural understanding in any way comprehend what love was, doubtless, I have ever since been a vassal to and paid tribute to Love, with entirely good intentions, and with great pleasure become his servant, body, heart, and soul, with good will. All this I committed to his service and did homage to him as my lord; and I prayed to him devoutly that he might employ my heart in such a way that it would be a delight to him and an honor to my dear lady.

"And I remained in his service many years before my heart was set anywhere in particular, and I knew not why; I believe it came to me naturally. Perhaps I was most capable in this respect, as is a white wall or slate, for it is ready to accept and receive anything that one will put there, whatever one wishes to paint or portray, no matter how elaborate the works may be.

"And at this time I fared well, so that I was able to have learned all about love, and I learned it as well or better than any other art or science; as love always came first in my mind, I never forgot it. I chose love as my first craft; therefore it has remained with me. Since I took it up at such a young age, my heart had no trouble with it, and time did not erase it, as I had studied too much for that to

---

[1] Medea and Jason. Knowing that her children would be slain by Jason's followers – since she had just slain Jason (unfaithful to her) and his bride – Medea slew her children.

[2] Dido and Aeneas. Their love is the topic of the opening books of Vergil's *Aeneid*. Though he pledged himself to Dido, Aeneas deserted her when he was reminded of his divine mission to found Rome.

[3] Echo and Narcissus. Narcissus, a beautiful youth, would love none but hit own reflection in the water. Echo loved him but died in despair because her love was unrequited.

[4] Samson and Dalilah. Biblical story in which the strong man Samson is betrayed by the enemy Dalilah, who seduces him to find out the secret of his strength (his hair).

happen. Up to that time, Youth, my governess, instructed me in idleness; for it was in my early youth, and I knew very little worth knowing then, for all my works were impermanent at that time, and all my thoughts were changeable. Everything that I knew then was equally good; but that is how it was.

"It happened that I came one day into a place where I saw truly the fairest company of ladies assembled in one place that ever a man had seen with eye. Shall I call it chance or grace that brought me there? No, only Fortune, who is so accustomed to lie, the false perverse traitoress! I wish to God I could call her worse, for now she makes me woeful, and I will soon tell you why.

"Among these ladies, to tell the truth, I saw one who was like none of the rest; for I dare swear, without a doubt, that as the summer's bright sun is fairer, clearer, and has more light than any other planet in the heavens, the moon or the seven stars,[1] so had she, for all the world, surmounted them all in beauty, in demeanor, in graciousness, in stature, in cheerfulness – in short, in excellence so well bestowed upon her – what more can I say? By God and his twelve apostles, this was my sweet, her very self. She had such a steadfast countenance, such noble deportment and bearing, and Love, who had listened so carefully to my request, had looked upon me so quickly, that she was, so help me God, so swiftly caught in my mind that I didn't need to ask for advice from anywhere, but only looked to her and to my heart; for when her eyes so gladly beheld my heart, I believe, my own thought then, without a doubt, said it would be better to serve her for nothing than to serve another and be well-rewarded. And it was so, for I will tell you why right now in full detail.

"I saw her dance so becomingly, to sing and join in carols so sweetly, to laugh and play so womanly, to carry herself so graciously, and to speak so friendly and kindly, that surely I believe that never was seen so blissful a treasure as she. For every hair on her head, to tell the truth, was not red or yellow or brown; it seemed most like gold.

"And what eyes my lady had! Stately, kind, glad, sincere, and true, well-proportioned, and not too wide. Thus her eyes looked directly, not aside or askance, but so carefully settled on things that they entirely ennobled everything they beheld. Her eyes seemed to say that she would have mercy[2] on me – fools would think so – but she would never do so hastily. But her look was not counterfeit; it was her own pure way of looking, a way in which the goddess, Lady Nature, had made her eyes open and close moderately; for even if she was delighted, her glances were not spread about foolishly or wildly, even if she was being playful; but, it seemed to me, her eyes said, 'By God, all of my ill-will is gone!'

"In this way she loved to live so fully that dullness was afraid of her. She was not too sober nor too glad; in all things she had more moderation, I believe, than any other creature. She hurt many men with her look, but that sat lightly on

---

[1] Seven stars. Probably the seven other known heavenly bodies in the Milky Way. Or, perhaps the Pleiades.
[2] Mercy. In the language of courtly love, for a woman to have mercy on a man is to allow him fully into her heart.

her heart, for she knew nothing of their thoughts; but whether she knew it or not, she nonetheless considered it as much as she would a piece of straw! To get her love, no nearer was he who dwelled at home than he who was in India; the first in line was always the last. But she loved good people, above all others, as one may love his brother; and she was very generous in this kind of love, especially in appropriate times and places.

"But what a face had she! Alas, my heart is so woeful that I can't describe it! I lack both the English and the wit to unfold it fully; and my spirits are also too dull for me to devise so great a thing. I have no wit that can suffice to comprehend her beauty. But I dare say this much, that she had a fresh, lively complexion, and every day her beauty renewed. And her face was nearly the best of all, for surely Nature had such desire to make that beautiful that truly she was the chief example and pattern of Nature's beauty – and of all her work; for though her image seems so dark and distant, I think I see her always. And, moreover, even if everyone who ever lived were now alive, they would be unable to discover any fault, any wicked sign, in her face, for it was sincere, honest, and kind.

"And such a fine, soft voice had my sweet one, the savior[1] of my life! So friendly, and so well-instructed, so well-grounded in reason, and so agreeable to all good people that, I dare well swear, by the cross, there was never found such eloquent speech, nor so sweet a tongue, nor one that scorned others less, nor could heal them more nor less falseness in her word, that in her simple promise alone was found as true as any bond or oath from any man's hand; nor could she chide anyone, not even one word. (I swear by the holy mass – even if the Pope himself sang it – that there was never any man nor woman harmed by her tongue; and as for her, all harm was hidden from her.) The whole world knows this well.

"But such a lovely neck had that sweet one, every inch perfectly shaped, without a blemish. It was white, smooth, straight, and even, without hollows or collar-bone, as it seems she had none. Her throat, as I remember, seemed a round tower of ivory, full, but not too full.

"And she was called the good faire "White"; truly that was my lady's name. She was both fair and bright; there was nothing inaccurate about her name. She had nice soft shoulders and a long body, and arms as well; every limb was well-rounded and fleshy, but not too much so; nice white hands, and red nails; round breasts; and firm broad hips; and a straight, flat back. I knew of no other fault, as far as I could tell, other than her limbs were not perfectly in proportion.

"She knew how to present herself so well, when she pleased, that I dare say that she was like a bright lamp from which everyone might receive an abundance of light, and never less. In manners and behavior my lady was so excellent that anyone who caught a glimpse of her remembered her fully; for I dare well swear, if she had been one among ten thousand standing in a row at a feast, she would have been, at the least, a chief paragon in the eyes of all; for wherever people gathered together without her, it seemed to me that the company was entirely lacking, like a crown without gemstones. Truly she was to my eye the solitary Phoenix of Arabia,[2] for there is only one of those, and I know of none other like

---

[1] Savior. Chaucer uses the word "leche," which means Physician or healer.

her.

"To speak of goodness, truly she had as much graciousness as ever had Esther[1] in the Bible, and more, if more were possible. And, to tell the truth, she had in this way a wit so congenial, so fully inclined to goodness, that all her thoughts were fixed, by the Cross, without malice and upon gladness; and thus I never saw one less harmful than she. I don't mean that she did not know what harm was, or else she would not have known so well what good was.

"And truly, speaking of truth, if she had not truth, it would have been a pity. She had such a great portion of truth – and I dare well swear it – that Truth himself had chosen her, over one and all, as his principal manor and resting place. And thus she gracefully and calmly persevered, reigning the most moderately I have ever seen, so kind and tolerant was her mind; and she gladly understood reason; and, of course, she knew goodness well. She used to do good deeds gladly; these were her custom in everything.

"Since she loved justice so well, she would do no wrong to anyone. No creature could do any shame to her, as she loved and honored her own name. She would not encourage anyone with false hopes, nor, be sure of this, would she strive to hold any creature in suspense with half-truths or false-seeming – unless anyone would lie about her. She sent no men to Rumania, Prussia, Mongolia, Alexandria, or Turkey, nor bid him to rush off and go bare-headed into the Gobi Desert and come home the long way, by the Kara-Nor, and say, 'Sir, be sure that you have praiseworthy deeds to report before you return here!' She used no such petty tricks.

"But why do I tell my tale? For this very reason, as I have said: my love was entirely set on her. For surely she was, this sweet wife, my source of contentment, my joy, my life, my good fortune, my health, and all my blessing, the welfare of the world, and my goddess, and I was wholly hers, body and soul."

"By our Lord," I said, "I well believe you! Assuredly, your love was well bestowed; I don't know how you might have done better."

"Better? No creature has ever done half so well," he said.

"I understand it well, sir," I said, "by God!"

"No, *believe* it well!"

"Sir, yes, I do; I believe you well, that truly you thought that she was the best, and the fairest of all to behold, for anyone who looked on her with your eyes."

"With *my eyes*? No, *all* saw her said and swore it was so. And even if they had not, I would still have loved my noble lady best. And even if I had had all the beauty that Alcibiades[2] ever had; all the strength of Hercules; all the worthiness of Alexander;[3] all the riches that ever were in Babylon, Carthage, Macedonia, Rome,

---

[2] Phoenix. In legends of the Phoenix, the bird which consumes itself in fire then is reborn of its own ashes, there is much emphasis placed on its solitary nature.

[1] Esther. Biblical model of wifely virtue. See Book of Esther.

[2] Alcibiades. Athenian politician, remembered mostly for his good looks.

[3] Alexander. Alexander the Great of Macedon, ruler of much of the Eastern Mediterranean in the fourth century B.C.

or Ninevah; all the courage of Hector[1] (whom Achilles slew at Troy, and so too was he slain in a temple, for both he and Antilochus were slain – so says Dares Frygius – for the love of Polixena);[2] or all the wisdom of Minerva, I would forever, without a doubt, have loved her, for I must.

"'*Must?*' No, truly, I speak nonsense now; Not '*must*' – and I will explain why: because my heart *wished* it through good *will*, and because I was obliged to love her as the fairest and the best. She was as good, God rest my soul, as ever was Penelope[3] of Greece, or as the noble wife Lucrece,[4] who was the best (so says the Roman, Titus Livus[5]). She was as good, though nothing like her, except in goodness (though their stories are true); nonetheless she was as faithful as she.

"But why don't I tell you about the first time I saw my lady? I was rather young, to tell the truth, and still in great need of learning; when my heart would yearn to love, it was a great enterprise. As fitting with my young childly mind, I boldly set all my mental energy, as well as my brain could manage, on loving her in the best way I knew how, to honor and serve her in the best way I knew at the time, I swear, without being false or slothful in any way, for I wished to see her more than anything. So greatly did seeing her affect me that when I first saw her in the morning I was cured of all my sorrow for the entire day; even into the evening it seemed nothing could grieve me, regardless of how painful my sorrows might be. And yet she sat so in my heart that, I swear, I would not for all the world leave this lady out of my thought; no, truly!"

"Now, I swear, sir," I said, "it seems to me you are in such a position to make your confession without repentance."

"Repentance? No, fy!" he said, "Should I now repent my love? No, surely! I'd be worse off than Achitophel,[6] or Antenor,[7] (the traitor who betrayed Troy), or the false Ganelon,[8] (who secured the treason of Roland and Oliver). No, while I am alive here, I will not forget her – nevermore."

"Now, good sir," I said then, "You have told me well before; there's no need to repeat again how you first saw her, and where. But would you tell me the manner in which you first spoke with her – this I ask you – and how she first came

---

[1] Hector. Trojan hero. His death at the hands of Achilles is the climax of *The Iliad.*

[2] Antilochus and Achilles. For the killing of Troilus and Hector, they were ambushed at the temple of Apollo where Achilles wished to marry Polixena.

[3] Penelope. Faithful wife of Odysseus, hero of *The Odyssey.* She waited him, though he was gone for over ten years and many men sought her hand.

[4] Lucrece. Faithful wife of Collatinus. Raped by Superbus, who cut out her tongue. She revealed the crime to him in her weaving, then took her life. Superbus' crime was then revenged.

[5] Titus Livius. Livy (59 BC – AD 17), author of *Ab Urbe Condita* (*From the Founding of the City*), which included the story of Lucrece, or Lucretia.

[6] Achitophel. Counseled Absalom to rebel against his father David. The rebellion failed and Absalom was killed in the Battle of Ephraim Wood. See 2 Samuel 17.

[7] Antenor. His treachery caused the downfall of Troy. As a peace offering, he sent the statue of Pallas Athene, the patron of Troy, to Ulysses.

[8] Ganelon. His treachery caused the great French hero Roland to be slain by the Saracens, as told in *The Song of Roland.*

to know your thoughts, whether you loved her or not? And tell me also what you have lost, as I heard you mention earlier."

"Yes!" he said, "you know not what you mean by your words; I have lost more than you think."

"What loss is that?" I said then; "Will she not love you? Is it so? Or have you done something wrong, that she has left you? Is it this? For God's love, tell me everything."

"Before God," he said, "I shall do so. I say, just as I have said, on her was all my love bestowed, and yet she did not know it, not a bit, not for a long time, believe me! For be assured, I wouldn't dare, not for all this world, reveal my thoughts to her, nor would I have upset her, truly. Would you like to know why? She had control over my body: as she held my heart, I could not escape. But to keep myself from idleness, I went about my business in making songs, as best I knew how, and often I sang them aloud; and I made a great number of songs, although I could not make them so well, as I didn't know all the art of it, as did Lamech's son Tubal,[1] who originated the art of song; for as his brother's hammers rang up and down upon the anvil, from this he took the first tune – though Greeks say it was Pythagoras[2] who was the founder of the art (Aurora[3] says so); but what does that matter? Nevertheless, I made songs from my feelings to gladden my heart. And listen, here was the first of all – and perhaps the worst of all:

'Lord, it makes my heart light
When I think on that sweet wight[4]
Who is so lovely to see;
And wish to God it might so be
That she would have me for her knight,
My lady, who is so fair and bright!'

"Now have I told you, to tell the truth, my first song. One day I thought to myself about the woe and sorrow I suffered to that point for her, and yet she knew nothing about it, nor did I yet tell her my thoughts.

"'Alas,' I thought, 'I know no remedy; unless I tell her, I am nothing but dead; and if I tell her, to tell the very truth, I am afraid she will be upset with me. Alas, what shall I do then?'

"I was so woeful in this debate, it seemed my heart would burst in two! So, at long last, to tell the truth, I determined that Nature never formed in any creature so much beauty, truly, and goodness, without mercy. In hope of that, I made my speech to her, but I told it badly and in a way that I never should have: for necessity, and against my own advising, I had to tell her, or die. I can hardly remember how I began; I can retell it only hazily; and, so help me God, I think it

---

[1] Lamech's son Tubal. Actually Jubal, called the "father of all such as handle the harp and organ" (Genesis 4.21).

[2] Pythagoras. Greek philosopher and ruler who greatly advanced fields of mathematics and geometry.

[3] Aurora. Twelfth-century versified Latin paraphrase and commentary on parts of the Bible by Peter of Riga (1140-1209).

[4] Wight. Creature, person.

was an unlucky day – there were *ten* wounds of Egypt that day[1] – for I skipped, out of pure fear, over many words in my speech, lest my words would be poorly said. With sorrowful heart and deadly wounds, meekly and quaking for pure fear and shame, and stammering in my speech for fear, and my hue growing entirely pale – I often grew both pale and red – bowing to her, I hung my head; I dared not once look on her, for my wits, manners, and everything were gone. I said 'Mercy!' and no more. It was not amusing; it sat sorely on me.

"So at last, to tell the truth, when my heart returned to me, to summarize, with all my heart I beseeched her to be my sweet lady; and swore, and promised her heartily to be always steadfast and true, and to love her always newly, freshly, and never have any other lady, and to preserve her honor, as best I could. I swore this to her: 'For your honor is all that ever there is for me evermore, my heart sweet! And I'll never be false to you, unless I am dreaming, so help me dear God!'

"And when I had completed my speech, God knows, she valued it not so much as a straw, so it seemed. To be brief, her answer, truly, was this – I can not now counterfeit her words, but this was the main point of her answer: she utterly said 'No.' Alas, the sorrow and the woe I suffered that day, so much so that truly Cassandra,[2] who so bewailed the destruction of Troy and of Ilium, never had such sorrow as I did then. I dared not say another word at that point, for pure fear, but stole away; and thus I lived many a day, so that truly I had no need to go further than the head of my bed to seek sorrow; I found sorrow readily every morning, as my love for her never wavered.

"So it happened, another year passed, and I thought I would try once to let her know and comprehend my woe; and she came to understand well that I intended nothing but good, and honor, and to preserve her name above all things; and that I dreaded her disdain; and was so eager to serve her; and it would be a pity if I should die, since, surely, I intended no harm. So when my lady knew all this, she gave me the noble gift of her mercy entirely, without ever any offense to her honor. Without a doubt, I would have it no other way.

And with that she gave me a ring; I think it was the most memorable thing; of course, there's no need to ask if my heart grew glad! So help me God, I was quickly raised, as if from death to life; of all possible fortunes, I found the best of all, the gladdest, and the most enjoyable. For truly that sweet creature, when I was wrong and she was right, would always forgive me so kindly and graciously. In all my youth, in all events, she took me into her service. And there she was always so true, and our joy was ever renewed; our hearts were so equally paired that never would either of us be contrary to the other for any woe. For truly, both our hearts shared one bliss and one sorrow alike; they were both glad and sad the same; all was one for us, without a doubt. And thus we lived many years so well I can not

---

[1] Ten wounds of Egypt. According to a late medieval belief, there were two unlucky days (*di[e]s mal* in French) per month, on which people were afflicted with wounds or plagues (as were the Egyptians in the time of Abraham). Black is having ten of these days at once.

[2] Cassandra. Trojan prophetess, sister of Hector and Troilus. Was given the gift of prophesy by Apollo, who, when she spurned his love, condemned her to the fate that no one would believe her predictions. Ilium. The citadel or fortress of Troy.

tell how."

"Sir," I said, "where is she now?"

"Now?" he said, and stopped at once. With that he grew as dead as stone and said, "Alas, that I was born! That was the loss that I told you before that I had lost. Remember how I said earlier, 'You know full little what you mean by your words; I have lost more than you think.' God knows, alas! She was that very person!"

"Alas, sir, how? How may that be?"

"She is dead!"

"No!"

"Yes, by my word!"

"Is that your loss? By God, that is such a pity!"

And with that word they quickly began to sound the hunting signal to head home; all the hart-hunting was done for that time.

With that I thought that this king began to ride homeward to an adjacent place which was a short way from us – a long castle with white walls, by Saint John, on a rich hill, so I dreamed; but thus it happened. I dreamed just as I tell you: in the castle there was a bell, and as it struck twelve, I awoke and found myself lying in my bed. And the book I had read, of Alcyone and Ceyx the king, and of the gods of sleep, I found wide open in my hand. I thought, "This is so strange a dream that I will, in the course of time, attempt to put this dream into rhyme as best I can, and do so soon."

This was my dream; now it is done.

The Tale of Griselda
Giovanni Boccaccio, 1313 – 1375
Francesco Petrarca, 1304 – 1374
Geoffrey Chaucer, c. 1340 – 1400

One of the most popular tales of the later Middle Ages and Renaissance was that of Griselda, the patient woman who accepted the will of her husband Walter (or Gualtieri), no matter what trials he set forth for her. She was used as the model for patience and associated with the Biblical figure of Job. In the following pages, there are three tellings of the tale of patient Griselda by three of the best story-tellers of the late Middle Ages, Boccaccio, Petrarch, and Chaucer. The first is a complete version of the tale, while the second and third are only the conclusions to it. Though all three authors overlap in their initial responses to the tale, they then move in very different directions.

∽
The Tale of Griselda
Giovanni Boccaccio, 1353
TRANSLATED BY GERARD P. NECASTRO, ADAPTED FROM J. M. RIGG

There was in olden days a certain Marquis of Saluzzo,[1] Gualtieri by name, a young man, but head of the house, who, having neither wife nor child, passed his time in nothing else but in hawking and hunting. He had no thought of taking a wife and having children. For this he should have been considered very wise, but his vassals, believing it foolish, often entreated him to take a wife, so that he might not die without an heir and that they would be left without a lord. They offered to find him one of such a model and of such parentage that he might marry with good hope and be well content with what would follow.

To their proposal, Gualtieri replied, "My friends, you are forcing me to do

---

[1] Saluzzo. A town in northeastern Italy in the Piedmont region, not far from the border of France.

what I had resolved never to do. I can see how hard it is to find a wife, whose ways accord well with one's own, and how many women there are who would not fit that plan, and how grievous a life one would lead who comes upon a lady that matches poorly with him. And to say that you think you know the daughters by the qualities of their fathers and mothers, and thereby – so you would argue – to provide me with a wife to my liking, is but folly; for I know not how you may penetrate the secrets of their mothers and fathers. And granted that you do know them, daughters oftentimes resemble neither of their parents. However, as you are determined to fasten these fetters upon me, I am content that it will be so; and so that I may have no cause to reproach any but myself, should it turn out badly, I am resolved that my wife shall be of my own choosing. But rest assured of this, that, no matter whom I choose, if she would not receive from you the honor due to a lady, it shall cost you dearly, seeing how sorely I resent being thus constrained by your importunity to take a wife against my will."

The noblemen replied that they were well content, provided that he would marry without more ado. And Gualtieri, who had long noted with approval the beauty, manners, and well-seeming virtues of a poor countryman's daughter, deemed that with her he might pass a tolerably happy life. Therefore he sought no further, but immediately resolved to marry her; and having sent for her father, who was a very poor man, he contracted with him to take her as his wife.

Having done this, Gualtieri assembled all the noblemen and friends he had in those parts, and said, "My friends, you were and determined that I should take a wife, and more to comply with your wishes than for any desire that I had to marry, I have made up my mind to do so. You remember the promise you gave me, namely, that, whomsoever I should take, you would pay her the honor due to a lady. This promise I now require you to keep, the time having come when I am to keep mine. I have found nearby here a maiden after my own heart, whom I intend to take as my wife, and to bring here to my house in the course of a few days. Therefore begin to plan how you may make the nuptial feast splendid, and welcome her with all honor, so that I may offer my full satisfaction with your observance of your promise, as you will be with my observance of mine."

The worthy men, one and all, answered with alacrity that they were well content, and that, whoever she might be, they would honor her as a lady and pay her all due respect as such. After this, they all promised to make a fine and grand and joyful celebration of the event, as did also Gualtieri. He arranged for a very stately and beautiful wedding, and invited to it large number of his friends and kinsfolk, and great gentlemen and others of the neighborhood. And for the wedding he ordered many fine and costly robes to be cut and fashioned to the figure of a girl who seemed to him to be of the same proportions as the girl that he purposed to wed, and he also purchased girdles, rings, a costly and beautiful crown, and all the other paraphernalia of a bride.

The day that Gualtieri had appointed for the wedding having come, about nine o'clock he mounted his horse, as did all the others who come to do him honor. Having made all necessary preparations, he said, "Gentlemen, it is time to go bring home the bride." And so away he rode with his company to the village; where, having arrived at the house of the girl's father, they found her re-

141

turning from the spring with a bucket of water, making all the haste she could, so that she might afterwards go with the other women to see Gualtieri's bride come by. When Gualtieri saw her, he called her by her name, that is to say, Griselda, and asked her where her father was. To this she modestly answered, "My Lord, he is in the house."

On this note Gualtieri dismounted and, having bidden the rest await him outside, entered the cottage alone; and meeting her father, whose name was Giannucolom he said, "I have come to wed Griselda, but first of all there are some matters I would like to hear from her own lips in your presence."

He then asked her, whether, if he took her as his wife, she would attempt to comply with his wishes, and be not angry, no matter what he might say or do, and be obedient; and be gentle, humble, and patient. He asked other similar questions as well, all of which she answered that she would do as he asked, as near as heaven and grace would enable her.

Upon hearing this, Gualtieri took her by the hand, led her forth, and, before the eyes of all his company and as many other folk as were there, having taken off all of her clothes with his own hands, clothed her with the garments that he had fashioned for her. And folding he hair over her shoulder, he set on her head a crown of gold, at which everyone stared in wonder. "Gentlemen," he said, "this is she whom I intend to make my wife, as she is willing to have me as a husband."

Then, as she stood abashed and astonished, he turned to her and said, "Griselda, will you have me for your husband?"

To him she answered, "Yes, my Lord."

"And I will have you as wife," he said, and married her before them all. And having set her upon a palfrey, he brought her home with pomp.

The wedding was beautiful and stately, and, had he married a daughter of the King of France, the feast could not have been more splendid. It seemed as if, with the change of her garb, the bride had acquired a new dignity of mind and manner. She was, as we have said, fair of form and feature; and furthermore she had now grown so engaging and gracious and debonair, that she seemed no longer to be a shepherdess and the daughter of Giannucolo, but the daughter of some noble lord, which caused many who had previously known her to marvel. Moreover, she was so obedient and devoted to her husband that he deemed himself the happiest and luckiest man in the world. And likewise she was so gracious and kindly to her husband's vassals that there was none of them who did not love her more dearly than himself. They were zealous to do her honor and prayed for her welfare and prosperity and long life; and instead of saying, as they had done earlier, that Gualtieri had acted foolishly to take her as his wife, they now swore that he had no equal in the world for wisdom and discernment, since, if it were not for him, her noble qualities would have always remained hidden under her sorry apparel and the garb of the peasant girl. And in short she so conducted herself in such a way that, not only the Marquis' realm it self, but all neighboring Provinces surrounding it, there was nothing spoken of her, but of her rare course of life, devotion, charity, and all her otherwise good actions, and, if anything had been said to the disadvantage of her husband when he married her, the judgment was now altogether to the contrary.

She had not been long with Gualtieri before she became pregnant and in due time she gave birth to a baby girl, at which Gualtieri had great joy. But, soon afterward, a strange humor took possession of him, namely, to put her patience to the trial by prolonged and intolerable hard tests: he began by afflicting her with his harsh words, putting on an angry air, and telling her that his vassals were most sorely dissatisfied with her because of her low birth. And especially now since they saw that she was a mother, they did nothing but make the most pitiful murmur at the birth of a daughter.

When Griselda heard these words, without the least change of countenance or sign of discomposure, she said, "My Lord, do with me as you may deem best for your own honor and comfort, for well I know that I am of less account than they, and unworthy of this honorable estate to which by your courtesy you have advanced me." Gualtieri was well pleased by this answer, knowing that she was in no degree puffed up with pride by his, or any other's, honorable respect for her.

A while afterwards, having told his wife in general terms that the vassals could not endure the daughter to whom she had given birth, he sent her a message by one of her servants. So the servant came to her and, with a very dolorous expression on his face and said, "Madam, as I value my life, I must carry out my Lord's command. He has bidden me take your daughter and..."

He could say no more, but from what the lady heard from his lips and read in his face, and remembered of her husband's words, she understood that he had been commanded to put the child to death. She then took the child from the cradle, and kissed and blessed her. She was very sore at heart, but she not changed in her countenance. She placed the girl in the servant's arms, saying, "Be sure that you leave nothing undone that my Lord and yours has charged you to do, but leave her not so that the beasts and the birds devour her, unless he has bidden this to you."

So the servant took the child and told Gualtieri what the lady had said; and Gualtieri, marveling at her constancy, sent him with the child to Bologna, to one of his kinswomen, whom he asked to raise and educate the child with great care, but never to let it be known whose child she was.

Soon afterward it happened that the lady again became pregnant and in due time gave birth to a son, at which Gualtieri was overjoyed. But, not content with what he had done, he now even more poignantly afflicted the lady. One day, with a ruffled appearance, he said to her, "Wife, since you gave birth to this boy, I may in no way live in peace with my vassals, so bitterly do they reproach me that a grandson of Giannucolo is to succeed me as their Lord. Therefore, I fear that, if I do not want to be driven out, I must do now as I did before, and in the end put you away and take another wife."

The lady heard him patiently, and answered only, "My honorable and gracious Lord, think only how you may content yourself and best please yourself, and waste no thought upon me, for there is nothing I desire except when I know that it is your pleasure."

Not many days after this, Gualtieri, in the same manner as he had sent for the daughter, sent for the son, and having made a show of putting him to death, provided for his, as for the girl's, well-being at Bologna. At this the lady showed no more discomposure in her expression or speech than at the loss of her daughter, which Gualtieri found more than strange. It affirmed to him that there was never another woman in the world that would have done so. And other than the fact that he had noticed that she was most tenderly affectionate towards her children, which was well pleasing to him, he had supposed that she was tired of them. He knew, however, that she was a truly virtuous mother and wisely able to endure with patience his severest impositions.

His subjects, who believed that he had put the children to death, held him mightily to blame for his cruelty and felt the utmost compassion for the lady. She, however, never said anything to the ladies who consoled her on the death of her children, except that the pleasure of the father of her children was her pleasure likewise.

Some years had passed since the girl's birth, when Gualtieri at length deemed the time come to put his wife's patience to the final proof. Accordingly, in the presence of a great company of his subjects he declared that in no way might he longer endure to have Griselda as his wife. He confessed that in taking her he had done a sorry thing, an act of a foolish young man, and that he therefore meant to do what he could to procure the Pope's dispensation to abandon Griselda and take another wife. With this he was much upbraided by many worthy men, but he made no other answer except that it must be so.

The lady, hearing this news and now deeming that she must look to go back to her poor father's house, and perhaps to tend the sheep, as she had once done, she came to understand that she would soon see him, to whom she was utterly devoted, loved by another woman. At this she grew sad inside, but still with the same composed appearance with which she had born Fortune's former buffets, she set herself to endure this last outrage. And it was not long before Gualtieri by counterfeit letters, which he arranged to be sent to him from Rome, made his subjects believe that the Pope had by these letters given him a dispensation to abandon Griselda away and take another wife.

Therefore, having ordered her to be brought before him, he said to her in the presence of many people, "Wife, by license granted me by the Pope, I am now free to abandon you, and take another wife; and, as my forbears have always been great gentlemen and lords of these parts, whereas yours have always been husbandmen, I intend that you go back to Giannucolo's house with the dowry that you brought me. After this I shall bring home a lady that I have found, and who is more suited in rank to be my wife and more pleasing to my people."

It was not without grief that the lady, as she heard this announcement, felt the great pain that any woman might feel at such a moment. Suppressing her tears, she answered, "My Lord, I have always known that my low degree was in no way congruous with your nobility, and I have always acknowledged that the rank I held with you was only through you and God, and I never made as if it were mine, or so esteem it, but only accounted it as a loan. It is your pleasure to recall it, and therefore it should be, and it is my pleasure to render it up to you.

So, here is your ring, with which you married me; take it back. You bid me take with me the dowry that I brought you; to do this will require neither paymaster on your part nor purse nor packhorse on mine; for I am not unmindful that I was naked when you first had me. And if you deem it appropriate that the body in which I have born children, begotten by you, should be beheld by all, naked will I depart. I pray you, nevertheless, if it please you, in reward for the virginity that I brought you and take not away, to allow me to bear hence upon my back a single shift – I crave no more – besides my dowry."

Gualtieri, whose heart wept, as his eyes would likewise have gladly yielded their natural tribute; hid everything with a pretended anger and said, "I allow you a shift to your back; so get you hence."

All that stood by begged him to give her a robe, so that she, who had been his wife for thirteen years and more, might not be seen to leave his house in so sorry and shameful a plight, having nothing on her but a shift. But their entreaties went for nothing: the lady in her shift, both barefoot and bareheaded, having bid them adieu, departed from the house, and went back to her father amid the tears and lamentations of all that saw her.

Giannucolo, who had always deemed it an incredible thing that Gualtieri should take his daughter as his wife and had looked for this abandonment to happen every day, had kept the clothes that she had taken off on the morning that Gualtieri had wedded her. He now brought them to her, and she, having put them on again, applied herself to the petty drudgery of her father's house, as she had been used to doing, enduring with fortitude this cruel visitation of adverse Fortune.

Now no sooner had Gualtieri dismissed Griselda than he gave his subjects to understand that he had taken as wife a daughter of one of the Counts of Panago. He accordingly made great preparations for the nuptials, during which he sent for Griselda. When she came, he said to her, "I am bringing here my new bride, and in this her first home-coming I intend to show her honor. You know that I have no women in this house that know how to set chambers in due order or to attend to the many other matters that so joyful an event requires. Therefore I sent for you to make the arrangements, as you know better than any other all the parts, provisions, and goods in the house and can set everything in such order as you shall think necessary. Invite such Ladies and Gentlemen as you may see fit, and receive them, as if you were the lady of the house. And when the wedding festivities have ended, you may go back to your cottage."

Although each of these words pierced Griselda's heart like a knife, since, in resigning her good fortune, she had not been able to renounce the love she bore Gualtieri, nevertheless she answered, "My Lord, I am ready and prompt to do your pleasure." And so, clad in the same sorry garments as she had worn in her father's house, she entered the house of Gualtieri, from which she had departed only a short time earlier in her shift. She began without delay to sweep the chambers, arrange the tapestries and cushions in the halls, prepare the kitchen, and set her hand to everything, as if she had been a common serving-wench. And she did not rest until she had brought everything into such proper and attractive appearance as the occasion demanded. This done, she invited in

Gualtieri's name all the ladies of those parts to be present at his nuptials, and awaited the event. The day having come, still wearing the sorry gray clothes of a commoner, but the heart and soul and demeanor of a lady, she received the ladies as they came and gave each a joyful greeting.

Now Gualtieri, as we said, had arranged for his two children to be carefully nurtured and brought up by a kinswoman of his at Bologna, who had married into the family of the Counts of Panago. Gualtieri had sent for his daughter, now twelve years old and the loveliest creature that ever was seen, and Gualtieri's son, having sent word to his kinswoman's husband at Bologna, praying him to please come with this girl and boy of his to Saluzzo, and to see that he brought a good and honorable company with him and to let all understand that he brought the girl to him as his wife, but in no way to disclose to any who she really was. The gentleman did as the Marquis asked him, and within a few days of his setting forth arrived at Saluzzo about breakfast-time with the girl, her brother, and a noble company, and found all the folk of those parts, and many other people as well, gathered there in expectation of Gualtieri's new bride.

The young woman, being received by the ladies, had no sooner come into the hall where the tables were seated than Griselda advanced to meet her, saying with hearty manner, "Welcome, my lady."

Then the ladies, who had with much instance, but in vain, begged Gualtieri either to let Griselda remain in another room or at any rate to furnish her with one of the robes that had been hers so that she might not present herself in such a sorry fashion before the strangers, were seated at the tables, where Griselda waited on them. The service having begun, the eyes of all were set on the girl, and every one said that Gualtieri had made an excellent exchange, and Griselda joined with the rest in greatly commending her, as did her little brother, though he did not know that she was his sister.

Now that Gualtieri was pleased at last with all that he had seen of his wife's patience, seeing that this new and strange turn made not the least alteration in her demeanor, and being well assured that it was not due to apathy or misunderstanding, for he knew her to be of excellent wisdom, deemed it time to relieve her of the suffering and give her such assurance as she ought to have.

Thus, having called her to him in presence of all the assembly, he said with a smile, "What do you think, Griselda, of our bride?"

"My Lord," replied Griselda, "I think mighty well of her; and if she is as discreet as she is beautiful – and so I believer her to be – I have no doubt that you may plan to lead with her a life of incomparable happiness. But with all earnestness I entreat you that you spare her those tribulations which you did once inflict upon another that was yours, for I scarce think she would be able to bear them as well because she is younger and she has been delicately nurtured, whereas the other had known no reprieve from hardship in her early life."

Seeing that Griselda had no doubt that the girl was to be his wife, and yet spoke never a bit less sweetly, Gualtieri asked her to sit down beside him, and he said, "Griselda, it is now time that you see the reward of your long patience, and that those, who have deemed me cruel and unjust and insensate should know that what I did was done with premeditated purpose. I intended to give both you and them a lesson, so that you might learn to be a wife, that they in like manner might learn how to take and keep a wife, and that I might gain perpetual peace with you for the rest of my life. Being in great fear when I came to take a wife, lest I should be disappointed, I therefore, to put the matter to the test, did – and how sorely you know – harass and afflict you. And since I never knew you either by deed or by word to deviate from my will, I now, deeming myself to have of you that assurance of happiness which I desired, intend to restore to you at once all that, step by step, I took from you, and by extremity of joy to compensate the tribulations that I inflicted on you. Receive, then, this girl, whom you suppose to be my bride, and her brother, with glad heart, as your children and mine. These are they, whom by you and many another it has long been supposed that I put ruthlessly to death. And I am your husband, who loves you more dearly than anything else, deeming that there is no man living could be as happy with his wife as I am."

Having said this, he embraced and kissed her; and then, while she wept for joy, they rose and hurried to sit with her daughter, who, like her brother, was greatly astonished at so rare a development. She embraced both of them tenderly, thus dispelling their confusion as well as that of many others who were present. Seeing this, the ladies, transported with delight, rose from table and brought Griselda to a chamber, and, with a much better view of the affair, divested her of her sorry garb and arrayed her in one of her own noble garments. And so, in guise of a lady (even though in her rags she had seemed no less), they led her back into the hall.

Wondrous was the joy which they shared with the children; and, entirely overjoyed at the event, they reveled and made great merry, and prolonged the festivities for several days. And they all pronounced Gualtieri to be very discreet, though they censured as intolerable the harsh probation to which he had subjected Griselda, and they accounted Griselda most discreet beyond all compare.

Some days afterward, the Count of Panago returned to Bologna, and Gualtieri took Giannucolo from his husbandry and established him in honor as his father-in-law, in which great comfort he lived for the rest of his days. Gualtieri himself, having matched his daughter with a husband of high degree, lived long and happily thereafter with Griselda, to whom he always paid great honor.

Now what shall we say in this case except that even into the cots of the poor the heavens let fall at times god-like spirits, as into the palaces of kings souls that are fitter to tend hogs than to exercise lordship over men? Who but Griselda had been able, with a tearless and cheerful countenance, to endure the hard and unheard-of trials to which Gualtieri subjected her?

It might have served Gualtieri right if he had married the kind of woman who, once driven out of her home in nothing but a shift, would have found another man to warm her robes in order to get herself a nice-looking dress out of the affair!

147

CB8O

Conclusion to the Tale of Griselda
Petrarch (Francesco Petrarca), 1373

TRANSLATED BY ROBERT D. FRENCH. ADAPTED BY GERARD P. NECASTRO

Almost out of her wits for joy and beside herself with maternal love, on hearing these words. Griselda rushed into her children's arms, shedding the most joyous tears. She wearied them with kisses and bedewed them with her loving tears. And straightway the ladies gathered about her with alacrity and affection; and when her vile apparel had been stripped off her, they clothed her in her accustomed garments and adorned her. The most joyous plaudits and auspicious words from all the throng resounded all about; and the day was the most renowned that ever was for its great joy and sorrow – more renowned, even, than the day of her nuptials dad been.

Many years later they lived in great peace and concord; and Gualtieri, who had appeared to neglect his father-in-law, lest he should stand in the way of the experiment Gualtieri had conceived, had the old man moved into the palace and held him in honor. He gave his own daughter in noble and honorable marriage, and his son he left behind him as his heir, happy in his wife and in his offspring.

This story it has seemed good to me to weave anew, in another tongue, not so much that it might stir the matrons of our times to imitate the patience of his wife – who seems to me scarcely imitable – as that it might stir all those who read it to imitate the woman's steadfastness, at least; so that they may have the resolution to perform for God what this woman performed for her husband. For God cannot be tempted by evil, as James the Apostle[1] says, and God himself tempts no man. Nevertheless God often tests us and allows us to be vexed with many a grievous scourge; not that He may know our spirit, for that he knew before we were made, but that our own frailty may be known to us through notable private signs. Therefore, I would assuredly enter on the list of steadfast men the name of anyone who endured for his God, without a murmur, what this obscure woman endured for her mortal husband.

---

[1] James. Author of the New Testament Book of James.

ᏮᏞᏋᎦ

Conclusion to the Tale of Griselda
Geoffrey Chaucer, 1390s
TRANSLATED BY GERARD P. NECASTRO

Chaucer inserted the Tale of Griselda into The Canterbury Tales, *where it is retold by the Clerk (the scholar). The Clerk uses it to repudiate the Wife of Bath, who has argued that women ought to be given complete control over men in marriage.*

Walter and Griselda lived together for many years in great happiness, peace, and agreement. Walter married his daughter richly to one of the finest lords in all of Italy, and Griselda's father was kept in peace and quiet at the court until the soul left his body. The son succeeded to his inheritance in peace and accord after Walter's day, and he was also fortunate in marriage, though he put his wife to no great test.

The world is not so strong, there is no denying it, as it was in olden times; listen, therefore to what my author[1] says: This story was not told so that wives will follow Griselda's example in humility, for that would be intolerable even if they wanted to, but so that everyone, according to his station, will be steadfast in adversity as Griselda was. It was with this purpose that Petrarch wrote this story, which is set down in high style. Since one woman was so patient towards a mortal man, the more we should receive with patience all that God sends us, for it is reasonable that He should test those whom He created. However, He will not tempt anyone whom he had redeemed, as St. James will tell you if you read his epistle. Undoubtedly God tests folk every day and causes us often to in various ways, for our own good, with the sharp lashes of adversity – not so He may know our qualities, for surely He knew all our weaknesses before we were ever born. His arrangements are all for our profit; let us live then in virtuous patience.

Hear but one more word, ladies and gentlemen, before I stop. Nowadays it would be very hard to find two or three like Griselda in a whole town. For if they were put to such tests, their gold is so badly alloyed with brass[2] that, though the coin appears to be good, it is more likely to break in two than bend. And so, because of my affection for the Wife of Bath – may God keep her and all her sex in supremacy: it would be a pity otherwise – with all lusty spirit, fresh and vigorous, I shall sing you a song which I think will please you. So let us stop this serious talk; listen to my song which goes like this:

At this point, something unusual happens to the text. Instead of getting the merry tune that we have been promised, we get something else. It is usually titled "Chaucer's Envoy."[3] Though it is possible that it was originally planned as an interruption by the Wife of Bath,[4] it is more likely a speech in which the Clerk

---

[1] My author. My source for this tale.

[2] Gold is so badly alloyed with brass. In other words, they are not pure or made entirely of the best elements.

[3] Envoy. Usually a short song of parting in which the poet tells his poem to fly off to his intended audience.

mocks the Wife and the advice that she has given to women a bit earlier in The Canterbury Tales. *In this case, we can take the following passage as being simultaneously serious and ridiculous.*

Griselda is dead, and her patience, too, and both are buried together in Italy. Therefore, I openly declare that no married man should be so harsh as to try his wife's patience in hope of finding another Griselda, for he shall certainly fail.

Oh, noble wives, full of high wisdom, let no humility nail down your tongue, and let no scholar have cause or reason to write so marvelous a story about you as the tale of patient Griselda, lest Chichevache,[1] the cow, swallow you into her belly. Follow the example of Echo,[2] who never keeps quiet but always answers back. Don't be tricked in your innocence; take the control into your own hands. Engrave this lesson deeply in your memories, for it will work to the common profit of mankind.

You wives, strong as big camels, stand up for your own rights; don't allow men to do injustices to you. And weak wives, feeble in battle, be fierce as a tiger, yonder in India; always chatter like a windmill, I advise you. Don't fear men or pay them respect, for though your husband may be dressed in armor, the arrows of your crabbed eloquence will pierce his breast and his helmet. I advise you to bind him with jealousy and you will make him cower like a quail. If you are pretty, show your face and your dress in company; if you are ugly, be unusually generous; always work hard to make friends. Be as gay in spirit as a linden leaf, and let him worry and weep, wring his hands and wail!

---

[4] Interruption by the Wife of Bath. This sort of interruption is fairly common throughout *The Canterbury Tales*. The Wife's advice to women earlier in *The Canterbury Tales* included the very strategies that the Clerk is about to name.

[1] Chichevache the cow. A lean cow fabled to have fed on patient wives, so it consequently (so the story goes) had little to eat.

[2] Echo. Mythological figure whose voice repeated the end of each of her utterances.

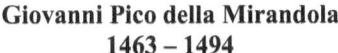

Giovanni Pico della Mirandola
1463 – 1494

During the Renaissance, the re-awakened interest in Greek and Latin writers provided such scholars as Giovanni Pico della Mirandola (usually referred to simply as Pico) with classical ideas of human dignity and human capability. Such Greeks as Plato and Aristotle contributed to the foundation of Renaissance humanism with their faith that the intellect can understand this world and how to live in it, and that humans are capable of working out their destinies.

Pico described himself as an explorer, and his depth of learning led him to value not only human potential, but also the wisdom of all ages and cultures. He believed that beneath the seeming differences of various philosophical and religious traditions there was a unitary thread binding them together. At the very center of this intellectual complex were his ideas about the dignity of human beings, ideas that became the standard for Renaissance humanism.

ଓଈଔ

On the Dignity of Man
Giovanni Pico della Mirandola, 1486
TRANSLATED BY THEODORE GRACYK

Most esteemed Fathers, I have read in the ancient writings of the Arabians that Abdala the Saracen on being asked what, on this stage, so to say, of the world, seemed to him most evocative of wonder. He replied that there was nothing to be seen more marvelous than man. As I reflected upon the basis assigned for these estimations, I was not fully persuaded by the diverse reasons advanced for the pre-eminence of human nature; that man is the intermediary between creatures, that he is the familiar of the gods above him as he is the lord of the beings beneath him...At long last, however, I feel that I have come to some understanding of why man is the most fortunate of living things and, consequently, deserving of all admiration...Hear then, oh Fathers, precisely what this condition of man is; and in the name of your humanity, grant me your benign audition as I pursue this theme.

God the Father, the Mightiest Architect, had already raised, according to the precepts of His hidden wisdom, this world we see, the cosmic dwelling of divinity, a temple most august. He had already adorned the super-celestial region with Intelligences, infused the heavenly globes with the life of immortal souls and set the fermenting dung-heap of the inferior world teeming with every form of animal life. But when this work was done, the Divine Artisan still longed for some creature which might comprehend the meaning of so vast an achievement, which might be moved with love at its beauty and smitten with awe at its grandeur....The truth was, however, that there remained no archetype according to which He might fashion a new offspring, nor in His treasure-houses the wherewithal to endow a new son with a fitting inheritance, nor any place, among the seats of the universe, where this new creature might dispose himself to contemplate the world. All space was already filled; all things had been distributed in the highest, the middle and the lowest orders. Still, it was not in the nature of the power of the Father to fail in this last creative élan; nor was it in the nature of that supreme Wisdom to hesitate through lack of counsel in so crucial a matter; nor, finally, in the nature of His beneficent love to compel the creature destined to praise the divine generosity in all other things to find it wanting in himself.

At last, the Supreme Maker decreed that this creature, to whom He could give nothing wholly his own, should have a share in the particular endowment of every other creature. Taking man, therefore, this creature of indeterminate image, He set him in the middle of the world and thus spoke to him: "We have given you, O Adam, no visage proper to yourself, nor endowment properly your own, in order that whatever place, whatever form, whatever gifts you may, with premeditation, select, these same you may have and possess through your own judgment and decision. The nature of all other creatures is defined and restricted within laws which We have laid down; you, by contrast, impeded by no such restrictions, may, by your own free will, to whose custody We have assigned you, trace for yourself the lineaments of your own nature. I have placed you at the very center of the world, so that from that vantage point you may with greater ease glance round about you on all that the world contains. We have made you a creature neither of heaven nor of earth, neither mortal nor immortal, in order that you may, as the free and proud shaper of your own being, fashion yourself in the form you may prefer. It will be in your power to descend to the lower, brutish forms of life; you will be able, through your own decision, to rise again to the superior orders whose life is divine...."

But what is the purpose of all this? That we may understand – since we have been born into this condition of being what we choose to be – that we ought to be sure above all else that it may never be said against us that, born to a high position, we failed to appreciate it, but fell instead to the estate of brutes and uncomprehending beasts of burden; and that the saying of Aspah the Prophet, "You are all Gods and sons of the Most High," might rather be true; and finally that we may not, through abuse of the generosity of a most indulgent Father, pervert the free option which he has given us from a saving to a damning gift. Let a certain saving ambition invade our souls so that, impatient of mediocrity, we pant after the highest things and (since, if we will, we can) bend all our efforts to their attainment. Let us disdain things of earth, hold as little worth even the astral orders and, putting behind us all the things of this world, hasten to that court beyond the world, closest to the most exalted Godhead. There, as the sacred mysteries tell us, the Seraphim, Cherubim and Thrones occupy the first places; but, unable to yield to them, and impatient of any second place, let us emulate their dignity and glory. And, if we will it, we shall be inferior to them in nothing.

Michel Eyquem de Montaigne
1533 – 1592

Michel Eyquem de Montaigne was a well-educated French aristocrat who served as a lawyer, court counselor, royal counselor, and diplomat and occasionally found himself, because his positions sometimes clashed with those in power, in difficult situations, even at times imprisoned.

He is best remembered for his massive volume of essays, simply referred to at the *Essais* (or *Essays*). He coined the term *essay*, which literally means an "attempt," and spent much of his life crafting these works. His encyclopedic knowledge and his thorough penetration of a broad spectrum of subjects from education and glory to cannibalism and drunkenness had great influence not only in France, but also in England, where his works were quoted by William Shakespeare and imitated by Francis Bacon.

ᘓᘔ

Of Repentance
Michel de Montaigne, 1580s
TRANSLATED BY CHARLES COTTON

The selection below is the first part of a much longer essay.

Others form man; I only report him: and represent a particular one, ill fashioned enough, and whom, if I had to model him anew, I should certainly make something else than what he is: but that's past recalling. Now, though the features of my picture alter and change, 'tis not, however, unlike: the world eternally turns round; all things therein are incessantly moving, the earth, the rocks of Caucasus, and the pyramids of Egypt, both by the public motion and their own. Even constancy itself is no other but a slower and more languishing motion. I cannot fix my object; 'tis always tottering and reeling by a natural giddiness: I take it as it is at the instant I consider it; I do not paint its being, I paint its passage; not a passing from one age to another, or, as the people say, from seven to seven years, but from day to day, from minute to minute.

I must accommodate my history to the hour: I may presently change, not only by fortune, but also by intention. 'Tis a counterpart of various and changeable accidents, and of irresolute imaginations, and, as it falls out, sometimes contrary: whether it be that I am then another self, or that I take subjects by other circumstances and considerations: so it is, that I may peradventure contradict myself, but, as Demades said, I never contradict the truth. Could my soul once take footing, I would not essay but resolve: but it is always learning and making trial.

I propose a life ordinary and without luster: 'tis all one; all moral philosophy may as well be applied to a common and private life, as to one of richer composition: every man carries the entire form of human condition. Authors communicate themselves to the people by some especial and extrinsic mark; I, the first of any, by my universal being; as Michel de Montaigne, not as a grammarian, a poet, or a lawyer. If the world find fault that I speak too much of myself, I find fault that they do not so much as think of themselves. But is it reason, that being so particular in my way of living, I should pretend to recommend myself to the public knowledge? And is it also reason that I should produce to the world, where art and handling have so much credit and authority, crude and simple effects of nature, and of a weak nature to boot? Is it not to build a wall without stone or brick, or some such thing, to write books without learning and without art? The fancies of music are carried on by art; mine by chance.

Martin Luther
1483 – 1546

Martin Luther was the central figure in the Reformation, an effort to reform the Roman Catholic Church from its many abuses. It began when Martin Luther, an Augustinian monk, shocked by the Church's corrupt practice of selling indulgences for saving souls, the worship of images and relics, and the proliferation of saints, wrote ninety-five theses of protest and nailed them on the church door in Wittenberg on October 31, 1517.

Luther, who taught theology at the University of Wittenberg, had discovered in Paul's letter to the Romans the doctrine that humans are justified by faith alone – not by works, not by priestly mediation, not by sacraments, and not by church membership. For Luther, reason and scripture were the keys to faith and thus to salvation.

Luther's defiance of the Church led to open confrontations. In 1520 he was called to the Diet of Worms (a hearing in the southwestern German city of Worms). Luther defended his writings to a crowded hall, giving the famous speech included below. Luther was declared a heretic, but thanks to Frederick the Wise of Saxony there was no further action. Luther went on to establish the Lutheran Church and live a rather calm life with his wife and children.

Major Works
Freedom of a Christian (1519)
On Good Works (1520)
Babylonian Captivity of the Church (1520)
Against the Murderous, Thieving Hordes of Peasants (1525)
On the Jews and Their Lies (1543)
The Luther Bible (Translation 1522, 1534)

ෆ৪৯

Speech at the Diet of Worms (Here I Stand)
Martin Luther, 1520
TRANSLATED BY CHARLES DUDLEY WARNER

"Most serene emperor, most illustrious princes, most clement lords, obedient to the time set for me yesterday evening, I appear before you, beseeching you, by the mercy of God, that your most serene majesty and your most illustrious lord-ships may deign to listen graciously to this my cause – which is, as I hope, a cause of justice and of truth. If through my inexperience I have either not given the proper titles to some, or have offended in some manner against court-customs and etiquette, I beseech you to kindly pardon me, as a man accustomed not to counts but to the cells of monks. I can bear no other witness about myself but that I have taught and written up to this time with simplicity of heart, as I had in view only the glory of God and the sound instruction of Christ's faithful.

"Most serene emperor, most illustrious princes, concerning those questions proposed to me yesterday on behalf of your serene majesty, whether I acknowledged as mine the books enumerated and published in my name and whether I wished to persevere in their defense or to retract them, I have given to the first question my full and complete answer, in which I still persist and shall persist forever. These books are mine and they have been published in my name by me, unless in the meantime, either through the craft or the mistaken wisdom of my emulators, something in them has been changed or wrongly cut out. For plainly I cannot acknowledge anything except what is mine alone and what has been written by me alone, to the exclusion of all interpretations of anyone at all.

"In replying to the second question, I ask that your most serene majesty and your lordships may deign to note that my books are not all of the same kind.

"For there are some in which I have discussed religious faith and morals simply and evangelically, so that even my enemies themselves are compelled to admit that these are useful, harmless, and clearly worthy to be read by Christians. Even the bull,[1] although harsh and cruel, admits that some of my books are inoffensive, and yet allows these also to be condemned with a judgment which is utterly monstrous. Thus, if I should begin to disavow them, I ask you, what would I be doing? Would not 1, alone of all men, be condemning the very truth upon which friends and enemies equally agree, striving alone against the harmonious confession of all?

"Another group of my books attacks the papacy and the affairs of the papists as those who both by their doctrines and very wicked examples have laid waste the Christian world with evil that affects the spirit and the body. For no one can deny or conceal this fact, when the experience of all and the complaints of everyone witness that through the decrees of the pope and the doctrines of men the consciences of the faithful have been most miserably entangled, tortured, and torn to pieces. Also, property and possessions, especially in this illustrious nation of Germany, have been devoured by an unbelievable tyranny and are being devoured to this time without letup and by unworthy means. [Yet

---

[1] Bull. A formal declaration authored by the pope.

the papists,] by their own decrees, warn that the papal laws and doctrines which are contrary to the gospel or the opinions of the fathers are to be regarded as erroneous and reprehensible.

"If, therefore, I should have retracted these writings, I should have done nothing other than to have added strength to this [papal] tyranny and I should have opened not only windows but also doors to such great godlessness. It would rage farther and more freely than ever it has dared up to this time. Yes, from the proof of such a revocation on my part, their wholly lawless and unrestrained kingdom of wickedness would become still more intolerable for the already wretched people; and their rule would be further strengthened and established, especially if it should be reported that this evil deed had been done by me by virtue of the authority of your most serene majesty and of the whole Roman Empire. Good God! What a cover for wickedness and tyranny I should have then become.

"I have written a third sort of book against some private and (as they say) distinguished individuals-those, namely, who strive to preserve the Roman tyranny and to destroy the godliness taught by me. Against these I confess I have been more violent than my religion or profession demands. But then, I do not set myself up as a saint; neither am I disputing about my life, but about the teaching of Christ. It is not proper for me to retract these works, because by this retraction it would again happen that tyranny and godlessness would, with my patronage, rule and rage among the people of God more violently than ever before.

"However, because I am a man and not God, I am not able to shield my books with any other protection than that which my Lord Jesus Christ himself offered for his teaching. When questioned before Annas about his teaching and struck by a servant, he said: 'If I have spoken wrongly, bear witness to the wrong' [John 18:19-23]. If the Lord himself, who knew that he could not err, did not refuse to hear testimony against his teaching, even from the lowliest servant, how much more ought I, who am the lowest scum and able to do nothing except err, desire and expect that somebody should want to offer testimony against my teaching! Therefore, I ask by the mercy of God, may your most serene majesty, most illustrious lordships, or anyone at all who is able, either high or low, bear witness, expose my errors, overthrowing them by the writings of the prophets and the evangelists. Once I have been taught I shall be quite ready to renounce every error, and I shall be the first to cast my books into the fire.

"From these remarks I think it is clear that I have sufficiently considered and weighed the hazards and dangers, as well as the excitement and dissensions aroused in the world as a result of my teachings, things about which I was gravely and forcefully warned yesterday. To see excitement and dissension arise because of the Word of God is to me clearly the most joyful aspect of all in these matters. For this is the way, the opportunity, and the result of the Word of God, just as He [Christ] said, 'I have not come to bring peace, but a sword. For I have come to set a man against his father,' etc. [Matt. 10:34-35]. Therefore, we ought to think how marvelous and terrible is our God in his counsels, lest by chance what is attempted for settling strife grows rather into an intolerable deluge of evils, if we begin by condemning the Word of God. And concern must be shown lest the reign of this most noble youth, Prince Charles (in whom after God is our great hope), become unhappy and inauspicious.

"I could illustrate this with abundant examples from Scripture – like Pharaoh, the king of Babylon, and the kings of Israel who, when they endeavored to pacify and strengthen their kingdoms by the wisest counsels, most surely destroyed themselves. For it is He who takes the wise in their own craftiness [Job 5:13] and overturns mountains before they know it [Job 9:5]. Therefore we must fear God. I do not say these things because there is a need of either my teachings or my warnings for such leaders as you, but because I must not withhold the allegiance which I owe my Germany. With these words I commend myself to your most serene majesty and to your lordships, humbly asking that I not be allowed through the agitation of my enemies, without cause, to be made hateful to you. I have finished."

When I had finished,[1] the speaker for the emperor said, as if in reproach, that I had not answered the question, that I ought not call into question those things which had been condemned and defined in councils; therefore what was sought from me was not a horned response, but a simple one, whether or not I wished to retract.

Here I answered: "Since then your serene majesty and your lordships seek a simple answer, I will give it in this manner, neither horned nor toothed: Unless I am convinced by the testimony of the Scriptures or by clear reason (for I do not trust either in the pope or in councils alone, since it is well known that they have often erred and contradicted themselves), I am bound by the Scriptures I have quoted and my conscience is captive to the Word of God. I cannot and I will not retract anything, since it is neither safe nor right to go against conscience.

"I cannot do otherwise, here I stand, may God help me, Amen."

---

[1] When I had finished. There is a break in the speech here because this reading is actually an excerpt from Luther's own account of the proceedings.

William Shakespeare
1564 – 1616

William Shakespeare is largely recognized as the greatest writer in the world, if not one of the very best. "The bard of Avon," still the most popular writer in the world, authored no less than thirty-seven plays, 154 sonnets, and three extended narrative poems, and ran the most successful theatre in Renaissance England.

His plays include comedies, histories, tragedies, romances, and "problem plays": the comedies range from farces such as *The Comedy of Errors* and *The Merry Wives of Windsor* to more philosophical plays like *As You Like It* and *Twelfth Night*; the tragedies include some of the most famous works in the world, *Romeo and Juliet*, *Hamlet*, *Othello*, *Macbeth*, and *King Lear*; and the history plays, which cover England's history from the late 1300s to the early 1500s, bring historical figures such as *Henry V* and *Richard III* to life in a way that no other writer has.

Many of Shakespeare's plays are difficult to classify, as he tinkered with the genres of drama, mixing elements of comedy into tragedies and histories, and tragedy into comedy and history: we laugh in the middle of *Romeo and Juliet* and *1 Henry IV*, and we are saddened at the end of *Richard II* and *Love's Labour's Lost*. His romances such as *Cymbeline* are a mixture of comedy, tragedy, and history; and his "problem plays," for example, *The Merchant of Venice*, so called because they seem to illustrate or discuss certain problems, are also mixes of different genres.

Shakespeare's achievement goes beyond the volume and variety of his works. Like his contemporary Christopher Marlowe, Shakespeare brought a new dimension of realism to the stage, creating characters that were not generalized types, but complex and often contradictory individual beings. Shakespeare also pushed the English language to new limits, crafting not only beautiful language, but language suited to every occasion; and when the language was insufficient he created new words, over 2000 of them.

As most courses in the Humanities will include a Shakespearean play, this volume does not present one. Instead, it includes only a few abbreviated scenes from *Romeo and Juliet* and *Hamlet* as well as a couple of his most famous sonnets.

Shakespeare's Plays

1589 *Comedy of Errors*
1590 *Henry VI, Part II*
1590 *Henry VI, Part III*
1591 *Henry VI, Part I*
1592 *Richard III*
1593 *Taming of the Shrew*
1593 *Titus Andronicus*
1594 *Romeo and Juliet*
1594 *Two Gentlemen of Verona*
1594 *Love's Labour's Lost*
1595 *Richard II*
1595 *Midsummer Night's Dream*
1596 *King John*
1596 *Merchant of Venice*
1597 *Henry IV, Part I*
1597 *Henry IV, Part II*
1598 *Henry V*
1598 *Much Ado about Nothing*
1599 *Twelfth Night*
1599 *As You Like It*
1599 *Julius Caesar*
1600 *Hamlet*
1600 *Merry Wives of Windsor*
1601 *Troilus and Cressida*
1602 *All's Well That Ends Well*
1604 *Othello*
1604 *Measure for Measure*
1605 *King Lear*
1605 *Macbeth*
1606 *Antony and Cleopatra*
1607 *Coriolanus*
1607 *Timon of Athens*
1608 *Pericles*
1609 *Cymbeline*
1610 *Winter's Tale*
1611 *Tempest*
1612 *Henry VIII*

Other Shakespeare Works

1593 Venus and Adonis
1594 The Rape of Lucrece
1609 The Lover's Complaint

161

Romeo and Juliet – Selected Passages
William Shakespeare, 1594

Act 1, Scene 5 (Romeo and Juliet's first meeting)

ROMEO If I profane with my unworthiest hand
This holy shrine, the gentle fine is this:
My lips, two blushing pilgrims, ready stand
To smooth that rough touch with a tender kiss.

JULIET Good pilgrim, you do wrong your hand too much,
Which mannerly devotion shows in this;
For saints have hands that pilgrims' hands do touch,
And palm to palm is holy palmers' kiss.

ROMEO Have not saints lips, and holy palmers too?

JULIET Ay, pilgrim, lips that they must use in prayer.

ROMEO O, then, dear saint, let lips do what hands do;
They pray, grant thou, lest faith turn to despair.

JULIET Saints do not move, though grant for prayers' sake.

ROMEO Then move not, while my prayer's effect I take.
Thus from my lips, by yours, my sin is purged.

JULIET Then have my lips the sin that they have took.

ROMEO Sin from thy lips? O trespass sweetly urged!
Give me my sin again.

JULIET You kiss by the book.

* * *

JULIET Wilt thou be gone? it is not yet near day:
It was the nightingale, and not the lark,
That pierced the fearful hollow of thine ear;
Nightly she sings on yon pomegranate-tree:
Believe me, love, it was the nightingale.

ROMEO It was the lark, the herald of the morn,
No nightingale: look, love, what envious streaks
Do lace the severing clouds in yonder east:
Night's candles are burnt out, and jocund day
Stands tiptoe on the misty mountain tops.
I must be gone and live, or stay and die.

JULIET Yon light is not day-light, I know it, I:
It is some meteor that the sun exhales,
To be to thee this night a torch-bearer,

And light thee on thy way to Mantua:
Therefore stay yet; thou need'st not to be gone.

ROMEO Let me be ta'en, let me be put to death;
I am content, so thou wilt have it so.
I'll say yon grey is not the morning's eye,
'Tis but the pale reflex of Cynthia's brow;
Nor that is not the lark, whose notes do beat
The vaulty heaven so high above our heads:
I have more care to stay than will to go:
Come, death, and welcome! Juliet wills it so.
How is't, my soul? let's talk; it is not day.

JULIET It is, it is: hie hence, be gone, away!
It is the lark that sings so out of tune,
Straining harsh discords and unpleasing sharps.
Some say the lark makes sweet division;
This doth not so, for she divideth us:
Some say the lark and loathed toad change eyes,
O, now I would they had changed voices too!
Since arm from arm that voice doth us affray,
Hunting thee hence with hunt's-up to the day,
O, now be gone; more light and light it grows.

☙❧

Hamlet – Selected Passages
William Shakespeare, 1600

Act 1, Scene 3

POLONIUS Yet here, Laertes! aboard, aboard, for shame!
The wind sits in the shoulder of your sail,
And you are stay'd for. There; my blessing with thee!
And these few precepts in thy memory
See thou character. Give thy thoughts no tongue,
Nor any unproportioned thought his act.
Be thou familiar, but by no means vulgar.
Those friends thou hast, and their adoption tried,
Grapple them to thy soul with hoops of steel;
But do not dull thy palm with entertainment
Of each new-hatch'd, unfledged comrade. Beware
Of entrance to a quarrel, but being in,
Bear't that the opposed may beware of thee.
Give every man thy ear, but few thy voice;
Take each man's censure, but reserve thy judgment.
Costly thy habit as thy purse can buy,
But not express'd in fancy; rich, not gaudy;
For the apparel oft proclaims the man,

And they in France of the best rank and station
Are of a most select and generous chief in that.
Neither a borrower nor a lender be;
For loan oft loses both itself and friend,
And borrowing dulls the edge of husbandry.
This above all: to thine ownself be true,
And it must follow, as the night the day,
Thou canst not then be false to any man.
Farewell: my blessing season this in thee!

* * *

Act 2, Scene 2

GUILDENSTERN My lord, we were sent for.

HAMLET I will tell you why; so shall my anticipation
prevent your discovery, and your secrecy to the king
and queen moult no feather. I have of late – but
wherefore I know not – lost all my mirth, forgone all
custom of exercises; and indeed it goes so heavily
with my disposition that this goodly frame, the
earth, seems to me a sterile promontory, this most
excellent canopy, the air, look you, this brave
o'erhanging firmament, this majestical roof fretted
with golden fire, why, it appears no other thing to
me than a foul and pestilent congregation of vapours.
What a piece of work is a man! how noble in reason!
how infinite in faculty! in form and moving how
express and admirable! in action how like an angel!
in apprehension how like a god! the beauty of the
world! the paragon of animals! And yet, to me,
what is this quintessence of dust? man delights not
me: no, nor woman neither, though by your smiling
you seem to say so.

* * *

(Later in the same scene, a description of the players)

POLONIUS The best actors in the world, either for tragedy,
comedy, history, pastoral, pastoral-comical,
historical-pastoral, tragical-historical, tragical-
comical-historical-pastoral, scene individable, or
poem unlimited: Seneca cannot be too heavy, nor
Plautus too light. For the law of writ and the
liberty, these are the only men.

* * *

Act 3, Scene 1

HAMLET To be, or not to be: that is the question:
Whether 'tis nobler in the mind to suffer
The slings and arrows of outrageous fortune,
Or to take arms against a sea of troubles,
And by opposing end them? To die: to sleep;
No more; and by a sleep to say we end
The heart-ache and the thousand natural shocks
That flesh is heir to, 'tis a consummation
Devoutly to be wish'd. To die, to sleep;
To sleep: perchance to dream: ay, there's the rub;
For in that sleep of death what dreams may come
When we have shuffled off this mortal coil,
Must give us pause: there's the respect
That makes calamity of so long life;
For who would bear the whips and scorns of time,
The oppressor's wrong, the proud man's contumely,
The pangs of despised love, the law's delay,
The insolence of office and the spurns
That patient merit of the unworthy takes,
When he himself might his quietus make
With a bare bodkin? who would fardels bear,
To grunt and sweat under a weary life,
But that the dread of something after death,
The undiscover'd country from whose bourn
No traveller returns, puzzles the will
And makes us rather bear those ills we have
Than fly to others that we know not of?
Thus conscience does make cowards of us all;
And thus the native hue of resolution
Is sicklied o'er with the pale cast of thought,
And enterprises of great pith and moment
With this regard their currents turn awry,
And lose the name of action. – Soft you now!
The fair Ophelia! Nymph, in thy orisons
Be all my sins remember'd.

* * *

Act 3, Scene 2

HAMLET Speak the speech, I pray you, as I pronounced
it to you, trippingly on the tongue: but if you mouth it,
as many of your players do, I had as lief the
town-crier spoke my lines. Nor do not saw the air
too much with your hand, thus, but use all gently;

for in the very torrent, tempest, and, as I may say,
the whirlwind of passion, you must acquire and beget
a temperance that may give it smoothness. O, it
offends me to the soul to hear a robustious
periwig-pated fellow tear a passion to tatters, to
very rags, to split the ears of the groundlings, who
for the most part are capable of nothing but
inexplicable dumbshows and noise: I would have such
a fellow whipped for o'erdoing Termagant; it
out-herods Herod: pray you, avoid it.

FIRST PLAYER I warrant your honour.

HAMLET Be not too tame neither, but let your own discretion
be your tutor: suit the action to the word, the
word to the action; with this special o'erstep not
the modesty of nature: for any thing so overdone is
from the purpose of playing, whose end, both at the
first and now, was and is, to hold, as 'twere, the
mirror up to nature; to show virtue her own feature,
scorn her own image, and the very age and body of
the time his form and pressure. Now this overdone,
or come tardy off, though it make the unskilful
laugh, cannot but make the judicious grieve; the
censure of the which one must in your allowance
o'erweigh a whole theatre of others. O, there be
players that I have seen play, and heard others
praise, and that highly, not to speak it profanely,
that, neither having the accent of Christians nor
the gait of Christian, pagan, nor man, have so
strutted and bellowed that I have thought some of
nature's journeymen had made men and not made them
well, they imitated humanity so abominably.

* * *

Act 5, Scene 2

HORATIO If your mind dislike any thing, obey it: I will
forestall their repair hither, and say you are not

HAMLET Not a whit, we defy augury: there's a special
providence in the fall of a sparrow. If it be now,
'tis not to come; if it be not to come, it will be
now; if it be not now, yet it will come: the
readiness is all: since no man has aught of what he
leaves, what is't to leave betimes?

ೞೞ
Selected Sonnets

Sonnet XVIII
William Shakespeare, 1590s

Shall I compare thee to a summer's day?
Thou art more lovely and more temperate:
Rough winds do shake the darling buds of May,
And summer's lease hath all too short a date:[1]
5   Sometime too hot the eye of heaven shines,
And often is his gold complexion dimm'd,
And every fair from fair[2] sometime declines,
By chance, or nature's changing course untrimm'd:[3]
But thy eternal summer shall not fade,
10   Nor lose possession of that fair thou ow'st,[4]
Nor shall death brag thou wander'st in his shade,
When in eternal lines to time thou grow'st,[5]
So long as men can breathe, or eyes can see,
So long lives this, and this gives life to thee.

ೞೞ
Sonnet CXXX
William Shakespeare, 1590s

My mistress' eyes are nothing like the sun;
Coral is far more red, than her lips red:
If snow be white, why then her breasts are dun;[6]
If hairs be wires,[7] black wires grow on her head.
5   I have seen roses damask'd,[8] red and white,
But no such roses see I in her cheeks;
And in some perfumes is there more delight
Than in the breath that from my mistress reeks.[9]
I love to hear her speak, yet well I know
10   That music hath a far more pleasing sound:
I grant I never saw a goddess go,[10] –
My mistress, when she walks, treads on the ground:
And yet by heaven, I think my love as rare,
As any she belied[11] with false compare.[12]

---

[1] Too short a date. I.e., too soon of an ending date.
[2] Fair from fair. Beautiful thing from beauty.
[3] Changing course untrimm'd. I.e., its orientation taken away.
[4] Thou ow'st. Which you own(est).
[5] Grow'st. Grow into, or become grafted upn.
[6] Dun. Dull grey or brown.
[7] Wires. Filament, as of gold.
[8] Damask'd. Variegated, set side by side.
[9] Reeks. Emanates.
[10] Go. Walk.

Michelangelo Buonarroti
1475 – 1564

Michelangelo is largely recognized as one of the finest artists the world has known. When many people think of his work, they think of his Sistine Chapel Ceiling or the *Last Judgment*, which also adorns the Sistine Chapel. Ironically, he never saw himself as a painter, but as a sculptor.

As the story goes, once he had completed his magnificent works *The Pietà* and the *David* (both before the age of thirty), a conspiracy of other artists arose to "slow him down" by convincing the Pope that he should paint the Sistine Chapel Ceiling, a project which took him four years to complete. After this project, however, for the remainder of his life Michelangelo took on mostly works of sculpture and architecture, with the exception of the *Last Judgment* (also in the Sistine Chapel), which took nearly six years to complete.

Michelangelo (pronounced Mee-kel-on-ge-lo, not My-kel-an-ge-lo) also wrote a series of poems about a variety of subjects, but mostly concerning matters of art and faith. In the selection below, he tells of the pain he experienced while painting the ceiling of the Sistine Chapel.

Major Works
The Pietà (1598 – 1599)
David (1501 – 1504)
Sistine Chapel Ceiling (1508 – 1512)
Tomb of Pope Julius II (1513 – 1532)
Moses (1513 – 1515)
Last Judgment (1535 – 1531)
Pope Julius' Tomb (1513 – 1532)
St. Peter's Basilica. (Architect; 1546 – 1564)

---

[11] Belied. Misrepresented, made false.
[12] Compare. Comparison.

On the Painting of the Sistine Chapel
Michelangelo Buonarroti, 1509
TRANSLATED BY JOHN ADDINGTON SYMONDS

I've grown a goiter by dwelling in this den –
As cats from stagnant streams in Lombardy,
Or in what other land they hap to be –
Which drives the belly close beneath the chin:
5   My beard turns up to heaven; my nape falls in,
Fixed on my spine: my breast-bone visibly
Grows like a harp: a rich embroidery
Bedews my face from brush-drops thick and thin.
My loins into my paunch like levers grind:
10 My buttock like a crupper[1] bears my weight;
My feet unguided wander to and fro;
In front my skin grows loose and long; behind,
By bending it becomes more taut and strait;
Crosswise I strain me like a Syrian bow:
15 Whence false and quaint, I know,
Must be the fruit of squinting brain and eye;
For ill can aim the gun that bends awry.
Come then, Giovanni,[2] try
To succor my dead pictures and my fame;
20 Since foul I fare and painting is my shame.

---

[1] Crupper. A strap attached to a saddle that winds under the a horse's tail and keeps the horse's saddle in place.
[2] Giovanni. The poem is addressed "to Giovanni of Pistoia," presumably Giovanni di Benedetto do Pistoia, who had likewise addressed several poems to Michelangelo.

Miguel de Cervantes Saavedra
1547 – 1616

Though Miguel de Cervantes Saavedra, Spain's greatest literary figure, began writing as a teenager, it was not until 1585 when, after twenty years of military service, he published his first work in prose, *La Galatea*. Before he began his most famous work, *Don Quixote*, he also wrote many works for the theater and a large number of short stories.

Don Quixote de la Mancha was published in two parts in Madrid, the first part appearing in 1605, and the second part in 1615. It was an immediate success. The fame of *Don Quixote* brought Cervantes to the attention of a wide audience, and he continued to write until his death in 1616.

Because of its unparalleled humor, story-telling, and intellectual ingenuity, *Don Quixote* is often considered the world's greatest novel.

Other Major Works
Exemplary Novels (1590 - 1612)
Voyage to Parnassus (1614)
The Labors of Persiles and Sigismunda (1616)

ℭℬ℘

Don Quixote
Miguel de Cervantes Saavedra, 1605
TRANSLATED BY JOHN ORMSBY

Chapter I
Which Treats of the Character and Pursuits of the
Famous Gentleman Don Quixote of La Mancha

In a village of La Mancha, the name of which I have no desire to call to mind, there lived not long since one of those gentlemen that keep a lance in the lance-rack, an old buckler, a lean hack, and a greyhound for coursing. On an cooking pot of rather more beef than mutton, a salad on most nights, scraps on Saturdays, lentils on Fridays, and a pigeon or so extra on Sundays, he spent three-quarters of his income. The rest of it went into a doublet of fine cloth and velvet breeches and shoes to match for holidays, while on week-days he made a brave figure in his best homespun. He had in his house a housekeeper past forty, a niece under twenty, and a lad for the field and market-place, who used to saddle the hack as well as handle the bill-hook. The age of this gentleman of ours was bordering on fifty; he was of a hardy habit, spare, gaunt-featured, a very early riser and a great sportsman. They will have it his surname was Quixada or Quesada (for here there is some difference of opinion among the authors who write on the subject), although from reasonable conjectures it seems plain that he was called Quexana. This, however, is of but little importance to our tale; it will be enough not to stray a hair's breadth from the truth in the telling of it.

You must know, then, that the above-named gentleman whenever he was at leisure (which was mostly all the year round) gave himself up to reading books of chivalry with such ardor and avidity that he almost entirely neglected the pursuit of his field-sports, and even the management of his property; and to such a pitch did his eagerness and infatuation go that he sold many an acre of tillage-land to buy books of chivalry to read, and brought home as many of them as he could get. But of all there were none he liked so well as those of the famous Feliciano de Silva's composition, for their lucidity of style and complicated conceits were as pearls in his sight, particularly when in his reading he came upon courtships and cartels, where he often found passages like "the reason of the unreason with which my reason is afflicted so weakens my reason that with reason I murmur at your beauty;" or again, "the high heavens, that of your divinity divinely fortify you with the stars, render you deserving of the desert your greatness deserves." Over conceits of this sort the poor gentleman lost his wits, and used to lie awake striving to understand them and worm the meaning out of them; meanings that Aristotle himself could not have made out or extracted had he come to life again for that special purpose.

He was not at all easy about the wounds which Don Belianis gave and took, because it seemed to him that, great as were the surgeons who had cured him, he must have had his face and body covered all over with seams and scars. He commended, however, the author's way of ending his book with the promise of that interminable adventure, and many a time was he tempted to take up his pen and finish it properly as is there proposed, which no doubt he would have done, and made a successful piece of work of it too, had not greater and more absorbing thoughts prevented him.

Many an argument did he have with the curate of his village (a learned man, and a graduate of Siguenza) as to which had been the better knight, Palmerin of England or Amadis of Gaul. Master Nicholas, the village barber, however, used to say that neither of them came up to the Knight of Phoebus, and that if there was any that could compare with him it was Don Galaor, the brother of Amadis of Gaul, because he had a spirit that was equal to every occasion, and was no finicky knight, nor lachrymose like his brother, while in the matter of valor he was not a whit behind him. In short, he became so absorbed in his books that he spent his nights from sunset to sunrise, and his days from dawn to dark, poring over them; and what with little sleep and much reading his brains got so dry that he lost his wits.

His fancy grew full of what he used to read about in his books, enchantments, quarrels, battles, challenges, wounds, wooings, loves, agonies, and all sorts of impossible nonsense; and it so possessed his mind that the whole fabric of invention and fancy he read of was true, that to him no history in the world had more reality in it. He used to say the Cid Ruy Diaz was a very good knight, but that he was not to be compared with the Knight of the Burning Sword who with one back-stroke cut in half two fierce and monstrous giants. He thought more of Bernardo del Carpio because at Roncesvalles he slew Roland in spite of enchantments, availing himself of the artifice of Hercules when he strangled Antaeus the son of Terra in his arms. He approved highly of the giant Morgante, because, although of the giant breed which is always arrogant and ill-conditioned, he alone was affable and well-bred. But above all he admired Reinaldos of Montalban, especially when he saw him sallying forth from his castle and robbing everyone he met, and when beyond the seas he stole that image of Mahomet which, as his history says, was entirely of gold. To have a bout of kicking at that traitor of a Ganelon he would have given his housekeeper, and his niece into the bargain.

In short, his wits being quite gone, he hit upon the strangest notion that ever madman in this world hit upon, and that was that he fancied it was right and requisite, as well for the support of his own honor as for the service of his country, that he should make a knight-errant of himself, roaming the world over in full armor and on horseback in quest of adventures, and putting in practice himself all that he had read of as being the usual practices of knights-errant; righting every kind of wrong, and exposing himself to peril and danger from which, in the issue, he was to reap eternal renown and fame. Already the poor man saw himself crowned by the might of his arm Emperor of Trebizond at least; and so, led away by the intense enjoyment he found in these pleasant fancies, he set himself forthwith to put his scheme into execution.

The first thing he did was to clean up some armor that had belonged to his great-grandfather, and had been for ages lying forgotten in a corner eaten with rust and covered with mildew. He scoured and polished it as best he could, but he perceived one great defect in it, that it had no closed helmet, nothing but a simple morion helmet. This deficiency, however, his ingenuity supplied, for he contrived a kind of half-helmet of pasteboard which, fitted on to the morion, looked like a whole one. It is true that, in order to see if it was strong and fit to stand a cut, he drew his sword and gave it a couple of slashes, the first of which undid in an instant what had taken him a week to do. The ease with which he had knocked it to pieces disconcerted him somewhat, and to guard against that danger he set to work again, fixing bars of iron on the inside until he was satisfied with its strength; and then, not caring to try any more experiments with it, he passed it and adopted it as a helmet of the most perfect construction.

He next proceeded to inspect his hack, which, with more quartos than a real and more blemishes than the steed of Gonela, that *"tantum pellis et ossa fuit,"*[1] surpassed in his eyes the Bucephalus of Alexander or the Babieca of the Cid. Four days were spent in thinking what name to give him, because (as he said to himself) it was not right that a horse belonging to a knight so famous, and one with such merits of his own, should be without some distinctive name, and he strove to adapt

---

[1] Tantum...fuit. He was all skin and bones

it so as to indicate what he had been before belonging to a knight-errant, and what he then was; for it was only reasonable that, his master taking a new character, he should take a new name, and that it should be a distinguished and full-sounding one, befitting the new order and calling he was about to follow. And so, after having composed, struck out, rejected, added to, unmade, and remade a multitude of names out of his memory and fancy, he decided upon calling him Rocinante, a name, to his thinking, lofty, sonorous, and significant of his condition as a hack before he became what he now was, the first and foremost of all the hacks in the world.

Having got a name for his horse so much to his taste, he was anxious to get one for himself, and he was eight days more pondering over this point, until at last he made up his mind to call himself "Don Quixote," whence, as has been already said, the authors of this veracious history have inferred that his name must have been beyond a doubt Quixada, and not Quesada as others would have it. Recollecting, however, that the valiant Amadis was not content to call himself curtly Amadis and nothing more, but added the name of his kingdom and country to make it famous, and called himself Amadis of Gaul, he, like a good knight, resolved to add on the name of his, and to style himself Don Quixote of La Mancha, whereby, he considered, he described accurately his origin and country, and did honor to it in taking his surname from it.

So then, his armor being furbished, his morion turned into a helmet, his hack christened, and he himself confirmed, he came to the conclusion that nothing more was needed now but to look out for a lady to be in love with; for a knight-errant without love was like a tree without leaves or fruit, or a body without a soul. As he said to himself, "If, for my sins, or by my good fortune, I come across some giant hereabouts, a common occurrence with knights-errant, and overthrow him in one onslaught, or cleave him asunder to the waist, or, in short, vanquish and subdue him, will it not be well to have some one I may send him to as a present, that he may come in and fall on his knees before my sweet lady, and in a humble, submissive voice say, 'I am the giant Caraculiambro, lord of the island of Malindrania, vanquished in single combat by the never sufficiently extolled knight Don Quixote of La Mancha, who has commanded me to present myself before your Grace, that your Highness dispose of me at your pleasure'?" Oh, how our good gentleman enjoyed the delivery of this speech, especially when he had thought of some one to call his Lady!

There was, so the story goes, in a village near his own a very good-looking farm-girl with whom he had been at one time in love, though, so far as is known, she never knew it nor gave a thought to the matter. Her name was Aldonza Lorenzo, and upon her he thought fit to confer the title of Lady of his Thoughts; and after some search for a name which should not be out of harmony with her own, and should suggest and indicate that of a princess and great lady, he decided upon calling her Dulcinea del Toboso – she being of El Toboso – a name, to his mind, musical, uncommon, and significant, like all those he had already bestowed upon himself and the things belonging to him.

Chapter II
Which Treats of the First Sally the Ingenious Don Quixote Made from Home

These preliminaries settled, he did not care to put off any longer the execution of his design, urged on to it by the thought of all the world was losing by his delay, seeing what wrongs he intended to right, grievances to redress, injustices to repair, abuses to remove, and duties to discharge. So, without giving notice of his intention to anyone, and without anybody seeing him, one morning before the dawning of the day (which was one of the hottest of the month of July) he donned his suit of armor, mounted Rocinante with his patched-up helmet on, braced his buckler, took his lance, and by the back door of the yard sallied forth upon the plain in the highest contentment and satisfaction at seeing with what ease he had made a beginning with his grand purpose.

But scarcely did he find himself upon the open plain, when a terrible thought struck him, one all but enough to make him abandon the enterprise at the very outset. It occurred to him that he had not been dubbed a knight, and that according to the law of chivalry he neither could nor ought to bear arms against any knight; and that even if he had been, still he ought, as a novice knight, to wear white armor, without a device upon the shield until by his prowess he had earned one. These reflections made him waver in his purpose, but his craze being stronger than any reasoning, he made up his mind to have himself dubbed a knight by the first one he came across, following the example of others in the same case, as he had read in the books that brought him to this pass. As for white armor, he resolved, on the first opportunity, to scour his until it was whiter than an ermine; and so comforting himself he pursued his way, taking that which his horse chose, for in this he believed lay the essence of adventures.

Thus setting out, our new-fledged adventurer paced along, talking to himself and saying, "Who knows but that in time to come, when the veracious history of my famous deeds is made known, the sage who writes it, when he has to set forth my first sally in the early morning, will do it after this fashion? 'Scarce had the rubicund Apollo spread o'er the face of the broad spacious earth the golden threads of his bright hair, scarce had the little birds of painted plumage attuned their notes to hail with dulcet and mellifluous harmony the coming of the rosy Dawn, that, deserting the soft couch of her jealous spouse, was appearing to mortals at the gates and balconies of the Manchegan horizon, when the renowned knight Don Quixote of La Mancha, quitting the lazy down, mounted his celebrated steed Rocinante and began to traverse the ancient and famous Campo de Montiel;'" which in fact he was actually traversing. "Happy the age, happy the time," he continued, "in which shall be made known my deeds of fame, worthy to be molded in brass, carved in marble, limned in pictures, for a memorial for ever. And thou, O sage magician, whoever thou art, to whom it shall fall to be the chronicler of this wondrous history, forget not, I entreat thee, my good Rocinante, the constant companion of my ways and wanderings." Presently he broke out again, as if he were love-stricken in earnest, "O Princess Dulcinea, lady of this captive heart, a grievous wrong hast thou done me to drive me forth with scorn, and with inexorable obduracy banish me from the presence of thy beauty. O lady, deign to hold in remembrance this heart, thy vassal, that thus in anguish pines for love of thee."

So he went on stringing together these and other absurdities, all in the style of those his books had taught him, imitating their language as well as he could; and all the while he rode so slowly and the sun mounted so rapidly and with such fervor that it was enough to melt his brains if he had any. Nearly all day he traveled without anything remarkable happening to him, at which he was in despair, for he was anxious to encounter some one at once upon whom to try the might of his strong arm.

Writers there are who say the first adventure he met with was that of Puerto Lapice; others say it was that of the windmills; but what I have ascertained on this point, and what I have found written in the annals of La Mancha, is that he was on the road all day, and towards nightfall his hack and he found themselves dead tired and hungry, when, looking all around to see if he could discover any castle or shepherd's shanty where he might refresh himself and relieve his sore wants, he perceived not far out of his road an inn, which was as welcome as a star guiding him to the portals, if not the palaces, of his redemption; and quickening his pace he reached it just as night was setting in. At the door were standing two young women, girls of the district as they call them, on their way to Seville with some carriers who had chanced to halt that night at the inn; and as, happen what might to our adventurer, everything he saw or imaged seemed to him to be and to happen after the fashion of what he read of, the moment he saw the inn he pictured it to himself as a castle with its four turrets and pinnacles of shining silver, not forgetting the drawbridge and moat and all the belongings usually ascribed to castles of the sort.

To this inn, which to him seemed a castle, he advanced, and at a short distance from it he checked Rocinante, hoping that some dwarf would show himself upon the battlements, and by sound of trumpet give notice that a knight was approaching the castle. But seeing that they were slow about it, and that Rocinante was in a hurry to reach the stable, he made for the inn door, and perceived the two gay damsels who were standing there, and who seemed to him to be two fair maidens or lovely ladies taking their ease at the castle gate.

At this moment it so happened that a swineherd who was going through the stubbles collecting a drove of pigs (for, without any apology, that is what they are called) gave a blast of his horn to bring them together, and forthwith it seemed to Don Quixote to be what he was expecting, the signal of some dwarf announcing his arrival; and so with prodigious satisfaction he rode up to the inn and to the ladies, who, seeing a man of this sort approaching in full armor and with lance and buckler, were turning in dismay into the inn, when Don Quixote, guessing their fear by their flight, raising his pasteboard visor, disclosed his dry dusty visage, and with courteous bearing and gentle voice addressed them, "Your ladyships need not fly or fear any rudeness, for that it belongs not to the order of knighthood which I profess to offer to anyone, much less to highborn maidens as your appearance proclaims you to be." The girls were looking at him and straining their eyes to make out the features which the clumsy visor obscured, but when they heard themselves called maidens, a thing so much out of their line, they could not restrain their laughter, which made Don Quixote wax indignant, and say, "Modesty becomes the fair, and moreover laughter that has little cause is great silliness; this, however, I say not to pain or anger you, for my desire is none other than to serve you."

The incomprehensible language and the unpromising looks of our cavalier only increased the ladies' laughter, and that increased his irritation, and matters might have gone farther if at that moment the landlord had not come out, who, being a very fat man, was a very peaceful one. He, seeing this grotesque figure clad in armor that did not match any more than his saddle, bridle, lance, buckler, or corselet, was not at all indisposed to join the damsels in their manifestations of amusement; but, in truth, standing in awe of such a complicated armament, he thought it best to speak him fairly, so he said, "Señor Caballero, if your worship wants lodging, bating the bed (for there is not one in the inn) there is plenty of everything else here." Don Quixote, observing the respectful bearing of the Alcaide of the fortress (for so innkeeper and inn seemed in his eyes), made answer,

"Sir Castellan, for me anything will suffice, for 'My armor is my only wear, My only rest the fray.'"

The host fancied he called him Castellan because he took him for a "worthy of Castile," though he was in fact an Andalusian, and one from the strand of San Lucar, as crafty a thief as Cacus and as full of tricks as a student or a page.

"In that case," said he, "'Your bed is on the flinty rock, Your sleep to watch always;' and if so, you may dismount and safely reckon upon any quantity of sleeplessness under this roof for a twelvemonth, not to say for a single night." So saying, he advanced to hold the stirrup for Don Quixote, who got down with great difficulty and exertion (for he had not broken his fast all day), and then charged the host to take great care of his horse, as he was the best bit of flesh that ever ate bread in this world. The landlord eyed him over but did not find him as good as Don Quixote said, nor even half as good; and putting him up in the stable, he returned to see what might be wanted by his guest, whom the damsels, who had by this time made their peace with him, were now relieving of his armor.

They had taken off his breastplate and back-piece, but they neither knew nor saw how to open his gorget[1] or remove his make-shift helmet, for he had fastened it with green ribbons, which, as there was no untying the knots, required to be cut. This, however, he would not by any means consent to, so he remained all the evening with his helmet on, the drollest and oddest figure that can be imagined; and while they were removing his armor, taking the baggages who were about it for ladies of high degree belonging to the castle, he said to them with great sprightliness:

"Oh, never, surely, was there knight
So served by hand of dame,
As served was he, Don Quixote hight,[2]
When from his town he came;
With maidens waiting on himself,
Princesses on his hack

– or Rocinante, for that, ladies mine, is my horse's name, and Don Quixote of La Mancha is my own; for though I had no intention of declaring myself until my achievements in your service and honor had made me known, the necessity of

---

[1] Gorget. Neckpiece or cloth worn about the neck.
[2] Hight. Was called.

adapting that old ballad of Lancelot to the present occasion has given you the knowledge of my name altogether prematurely. A time, however, will come for your ladyships to command and me to obey, and then the might of my arm will show my desire to serve you."

The girls, who were not used to hearing rhetoric of this sort, had nothing to say in reply; they only asked him if he wanted anything to eat. "I would gladly eat a bit of something," said Don Quixote, "for I feel it would come very seasonably." The day happened to be a Friday, and in the whole inn there was nothing but some pieces of the fish they call in Castile "abadejo," in Andalusia "bacallao," and in some places "curadillo," and in others "troutlet;" so they asked him if he thought he could eat troutlet, for there was no other fish to give him. "If there be troutlets enough," said Don Quixote, "they will be the same thing as a trout; for it is all one to me whether I am given eight reals in small change or a piece of eight; moreover, it may be that these troutlets are like veal, which is better than beef, or kid, which is better than goat. But whatever it be let it come quickly, for the burden and pressure of arms cannot be borne without support to the inside."

They laid a table for him at the door of the inn for the sake of the air, and the host brought him a portion of ill-soaked and worse cooked stockfish, and a piece of bread as black and moldy as his own armor; but a laughable sight it was to see him eating, for having his helmet on and the beaver up, he could not with his own hands put anything into his mouth unless some one else placed it there, and this service one of the ladies rendered him. But to give him anything to drink was impossible, or would have been so had not the landlord bored a reed, and putting one end in his mouth poured the wine into him through the other; all which he bore with patience rather than sever the ribbons of his helmet.

While this was going on there came up to the inn a pig gelder, who, as he approached, sounded his reed pipe four or five times, and thereby completely convinced Don Quixote that he was in some famous castle, and that they were regaling him with music, and that the stockfish was trout, the bread the whitest, the wenches ladies, and the landlord the castellan of the castle; and consequently he held that his enterprise and sally had been to some purpose. But still it distressed him to think he had not been dubbed a knight, for it was plain to him he could not lawfully engage in any adventure without receiving the order of knighthood.

Chapter VIII
Of the Good Fortune Which the Valiant Don Quixote Had in the Terrible and Undreamt-Of Adventure of the Windmills, With Other Occurrences Worthy to Be Fitly Recorded

At this point they came in sight of thirty forty windmills that there are on plain, and as soon as Don Quixote saw them he said to his squire, "Fortune is arranging matters for us better than we could have shaped our desires ourselves, for look there, friend Sancho Panza, where thirty or more monstrous giants present themselves, all of whom I mean to engage in battle and slay, and with whose spoils we shall begin to make our fortunes; for this is righteous warfare, and it is God's good service to sweep so evil a breed from off the face of the earth."

"What giants?" said Sancho Panza.

"Those thou seest there," answered his master, "with the long arms, and some have them nearly two leagues long."

"Look, your worship," said Sancho; "what we see there are not giants but windmills, and what seem to be their arms are the sails that turned by the wind make the millstone go."

"It is easy to see," replied Don Quixote, "that thou art not used to this business of adventures; those are giants; and if thou art afraid, away with thee out of this and betake thyself to prayer while I engage them in fierce and unequal combat."

So saying, he gave the spur to his steed Rocinante, heedless of the cries his squire Sancho sent after him, warning him that most certainly they were windmills and not giants he was going to attack. He, however, was so positive they were giants that he neither heard the cries of Sancho, nor perceived, near as he was, what they were, but made at them shouting, "Fly not, cowards and vile beings, for a single knight attacks you."

A slight breeze at this moment sprang up, and the great sails began to move, seeing which Don Quixote exclaimed, "Though ye flourish more arms than the giant Briareus, ye have to reckon with me."

So saying, and commending himself with all his heart to his lady Dulcinea, imploring her to support him in such a peril, with lance in rest and covered by his buckler, he charged at Rocinante's fullest gallop and fell upon the first mill that stood in front of him; but as he drove his lance-point into the sail the wind whirled it round with such force that it shivered the lance to pieces, sweeping with it horse and rider, who went rolling over on the plain, in a sorry condition. Sancho hastened to his assistance as fast as his ass could go, and when he came up found him unable to move, with such a shock had Rocinante fallen with him.

"God bless me!" said Sancho, "did I not tell your worship to mind what you were about, for they were only windmills? and no one could have made any mistake about it but one who had something of the same kind in his head."

"Hush, friend Sancho," replied Don Quixote, "the fortunes of war more than any other are liable to frequent fluctuations; and moreover I think, and it is the truth, that that same sage Friston who carried off my study and books, has turned these giants into mills in order to rob me of the glory of vanquishing them, such is the enmity he bears me; but in the end his wicked arts will avail but little against my good sword."

"God order it as he may," said Sancho Panza, and helping him to rise got him up again on Rocinante, whose shoulder was half out; and then, discussing the late adventure, they followed the road to Puerto Lapice, for there, said Don Quixote, they could not fail to find adventures in abundance and variety, as it was a great thoroughfare. For all that, he was much grieved at the loss of his lance, and saying so to his squire, he added, "I remember having read how a Spanish knight, Diego Perez de Vargas by name, having broken his sword in battle, tore from an oak a ponderous bough or branch, and with it did such things that day, and pounded so many Moors, that he got the surname of Machuca, and he and his descendants from that day forth were called Vargas y Machuca. I mention this because from the first oak I see I mean to rend such another branch, large and stout like that, with which I am determined and resolved to do such deeds that thou mayest deem thyself very fortunate in being found worthy to come and see them, and be an eyewitness of things that will with difficulty be believed."

"Be that as God will," said Sancho, "I believe it all as your worship says it; but straighten yourself a little, for you seem all on one side, may be from the shaking of the fall."

"That is the truth," said Don Quixote, "and if I make no complaint of the pain it is because knights-errant are not permitted to complain of any wound, even though their bowels be coming out through it."

"If so," said Sancho, "I have nothing to say; but God knows I would rather your worship complained when anything ailed you. For my part, I confess I must complain however small the ache may be; unless this rule about not complaining extends to the squires of knights-errant also."

Don Quixote could not help laughing at his squire's simplicity, and he assured him he might complain whenever and however he chose, just as he liked, for, so far, he had never read of anything to the contrary in the order of knighthood.

Sancho bade him remember it was dinner-time, to which his master answered that he wanted nothing himself just then, but that he might eat when he had a mind. With this permission Sancho settled himself as comfortably as he could on his beast, and taking out of the saddlebag what he had stowed away in them, he jogged along behind his master munching deliberately, and from time to time taking a pull at the wine bottle with a relish that the thirstiest tapster in Malaga might have envied; and while he went on in this way, gulping down draught after draught, he never gave a thought to any of the promises his master had made him, nor did he rate it as hardship but rather as recreation going in quest of adventures, however dangerous they might be.

Finally they passed the night among some trees, from one of which Don Quixote plucked a dry branch to serve him after a fashion as a lance, and fixed on it the head he had removed from the broken one. All that night Don Quixote lay awake thinking of his lady Dulcinea, in order to conform to what he had read in his books, how many a night in the forests and deserts knights used to lie sleepless supported by the memory of their mistresses. Not so did Sancho Panza spend it, for having his stomach full of something stronger than chicory water he made but one sleep of it, and, if his master had not called him, neither the rays of the sun beating on his face nor all the cheery notes of the birds welcoming the approach of day would have had power to waken him. On getting up he tried the wine bottle and found it somewhat less full than the night before, which grieved his heart because they did not seem to be on the way to remedy the deficiency readily. Don Quixote did not care to break his fast, for, as has been already said, he confined himself to savory recollections for nourishment.

They returned to the road they had set out with, leading to Puerto Lapice, and at three in the afternoon they came in sight of it. "Here, brother Sancho Panza," said Don Quixote when he saw it, "we may plunge our hands up to the elbows in what they call adventures; but observe, even shouldst thou see me in the greatest danger in the world, thou must not put a hand to thy sword in my defense, unless indeed thou perceivest that those who assail me are rabble or base folk; for in that case thou mayest very properly aid me; but if they be knights it is on no account permitted or allowed thee by the laws of knighthood to help me until thou hast been dubbed a knight."

"Most certainly, señor," replied Sancho, "your worship shall be fully obeyed in this matter; all the more as of myself I am peaceful and no friend to mixing in strife and quarrels: it is true that as regards the defense of my own person I shall not give much heed to those laws, for laws human and divine allow each one to defend himself against any assailant whatever."

"That I grant," said Don Quixote, "but in this matter of aiding me against knights thou must put a restraint upon thy natural impetuosity."

"I will do so, I promise you," answered Sancho, "and will keep this precept as carefully as Sunday."

While they were thus talking there appeared on the road two friars of the order of St. Benedict, mounted on two dromedaries, for not less tall were the two mules they rode on. They wore traveling spectacles and carried sunshades; and behind them came a coach attended by four or five persons on horseback and two muleteers on foot. In the coach there was, as afterwards appeared, a Biscay lady on her way to Seville, where her husband was about to take passage for the Indies with an appointment of high honor. The friars, though going the same road, were not in her company; but the moment Don Quixote perceived them he said to his squire, "Either I am mistaken, or this is going to be the most famous adventure that has ever been seen, for those black bodies we see there must be, and doubtless are, magicians who are carrying off some stolen princess in that coach, and with all my might I must undo this wrong."

"This will be worse than the windmills," said Sancho. "Look, señor; those are friars of St. Benedict, and the coach plainly belongs to some travelers: I tell you to mind well what you are about and don't let the devil mislead you."

"I have told thee already, Sancho," replied Don Quixote, "that on the subject of adventures thou knowest little. What I say is the truth, as thou shalt see presently."

So saying, he advanced and posted himself in the middle of the road along which the friars were coming, and as soon as he thought they had come near enough to hear what he said, he cried aloud, "Devilish and unnatural beings, release instantly the highborn princesses whom you are carrying off by force in this coach, else prepare to meet a speedy death as the just punishment of your evil deeds."

The friars drew rein and stood wondering at the appearance of Don Quixote as well as at his words, to which they replied, "Señor Caballero, we are not devilish or unnatural, but two brothers of St. Benedict following our road, nor do we know whether or not there are any captive princesses coming in this coach."

"No soft words with me, for I know you, lying rabble," said Don Quixote, and without waiting for a reply he spurred Rocinante and with leveled lance charged the first friar with such fury and determination, that, if the friar had not flung himself off the mule, he would have brought him to the ground against his will, and sore wounded, if not killed outright. The second brother, seeing how his comrade was treated, drove his heels into his castle of a mule and made off across the country faster than the wind.

Sancho Panza, when he saw the friar on the ground, dismounting briskly from his ass, rushed towards him and began to strip off his gown. At that instant the friar's muleteers came up and asked what he was stripping him for. Sancho answered them that this fell to him lawfully as spoil of the battle which his lord Don Quixote had won. The muleteers, who had no idea of a joke and did not understand all this about battles and spoils, seeing that Don Quixote was some distance off talking to the travellers in the coach, fell upon Sancho, knocked him down, and leaving hardly a hair in his beard, belabored him with kicks and left him stretched breathless and senseless on the ground; and without any more delay helped the friar to mount, who, trembling, terrified, and pale, as soon as he found himself in the saddle, spurred after his companion, who was standing at a distance looking on, watching the result of the onslaught; then, not caring to wait for the end of the affair just begun, they pursued their journey making more crosses than if they had the devil after them.

Don Quixote was, as has been said, speaking to the lady in the coach: "Your beauty, lady mine," said he, "may now dispose of your person as may be most in accordance with your pleasure, for the pride of your ravishers lies prostrate on the ground through this strong arm of mine; and lest you should be pining to know the name of your deliverer, know that I am called Don Quixote of La Mancha, knight-errant and adventurer, and captive to the peerless and beautiful lady Dulcinea del Toboso: and in return for the service you have received of me I ask no more than that you should return to El Toboso, and on my behalf present yourself before that lady and tell her what I have done to set you free."

One of the squires in attendance upon the coach, a Biscayan, was listening to all Don Quixote was saying, and, perceiving that he would not allow the coach to go on, but was saying it must return at once to El Toboso, he made at him, and seizing his lance addressed him in bad Castilian and worse Biscayan after his fashion, "Begone, caballero, and ill go with thee; by the God that made me, unless thou quittest coach, slayest thee as art here a Biscayan."

Don Quixote understood him quite well, and answered him very quietly, "If thou wert a knight, as thou art none, I should have already chastised thy folly and rashness, miserable creature."

To which the Biscayan returned, "I, no gentleman! – I swear to God thou liest, as I am Christian: if thou droppest lance and drawest sword, soon shalt thou see thou art carrying water to the cat: Biscayan on land, hidalgo at sea, hidalgo at the devil, and look, if thou sayest otherwise thou liest."

"You will see presently," replied Don Quixote; and throwing his lance on the ground he drew his sword, braced his buckler on his arm, and attacked the Biscayan, bent upon taking his life.

The Biscayan, when he saw him coming on, though he wished to dismount from his mule, in which, being one of those sorry ones let out for hire, he had no confidence, had no choice but to draw his sword; it was lucky for him, however, that he was near the coach, from which he was able to snatch a cushion that served him for a shield; and they went at one another as if they had been two mortal enemies. The others strove to make peace between them, but could not, for the Biscayan declared in his disjointed phrase that if they did not let him finish his battle he would kill his mistress and everyone that strove to prevent him. The lady in the coach, amazed and terrified at what she saw, ordered the coachman to draw aside a little, and set herself to watch this severe struggle, in the course of which the Biscayan smote Don Quixote a mighty stroke on the shoulder over the top of his buckler, which, given to one without armor, would have cleft him to the waist.

Don Quixote, feeling the weight of this prodigious blow, cried aloud, saying, "O lady of my soul, Dulcinea, flower of beauty, come to the aid of this your knight, who, in fulfilling his obligations to your beauty, finds himself in this extreme peril." To say this, to lift his sword, to shelter himself well behind his buckler, and to assail the Biscayan was the work of an instant, determined as he was to venture all upon a single blow. The Biscayan, seeing him come on in this way, was convinced of his courage by his spirited bearing, and resolved to follow his example, so he waited for him keeping well under cover of his cushion, being unable to execute any sort of maneuver with his mule, which, dead tired and never meant for this kind of game, could not stir a step.

On, then, as aforesaid, came Don Quixote against the wary Biscayan, with uplifted sword and a firm intention of splitting him in half, while on his side the Biscayan waited for him sword in hand, and under the protection of his cushion; and all present stood trembling, waiting in suspense the result of blows such as threatened to fall, and the lady in the coach and the rest of her following were making a thousand vows and offerings to all the images and shrines of Spain, that God might deliver her squire and all of them from this great peril in which they found themselves.

But it spoils all, that at this point and crisis the author of the history leaves this battle impending, giving as excuse that he could find nothing more written about these achievements of Don Quixote than what has been already set forth. It is true the second author of this work was unwilling to believe that a history so curious could have been allowed to fall under the sentence of oblivion, or that the wits of La Mancha could have been so undiscerning as not to preserve in their archives or registries some documents referring to this famous knight; and this being his persuasion, he did not despair of finding the conclusion of this pleasant history, which, heaven favoring him, he did find in a way that shall be related in the Second Part.

Chapter XX
Of the Unexampled and Unheard-Of Adventure Which Was Achieved by the Valiant Don Quixote of La Mancha With Less Peril Than Any Ever Achieved by Any Famous Knight in the World

"It cannot be, señor, but that this grass is a proof that there must be hard by some spring or brook to give it moisture, so it would be well to move a little farther on, that we may find some place where we may quench this terrible thirst that plagues us, which beyond a doubt is more distressing than hunger."

The advice seemed good to Don Quixote, and, he leading Rocinante by the bridle and Sancho the ass by the halter, after he had packed away upon him the remains of the supper, they advanced the meadow feeling their way, for the darkness of the night made it impossible to see anything; but they had not gone two hundred paces when a loud noise of water, as if falling from great rocks, struck their ears. The sound cheered them greatly; but halting to make out by listening from what quarter it came they heard unseasonably another noise which spoiled the satisfaction the sound of the water gave them, especially for Sancho, who was by nature timid and faint-hearted. They heard, I say, strokes falling with a measured beat, and a certain rattling of iron and chains that, together with the furious din of the water, would have struck terror into any heart but Don Quixote's. The night was, as has been said, dark, and they had happened to reach a spot in among some tall trees, whose leaves stirred by a gentle breeze made a low ominous sound; so that, what with the solitude, the place, the darkness, the noise of the water, and the rustling of the leaves, everything inspired awe and dread; more especially as they perceived that the strokes did not cease, nor the wind lull, nor morning approach; to all which might be added their ignorance as to where they were.

But Don Quixote, supported by his intrepid heart, leaped on Rocinante, and bracing his buckler on his arm, brought his pike to the slope, and said, "Friend Sancho, know that I by Heaven's will have been born in this our iron age to revive in it the age of gold, or the golden as it is called; I am he for whom perils, mighty achievements, and valiant deeds are reserved; I am, I say again, he who is to revive the Knights of the Round Table, the Twelve of France and the Nine Worthies; and he who is to consign to oblivion the Platirs, the Tablantes, the Olivantes and Tirantes, the Phoebuses and Belianises, with the whole herd of famous knights-errant of days gone by, performing in these in which I live such exploits, marvels, and feats of arms as shall obscure their brightest deeds.

"Thou dost mark well, faithful and trusty squire, the gloom of this night, its strange silence, the dull confused murmur of those trees, the awful sound of that water in quest of which we came, that seems as though it were precipitating and dashing itself down from the lofty mountains of the Moon, and that incessant hammering that wounds and pains our ears; which things all together and each of itself are enough to instill fear, dread, and dismay into the breast of Mars himself, much more into one not used to hazards and adventures of the kind. Well, then, all this that I put before thee is but an incentive and stimulant to my spirit, making my heart burst in my bosom through eagerness to engage in this adventure, arduous as it promises to be; therefore tighten Rocinante's girths a little, and God be with thee; wait for me here three days and no more, and if in that time I come not back, thou canst return to our village, and thence, to do me a favor and a service, thou wilt go to El Toboso, where thou shalt say to my incomparable lady Dulcinea that her captive knight hath died in attempting things that might make him worthy of being called hers."

When Sancho heard his master's words he began to weep in the most pathetic way, saying:

"Señor, I know not why your worship wants to attempt this so dreadful adventure; it is night now, no one sees us here, we can easily turn about and take ourselves out of danger, even if we don't drink for three days to come; and as there is no one to see us, all the less will there be anyone to set us down as cowards; besides, I have many a time heard the curate of our village, whom your worship knows well, preach that he who seeks danger perishes in it; so it is not right to tempt God by trying so tremendous a feat from which there can be no escape save by a miracle, and Heaven has performed enough of them for your worship in delivering you from being blanketed as I was, and bringing you out victorious and safe and sound from among all those enemies that were with the dead man; and if all this does not move or soften that hard heart, let this thought and reflection move it, that you will have hardly quitted this spot when from pure fear I shall yield my soul up to anyone that will take it.

"I left home and wife and children to come and serve your worship, trusting to do better and not worse; but as covetousness bursts the bag, it has rent my hopes asunder, for just as I had them highest about getting that wretched unlucky island your worship has so often promised me, I see that instead and in lieu of it you mean to desert me now in a place so far from human reach: for God's sake, master mine, deal not so unjustly by me, and if your worship will not entirely give up attempting this feat, at least put it off until morning, for by what the lore I learned when I was a shepherd tells me it cannot want three hours of dawn now, because the mouth of the Horn is overhead and makes midnight in the line of the left arm."

"How canst thou see, Sancho," said Don Quixote, "where it makes that line, or where this mouth or this occiput[1] is that thou talkest of, when the night is so dark that there is not a star to be seen in the whole heaven?"

"That's true," said Sancho, "but fear has sharp eyes, and sees things underground, much more above in heavens; besides, there is good reason to show that it now wants but little of day."

"Let it want what it may," replied Don Quixote, "it shall not be said of me now or at any time that tears or entreaties turned me aside from doing what was in accordance with knightly usage; and so I beg of thee, Sancho, to hold thy peace, for God, who has put it into my heart to undertake now this so unexampled and terrible adventure, will take care to watch over my safety and console thy sorrow; what thou hast to do is to tighten Rocinante's girths well, and wait here, for I shall come back shortly, alive or dead."

Sancho perceiving it his master's final resolve, and how little his tears, counsels, and entreaties prevailed with him, determined to have recourse to his own ingenuity and compel him, if he could, to wait until daylight; and so, while tightening the girths of the horse, he quietly and without being felt, with his ass' halter tied both Rocinante's legs, so that when Don Quixote strove to go he was unable as the horse could only move by jumps. Seeing the success of his trick, Sancho Panza said:

"See there, señor! Heaven, moved by my tears and prayers, has so ordered it that Rocinante cannot stir; and if you will be obstinate, and spur and strike him, you will only provoke fortune, and kick, as they say, against the pricks."

Don Quixote at this grew desperate, but the more he drove his heels into the horse, the less he stirred him; and not having any suspicion of the tying, he was fain to resign himself and wait until daybreak or until Rocinante could move, firmly persuaded that all this came of something other than Sancho's ingenuity. So he said to him, "As it is so, Sancho, and as Rocinante cannot move, I am content to wait until dawn smiles upon us, even though I weep while it delays its coming."

"There is no need to weep," answered Sancho, "for I will amuse your worship by telling stories from this until daylight, unless indeed you like to dismount and lie

---

[1] Occiput. Back of the head or skull.

down to sleep a little on the green grass after the fashion of knights-errant, so as to be fresher when day comes and the moment arrives for attempting this extraordinary adventure you are looking forward to."

"What art thou talking about dismounting or sleeping for?" said Don Quixote. "Am I, thinkest thou, one of those knights that take their rest in the presence of danger? Sleep thou who art born to sleep, or do as thou wilt, for I will act as I think most consistent with my character."

"Be not angry, master mine," replied Sancho, "I did not mean to say that;" and coming close to him he laid one hand on the pommel of the saddle and the other on the cantle so that he held his master's left thigh in his embrace, not daring to separate a finger's width from him; so much afraid was he of the strokes which still resounded with a regular beat. Don Quixote bade him tell some story to amuse him as he had proposed, to which Sancho replied that he would if his dread of what he heard would let him.

"Still," said Sancho, "I will strive to tell a story which, if I can manage to relate it, and nobody interferes with the telling, is the best of stories, and let your worship give me your attention, for here I begin. What was, was; and may the good that is to come be for all, and the evil for him who goes to look for it – your worship must know that the beginning the old folk used to put to their tales was not just as each one pleased; it was a maxim of Cato Zonzorino the Roman, that says 'the evil for him that goes to look for it,' and it comes as pat to the purpose now as ring to finger, to show that your worship should keep quiet and not go looking for evil in any quarter, and that we should go back by some other road, since nobody forces us to follow this in which so many terrors affright us."

"Go on with thy story, Sancho," said Don Quixote, "and leave the choice of our road to my care."

"I say then," continued Sancho, "that in a village of Estremadura there was a goat-shepherd – that is to say, one who tended goats – which shepherd or goatherd, as my story goes, was called Lope Ruiz, and this Lope Ruiz was in love with a shepherdess called Torralva, which shepherdess called Torralva was the daughter of a rich grazier, and this rich grazier -"

"If that is the way thou tellest thy tale, Sancho," said Don Quixote, "repeating twice all thou hast to say, thou wilt not have done these two days; go straight on with it, and tell it like a reasonable man, or else say nothing."

"Tales are always told in my country in the very way I am telling this," answered Sancho, "and I cannot tell it in any other, nor is it right of your worship to ask me to make new customs."

"Tell it as thou wilt," replied Don Quixote; "and as fate will have it that I cannot help listening to thee, go on."

"And so, lord of my soul," continued Sancho, as I have said, this shepherd was in love with Torralva the shepherdess, who was a wild buxom lass with something of the look of a man about her, for she had little moustaches; I fancy I see her now."

"Then you knew her?" said Don Quixote.

"I did not know her," said Sancho, "but he who told me the story said it was so true and certain that when I told it to another I might safely declare and swear I had seen it all myself. And so in course of time, the devil, who never sleeps and puts everything in confusion, contrived that the love the shepherd bore the shepherdess turned into hatred and ill-will, and the reason, according to evil tongues, was some little jealousy she caused him that crossed the line and trespassed on forbidden ground; and so much did the shepherd hate her from that time forward that, in order to escape from her, he determined to quit the country and go where he should never set eyes on her again. Torralva, when she found herself spurned by Lope, was immediately smitten with love for him, though she had never loved him before."

"That is the natural way of women," said Don Quixote, "to scorn the one that loves them, and love the one that hates them: go on, Sancho."

"It came to pass," said Sancho, "that the shepherd carried out his intention, and driving his goats before him took his way across the plains of Estremadura to pass over into the Kingdom of Portugal. Torralva, who knew of it, went after him, and on foot and barefoot followed him at a distance, with a pilgrim's staff in her hand and a scrip round her neck, in which she carried, it is said, a bit of looking-glass and a piece of a comb and some little pot or other of paint for her face; but let her carry what she did, I am not going to trouble myself to prove it; all I say is, that the shepherd, they say, came with his flock to cross over the river Guadiana, which was at that time swollen and almost overflowing its banks, and at the spot he came to there was neither ferry nor boat nor anyone to carry him or his flock to the other side, at which he was much vexed, for he perceived that Torralva was approaching and would give him great annoyance with her tears and entreaties; however, he went looking about so closely that he discovered a fisherman who had alongside of him a boat so small that it could only hold one person and one goat; but for all that he spoke to him and agreed with him to carry himself and his three hundred goats across.

The fisherman got into the boat and carried one goat over; he came back and carried another over; he came back again, and again brought over another – let your worship keep count of the goats the fisherman is taking across, for if one escapes the memory there will be an end of the story, and it will be impossible to tell another word of it. To proceed, I must tell you the landing place on the other side was miry and slippery, and the fisherman lost a great deal of time in going and coming; still he returned for another goat, and another, and another."

"Take it for granted he brought them all across," said Don Quixote, "and don't keep going and coming in this way, or thou wilt not make an end of bringing them over this twelvemonth."

"How many have gone across so far?" said Sancho.

"How the devil do I know?" replied Don Quixote.

"There it is," said Sancho, "what I told you, that you must keep a good count; well then, by God, there is an end of the story, for there is no going any farther."

"How can that be?" said Don Quixote; "is it so essential to the story to know to a nicety the goats that have crossed over, that if there be a mistake of one in the reckoning, thou canst not go on with it?"

"No, señor, not a bit," replied Sancho; "for when I asked your worship to tell me how many goats had crossed, and you answered you did not know, at that very instant all I had to say passed away out of my memory, and, faith, there was much virtue in it, and entertainment."

"So, then," said Don Quixote, "the story has come to an end?"

"As much as my mother has," said Sancho.

"In truth," said Don Quixote, "thou hast told one of the rarest stories, tales, or histories, that anyone in the world could have imagined, and such a way of telling it and ending it was never seen nor will be in a lifetime; though I expected nothing else from thy excellent understanding. But I do not wonder, for perhaps those ceaseless strokes may have confused thy wits."

"All that may be," replied Sancho, "but I know that as to my story, all that can be said is that it ends there where the mistake in the count of the passage of the goats begins."

"Let it end where it will, well and good," said Don Quixote, "and let us see if Rocinante can go;" and again he spurred him, and again Rocinante made jumps and remained where he was, so well tied was he.

Just then, whether it was the cold of the morning that was now approaching, or that he had eaten something laxative at supper, or that it was only natural (as is most likely), Sancho felt a desire to do what no one could do for him; but so great was the fear that had penetrated his heart, he dared not separate himself from his master by as much as the black of his nail; to escape doing what he wanted was, however, also impossible; so what he did for peace's sake was to remove his right hand, which held the back of the saddle, and with it to untie gently and silently the running string which alone held up his breeches, so that on loosening it they at once fell down round his feet like fetters; he then raised his shirt as well as he could and bared his hind quarters, no slim ones.

But, this accomplished, which he fancied was all he had to do to get out of this terrible strait and embarrassment, another still greater difficulty presented itself, for it seemed to him impossible to relieve himself without making some noise, and he ground his teeth and squeezed his shoulders together, holding his breath as much as he could; but in spite of his precautions he was unlucky enough after all to make a little noise, very different from that which was causing him so much fear.

Don Quixote, hearing it, said, "What noise is that, Sancho?"

"I don't know, señor," said he; "it must be something new, for adventures and misadventures never begin with a trifle." Once more he tried his luck, and succeeded so well, that without any further noise or disturbance he found himself relieved of the burden that had given him so much discomfort. But as Don Quixote's sense of smell was as acute as his hearing, and as Sancho was so closely linked with him that the fumes rose almost in a straight line, it could not be but that some should reach his nose, and as soon as they did he came to its relief by compressing it between his fingers, saying in a rather snuffing tone, "Sancho, it strikes me thou art in great fear."

"I am," answered Sancho; "but how does your worship perceive it now more than ever?"

"Because just now thou smellest stronger than ever, and not of ambergris," answered Don Quixote.

"Very likely," said Sancho, "but that's not my fault, but your worship's, for leading me about at unseasonable hours and at such unwonted paces."

"Then go back three or four, my friend," said Don Quixote, all the time with his fingers to his nose; "and for the future pay more attention to thy person and to what thou owest to mine; for it is my great familiarity with thee that has bred this contempt."

"I'll bet," replied Sancho, "that your worship thinks I have done something I ought not with my person."

"It makes it worse to stir it, friend Sancho," returned Don Quixote.

Chapter XXV
Which Treats of the Strange Things That Happened to the
Stout Knight of La Mancha in the Sierra Morena

Don Quixote took out the note-book, and, retiring to one side, very deliberately began to write the letter, and when he had finished it he called to Sancho, saying he wished to read it to him, so that he might commit it to memory, in case of losing it on the road; for with evil fortune like his anything might be apprehended. To which Sancho replied, "Write it two or three times there in the book and give it to me, and I will carry it very carefully, because to expect me to keep it in my memory is all nonsense, for I have such a bad one that I often forget my own name; but for all that repeat it to me, as I shall like to hear it, for surely it will run as if it was in print."

"Listen," said Don Quixote, "this is what it says:

Don Quixote's Letter to Dulcinea Del Toboso
Sovereign and exalted Lady,
The pierced by the point of absence, the wounded to the heart's core, sends thee, sweetest Dulcinea del Toboso, the health that he himself enjoys not. If thy beauty despises me, if thy worth is not for me, if thy scorn is my affliction, though I be sufficiently long-suffering, hardly shall I endure this anxiety, which, besides being oppressive, is protracted. My good squire Sancho will relate to thee in full, fair ingrate, dear enemy, the condition to which I am reduced on thy account: if it be thy pleasure to give me relief, I am thine; if not, do as may be pleasing to thee; for by ending my life I shall satisfy thy cruelty and my desire.
Thine until death,
The Knight of the Rueful Countenance.

"By the life of my father," said Sancho, when he heard the letter, "it is the loftiest thing I ever heard. Body of me! how your worship says everything as you like in it! And how well you fit in 'The Knight of the Rueful Countenance' into the signature. I declare your worship is indeed the very devil, and there is nothing you don't know."

"Everything is needed for the calling I follow," said Don Quixote.

"Now then," said Sancho, "let your worship put the order for the three ass-colts on the other side, and sign it very plainly, that they may recognize it at first sight."

"With all my heart," said Don Quixote, and as he had written it he read it to this effect:

> Mistress Niece,
> By this first of ass-colts please pay to Sancho Panza, my squire, three of the five I left at home in your charge: said three ass-colts to be paid and delivered for the same number received here in hand, which upon this and upon his receipt shall be duly paid. Done in the heart of the Sierra Morena, the twenty-seventh of August of this present year.

"That will do," said Sancho; "now let your worship sign it."

"There is no need to sign it," said Don Quixote, "but merely to put my flourish, which is the same as a signature, and enough for three asses, or even three hundred."

"I can trust your worship," returned Sancho; "let me go and saddle Rocinante, and be ready to give me your blessing, for I mean to go at once without seeing the fooleries your worship is going to do; I'll say I saw you do so many that she will not want any more."

"At any rate, Sancho," said Don Quixote, "I should like – and there is reason for it – I should like thee, I say, to see me stripped to the skin and performing a dozen or two of insanities, which I can get done in less than half an hour; for having seen them with thine own eyes, thou canst then safely swear to the rest that thou wouldst add; and I promise thee thou wilt not tell of as many as I mean to perform."

"For the love of God, master mine," said Sancho, "let me not see your worship stripped, for it will sorely grieve me, and I shall not be able to keep from tears, and my head aches so with all I shed last night for Dapple, that I am not fit to begin any fresh weeping; but if it is your worship's pleasure that I should see some insanities, do them in your clothes, short ones, and such as come readiest to hand; for I myself want nothing of the sort, and, as I have said, it will be a saving of time for my return, which will be with the news your worship desires and deserves. If not, let the lady Dulcinea look to it; if she does not answer reasonably, I swear as solemnly as I can that I will fetch a fair answer out of her stomach with kicks and cuffs; for why should it be borne that a knight-errant as famous as your worship should go mad without rhyme or reason for a – ? Her ladyship had best not drive me to say it, for by God I will speak out and let off everything cheap, even if it doesn't sell: I am pretty good at that! she little knows me; faith, if she knew me she'd be in awe of me."

"In faith, Sancho," said Don Quixote, "to all appearance thou art no sounder in thy wits than I."

"I am not so mad," answered Sancho, "but I am more peppery; but apart from all this, what has your worship to eat until I come back? Will you sally out on the road like Cardenio to force it from the shepherds?"

"Let not that anxiety trouble thee," replied Don Quixote, "for even if I had it I should not eat anything but the herbs and the fruits which this meadow and these trees may yield me; the beauty of this business of mine lies in not eating, and in performing other mortifications."

"Do you know what I am afraid of?" said Sancho upon this; "that I shall not be able to find my way back to this spot where I am leaving you, it is such an out-of-the-way place."

"Observe the landmarks well," said Don Quixote, "for I will try not to go far from this neighborhood, and I will even take care to mount the highest of these rocks to see if I can discover thee returning; however, not to miss me and lose thyself, the best plan will be to cut some branches of the broom that is so abundant about here, and as thou goest to lay them at intervals until thou hast come out upon the plain; these will serve thee, after the fashion of the ball of string in the labyrinth of Theseus, as marks and signs for finding me on thy return."

"So I will," said Sancho Panza, and having cut some, he asked his master's blessing, and not without many tears on both sides, took his leave of him, and mounting Rocinante, of whom Don Quixote charged him earnestly to have as much care as of his own person, he set out for the plain, strewing at intervals the branches of broom as his master had recommended him; and so he went his way, though Don Quixote still entreated him to see him do were it only a couple of mad acts. He had not gone a hundred paces, however, when he returned and said:

"I must say, señor, your worship said quite right, that in order to be able to swear without a weight on my conscience that I had seen you do mad things, it would be well for me to see if it were only one; though in your worship's remaining here I have seen a very great one."

"Did I not tell thee so?" said Don Quixote. "Wait, Sancho, and I will do them in the saying of a credo," and pulling off his breeches in all haste he stripped himself to his skin and his shirt, and then, without more ado, he cut a couple of gambados in the air, and a couple of somersaults, heels over head, making such a display that, not to see it a second time, Sancho wheeled Rocinante round, and felt easy, and satisfied in his mind that he could swear he had left his master mad; and so we will leave him to follow his road until his return, which was a quick one.

Chapter XXXI
Of the Delectable Discussion Between Don Quixote and Sancho Panza, His Squire, Together with Other Incidents

"All that is not unsatisfactory to me," said Don Quixote. "Go on; thou didst reach her; and what was that queen of beauty doing? Surely thou didst find her stringing pearls, or embroidering some device in gold thread for this her enslaved knight."

"I did not," said Sancho, "but I found her winnowing two bushels of wheat in the yard of her house."

"Then depend upon it," said Don Quixote, "the grains of that wheat were pearls when touched by her hands; and didst thou look, friend? was it white wheat or brown?"

"It was neither, but red," said Sancho.

"Then I promise thee," said Don Quixote, "that, winnowed by her hands, beyond a doubt the bread it made was of the whitest; but go on; when thou gavest her my letter, did she kiss it? Did she place it on her head? Did she perform any ceremony befitting it, or what did she do?"

"When I went to give it to her," replied Sancho, "she was hard at it swaying from side to side with a lot of wheat she had in the sieve, and she said to me, 'Lay the letter, friend, on the top of that sack, for I cannot read it until I have done sifting all this."

"Discreet lady!" said Don Quixote; "that was in order to read it at her leisure and enjoy it; proceed, Sancho; while she was engaged in her occupation what converse did she hold with thee? What did she ask about me, and what answer didst thou give? Make haste; tell me all, and let not an atom be left behind in the ink-bottle."

"She asked me nothing," said Sancho; "but I told her how your worship was left doing penance in her service, naked from the waist up, in among these mountains like a savage, sleeping on the ground, not eating bread off a tablecloth nor combing your beard, weeping and cursing your fortune."

"In saying I cursed my fortune thou saidst wrong," said Don Quixote; "for rather do I bless it and shall bless it all the days of my life for having made me worthy of aspiring to love so lofty a lady as Dulcinea del Toboso."

"And so lofty she is," said Sancho, "that she overtops me by more than a hand's-breadth."

"What! Sancho," said Don Quixote, "didst thou measure with her?"

"I measured in this way," said Sancho; "going to help her to put a sack of wheat on the back of an ass, we came so close together that I could see she stood more than a good palm over me."

"Well!" said Don Quixote, "and doth she not of a truth accompany and adorn this greatness with a thousand million charms of mind! But one thing thou wilt not deny, Sancho; when thou camest close to her didst thou not perceive a Sabaean odor, an aromatic fragrance, a, I know not what, delicious, that I cannot find a name for; I mean a redolence, an exhalation, as if thou wert in the shop of some dainty glover?"

"All I can say is," said Sancho, "that I did perceive a little odor, something goaty; it must have been that she was all in a sweat with hard work."

"It could not be that," said Don Quixote, "but thou must have been suffering from cold in the head, or must have smelt thyself; for I know well what would be the scent of that rose among thorns, that lily of the field, that dissolved amber."

"Maybe so," replied Sancho; "there often comes from myself that same odor which then seemed to me to come from her grace the lady Dulcinea; but that's no wonder, for one devil is like another."

"Well then," continued Don Quixote, "now she has done sifting the corn and sent it to the mill; what did she do when she read the letter?"

"As for the letter," said Sancho, "she did not read it, for she said she could neither read nor write; instead of that she tore it up into small pieces, saying that she did not want to let anyone read it lest her secrets should become known in the village, and that what I had told her by word of mouth about the love your worship bore her, and the extraordinary penance you were doing for her sake, was enough; and, to make an end of it, she told me to tell your worship that she kissed your hands, and that she had a greater desire to see you than to write to you; and that therefore she entreated and commanded you, on sight of this present, to come out of these thickets, and to have done with carrying on absurdities, and to set out at once for El Toboso, unless something else of greater importance should happen, for she had a great desire to see your worship.

She laughed greatly when I told her how your worship was called The Knight of the Rueful Countenance; I asked her if that Biscayan the other day had been there; and she told me he had, and that he was an honest fellow; I asked her too about the galley slaves, but she said she had not seen any as yet."

"So far all goes well," said Don Quixote; "but tell me what jewel was it that she gave thee on taking thy leave, in return for thy tidings of me? For it is a usual and ancient custom with knights and ladies errant to give the squires, damsels, or dwarfs who bring tidings of their ladies to the knights, or of their knights to the ladies, some rich jewel as a guerdon for good news,' and acknowledgment of the message."

"That is very likely," said Sancho, "and a good custom it was, to my mind; but that must have been in days gone by, for now it would seem to be the custom only to give a piece of bread and cheese; because that was what my lady Dulcinea gave me over the top of the yard-wall when I took leave of her; and more by token it was sheep's-milk cheese."

"She is generous in the extreme," said Don Quixote, "and if she did not give thee a jewel of gold, no doubt it must have been because she had not one nearby to give thee; but sleeves are good after Easter; I shall see her and all shall be made right. But knowest thou what amazes me, Sancho? It seems to me thou must have gone and come through the air, for thou hast taken but little more than three days to go to El Toboso and return, though it is more than thirty leagues from here to there. From which I am inclined to think that the sage magician who is my friend, and watches over my interests (for of necessity there is and must be one, or else I should not be a right knight-errant), that this same, I say, must have helped thee to travel without thy knowledge . . .

The Metaphysical Poets

John Donne, 1572 – 1631

Andrew Marvell, 1621 – 1678

The Metaphysical Poets is a name given to a group of seventeenth-century poets (chiefly John Donne, George Herbert, Henry Vaughan, Andrew Marvell, and Richard Crashaw), who, though they did not for the most part know one another, shared certain qualities in their work, especially an inventive use of extended metaphors (or conceits) and a speculative approach to love and religion, especially combined together.

The two poets included here, John Donne and Andrew Marvell, though starkly different in their careers, seemed to overlap a good deal in their poetry. Donne, though born a Catholic, converted to Anglicanism, was ordained a priest, served as chaplain to James I, and was named dean of St. Paul's Cathedral. Andrew Marvell found himself near the center of British politics, as tutor to Oliver Cromwell's ward, as secretary to Cromwell's Council of State, and a long-term member of Parliament. In both cases, despite their prominent careers, they managed to write poetry about love in ways that had never been achieved and have not since.

C×ৎ৩

Batter My Heart, Three-Person'd God
John Donne, 1633

Batter my heart, three-person'd God, for you
As yet but knock, breathe, shine, and seek to mend;
That I may rise and stand, o'erthrow me, and bend
Your force to break, blow, burn, and make me new.
5   I, like an usurp'd town to'another[1] due,
Labor to'admit you, but oh, to no end;
Reason, your viceroy in me, me should defend,
But is captiv'd, and proves weak or untrue.
Yet dearly'I love you, and would be lov'd fain,
10 But am betroth'd unto your enemy;

---

[1] To'another. The reader is to merge these words, so that there are three syllables instead of four. This unusual use of apostrophes appears throughout the work of Donne and his contemporaries.

193

Divorce me, 'untie or break that knot again,
Take me to you, imprison me, for I,
Except you'enthrall me, never shall be free,
Nor ever chaste, except you ravish me.

∞

The Flea
John Donne, 1633

Mark but this flea, and mark in this,
How little that which thou deny'st me is;
It sucked me first, and now sucks thee,
And in this flea our two bloods mingled be;
5 Thou know'st that this cannot be said
A sin, nor shame, nor loss of maidenhead;
Yet this enjoys before it woo,
And pampered swells with one blood made of two,
And this, alas, is more than we would do.

10 Oh stay, three lives in one flea spare,
Where we almost, yea, more than married are.
This flea is you and I, and this
Our marriage bed, and marriage temple is;
Though parents grudge, and you, w' are met,
15 And cloistered in these living walls of jet.
Though use make you apt to kill me,
Let not to that, self-murder added be,
And sacrilege, three sins in killing three.

Cruel and sudden, hast thou since
20 Purpled thy nail in blood of innocence?
Wherein could this flea guilty be,
Except in that drop which it sucked from thee?
Yet thou triumph'st and say'st that thou
Find'st not thyself, nor me the weaker now;
25 'Tis true, then learn how false fears be:
Just so much honor, when thou yield'st to me,
Will waste, as this flea's death took life from thee.

∞

A Valediction: Forbidding Mourning
John Donne, 1633

As virtuous men pass mildly away,
And whisper to their souls, to go,
Whilst some of their sad friends do say,
"The breath goes now," and some say, "No:"

5 So let us melt, and make no noise,
No tear-floods, nor sigh-tempests move;

'Twere profanation of our joys
To tell the laity our love.

Moving of th' earth brings harms and fears;
10 Men reckon what it did, and meant;
But trepidation of the spheres,
Though greater far, is innocent.

Dull sublunary lovers' love
(Whose soul is sense) cannot admit
15 Absence, because it doth remove
Those things which elemented it.

But we by a love so much refin'd,
That ourselves know not what it is,
Inter-assured of the mind,
20 Care less, eyes, lips, and hands to miss.

Our two souls therefore, which are one,
Though I must go, endure not yet
A breach, but an expansion,
Like gold to airy thinness beat.

25 If they be two, they are two so
As stiff twin compasses are two;
Thy soul, the fix'd foot, makes no show
To move, but doth, if th' other do.

And though it in the centre sit,
30 Yet when the other far doth roam,
It leans, and hearkens after it,
And grows erect, as that comes home.

Such wilt thou be to me, who must
Like th' other foot, obliquely run;
35 Thy firmness makes my circle just,
And makes me end, where I begun.

ભ્ટજ

To His Coy Mistress
Andrew Marvell, 1681

Had we but world enough, and time,
This coyness, lady, were no crime.
We would sit down and think which way
To walk, and pass our long love's day;
5 Thou by the Indian Ganges' side
Should'st rubies find; I by the tide
Of Humber would complain. I would
Love you ten years before the Flood;
And you should, if you please, refuse
10 Till the conversion of the Jews.

195

My vegetable love should grow
Vaster than empires, and more slow.
An hundred years should go to praise
Thine eyes, and on thy forehead gaze;
15 Two hundred to adore each breast,
But thirty thousand to the rest;
An age at least to every part,
And the last age should show your heart.
For, lady, you deserve this state,
20 Nor would I love at lower rate.

But at my back I always hear
Time's winged chariot hurrying near;
And yonder all before us lie
Deserts of vast eternity.
25 Thy beauty shall no more be found,
Nor, in thy marble vault, shall sound
My echoing song; then worms shall try
That long preserv'd virginity,
And your quaint honour turn to dust,
30 And into ashes all my lust.
The grave's a fine and private place,
But none I think do there embrace.

Now therefore, while the youthful hue
Sits on thy skin like morning dew,
35 And while thy willing soul transpires
At every pore with instant fires,
Now let us sport us while we may;
And now, like am'rous birds of prey,
Rather at once our time devour,
40 Than languish in his slow-chapp'd[1] power.
Let us roll all our strength, and all
Our sweetness, up into one ball;
And tear our pleasures with rough strife
Through the iron gates of life.
45 Thus, though we cannot make our sun
Stand still, yet we will make him run

---

[1] Slow-chapp'd. Slow-jawed, or chewing slowly.

John Milton
1608 - 1674

After Chaucer and Shakespeare, John Milton is the most celebrated and influential writer in the English language. A brilliant scholar from youth, he wrote poetry in Latin and Italian as well as English, read voraciously, and remembered most everything.

His greatest work, *Paradise Lost*, is one of the longest works of poetry in the English language and the work that pushes the language to its limits. In this epic poem, John Milton attempts to, as he puts it, "justify the ways of God to men." In order to carry out this project, Milton chooses the subject of the beginning of time, particularly the war in the heavens between the good and bad (or rebel) angels, led by Satan, and the creation and fall of Adam and Eve.

In Milton's time, *Paradise Lost* had a mixed reception, as Milton, a well-known admirer of those who had revolted against Charles I and follower of the revolutionary leader Oliver Cromwell (on whom some say that Satan is modeled), was much scrutinized by the court of Charles II, who had been restored to the throne seven years before the publication of the poem.

Major Works
Paradise Lost (1667)
Paradise Regained (1671)
Samson Agonistes (1671)

∞
Paradise Lost, Book 1
John Milton, 1667

The first passage is the very beginning of the poem. Here Milton outlines his topic for the poem, asks for the strength to carry out his task, and names his purpose.

Of Mans First Disobedience, and the Fruit
Of that Forbidden Tree, whose mortal tast

Brought Death into the World, and all our woe,
With loss of Eden, till one greater Man
5   Restore us, and regain the blissful Seat,
Sing Heav'nly Muse, that on the secret top
Of Oreb, or of Sinai, didst inspire
That Shepherd, who first taught the chosen Seed,
In the Beginning how the Heav'ns and Earth
10 Rose out of Chaos: Or if Sion Hill
Delight thee more, and Siloa's Brook that flow'd
Fast by the Oracle of God; I thence
Invoke thy aid to my adventrous Song,
That with no middle flight intends to soar
15 Above th' Aonian Mount, while it pursues
Things unattempted yet in Prose or Rhime.
And chiefly Thou O Spirit, that dost prefer
Before all Temples th'upright heart and pure,
Instruct me, for Thou know'st; Thou from the first
20 Wast present, and with mighty wings outspread
Dove-like satst brooding on the vast Abyss
And mad'st it pregnant: What in me is dark
Illumin, what is low raise and support;
That to the height of this great Argument
25 I may assert Eternal Providence,
And justify the wayes of God to men.

Paradise Lost, Book 1

In the second passage, we see Satan not as the wicked corrupter of humankind that we normally see him as, but as a tenacious leader who speaks with as much skill and charisma as the greatest of statesmen. Though he and his followers (the fallen angels) have been driven out of heaven and into hell, he argues that it is better "to reign in hell than to serve in heaven." He exhorts his followers to continue their struggle, though they have just lost the battle to the good angels.

Is this the Region, this the Soil, the Clime,
Said then the lost Arch-Angel, this the seat
That we must change for Heav'n, this mournful gloom
For that celestial light? Be it so, since he
5   Who now is Sovran can dispose and bid
What shall be right: farthest from him is best
Whom reason hath equaled, force hath made supreme
Above his equals. Farewell happy Fields
Where Joy for ever dwells: Hail horrours, hail
10 Infernal world, and thou profoundest Hell
Receive thy new Possessor: One who brings
A mind not to be chang'd by Place or Time.
The mind is its own place, and in it self

Can make a Heav'n of Hell, a Hell of Heav'n.
15 What matter where, if I be still the same,
And what I should be, all but less then he
Whom Thunder hath made greater? Here at least
We shall be free; th' Almighty hath not built
Here for his envy, will not drive us hence:
20 Here we may reign secure, and in my choice
To reign is worth ambition though in Hell:
Better to reign in Hell, then serve in Heav'n.
But wherefore let we then our faithful friends,
Th'associates and copartners of our loss
25 Lie thus astonished on th'oblivious Pool,
And call them not to share with us their part
In this unhappy Mansion, or once more
With rallied Arms to try what may be yet
Regained in Heav'n, or what more lost in Hell?

Paradise Lost, Book 4

In the third passage, we see Satan at a different phase of the poem. The fallen rebel angels have decided that, rather than continue the battle they have just lost, they would seek revenge by spoiling God's new creation, the human race. Satan, with heroic effort and unsurpassed guile, has reached the Garden of Eden and seen how wonderful is God's new creation. As he watches Adam and Eve, he shows his jealousy and malice, in contrast with the heroism and strength he showed early in the poem.

O Hell! what doe mine eyes with grief behold,
Into our room of bliss thus high advanc't
Creatures of other mould, earth-born perhaps,
Not Spirits, yet to heav'nly Spirits bright
5 Little inferior; whom my thoughts pursue
With wonder, and could love, so lively shines
In them Divine resemblance, and such grace
The hand that formed them on their shape hath poured.
Ah gentle pair, yee little think how nigh
10 Your change approaches, when all these delights
Will vanish and deliver ye to woe,
More woe, the more your taste is now of joy;
Happy, but for so happy ill secur'd
Long to continue, and this high seat your Heav'n
15 Ill fenc't for Heav'n to keep out such a foe
As now is entered; yet no purpos'd foe
To you whom I could pity thus forlorn
Though I unpittied: League with you I seek,
And mutual amity so straight, so close,
20 That I with you must dwell, or you with me

Henceforth; my dwelling haply may not please
Like this fair Paradise, your sense, yet such
Accept your Makers work; he gave it me,
Which I as freely give; Hell shall unfold,
25   To entertain you two, her widest Gates,
And send forth all her Kings; there will be room,
Not like these narrow limits, to receive
Your numerous offspring; if no better place,
Thank him who puts me loath to this revenge
30   On you who wrong me not for him who wronged.
And should I at your harmless innocence
Melt, as I do, yet public reason just,
Honour and Empire with revenge enlarg'd,
By conquering this new World, compels me now
35   To do what else though dammed I should abhor.

Paradise Lost, Book 9

In the fourth passage, we see Satan, having taken the shape of a serpent (he can take any shape he likes), greets Eve and begins to convince her that she should eat of the fruit of the tree of the knowledge of good and evil.

Wonder not, Sovereign Mistress, if perhaps
Thou canst, who art sole Wonder, much less arm
Thy looks, the Heav'n of mildness, with disdain,
Displeas'd that I approach thee thus, and gaze
5   Insatiate, I thus single, nor have feared
Thy awful brow, more awful thus retir'd.
Fairest resemblance of thy Maker faire,
Thee all things living gaze on, all things thine
By gift, and thy Celestial Beauty adore
10 With ravishment beheld, there best beheld
Where universally admir'd; but here
In this enclosure wild, these Beasts among,
Beholders rude, and shallow to discern
Half what in thee is fair, one man except,
15 Who sees thee? (and what is one?) who shouldst be seen
A Goddess among Gods, ador'd and serv'd
By Angels numberless, thy daily Train.

Aphra Behn
1640 – 1689

Born in England and raised in Suriname, West Indies, Aphra Behn returned to England, married, worked as a spy in Antwerp during the war of 1665 to 1667 against the Dutch, was jailed briefly for debt (because she was not paid), turned to writing for a living, and became probably the first professional female writer in England. Though a versatile and productive writer, she suffered accusations of plagiarism and lewdness, mostly because she was a woman in a male profession. Nonetheless, she wrote eighteen plays and four novels, including *Oroonoko*, one of the first depictions of the "noble savage."

Major Works
The Rover (1677, 1681)
The City Heiress (1682)
The Luck Chance (1686)
Oroonoko (1688)

ༀ

Love Armed
Aphra Behn, 1684

    Love in fantastic triumph sat,
      Whilst bleeding hearts around him flow'd,
    For whom fresh pains he did create,
      And strange tyrannic power he shew'd;
5   From thy bright eyes he took his fire,
      Which round about in sport he hurl'd;
    But 'twas from mine he took desire
      Enough to undo the amorous world.

    From me he took his sighs and tears,
10   From thee his pride and cruelty;
    From me his languishments and fears,
      And every killing dart from thee;

Thus thou and I the God have arm'd,
    And set him up a Deity;
15 But my poor heart alone is harm'd,
    Whilst thine the victor is, and free.

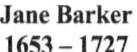

Jane Barker
1653 – 1727

Jane Barker was part of a large swell of mostly unrecognized writing by British women in the early eighteenth century. She wrote several novels and at least one volume of poetry. Her most intriguing work is the *Patchwork Trilogy*, containing *Love Intrigues*, *The Patchwork Screen for the Ladies*, and *The Lining of the Patchwork Screen*. In it she relates the love between Bosvil and Galesia (distant cousins), their split, and Galesia's further life and inclusion in a community of women. Most of the second and third novels contain short tales, poems, and other items, which are pieced together like a patchwork screen.

CR&O

Love Intrigues, Or The Amours of Bosvil and Galesia (*Selections*)
Jane Barker, 1713

Galesia has just learned that her beloved Bosvil has been false to her.

Now whether this Affliction was laid on me by the immediate Hand of Providence, or that Fate, or my Constellations produced it by secondary Causes,[1] I knew not; but Innocence was my Consolation; for I had nothing wherewith to reproach my self; I had acted justly, and honourably towards him; he could not upbraid me either with Coyness, or Kindness; for tho' I had squar'd my Actions, by the exact Rules of Vertue, and Modesty; yet I did not exclude Civility, and good Nature; for I always stay'd in his Company, heard him, laugh'd fool'd, and jested with him; yet not so freely as to transgress good Manners, or break Respect on either side; all which might assure a Person less judicious than himself, that neither his Person, nor Proposals, were disagreeable. All these Considerations served to render his Coldness the more surprizing; but it pleas'g God to have it thus; Bosvil perhaps was my Idol, and rival'd Heaven in my Affections, that I might say to him, as

---

[1] Causes. Please note that the unusual capitalization and spelling in this selection has been retained from the original text to illustrate the typical formatting of texts in this era.

Cowley to his Mistress.

> Thou even my Prayers dost steal from me,
> For I with wild Idolatry,
> Begin to God, and end 'em all in Thee.

This Vicissitude in my Affairs, made me reflect on those Verses, or Vision, which said, Hymen and Fortune are thy Foes, &c. In which I endeavour'd to be resign'd, saying, It is the Lord's Doing, tho' marvellous in my Eyes. Tho' nothing could be harsher, than to be thus abandoned in the Flower of my Youth, and that my own Relation, who ought to have sustain'd me against any false Pretender: I endeavour'd to detach my Thoughts from him; or if it was so that i must needs think on him, I resolved it shou'd be on his Crimes, Falshood, and Cruelty.

Thus by degrees his Company became troublesom, and his Presence ungrateful. Yet cou'd I not avoid either, for I had no Reason to quarrel with him, unless for not courting me, as formerly: And that was turning the Tables, and making my self the Lover, instead of the Person beloved; which was not only contradictory to my haughty Humour, but seem'd in a manner to invert Nature; nevertheless I forced my self to bear it, with a seeming Equality of Mind, till a fit Occasion wou'd offer it self to my Revenge. Like the Quaker that is smitten on the one Cheek, turns the other also; but after that heving (as he thinks) fulfill'd the Law, can beat his Adversary as well as any carnal Man: so I waited but for a left Cheek-blow; some ungrateful Action, that might give at least a seeming just Cause to quarrel, so as to take occasion to banish him; his Presence being as disagreeable to me as a Specter; for it's natural enough, that the Cause of Grief, shou'd be the Object of Aversion.

I remain'd full of this Wish many Months; at last Fortune was a little propitious to my Desires, at least I wrested an Occasion to my Caprice, which was thus.

Bosvil and another young Gentleman his Friend, met my Father at a certain Place over a Bottle; here Bosvil proposed his Friend to my Father as an Husband for me, all Conditions of Portion and Joynture were there propos'd, and approv'd on both sides, and the Day appointed on which the Gentleman shou'd come to visit me, which was to be the Week following. This my Father told me with Satisfaction, withal minding me, how much I was obliged to my Cousin Bosvil: To which my Answers were few, dubious, and obscure; which pass'd with my good Father, for a little Virgin Surprize; which Discourses of this nature are apt to raise the Hearts of young Creatures.

But, O my Lucasia! I cannot tell you what I suffer'd whan I was alone, Rage and Madness seiz'd me; Malice and Revenge were all I thought on: I inspired an evil Genius, resolv'd his Death, and pleas'd my self in the Fancy of a barbarous Revenge: I shall delight my self, to see the Blood pour out of his false Heart: In order to accomplish this detestable Freak, I went towards the Place of his Abode, supposing a Rapier in my hand, and saying to my self; The false Bosvil shou'd now disquiet me no more, nor any other of our Sex; in him I will end his Race, no more of them shall come to disturb, or affront Womankind; this only Son, shall dye by the hands of me an only Daughter; and however the World may call it Cruely, or barbarous; I am sure our sex will have reason to thank me, and keep an Annual

Festival, on which a Criminal like him is executed: The Example perhaps will deter others, and secure many from the Wrongs of such false Traitors; and I be magnified in future times; for it was for ridding the World of a Monster, that Hercules was esteem'd so great a Hero, and George a Saint. Then sure I shall be rank'd in the Catalogue of Heroines, for such a Service done to my Sex: for certainly the Deserts of Arabia never produced a more formidable Monster, than this unaccountable Bosvil. Behold what Sophisms one can find to justify any mad Attempt, and how for the gratifying our Fancy, we are ready to affront, if not quite reverse the Laws of Nature: that, if the Feebleness of our Hands did not moderate the Fury of our Heads, Woman sometimes wou'd exceed the fiercest Savages; especially, when affronted in her Amours; which brings into my Mind a Verse or two on such an Occasion.

> A slighted Woman oft a Fury grows,
> And for Revenge quits her Baptismal Vows,
> Becomes a Witch, and does a Fiend espouse.

In these wild Thoughts I wander'd, till Weariness made me know my own Weakness, and Incapacity of performing, what Fury had inspir'd; and forc'd me to seek Repose under the first Shade; where my flowing Tears mitigated the Heat of my Rage, washing away those extravagant Thoughts, and made me turn my Anger against my self, my wretched self, that woful and unworthy thing; the Scorn of my Kinsman, Lover, Friend, &c. A thousand times I wished that some kind of Serpent wou'd creep out of its Hole and sting me to Death, or that Thunder wou'd descend, and strike me into the Earth; and so at once perform my Death, and Funeral! O no (said I) that wou'd render Bosvil too happy. I must go home and write the whole Scene of his Treachery, and then on my self act the last part of the Tragedy. With these Thoughts I bubled my froward Fancy, and so returning home very weary, I threw my self on my Bed, where all my Resentment became a Prey to gentle Slumbers; which much refresh'd my weary Body, and more weary Mind; rendering me a little capable of acting according to the Dictates of Reason; but not without a large Mixture of Passion; that when I awak'd, I writ to him after this Bizar manner.

Cousin;

> *I Thought you had been so well acquainted with my Humour, touching a Married Life, as to know it to be my Aversion, therefore wonder you shou'd make such a Proposal to my Father on your Friends Behalf: perhaps you will say it was but in jest, and I believe it was no more; but I beg you to make something else the Subject of your Raillery, and leave me out, till Misbehaviour render me the proper Object of Ridicule, which has not hitherto; for I have done nothing dishonourable to my self, nor disobliging to you; therefore ought rather to be the Object of Civility than Banter, which perhaps, Distance and Absence may accomplish; therefore I beg you will see me no more, till Fortune commission you by the Change of your Condition; in the mean time I shall remain,*

> Your Kinswoman,
> and humble Servant,
> Galesia.

Alexander Pope
1688 – 1744

Born into a London merchant-class family, Alexander Pope was a Catholic in a time of intense anti-Catholic sentiment in England. Because his family was Catholic, they were forced to move from London, and young Alexander, though he did gain an education in Catholic schools, which were illegal, was not allowed to enter a university. From the age of twelve, Pope suffered much physical illness, especially from Pott's Disease (tuberculosis of the bone), which led to a deformed spine (a hunchback), respiratory problems, and chronic pain.

Despite all of this, Pope was arguably the most ingenious writer of his age, producing poetry as polished as any that has been written in English. Much of his life was lived in a genteel fashion at his villa in Twickenham, where he continued to garden, write poetry, and attack many of his literary contemporaries (except his friends Swift and Gay).

In the selection that follows, the first of four epistles (letters) that make up *An Essay on Man*, Pope, at the behest of his patron Herbert St. John, Lord Bolingbroke (as noted in the first line of the poem), takes on the nearly impossible task of explaining why there is tragedy in this world (much like Milton's attempt to "justify the ways of God to men"). The poem is also memorable for its description of the "great chain of being."

Major Works
Essay on Criticism (1711)
Rape of the Lock (1714)
Dunciad (1728)
Essay on Man (1734)

03&0

From An Essay On Man (*Epistle I*)
Alexander Pope, 1733 – 34

Awake, my St. John! leave all meaner things
To low ambition, and the pride of kings.
Let us (since life can little more supply
Than just to look about us and to die)
5   Expatiate free o'er all this scene of man;

A mighty maze! but not without a plan;
A wild, where weeds and flow'rs promiscuous shoot;
Or garden, tempting with forbidden fruit.
Together let us beat this ample field,
10 Try what the open, what the covert yield;
The latent tracts, the giddy heights explore
Of all who blindly creep, or sightless soar;
Eye Nature's walks, shoot folly as it flies,
And catch the manners living as they rise;
15 Laugh where we must, be candid where we can;
But vindicate the ways of God to man.
Say first, of God above, or man below,
What can we reason, but from what we know?
Of man what see we, but his station here,
20 From which to reason, or to which refer?
Through worlds unnumber'd though the God be known,
'Tis ours to trace him only in our own.
He, who through vast immensity can pierce,
See worlds on worlds compose one universe,
25 Observe how system into system runs,
What other planets circle other suns,
What varied being peoples ev'ry star,
May tell why Heav'n has made us as we are.
But of this frame the bearings, and the ties,
30 The strong connections, nice dependencies,
Gradations just, has thy pervading soul
Look'd through? or can a part contain the whole?
Is the great chain, that draws all to agree,
And drawn supports, upheld by God, or thee?
35 Presumptuous man! the reason wouldst thou find,
Why form'd so weak, so little, and so blind?
First, if thou canst, the harder reason guess,
Why form'd no weaker, blinder, and no less?
Ask of thy mother earth, why oaks are made
40 Taller or stronger than the weeds they shade?
Or ask of yonder argent fields above,
Why Jove's satellites are less than Jove?
Of systems possible, if 'tis confest
That Wisdom infinite must form the best,
45 Where all must full or not coherent be,
And all that rises, rise in due degree;
Then, in the scale of reas'ning life, 'tis plain
There must be somewhere, such a rank as man:
And all the question (wrangle e'er so long)
50 Is only this, if God has plac'd him wrong?
Respecting man, whatever wrong we call,

May, must be right, as relative to all.
In human works, though labour'd on with pain,
A thousand movements scarce one purpose gain;
55 In God's, one single can its end produce;
Yet serves to second too some other use.
So man, who here seems principal alone,
Perhaps acts second to some sphere unknown,
Touches some wheel, or verges to some goal;
60 'Tis but a part we see, and not a whole.
When the proud steed shall know why man restrains
His fiery course, or drives him o'er the plains:
When the dull ox, why now he breaks the clod,
Is now a victim, and now Egypt's God:
65 Then shall man's pride and dulness comprehend
His actions', passions', being's, use and end;
Why doing, suff'ring, check'd, impell'd; and why
This hour a slave, the next a deity.
Then say not man's imperfect, Heav'n in fault;
70 Say rather, man's as perfect as he ought:
His knowledge measur'd to his state and place;
His time a moment, and a point his space.
If to be perfect in a certain sphere,
What matter, soon or late, or here or there?
75 The blest today is as completely so,
As who began a thousand years ago.
Heav'n from all creatures hides the book of fate,
All but the page prescrib'd, their present state:
From brutes what men, from men what spirits know:
80 Or who could suffer being here below?
The lamb thy riot dooms to bleed today,
Had he thy reason, would he skip and play?
Pleas'd to the last, he crops the flow'ry food,
And licks the hand just rais'd to shed his blood.
85 Oh blindness to the future! kindly giv'n,
That each may fill the circle mark'd by Heav'n:
Who sees with equal eye, as God of all,
A hero perish, or a sparrow fall,
Atoms or systems into ruin hurl'd,
90 And now a bubble burst, and now a world.
Hope humbly then; with trembling pinions soar;
Wait the great teacher Death; and God adore.
What future bliss, he gives not thee to know,
But gives that hope to be thy blessing now.
95 Hope springs eternal in the human breast:
Man never is, but always to be blest:
The soul, uneasy and confin'd from home,

Rests and expatiates in a life to come.
Lo! the poor Indian, whose untutor'd mind
100 Sees God in clouds, or hears him in the wind;
His soul, proud science never taught to stray
Far as the solar walk, or milky way;
Yet simple nature to his hope has giv'n,
Behind the cloud topp'd hill, an humbler heav'n;
105 Some safer world in depth of woods embrac'd,
Some happier island in the wat'ry waste,
Where slaves once more their native land behold,
No fiends torment, no Christians thirst for gold.
To be, contents his natural desire,
110 He asks no angel's wing, no seraph's fire;
But thinks, admitted to that equal sky,
His faithful dog shall bear him company.
Go, wiser thou! and, in thy scale of sense
Weigh thy opinion against Providence;
115 Call imperfection what thou fanciest such,
Say, here he gives too little, there too much:
Destroy all creatures for thy sport or gust,
Yet cry, if man's unhappy, God's unjust;
If man alone engross not Heav'n's high care,
120 Alone made perfect here, immortal there:
Snatch from his hand the balance and the rod,
Rejudge his justice, be the God of God.
In pride, in reas'ning pride, our error lies;
All quit their sphere, and rush into the skies.
125 Pride still is aiming at the blest abodes,
Men would be angels, angels would be gods.
Aspiring to be gods, if angels fell,
Aspiring to be angels, men rebel:
And who but wishes to invert the laws
130 Of order, sins against th' Eternal Cause.
Ask for what end the heav'nly bodies shine,
Earth for whose use? Pride answers, "'Tis for mine:
For me kind Nature wakes her genial pow'r,
Suckles each herb, and spreads out ev'ry flow'r;
135 Annual for me, the grape, the rose renew,
The juice nectareous, and the balmy dew;
For me, the mine a thousand treasures brings;
For me, health gushes from a thousand springs;
Seas roll to waft me, suns to light me rise;
140 My foot-stool earth, my canopy the skies."
But errs not Nature from this gracious end,
From burning suns when livid deaths descend,
When earthquakes swallow, or when tempests sweep

Towns to one grave, whole nations to the deep?
145 "No, ('tis replied) the first Almighty Cause
Acts not by partial, but by gen'ral laws;
Th' exceptions few; some change since all began:
And what created perfect?" – Why then man?
If the great end be human happiness,
150 Then Nature deviates; and can man do less?
As much that end a constant course requires
Of show'rs and sunshine, as of man's desires;
As much eternal springs and cloudless skies,
As men for ever temp'rate, calm, and wise.
155 If plagues or earthquakes break not Heav'n's design,
Why then a Borgia, or a Catiline?
Who knows but he, whose hand the lightning forms,
Who heaves old ocean, and who wings the storms;
Pours fierce ambition in a Caesar's mind,
160 Or turns young Ammon loose to scourge mankind?
From pride, from pride, our very reas'ning springs;
Account for moral, as for nat'ral things:
Why charge we Heav'n in those, in these acquit?
In both, to reason right is to submit.
165 Better for us, perhaps, it might appear,
Were there all harmony, all virtue here;
That never air or ocean felt the wind;
That never passion discompos'd the mind.
But ALL subsists by elemental strife;
170 And passions are the elements of life.
The gen'ral order, since the whole began,
Is kept in nature, and is kept in man.
What would this man? Now upward will he soar,
And little less than angel, would be more;
175 Now looking downwards, just as griev'd appears
To want the strength of bulls, the fur of bears.
Made for his use all creatures if he call,
Say what their use, had he the pow'rs of all?
Nature to these, without profusion, kind,
180 The proper organs, proper pow'rs assign'd;
Each seeming want compensated of course,
Here with degrees of swiftness, there of force;
All in exact proportion to the state;
Nothing to add, and nothing to abate.
185 Each beast, each insect, happy in its own:
Is Heav'n unkind to man, and man alone?
Shall he alone, whom rational we call,
Be pleas'd with nothing, if not bless'd with all?
The bliss of man (could pride that blessing find)

190 Is not to act or think beyond mankind;
    No pow'rs of body or of soul to share,
    But what his nature and his state can bear.
    Why has not man a microscopic eye?
    For this plain reason, man is not a fly.
195 Say what the use, were finer optics giv'n,
    T' inspect a mite, not comprehend the heav'n?
    Or touch, if tremblingly alive all o'er,
    To smart and agonize at ev'ry pore?
    Or quick effluvia darting through the brain,
200 Die of a rose in aromatic pain?
    If nature thunder'd in his op'ning ears,
    And stunn'd him with the music of the spheres,
    How would he wish that Heav'n had left him still
    The whisp'ring zephyr, and the purling rill?
205 Who finds not Providence all good and wise,
    Alike in what it gives, and what denies?
    Far as creation's ample range extends,
    The scale of sensual, mental pow'rs ascends:
    Mark how it mounts, to man's imperial race,
210 From the green myriads in the peopled grass:
    What modes of sight betwixt each wide extreme,
    The mole's dim curtain, and the lynx's beam:
    Of smell, the headlong lioness between,
    And hound sagacious on the tainted green:
215 Of hearing, from the life that fills the flood,
    To that which warbles through the vernal wood:
    The spider's touch, how exquisitely fine!
    Feels at each thread, and lives along the line:
    In the nice bee, what sense so subtly true
220 From pois'nous herbs extracts the healing dew?
    How instinct varies in the grov'lling swine,
    Compar'd, half-reas'ning elephant, with thine!
    'Twixt that, and reason, what a nice barrier;
    For ever sep'rate, yet for ever near!
225 Remembrance and reflection how allied;
    What thin partitions sense from thought divide:
    And middle natures, how they long to join,
    Yet never pass th' insuperable line!
    Without this just gradation, could they be
230 Subjected, these to those, or all to thee?
    The pow'rs of all subdu'd by thee alone,
    Is not thy reason all these pow'rs in one?
    See, through this air, this ocean, and this earth,
    All matter quick, and bursting into birth.
235 Above, how high, progressive life may go!

Around, how wide! how deep extend below!
Vast chain of being, which from God began,
Natures ethereal, human, angel, man,
Beast, bird, fish, insect! what no eye can see,
240 No glass can reach! from infinite to thee,
From thee to nothing! – On superior pow'rs
Were we to press, inferior might on ours:
Or in the full creation leave a void,
Where, one step broken, the great scale's destroy'd:
245 From nature's chain whatever link you strike,
Tenth or ten thousandth, breaks the chain alike.
And, if each system in gradation roll
Alike essential to th' amazing whole,
The least confusion but in one, not all
250 That system only, but the whole must fall.
Let earth unbalanc'd from her orbit fly,
Planets and suns run lawless through the sky;
Let ruling angels from their spheres be hurl'd,
Being on being wreck'd, and world on world;
255 Heav'n's whole foundations to their centre nod,
And nature trembles to the throne of God.
All this dread order break – for whom? for thee?
Vile worm! – Oh madness, pride, impiety!
What if the foot ordain'd the dust to tread,
260 Or hand, to toil, aspir'd to be the head?
What if the head, the eye, or ear repin'd
To serve mere engines to the ruling mind?
Just as absurd for any part to claim
To be another, in this gen'ral frame:
265 Just as absurd, to mourn the tasks or pains,
The great directing Mind of All ordains.
All are but parts of one stupendous whole,
Whose body Nature is, and God the soul;
That, chang'd through all, and yet in all the same,
270 Great in the earth, as in th' ethereal frame,
Warms in the sun, refreshes in the breeze,
Glows in the stars, and blossoms in the trees,
Lives through all life, extends through all extent,
Spreads undivided, operates unspent,
275 Breathes in our soul, informs our mortal part,
As full, as perfect, in a hair as heart;
As full, as perfect, in vile man that mourns,
As the rapt seraph that adores and burns;
To him no high, no low, no great, no small;
280 He fills, he bounds, connects, and equals all.
Cease then, nor order imperfection name:

Our proper bliss depends on what we blame.
Know thy own point: This kind, this due degree
Of blindness, weakness, Heav'n bestows on thee.
285 Submit. – In this, or any other sphere,
Secure to be as blest as thou canst bear:
Safe in the hand of one disposing pow'r,
Or in the natal, or the mortal hour.
All nature is but art, unknown to thee;
290 All chance, direction, which thou canst not see;
All discord, harmony, not understood;
All partial evil, universal good:
And, spite of pride, in erring reason's spite,
One truth is clear, Whatever is, is right.

Thomas Jefferson
1743 – 1826

Thomas Jefferson, best known as the third President of the United States and the author of the Declaration of Independence, was also an inventor with interests in agriculture, science, religion, and architecture. Though he spent a great deal of time in politics, he always enjoyed returning to his beloved estate of Monticello where he could carry out his studies and experiments.

The Declaration of Independence stands among the world's great documents as a testament of rational thought in a time of crisis, and it has served as a model, source, or inspiration for hundreds of important political or governmental documents around the world.

C3£0

The Declaration of Independence
Thomas Jefferson, 1776

When in the course of human events, it becomes necessary for one people to dissolve the political bands which have connected them with another, and to assume the Powers of the earth, the separate and equal station to which the Laws of Nature and of Nature's God entitle them, a decent respect to the opinions of mankind requires that they should declare the causes which impel them to the separation.

We hold these truths to be self-evident, that all men are created equal, that they are endowed by their Creator with certain unalienable rights, that among these are Life, Liberty, and the pursuit of Happiness. That to secure these rights, Governments are instituted among Men, deriving their just powers from the consent of the governed. That whenever any Form of Government becomes destructive of these ends, it is the Right of the People to alter or to abolish it, and to institute new Government, laying its foundation on such principles and organizing its powers in such form, as to them shall seem most likely to effect their Safety and Happiness. Prudence, indeed, will dictate that Governments long established should not be changed for light and transient causes; and accordingly all experience hath shown, that mankind are more disposed to suffer, while evils are sufferable, than to right themselves by abolishing the forms to which they are accustomed. But when a long train of abuses and usurpations, pursuing invariably the same Object evinces a design to reduce them under absolute Despotism, it is their right, it is their duty, to throw off such Government, and to provide new Guards for their future security. – Such has been the patient sufferance of these Colonies; and such is now the necessity which constrains them to alter their former Systems of Government. The history of the present King of Great Britain is a history of repeated injuries and usurpations, all having in direct object the establishment of an absolute Tyranny over these States. To prove this, let Facts be submitted to a candid world. He has refused his Assent to Laws, the most wholesome and necessary for the public good.

He has forbidden his Governors to pass Laws of immediate and pressing importance, unless suspended in their operation till his Assent should be obtained; and when so suspended, he has utterly neglected to attend to them.

He has refused to pass other Laws for the accommodation of large districts of people, unless those people would relinquish the right of Representation in the Legislature, a right inestimable to them and formidable to tyrants only.

He has called together legislative bodies at places unusual, uncomfortable and distant from the depository of their public Records, for the sole purpose of fatiguing them into compliance with his measures.

He has dissolved Representative Houses repeatedly, for opposing with manly firmness his invasions on the rights of the people.

He has refused for a long time, after such dissolutions, to cause others to be elected; whereby the Legislative powers, incapable of Annihilation, have returned to the People at large for their exercise; the State remaining in the mean time exposed to all dangers of invasion from without, and convulsions within.

He has endeavoured to prevent the population of these States; for that purpose obstructing the Laws of Naturalization of Foreigners; refusing to pass others to encourage their migrations hither, and raising the conditions of new Appropriations of Lands.

He has obstructed the Administration of Justice, by refusing his Assent to Laws for establishing Judiciary powers.

He has made Judges dependent on his Will alone, for the tenure of their offices, and the amount and payment of their salaries. He has erected a multitude of New Offices, and sent hither swarms of Officers to harass our People, and eat out their substance. He has kept among us, in times of peace, Standing Armies without the Consent of our legislature.

He has affected to render the Military independent of and superior to the Civil Power.

He has combined with others to subject us to a jurisdiction foreign to our constitution, and unacknowledged by our laws; giving his Assent to their Acts of pretended Legislation:

For quartering large bodies of armed troops among us:

For protecting them, by a mock Trial, from Punishment for any Murders which they should commit on the Inhabitants of these States: For cutting off our Trade with all parts of the world:

For imposing taxes on us without our Consent:

For depriving us of many cases, of the benefits of Trial by Jury: For transporting us beyond Seas to be tried for pretended offences:

For abolishing the free System of English Laws in a neighbouring Province, establishing therein an Arbitrary government, and enlarging its Boundaries so as to render it at once an example and fit instrument for introducing the same absolute rule into these Colonies:

For taking away our Charters, abolishing our most valuable Laws, and altering fundamentally the Forms of our Governments: For suspending our own Legislatures, and declaring themselves invested with Power to legislate for us in all cases whatsoever. He has abdicated Government here, by declaring us out of his Protection and waging War against us.

He has plundered our seas, ravaged our Coasts, burnt our towns, and destroyed the lives of our people.

He is at this time transporting large armies of foreign mercenaries to compleat the works of death, desolation, and tyranny, already begun with circumstances of Cruelty & perfidy scarcely parallelled in the most barbarous ages, and totally unworthy the Head of a civilized nation.

He has constrained our fellow Citizens taken Captive on the high Seas to bear Arms against their Country, to become the executioners of their friends and Brethren, or to fall themselves by their Hands.

He has excited domestic insurrections amongst us, and has endeavoured to bring on the inhabitants of our frontiers, the merciless Indian savages, whose known rule of warfare, is an undistinguished destruction of all ages, sexes, and conditions.

In every stage of these Oppressions We have Petitioned for Redress in the most humble terms: Our repeated Petitions have been answered only by repeated injury. A Prince, whose character is thus marked by every act which may define a Tyrant, is unfit to be the ruler of a free people.

Nor have We been wanting in attention to our British brethren. We have warned them from time to time of attempts by their legislature to extend an unwarrantable jurisdiction over us. We have reminded them of the circumstances of our emigration and settlement here. We have appealed to their native justice and magnanimity, and we have conjured them by the ties of our common kindred to disavow these usurpations, which, would inevitably interrupt our connections and correspondence. They too must have been deaf to the voice of justice and of consanguinity. We must, therefore, acquiesce in the necessity, which denounces our Separation, and hold them, as we hold the rest of mankind, Enemies in War, in Peace Friends.

We, therefore, the Representatives of the United States of America, in General Congress, Assembled, appealing to the Supreme Judge of the world for the rectitude of our intentions, do, in the Name, and by Authority of the good People of these Colonies, solemnly publish and declare, That these United Colonies are, and of Right ought to be free and independent states; that they are Absolved from all Allegiance to the British Crown, and that all political connection between them and the State of Great Britain, is and ought to be totally dissolved; and that as Free and Independent States, they have full Power to levy War, conclude Peace, contract Alliances, establish Commerce, and to do all other Acts and Things which Independent States may of right do. And for the support of this Declaration, with a firm reliance on the Protection of Divine Providence, we mutually pledge to each other our Lives, our Fortunes, and our sacred Honor.

William Blake
1757 – 1827

William Blake, the first of the major English Romantic poets, as well as a painter, engraver, and printer, largely self-taught, began writing with collections of very short poems and moved toward lengthy mystical visions, which he illustrated and printed as well.

Blake's poetry, always memorable, takes on two distinct dimensions. *The Marriage of Heaven and Hell* and *Jerusalem* mystical or prophetic aspect, following the models of the Biblical prophets Isaiah and Elijah and the epic poets Vergil and Milton. His shorter works show concern for the victims of contemporary social problems, as in the poem "London," included below. He reminds us that the root of these problems is that we are enslaved in "mind-forg'd manacles." He believed that all people ought to think for themselves and not follow the crowds; as he put it in his poem *Jerusalem*, "I must Create a System, or be enslav'd by another Man's."

Major Works

Songs of Innocence (1789) and *Songs of Experience* (1794)
The Marriage of Heaven and Hell (1790 – 1793)
Jerusalem: The Emanation of the Giant Albion (1804 – 1820)

 softbreak

ത⁊ø

The Tyger
William Blake, 1794

Tyger! Tyger! burning bright
In the forests of the night,
What immortal hand or eye
Could frame thy fearful symmetry?

5   In what distant deeps or skies
Burnt the fire of thine eyes?
On what wings dare he aspire?
What the hand dare seize the fire?

And what shoulder, and what art,
10 Could twist the sinews of thy heart,
And when thy heart began to beat,
What dread hand? and what dread feet?

What the hammer? what the chain?
In what furnace was thy brain?
15 What the anvil? what dread grasp
Dare its deadly terrors clasp?

When the stars threw down their spears,
And water'd heaven with their tears,
Did he smile his work to see?
20 Did he who made the Lamb make thee?

Tyger! Tyger! burning bright
In the forests of the night,
What immortal hand or eye,
Dare frame thy fearful symmetry?

⋘⋙
And Did Those Feet in Ancient Time
William Blake, 1808

And did those feet in ancient time
Walk upon England's mountains green?
And was the holy Lamb of God
On England's pleasant pastures seen?

5 And did the Countenance Divine
Shine forth upon our clouded hills?
And was Jerusalem builded here
Among these dark Satanic mills?

Bring me my bow of burning gold:
10 Bring me my arrows of desire:
Bring me my spear: O clouds unfold!
Bring me my chariot of fire.

I will not cease from mental fight,
Nor shall my sword sleep in my hand
15 Till we have built Jerusalem
In England's green and pleasant land.

⋘⋙
London
William Blake, 1794

I wander thro' each charter'd street,
Near where the charter'd Thames does flow,
And mark in every face I meet
Marks of weakness, marks of woe.

5   In every cry of every Man,
      In every Infant's cry of fear,
      In every voice, in every ban,
      The mind-forg'd manacles I hear.

      How the Chimney-sweeper's cry
10 Every black'ning Church appalls;
      And the hapless Soldier's sigh
      Runs in blood down Palace walls.

      But most thro' midnight streets I hear
      How the youthful Harlot's curse
15 Blasts the new born Infant's tear,
      And blights with plagues the Marriage hearse.

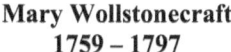

Mary Wollstonecraft
1759 – 1797

Mary Wollstonecraft, a British writer, philosopher, and novelist, is considered by many to be the mother of the British women's suffrage movement. Her *Vindication of the Rights of Women* argues that women need political power in the form of the vote, financial power in the form of personal property, and physical strength, which can come through more fresh air and exercise. She was also the wife of British philosopher, William Godwin, and mother of Mary Shelley, author of *Frankenstein.*

Major Works
A Vindication of the Rights of Men (1790)
A Vindication of the Rights of Women (1792)
Maria, or the Wrongs of Women (1798)

03&0

Observations on the State of Degradation to
Which Woman Is Reduced by Various Causes
***From* A Vindication of the Rights of Women (*Chapter IV*)**
Mary Wollstonecraft, 1792

That woman is naturally weak, or degraded by a concurrence of circumstances, is, I think, clear. But this position I shall simply contrast with a conclusion, which I have frequently heard fall from sensible men in favour of an aristocracy: that the mass of mankind cannot be any thing, or the obsequious slaves, who patiently allow themselves to be penned up, would feel their own consequence, and spurn their chains. Men, they further observe, submit every where to oppression, when they have only to lift up their heads to throw off the yoke; yet, instead of asserting their birthright, they quietly lick the dust, and say, let us eat and drink, for tomorrow we die. Women, I argue from analogy, are degraded by the same propensity to enjoy the present moment; and, at last, despise the freedom which they have not sufficient virtue to struggle to attain. But I must be more explicit.

With respect to the culture of the heart, it is unanimously allowed that sex is out of the question; but the line of subordination in the mental powers is never to be passed over. Only "absolute in loveliness," the portion of rationality granted to woman, is indeed very scanty; for, denying her genius and judgment, it is scarcely possible to divine what remains to characterize intellect.

The stamina of immortality, if I may be allowed the phrase is the perfectibility of human reason: for, was man created perfect, or did a flood of knowledge break in upon him, when he arrived at maturity, that precluded error, I should doubt whether his existence would be continued after the dissolution of the body. But, in the present state of things, every difficulty in morals that escapes from human discussion, and equally baffles the investigation of profound thinking, and the lightning glance of genius, is an argument on which I build my belief of the immortality of the soul. Reason is, consequentially, the simple power of improvement; or, more properly speaking, of discerning truth. Every individual is in this respect a world in itself. More or less may be conspicuous in one being than another; but the nature of reason must be the same in all, if it be an emanation of divinity, the tie that connects the creature with the Creator; for, can that soul be stamped with the heavenly image, that is not perfected by the exercise of its own reason?

Yet outwardly ornamented with elaborate care, and so adorned to delight man, "that with honour he may love," the soul of woman is not allowed to have this distinction, and man, ever placed between her and reason, she is always represented as only created to see through a gross medium, and to take things on trust. But, dismissing these fanciful theories, and considering woman as a whole, let it be what it will, instead of a part of man, the inquiry is whether she has reason or not. If she has, which, for a moment, I will take for granted, she was not created merely to be the solace of man, and the sexual should not destroy the human character.

Into this error men have, probably, been led by viewing education in a false light; not considering it as the first step to form a being advancing gradually towards perfection; but only as a preparation for life. On this sensual error, for I must call it so, has the false system of female manners been reared, which robs the whole sex of its dignity, and classes the brown and fair with the smiling flowers that only adorns the land. This has ever been the language of men, and the fear of departing from a supposed sexual character, has made even women of superior sense adopt the same sentiments.

Thus understanding, strictly speaking, has been denied to woman; and instinct, sublimated into wit and cunning, for the purposes of life, has been substituted in its stead. The power of generalizing ideas, of drawing comprehensive conclusions from individual observations, is the only acquirement, for an immortal being, that really deserves the name of knowledge. Merely to observe, without endeavouring to account for any thing, may (in a very incomplete manner) serve as the common sense of life; but where is the store laid up that is to clothe the soul when it leaves the body?...

I lament that women are systematically degraded by receiving the trivial attentions, which men think it manly to pay to the sex, when, in fact, they are insultingly supporting their own superiority. It is not condescension to bow to an inferiour. So ludicrous, in fact, do these ceremonies appear to me, that I scarcely am able to govern my muscles, when I see a man start with eager, and serious solicitude to lift a handkerchief, or shut a door, when the lady could have done it herself, had she only moved a pace or two....

Women, commonly called Ladies, are not to be contradicted in company, are not allowed to exert any manual strength; and from them the negative virtues only are expected, when any virtues are expected, patience, docility, good-humour, and flexibility; virtues incompatible with any vigorous exertion of intellect. Besides, by living more with each other, and being seldom absolutely alone, they are more under the influence of sentiments than passions. Solitude and reflection are necessary to give to wishes the force of passions, and to enable the imagination to enlarge the object, and make it the most desirable. The same may be said of the rich; they do not sufficiently deal in general ideas, collected by impassioned thinking, or calm investigation, to acquire that strength of character on which great resolves are built. But hear what an acute observer says of the great....

And all this is built on her loveliness! In the middle rank of life, to continue the comparison, men, in their youth, are prepared for professions, and marriage is not considered as the grand feature in their lives; whilst women, on the contrary, have no other scheme to sharpen their faculties. It is not business, extensive plans, or any of the excursive flights of ambition, that engross their attention; no, their thoughts are not employed in rearing such noble structures. To rise in the world, and have the liberty of running from pleasure to pleasure, they must marry advantageously, and to this object their time is sacrificed, and their persons often legally prostituted.

A man when he enters any profession has his eye steadily fixed on some future advantage (and the mind gains great strength by having all its efforts directed to one point) and, full of his business, pleasure is considered as mere relaxation; whilst women seek for pleasure as the main purpose of existence. In fact, from the education, which they receive from society, the love of pleasure may be said to govern them all; but does this prove that there is a sex in souls? It would be just as rational to declare that the courtiers in France, when a destructive system of despotism had formed their character, were not men, because liberty, virtue, and humanity, were sacrificed to pleasure and vanity. – Fatal passions, which have ever domineered over the whole race!...

In short, women, in general, as well as the rich of both sexes, have acquired all the follies and vices of civilization, and missed the useful fruit. It is not necessary for me always to premise, that I speak of the condition of the whole sex, leaving exceptions out of the question. Their senses are inflamed, and their understandings neglected, consequently they become the prey of their senses, delicately termed sensibility, and are blown about by every momentary gust of feeling. They are, therefore, in a much worse condition than they would be in were they in a state nearer to nature. Ever restless and anxious, their over exercised sensibility not only renders them uncomfortable themselves, but troublesome, to use a soft phrase, to others.

All their thoughts turn on things calculated to excite emotion; and feeling, when they should reason, their conduct is unstable, and their opinions are wavering – not the wavering produced by deliberation or progressive views, but by contradictory emotions. By fits and starts they are warm in many pursuits; yet this warmth, never concentrated into perseverance, soon exhausts itself; exhaled by its own heat, or meeting with some other fleeting passion, to which reason has never given any specific gravity, neutrality ensues. Miserable, indeed, must be that being whose cultivation of mind has only tended to inflame its passions! A distinction should be made between inflaming and strengthening them. The passions thus pampered, whilst the judgment is left unformed, what can be expected to ensue? – Undoubtedly, a mixture of madness and folly!

This observation should not be confined to the fair sex; however, at present, I only mean to apply it to them.

Novels, music, poetry, and gallantry, all tend to make women the creatures of sensation, and their character is thus formed during the time they are acquiring accomplishments, the only improvement they are excited, by their station in society, to acquire. This overstretched sensibility naturally relaxes the other powers of the mind, and prevents intellect from attaining that sovereignty which it ought to attain to render a rational creature useful to others, and content with its own station: for the exercise of the understanding, as life advances, is the only method pointed out by nature to calm the passions....

It would be an endless task to trace the variety of meannesses, cares, and sorrows, into which women are plunged by the prevailing opinion, that they were created rather to feel than reason, and that all the power they obtain, must be obtained by their charms and weakness:

"Fine by defect, and amiably weak!"

And, made by this amiable weakness entirely dependent, excepting what they gain by illicit sway, on man, not only for protection, but advice, is it surprising that, neglecting the duties that reason alone points out, and shrinking from trials calculated to strengthen their minds, they only exert themselves to give their defects a graceful covering, which may serve to heighten their charms in the eye of the voluptuary, though it sink them below the scale of moral excellence?

Fragile in every sense of the word, they are obliged to look up to man for every comfort. In the most trifling danger they cling to their support, with parasitical tenacity, piteously demanding succour; and their natural protector extends his arm, or lifts up his voice, to guard the lovely trembler – from what? Perhaps the frown of an old cow, or the jump of a mouse; a rat, would be a serious danger. In the name of reason, and even common sense, what can save such beings from contempt; even though they be soft and fair?

These fears, when not affected, may be very pretty; but they shew a degree of imbecility that degrades a rational creature in a way women are not aware of – for love and esteem are very distinct things.

I am fully persuaded that we should hear of none of these infantile airs, if girls were allowed to take sufficient exercise, and not confined in close rooms till their muscles are relaxed, and their powers of digestion destroyed. To carry the remark still further, if fear in girls, instead of being cherished, perhaps, created, was treated in the same manner as cowardice in boys, we should quickly see women with more dignified aspects. It is true, they could not then with equal propriety be termed the sweet flowers that smile in the walk of man; but they would be more respectable members of society, and discharge the important duties of life by the light of their own reason. "Educate women like men," says Rousseau, "and the more they resemble our sex the less power will they have over us." This is the very point I aim at. I do not wish them to have power over men; but over themselves.

In the same strain have I heard men argue against instructing the poor; for many are the forms that aristocracy assumes. "Teach them to read and write," say they, "and you take them out of the station assigned them by nature." An eloquent Frenchman has answered them, I will borrow his sentiments. But they know not, when they make man a brute, that they may expect every instant to see him transformed into a ferocious beast. Without knowledge there can be no morality!

Ignorance is a frail base for virtue! Yet, that it is the condition for which woman was organized, has been insisted upon by the writers who have most vehemently argued in favour of the superiority of man; a superiority not in degree, but offence; though, to soften the argument, they have laboured to prove, with chivalrous generosity, that the sexes ought not to be compared; man was made to reason, woman to feel; and that together, flesh and spirit, they make the most perfect whole, by blending happily reason and sensibility into one character.

William Wordsworth
1770 – 1850

Perhaps the most representative of the English Romantic poets in their close observation of nature and their understanding of its importance, William Wordsworth, with the help of his friend Samuel Taylor Coleridge, brought to poetry the notion that simple diction was necessary to make poetry more useful to its readers. In their Preface to their edition of *Lyrical Ballads*, they outlined their project to write poetry in the "real language of men," which is in line with the "real language of nature," unlike the artificial language that had developed in poetry in recent centuries.

The selection below, "Lines Composed a Few Miles above Tintern Abbey," published in *Lyrical Ballads*, explores the interactions of the mind and heart with Nature, as revealed by the memory.

Major Works
Lyrical Ballads, with a Few Other Poems (1798, 1800)
Poems, in Two Volumes (1807)
Guide to the Lakes (1810)
The Excursion (1814)
The Prelude (1799, 1805, 1850)

෴

Lines Composed a Few Miles Above Tintern Abbey, On Revisiting the Banks of the Wye During a Tour. July 13, 1798
William Wordsworth

Five years have past; five summers, with the length
Of five long winters! and again I hear
These waters, rolling from their mountain-springs
With a soft inland murmur – Once again
5   Do I behold these steep and lofty cliffs,
That on a wild secluded scene impress
Thoughts of more deep seclusion; and connect
The landscape with the quiet of the sky.

The day is come when I again repose
10 Here, under this dark sycamore, and view
These plots of cottage-ground, these orchard-tufts,
Which at this season, with their unripe fruits,
Are clad in one green hue, and lose themselves
'Mid groves and copses. Once again I see
15 These hedge-rows, hardly hedge-rows, little lines
Of sportive wood run wild: these pastoral farms,
Green to the very door; and wreaths of smoke
Sent up, in silence, from among the trees!
With some uncertain notice, as might seem
20 Of vagrant dwellers in the houseless woods,
Or of some Hermit's cave, where by his fire
The Hermit sits alone.
                              These beauteous forms,
Through a long absence, have not been to me
As is a landscape to a blind man's eye:
25 But oft, in lonely rooms, and 'mid the din
Of towns and cities, I have owed to them
In hours of weariness, sensations sweet,
Felt in the blood, and felt along the heart;
And passing even into my purer mind,
30 With tranquil restoration: – feelings too
Of unremembered pleasure: such, perhaps,
As have no slight or trivial influence
On that best portion of a good man's life,
His little, nameless, unremembered, acts
35 Of kindness and of love. Nor less, I trust,
To them I may have owed another gift,
Of aspect more sublime; that blessed mood,
In which the burthen of the mystery,
40 In which the heavy and the weary weight
Of all this unintelligible world,
Is lightened: – that serene and blessed mood,
In which the affections gently lead us on, –
Until, the breath of this corporeal frame
And even the motion of our human blood
45 Almost suspended, we are laid asleep
In body, and become a living soul:
While with an eye made quiet by the power
Of harmony, and the deep power of joy,
We see into the life of things.
                              If this
50 Be but a vain belief, yet, oh! how oft –
In darkness and amid the many shapes
Of joyless daylight; when the fretful stir

Unprofitable, and the fever of the world,
Have hung upon the beatings of my heart –
55 How oft, in spirit, have I turned to thee,
O sylvan Wye! thou wanderer thro' the woods,
How often has my spirit turned to thee!

And now, with gleams of half-extinguished thought,
With many recognitions dim and faint,
60 And somewhat of a sad perplexity,
The picture of the mind revives again:
While here I stand, not only with the sense
Of present pleasure, but with pleasing thoughts
That in this moment there is life and food
65 For future years. And so I dare to hope,
Though changed, no doubt, from what I was when first
I came among these hills; when like a roe
I bounded o'er the mountains, by the sides
Of the deep rivers, and the lonely streams,
70 Wherever nature led: more like a man
Flying from something that he dreads, than one
Who sought the thing he loved. For nature then
(The coarser pleasures of my boyish days,
And their glad animal movements all gone by)
75 To me was all in all. – I cannot paint
What then I was. The sounding cataract
Haunted me like a passion: the tall rock,
The mountain, and the deep and gloomy wood,
Their colours and their forms, were then to me
80 An appetite; a feeling and a love,
That had no need of a remoter charm,
By thought supplied, nor any interest
Unborrowed from the eye. – That time is past,
And all its aching joys are now no more,
85 And all its dizzy raptures. Not for this
Faint I, nor mourn nor murmur, other gifts
Have followed; for such loss, I would believe,
Abundant recompence. For I have learned
To look on nature, not as in the hour
90 Of thoughtless youth; but hearing oftentimes
The still, sad music of humanity,
Nor harsh nor grating, though of ample power
To chasten and subdue. And I have felt
A presence that disturbs me with the joy
95 Of elevated thoughts; a sense sublime
Of something far more deeply interfused,
Whose dwelling is the light of setting suns,
And the round ocean and the living air,

And the blue sky, and in the mind of man;
100 A motion and a spirit, that impels
All thinking things, all objects of all thought,
And rolls through all things. Therefore am I still
A lover of the meadows and the woods,
And mountains; and of all that we behold
105 From this green earth; of all the mighty world
Of eye, and ear, – both what they half create,
And what perceive; well pleased to recognise
In nature and the language of the sense,
The anchor of my purest thoughts, the nurse,
110 The guide, the guardian of my heart, and soul
Of all my moral being.
                                        Nor perchance,
If I were not thus taught, should I the more
Suffer my genial spirits to decay:
For thou art with me here upon the banks
115 Of this fair river; thou my dearest Friend,
My dear, dear Friend; and in thy voice I catch
The language of my former heart, and read
My former pleasures in the shooting lights
Of thy wild eyes. Oh! yet a little while
120 May I behold in thee what I was once,
My dear, dear Sister! and this prayer I make,
Knowing that Nature never did betray
The heart that loved her; 'tis her privilege,
Through all the years of this our life, to lead
125 From joy to joy: for she can so inform
The mind that is within us, so impress
With quietness and beauty, and so feed
With lofty thoughts, that neither evil tongues,
Rash judgments, nor the sneers of selfish men,
130 Nor greetings where no kindness is, nor all
The dreary intercourse of daily life,
Shall e'er prevail against us, or disturb
Our cheerful faith, that all which we behold
Is full of blessings. Therefore let the moon
135 Shine on thee in thy solitary walk;
And let the misty mountain-winds be free
To blow against thee: and, in after years,
When these wild ecstasies shall be matured
Into a sober pleasure; when thy mind
140 Shall be a mansion for all lovely forms,
Thy memory be as a dwelling-place
For all sweet sounds and harmonies; oh! then,
If solitude, or fear, or pain, or grief,

Should be thy portion, with what healing thoughts
145 Of tender joy wilt thou remember me,
And these my exhortations! Nor, perchance –
If I should be where I no more can hear
Thy voice, nor catch from thy wild eyes these gleams
Of past existence – wilt thou then forget
150 That on the banks of this delightful stream
We stood together; and that I, so long
A worshipper of Nature, hither came
Unwearied in that service: rather say
With warmer love – oh! with far deeper zeal
155 Of holier love. Nor wilt thou then forget,
That after many wanderings, many years
Of absence, these steep woods and lofty cliffs,
And this green pastoral landscape, were to me
More dear, both for themselves and for thy sake!

Percy Bysshe Shelley
1792 – 1822

Percy Bysshe Shelley, expelled from University College in 1811 for writing *The Necessity of Atheism*, took up a number of revolutionary causes. Surrounded by tragedy and death, including that of his friend John Keats, for whom he wrote the elegy "Adonais," his work often contemplates the nature of our fleeting existence and the poet's role in such a world. Though he found happiness in 1816 when he married Mary Godwin Shelley, author of *Frankenstein*, he died in 1822 off the coast of northern Italy, where he had relocated because of bankruptcy, when, after visiting fellow poet Lord Byron, his yacht sank in a storm.

Though many agree that Shelley's best work is in his shorter pieces, such as "Mont Blanc," "Ode to the West Wind," "To a Skylark," and "The Cloud," he was more passionate about his longer and more political works, including *The Cenci* and *Prometheus Unbound*.

Major Works
Alastor, or The Spirit of Solitude (1815)
The Cenci, A Tragedy, in Five Acts (1819)
Prometheus Unbound, A Lyrical Drama, in Four Acts (1820)
The Witch of Atlas (1820, 1824)

ೞಜಿ
Ozymandias[1]
Percy Bysshe Shelley, 1821

 I met a traveller from an antique land
 Who said: Two vast and trunkless legs of stone
 Stand in the desert. Near them, on the sand,
 Half sunk, a shattered visage lies, whose frown,
5 And wrinkled lip, and sneer of cold command,
 Tell that its sculptor well those passions read
 Which yet survive, stamped on these lifeless things,
 The hand that mocked them, and the heart that fed;

---

[1] Ozymandias. Greek name for Ramses II of Egypt, 13th century B.C.

And on the pedestal these words appear:
10   "My name is Ozymandias, king of kings:
Look on my works, ye Mighty, and despair!"
Nothing beside remains. Round the decay
Of that colossal wreck, boundless and bare
The lone and level sands stretch far away.

ঙ৪৪১

A Defence of Poetry (*The Conclusion*)
Percy Bysshe Shelley, 1840

For the Literature of England, an energetic development of which has ever pre-ceded or accompanied a great and free development of the national will, has arisen as it were from a new birth. In spite of the low-thoughted envy which would undervalue contemporary merit, our own will be a memorable age in in-tellectual achievements, and we live among such philosophers and poets as sur-pass beyond comparison any who have appeared since the last national struggle for civil and religious liberty.[1] The most unfailing herald, companion, and fol-lower of the awakening of a great people to work a beneficial change in opinion or institution, is Poetry.

At such periods there is an accumulation of the power of communicating and receiving intense and impassioned conceptions respecting man and nature. The persons in whom this power resides, may often, as far as regards many portions of their nature, have little apparent correspondence with that spirit of good of which they are the ministers. But even whilst they deny and abjure, they are yet compelled to serve, the power which is seated upon the throne of their own soul.

It is impossible to read the compositions of the most celebrated writers of the day without being startled with the electric life which burns within their words. They measure the circumference and sound the depths of human nature with a comprehensive and all-penetrating spirit, and they are themselves perhaps the most sincerely astonished at its manifestations, for it is less their spirit than the spirit of the age.

Poets are the hierophants[2] of an unapprehended inspiration, the mirrors of the gigantic shadows which futurity casts upon the present, the words which express what they understand not; the trumpets which sing to battle, and feel not what they inspire: the influence which is moved not, but moves. Poets are the unacknowledged legislators of the world.

---

[1] Since the last…liberty. Perhaps the mid-1600s.
[2] Hierophants. Priests, in a sense, who reveal mysteries.

John Keats
1795 – 1821

At the age of fifteen John Keats was apprenticed to a surgeon and in 1816 became a dresser (an assistant surgeon) at Guy's Hospital (King's College). He was drawn, however, to poetry, and published his first book, *Poems*, in 1817, and *Endymion* in 1818. The latter was so severely condemned by one critic that some believed that it caused his death; Shelley based his elegy of Keats, "Adonais," on this belief.

As Keats recognized throughout his entire short writing career that his ill-health might bring an early death, most of his poems give attention to the brevity and preciousness of life. Though Keats had only been publishing poetry for four years at the time of his death from consumption (tuberculosis), and thoughsome of his works were poorly received, he soon became, and still remains, one of the most respected of English poets.

Major Works
Hyperion (1819)
The Eve of St. Agnes (1820)
Lamia (1820)

ೞഔ

John Keats
Ode on a Grecian Urn, 1820

    Thou still unravish'd bride of quietness
    Thou foster-child of silence and slow time,
    Sylvan historian, who canst thus express
    A flowery tale more sweetly than our rhyme:
5   What leaf-fring'd legend haunts about thy shape
    Of deities or mortals, or of both,
    In Tempe or the dales of Arcady?
    What men or gods are these? What maidens loth?
    What mad pursuit? What struggle to escape?
10   What pipes and timbrels? What wild ecstasy?

Heard melodies are sweet, but those unheard
Are sweeter; therefore, ye soft pipes, play on;
Not to the sensual ear, but, more endear'd,
Pipe to the spirit ditties of no tone:
15 Fair youth, beneath the trees, thou canst not leave
Thy song, nor ever can those trees be bare;
Bold Lover, never, never canst thou kiss,
Though winning near the goal yet, do not grieve;
She cannot fade, though thou hast not thy bliss,
20 For ever wilt thou love, and she be fair!

Ah, happy, happy boughs! that cannot shed
Your leaves, nor ever bid the Spring adieu;
And, happy melodist, unwearied,
For ever piping songs for ever new;
25 More happy love! more happy, happy love!
For ever warm and still to be enjoy'd,
For ever panting, and for ever young;
All breathing human passion far above,
That leaves a heart high-sorrowful and cloy'd,
30 A burning forehead, and a parching tongue.

Who are these coming to the sacrifice?
To what green altar, O mysterious priest,
Lead'st thou that heifer lowing at the skies,
And all her silken flanks with garlands drest?
35 What little town by river or sea shore,
Or mountain-built with peaceful citadel,
Is emptied of this folk, this pious morn?
And, little town, thy streets for evermore
Will silent be; and not a soul to tell
40 Why thou art desolate, can e'er return.

O Attic shape! Fair attitude! with brede
Of marble men and maidens overwrought,
With forest branches and the trodden weed;
Thou, silent form, dost tease us out of thought
45 As doth eternity: Cold Pastoral!
When old age shall this generation waste,
Thou shalt remain, in midst of other woe
Than ours, a friend to man, to whom thou say'st,
"Beauty is truth, truth beauty, – that is all
50 Ye know on earth, and all ye need to know.

ଔଞ
La Belle Dame Sans Merci[1]
John Keats, 1819

Ah, what can ail thee, wretched wight,
Alone and palely loitering;
The sedge is wither'd from the lake,
And no birds sing.

5   Ah, what can ail thee, wretched wight,
So haggard and so woe-begone?
The squirrel's granary is full,
And the harvest's done.

I see a lily on thy brow,
10 With anguish moist and fever dew;
And on thy cheek a fading rose
Fast withereth too.

I met a lady in the meads
Full beautiful, a faery's child;
15 Her hair was long, her foot was light,
And her eyes were wild.

I set her on my pacing steed,
And nothing else saw all day long;
For sideways would she lean, and sing
20 A faery's song.

I made a garland for her head,
And bracelets too, and fragrant zone;
She look'd at me as she did love,
And made sweet moan.

25 She found me roots of relish sweet,
And honey wild, and manna dew;
And sure in language strange she said,
I love thee true.

She took me to her elfin grot,
30 And there she gaz'd and sighed deep,
And there I shut her wild sad eyes –
So kiss'd to sleep.

And there we slumber'd on the moss,
And there I dream'd, ah woe betide,
35 The latest dream I ever dream'd
On the cold hill side.

I saw pale kings, and princes too,

---

[1] *La Belle Dame Sans Merci*. The Beautiful Woman Without Pity.

Pale warriors, death-pale were they all;
Who cry'd – "La belle Dame sans merci
40   Hath thee in thrall!"

I saw their starv'd lips in the gloam
With horrid warning gaped wide,
And I awoke, and found me here
On the cold hill side.

45   And this is why I sojourn here
Alone and palely loitering,
Though the sedge is wither'd from the lake,
And no birds sing

Charles Darwin
1809 – 1882

Charles Darwin, an English naturalist and writer, was the pioneer of the biological theory of evolution, the process by which various forms of living organisms develop and diversify from earlier forms. This concept, often misunderstood, results from natural selection, the gradual process by which individuals' inherited needs and abilities are matched to resources present in their environment and passed to future generations. Only five years after Darwin's original publication, the biologist and political theorist Herbert Spencer misused the phrase "survival of the fittest" to mean "the preservation of favoured races in the struggle for life,"[1] which Darwin corrected to mean "better adapted for immediate, local environment."[2] A species' survival was a function of its suitability to its environment: for example, a "peppered moth" survives where it can hide among a similarly colored environment; and a tree will not survive in latitudes where temperature and light will not allow it.

Major Works
The Voyage of the Beagle (1839)
On the Origin of Species (1859)

೧೮೩೦
The Origin of the Species (*Selections*)
Chapter 4 Natural Selection
How will the struggle for existence, discussed too briefly in the last chapter, act in regard to variation? Can the principle of selection, which we have seen is so potent in the hands of man, apply in nature? I think we shall see that it can act most effectually. Let it be borne in mind in what an endless number of strange peculiarities our domestic productions, and, in a lesser degree, those under nature, vary; and how strong the hereditary tendency is. Under domestication, it may be truly said that the, whole organisation becomes in some degree plastic. Let it be borne in mind how infinitely complex and close-fitting are the mutual relations of all organic beings to each other and to their physical conditions of

---

[1] Herbert Spencer. *Principles of Biology*, 1864, vol. 1, page 444.
[2] Charles Darwin. *Origin of the Species*. 1859.

life. Can it, then, be thought improbable, seeing that variations useful to man have undoubtedly occurred, that other variations useful in some way to each being in the great and complex battle of life, should sometimes occur in the course of thousands of generations? If such do occur, can we doubt (remembering that many more individuals are born than can possibly survive) that individuals having any advantage, however slight, over others, would have the best chance of surviving and of procreating their kind? On the other hand, we may feel sure that any variation in the least degree injurious would be rigidly destroyed. This preservation of favourable variations and the rejection of injurious variations, I call Natural Selection. Variations neither useful nor injurious would not be affected by natural selection, and would be left a fluctuating element, as perhaps we see in the species called polymorphic, or would ultimately become fixed, owing to the nature of the organism and the nature of the conditions.

We shall best understand the probable course of natural selection by taking the case of a country undergoing some physical change, for instance, of climate. The proportional numbers of its inhabitants would almost immediately undergo a change, and some species might become extinct. We may conclude, from what we have seen of the intimate and complex manner in which the inhabitants of each country are bound together, that any change in the numerical proportions of some of the inhabitants, independently of the change of climate itself, would most seriously affect many of the others. If the country were open on its borders, new forms would certainly immigrate, and this also would seriously disturb the relations of some of the former inhabitants. Let it be remembered how powerful the influence of a single introduced tree or mammal has been shown to be. But in the case of an island, or of a country partly surrounded by barriers, into which new and better adapted forms could not freely enter, we should then have places in the economy of nature which would assuredly be better filled up, if some of the original inhabitants were in some manner modified; for, had the area been open to immigration, these same places would have been seized on by intruders. In such case, every slight modification, which in the course of ages chanced to arise, and which in any way favoured the individuals of any of the species, by better adapting them to their altered conditions, would tend to be preserved; and natural selection would thus have free scope for the work of improvement.

We have reason to believe, as stated in the first chapter, that a change in the conditions of life, by specially acting on the reproductive system, causes or increases variability; and in the foregoing case the conditions of life are supposed to have undergone a change, and this would manifestly be favourable to natural selection, by giving a better chance of profitable variations occurring; and unless profitable variations do occur, natural selection can do nothing. Not that, as I believe, any extreme amount of variability is necessary; as man can certainly produce great results by adding up in any given direction mere individual differences, so could Nature, but far more easily, from having incomparably longer time at her disposal. Nor do I believe that any great physical change, as of climate, or any unusual degree of isolation to check immigration, is actually necessary to produce new and unoccupied places for natural selection to fill up by modifying and improving some of the varying inhabitants. For as all the inhabitants of each country are struggling together with nicely balanced forces, extremely slight modifications in the structure or habits of one inhabitant would often give it an advantage over others; and still further modifications of the same kind would often still further increase the advantage. No country can be named in which all the native inhabitants are now so perfectly adapted to each other and to the physical conditions under which they live, that none of them could anyhow be improved; for in all countries, the natives have been so far conquered by naturalised productions, that they have allowed foreigners to take firm possession of the land. And as foreigners have thus everywhere beaten some of the natives, we may safely conclude that the natives might have been modified with advantage, so as to have better resisted such intruders.

As man can produce and certainly has produced a great result by his methodical and unconscious means of selection, what may not nature effect? Man can act only on external and visible characters: nature cares nothing for appearances, except in so far as they may be useful to any being. She can act on every internal organ, on every shade of constitutional difference, on the whole machinery of life. Man selects only for his own good; Nature only for that of the being which she tends. Every selected character is fully exercised by her; and the being is placed under well-suited conditions of life. Man keeps the natives of many climates in the same country; he seldom exercises each selected character in some peculiar and fitting manner; he feeds a long and a short beaked pigeon on the same food; he does not exercise a long-backed or long-legged quadruped in any peculiar manner; he exposes sheep with long and short wool to the same climate. He does not allow the most vigorous males to struggle for the females. He does not rigidly destroy all inferior animals, but protects during each varying season, as far as lies in his power, all his productions. He often begins his selection by some half-monstrous form; or at least by some modification prominent enough to catch his eye, or to be plainly useful to him. Under nature, the slightest difference of structure or constitution may well turn the nicely-balanced scale in the struggle for life, and so be preserved. How fleeting are the wishes and efforts of man! how short his time! and consequently how poor will his products be, compared with those accumulated by nature during whole geological periods. Can we wonder, then, that nature's productions should be far 'truer' in character than man's productions; that they should be infinitely better adapted to the most complex conditions of life, and should plainly bear the stamp of far higher workmanship?

In order to make it clear how, as I believe, natural selection acts, I must beg permission to give one or two imaginary illustrations. Let us take the case of a wolf, which preys on various animals, securing some by craft, some by strength, and some by fleetness; and let us suppose that the fleetest prey, a deer for instance, had from any change in the country increased in numbers, or that other prey had decreased in numbers, during that season of the year when the wolf is hardest pressed for food. I can under such circumstances see no reason to doubt that the swiftest and slimmest wolves would have the best chance of surviving, and so be preserved or selected, provided always that they retained strength to master their prey at this or at some other period of the year, when they might be compelled to prey on other animals. I can see no more reason to doubt this, than that man can improve the fleetness of his greyhounds by careful and methodical selection, or by that unconscious selection which results from each man trying to keep the best dogs without any thought of modifying the breed.

Chapter 14 Recapitulation and Conclusion

Authors of the highest eminence seem to be fully satisfied with the view that each species has been independently created. To my mind it accords better with what we know of the laws impressed on matter by the Creator, that the production and extinction of the past and present inhabitants of the world should have been due to secondary causes, like those determining the birth and death of the individual. When I view all beings not as special creations, but as the lineal descendants of some few beings which lived long before the first bed of the Silurian system was deposited, they seem to me to become ennobled. Judging from the past, we may safely infer that not one living species will transmit its unaltered likeness to a distant futurity. And of the species now living very few will transmit progeny of any kind to a far distant futurity; for the manner in which all organic beings are grouped, shows that the greater number of species of each genus, and all the species of many genera, have left no descendants, but have become utterly extinct. We can so far take a prophetic glance into futurity as to foretel that it will be the common and widely-spread species, belonging to the larger and dominant groups, which will ultimately prevail and procreate new and dominant species. As all the living forms of life are the lineal descendants of those which lived long before the Silurian epoch, we may feel certain that the ordinary succession by generation has never once been broken, and that no cataclysm has desolated the whole world. Hence we may look with some confidence to a secure future of equally inappreciable length. And as natural selection works solely by and for the good of each being, all corporeal and mental endowments will tend to progress towards perfection.

It is interesting to contemplate an entangled bank, clothed with many plants of many kinds, with birds singing on the bushes, with various insects flitting about, and with worms crawling through the damp earth, and to reflect that these elaborately constructed forms, so different from each other, and dependent on each other in so complex a manner, have all been produced by laws acting around us. These laws, taken in the largest sense, being Growth with Reproduction; inheritance which is almost implied by reproduction; Variability from the indirect and direct action of the external conditions of life, and from use and disuse; a Ratio of Increase so high as to lead to a Struggle for Life, and as a consequence to Natural Selection, entailing Divergence of Character and the Extinction of less-improved forms. Thus, from the war of nature, from famine and death, the most exalted object which we are capable of conceiving, namely, the production of the higher animals, directly follows. There is grandeur in this view of life, with its several powers, having been originally breathed into a few forms or into one; and that, whilst this planet has gone cycling on according to the fixed law of gravity, from so simple a beginning endless forms most beautiful and most wonderful have been, and are being, evolved.

Alfred, Lord Tennyson
1809 – 1892

Alfred, Lord Tennyson, prolific British poet, was Poet Laureate of Great Britain from 1850 to 1892 under Queen Victoria, whose reign marked the high point of the British Empire. His work seems to simultaneously celebrate and criticize the imperial ambitions of his nation, which might be seen in the in the poem "Ulysses," presented below.

Another factor that influenced Tennyson's writing was the death of his close friend Arthur Hallam, for whom he wrote *In Memoriam*. "Ulysses" was written shortly after Hallam's death and shows a certain doubt about the necessity of going forward and braving the challenges of life. Based on passages in Book XI of Homer's *Odyssey* and Canto XXVI of Dante's *Inferno* (included earlier in this volume), which Hallam had encouraged Tennyson to study, Tennyson characterizes the restless spirit of the wandering hero.

Major Works
In Memoriam A.H.H. (1849)
Enoch Arden and Other Poems (1864)
Idylls of the King (1874)

ᏣᏍᏅ
Alfred Lord Tennyson
Ulysses, 1842

It little profits that an idle king,
By this still hearth, among these barren crags,
Match'd with an aged wife, I mete and dole
Unequal laws unto a savage race,
5   That hoard, and sleep, and feed, and know not me.
I cannot rest from travel: I will drink
Life to the lees: All times I have enjoy'd
Greatly, have suffer'd greatly, both with those
That loved me, and alone, on shore, and when
10 Thro' scudding drifts the rainy Hyades[1]

Vext the dim sea: I am become a name;
For always roaming with a hungry heart
Much have I seen and known; cities of men
And manners, climates, councils, governments,
15 Myself not least, but honour'd of them all;
And drunk delight of battle with my peers,
Far on the ringing plains of windy Troy.
I am a part of all that I have met;
Yet all experience is an arch wherethro'
20 Gleams that untravell'd world whose margin fades
For ever and forever when I move.
How dull it is to pause, to make an end,
To rust unburnish'd, not to shine in use!
As tho' to breathe were life! Life piled on life
25 Were all too little, and of one to me
Little remains: but every hour is saved
From that eternal silence, something more,
A bringer of new things; and vile it were
For some three suns to store and hoard myself,
30 And this gray spirit yearning in desire
To follow knowledge like a sinking star,
Beyond the utmost bound of human thought.

This is my son, mine own Telemachus,
To whom I leave the sceptre and the isle,[1] –
35 Well-loved of me, discerning to fulfil
This labour, by slow prudence to make mild
A rugged people, and thro' soft degrees
Subdue them to the useful and the good.
Most blameless is he, centred in the sphere
40 Of common duties, decent not to fail
In offices of tenderness, and pay
Meet adoration to my household gods,
When I am gone. He works his work, I mine.

There lies the port; the vessel puffs her sail:
45 There gloom the dark, broad seas. My mariners,
Souls that have toil'd, and wrought, and thought with me –
That ever with a frolic welcome took
The thunder and the sunshine, and opposed
Free hearts, free foreheads – you and I are old;
50 Old age hath yet his honour and his toil;
Death closes all: but something ere the end,
Some work of noble note, may yet be done,

---

[1] Rainy Hyades. A group of stars that rise with the sun in Spring in the rainy season.
[1] The isle. Ithaca, where Ulysses reigned as king before and after the Trojan War.

Not unbecoming men that strove with Gods.
The lights begin to twinkle from the rocks:
55 The long day wanes: the slow moon climbs: the deep
Moans round with many voices. Come, my friends,
'Tis not too late to seek a newer world.
Push off, and sitting well in order smite
The sounding furrows; for my purpose holds
60 To sail beyond the sunset, and the baths[1]
Of all the western stars, until I die.
It may be that the gulfs will wash us down:[2]
It may be we shall touch the Happy Isles,[3]
And see the great Achilles, whom we knew.
65 Tho' much is taken, much abides; and tho'
We are not now that strength which in old days
Moved earth and heaven, that which we are, we are;
One equal temper of heroic hearts,
Made weak by time and fate, but strong in will
70 To strive, to seek, to find, and not to yield.

---

[1] The baths. The place where the stars seem to fall into the ocean.

[2] Wash us down. The ocean was imagined by Homer as a river encompassing the earth, and on the west plunging down a vast chasm where was the entrance of Hades. The irony is that this is the fate of Ulysses and his men.

[3] The Happy Isles. The islands of the blessed, which are supposed to lie to the west of the Pillars of Hercules (the rocks flanking the Strait of Gibraltar), i.e., in the Atlantic.

Karl Marx	Friedrich Engels
1818 – 1883	1820 – 1895

Karl Marx and Friedrich Engels are best known as the authors of *The Communist Manifesto*, selections from which are included below. Marx and Engels were German philosophers, economists, sociologists, historians, journalists, and revolutionary socialists, most famous as the founders of Communism. Their work, both in collaboration and individually, has changed the way that we look at ourselves; not only are we more conscious of class conflict and the distribution of wealth, we are also able to see how the economic structure of society constantly shapes our ideology.

Marx's Other Major Works
Wage Labor and Capital (1847)
The Eighteenth Brumaire of Louis Napoleon (1852)
Capital, Volumes I, II, & III (*Das Kapital*) (1867, 1885, 1894)

Engels' Other Major Works
The Condition of the Working Class in England (1844)
Socialism: Utopian and Scientific (1880)
The Origin of the Family, Private Property and the State (1884)

ᘓᘔ

Manifesto of the Communist Party (*Selections*)
Karl Marx and Friedrich Engels, 1848
TRANSLATED BY SAMUEL MOORE

A specter is haunting Europe – the specter of communism. All the powers of old Europe have entered into a holy alliance to exorcise this specter: Pope and Tsar, Metternich and Guizot, French Radicals and German police-spies.

Where is the party in opposition that has not been decried as communistic by its opponents in power? Where is the opposition that has not hurled back the branding reproach of communism, against the more advanced opposition parties, as well as against its reactionary adversaries?

Two things result from this fact:

I. Communism is already acknowledged by all European powers to be itself a power.

II. It is high time that Communists should openly, in the face of the whole world, publish their views, their aims, their tendencies, and meet this nursery tale of the specter of communism with a manifesto of the party itself.

To this end, Communists of various nationalities have assembled in London and sketched the following manifesto, to be published in the English, French, German, Italian, Flemish and Danish languages.

Bourgeois and Proletarians
The history of all hitherto existing society is the history of class struggles.

Freeman and slave, patrician and plebian, lord and serf, guild-master and journeyman, in a word, oppressor and oppressed, stood in constant opposition to one another, carried on an uninterrupted, now hidden, now open fight, a fight that each time ended, either in a revolutionary reconstitution of society at large, or in the common ruin of the contending classes.

In the earlier epochs of history, we find almost everywhere a complicated arrangement of society into various orders, a manifold gradation of social rank. In ancient Rome we have patricians, knights, plebeians, slaves; in the Middle Ages, feudal lords, vassals, guild-masters, journeymen, apprentices, serfs; in almost all of these classes, again, subordinate gradations.

The modern bourgeois society that has sprouted from the ruins of feudal society has not done away with class antagonisms. It has but established new classes, new conditions of oppression, new forms of struggle in place of the old ones.

Our epoch, the epoch of the bourgeoisie, possesses, however, this distinct feature: it has simplified class antagonisms. Society as a whole is more and more splitting up into two great hostile camps, into two great classes directly facing each other – bourgeoisie and proletariat.

Proletarians and Communists
The immediate aim of the Communists is the same as that of all other proletarian parties: Formation of the proletariat into a class, overthrow of the bourgeois supremacy, conquest of political power by the proletariat.

* * *

The distinguishing feature of communism is not the abolition of property generally, but the abolition of bourgeois property. But modern bourgeois private property is the final and most complete expression of the system of producing and appropriating products that is based on class antagonisms, on the exploitation of the many by the few.

In this sense, the theory of the Communists may be summed up in the single sentence: Abolition of private property.

We Communists have been reproached with the desire of abolishing the right of personally acquiring property as the fruit of a man's own labor, which property is alleged to be the groundwork of all personal freedom, activity and independence.

Hard-won, self-acquired, self-earned property! Do you mean the property of petty artisan and of the small peasant, a form of property that preceded the bourgeois form? There is no need to abolish that; the development of industry has to a great extent already destroyed it, and is still destroying it daily.

Or do you mean the modern bourgeois private property?

But does wage labor create any property for the laborer? Not a bit. It creates capital, i.e., that kind of property which exploits wage labor, and which cannot increase except upon conditions of begetting a new supply of wage labor for fresh exploitation. Property, in its present form, is based on the antagonism of capital and wage labor. Let us examine both sides of this antagonism.

To be a capitalist, is to have not only a purely personal, but a social STATUS in production. Capital is a collective product, and only by the united action of many members, nay, in the last resort, only by the united action of all members of society, can it be set in motion. Capital is therefore not only personal; it is a social power.

When, therefore, capital is converted into common property, into the property of all members of society, personal property is not thereby transformed into social property. It is only the social character of the property that is changed. It loses its class character.

Let us now take wage labor.

The average price of wage labor is the minimum wage, i.e., that quantum of the means of subsistence which is absolutely requisite to keep the laborer in bare existence as a laborer. What, therefore, the wage laborer appropriates by means of his labor merely suffices to prolong and reproduce a bare existence. We by no means intend to abolish this personal appropriation of the products of labor, an appropriation that is made for the maintenance and reproduction of human life, and that leaves no surplus wherewith to command the labor of others. All that we want to do away with is the miserable character of this appropriation, under which the laborer lives merely to increase capital, and is allowed to live only in so far as the interest of the ruling class requires it.

In bourgeois society, living labor is but a means to increase accumulated labor. In communist society, accumulated labor is but a means to widen, to enrich, to promote the existence of the laborer.

In bourgeois society, therefore, the past dominates the present; in communist society, the present dominates the past. In bourgeois society, capital is independent and has individuality, while the living person is dependent and has no individuality.

And the abolition of this state of things is called by the bourgeois, abolition of individuality and freedom! And rightly so. The abolition of bourgeois individuality, bourgeois independence, and bourgeois freedom is undoubtedly aimed at. By freedom is meant, under the present bourgeois conditions of production, free trade, free selling and buying.

But if selling and buying disappears, free selling and buying disappears also. This talk about free selling and buying, and all the other "brave words" of our bourgeois about freedom in general, have a meaning, if any, only in contrast with restricted selling and buying, with the fettered traders of the Middle Ages, but have no meaning when opposed to the communist abolition of buying and selling, or the bourgeois conditions of production, and of the bourgeoisie itself.

You are horrified at our intending to do away with private property. But in your existing society, private property is already done away with for nine-tenths of the population; its existence for the few is solely due to its non-existence in the hands of those nine-tenths. You reproach us, therefore, with intending to do away with a form of property, the necessary condition for whose existence is the non-existence of any property for the immense majority of society.

In one word, you reproach us with intending to do away with your property. Precisely so; that is just what we intend.

From the moment when labor can no longer be converted into capital, money, or rent, into a social power capable of being monopolized, i.e., from the moment when individual property can no longer be transformed into bourgeois property, into capital, from that moment, you say, individuality vanishes.

You must, therefore, confess that by "individual" you mean no other person than the bourgeois, than the middle-class owner of property. This person must, indeed, be swept out of the way, and made impossible.

* * *

But you Communists would introduce community or women, screams the bourgeoisie in chorus.

The bourgeois sees his wife a mere instrument of production. He hears that the instruments of production are to be exploited in common, and, naturally, can come to no other conclusion that the lot of being common to all will likewise fall to the women.

He has not even a suspicion that the real point aimed at is to do away with the status of women as mere instruments of production.

For the rest, nothing is more ridiculous than the virtuous indignation of our bourgeois at the community of women which, they pretend, is to be openly and officially established by the Communists. The Communists have no need to introduce free love; it has existed almost from time immemorial.

Our bourgeois, not content with having wives and daughters of their proletarians at their disposal, not to speak of common prostitutes, take the greatest pleasure in seducing each other's wives. (Ah, those were the days!)

Bourgeois marriage is, in reality, a system of wives in common and thus, at the most, what the Communists might possibly be reproached with is that they desire to introduce, in substitution for a hypocritically concealed, an openly legalized system of free love. For the rest, it is self-evident that the abolition of the present system of production must bring with it the abolition of free love springing from that system, i.e., of prostitution both public and private.

The Communists are further reproached with desiring to abolish countries and nationality.

The working men have no country. We cannot take from them what they have not got. Since the proletariat must first of all acquire political supremacy, must rise to be the leading class of the nation, must constitute itself *the* nation, it is, so far, itself national, though not in the bourgeois sense of the word.

National differences and antagonism between peoples are daily more and more vanishing, owing to the development of the bourgeoisie, to freedom of commerce, to the world market, to uniformity in the mode of production and in the conditions of life corresponding thereto.

The supremacy of the proletariat will cause them to vanish still faster. United action of the leading civilized countries at least is one of the first conditions for the emancipation of the proletariat.

In proportion as the exploitation of one individual by another will also be put an end to, the exploitation of one nation by another will also be put an end to. In proportion as the antagonism between classes within the nation vanishes, the hostility of one nation to another will come to an end.

* * *

"Undoubtedly," it will be said, "religious, moral, philosophical, and juridical ideas have been modified in the course of historical development. But religion, morality, philosophy, political science, and law, constantly survived this change."

"There are, besides, eternal truths, such as Freedom, Justice, etc., that are common to all states of society. But communism abolishes eternal truths, it abolishes all religion, and all morality, instead of constituting them on a new basis; it therefore acts in contradiction to all past historical experience."

What does this accusation reduce itself to? The history of all past society has consisted in the development of class antagonisms, antagonisms that assumed different forms at different epochs.

But whatever form they may have taken, one fact is common to all past ages, viz., the exploitation of one part of society by the other. No wonder, then, that the social consciousness of past ages, despite all the multiplicity and variety it displays, moves within certain common forms, or general ideas, which cannot completely vanish except with the total disappearance of class antagonisms.

The communist revolution is the most radical rupture with traditional relations; no wonder that its development involved the most radical rupture with traditional ideas.

* * *

Position of the Communists in Relation to the Various Existing Opposition Parties

The Communists disdain to conceal their views and aims. They openly declare that their ends can be attained only by the forcible overthrow of all existing social conditions. Let the ruling classes tremble at a communist revolution. The proletarians have nothing to lose but their chains. They have a world to win.

Workers of all countries, unite!

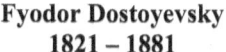

Fyodor Dostoyevsky
1821 – 1881

Fyodor Dostoyevsky, one of the world's greatest novelists, was born in Moscow
and educated at the School of Military Engineering in Saint Petersburg, but
abandoned his military career in 1844 to devote himself to literature. His first
novels, *Poor Folk* and *The Double*, won praise but were soon forgotten. In the
late 1840s Dostoyevsky became involved with a group of intellectuals interested
in social reform, which was crushed when Czar Nicholas I, fearing revolution,
arrested Dostoyevsky and the others and condemned them to death; on their way
to the gallows, however, their sentences were changed to imprisonment in Sibe-
ria. This reprieve and the next four years he spent in hard labor alongside many
hardened criminals changed his life. Soon after he was released, he was married
and resumed his writing career, creating intense novels that dramatize religious,
moral, political, and psychological issues. His life was not easy: he suffered severe financial problems brought on by his ill health and a gambling addiction.
None of this stopped him from writing some of the finest novels in the world,
especially *Crime and Punishment* and *The Brothers Karamazov.*

The selection below, "The Grand Inquisitor," is taken from Book 5 of *The
Brothers Karamozov*, a novel about the murder of a father and the lives of the
his four sons, all of whom have a motive for the crime. In this part, a leader of
the Spanish Inquisition interrogates Jesus Christ about why Jesus has returned to
the world.

Major Works
The Double (1846)
Notes from Underground (1864)
Crime and Punishment (1866)
The Idiot (1869)
The Brothers Karamazov (1880)

og&ⅽ

The Grand Inquisitor
From The Brothers Karamazov
Fyodor Dostoyevsky, 1880
TRANSLATED BY CONSTANCE GARNETT

"Even this must have a preface – that is, a literary preface," laughed Ivan, "and I am a poor hand at making one. You see, my action takes place in the sixteenth century, and at that time, as you probably learnt at school, it was customary in poetry to bring down heavenly powers on earth. Not to speak of Dante, in France, clerks, as well as the monks in the monasteries, used to give regular performances in which the Madonna, the saints, the angels, Christ, and God Himself were brought on the stage. In those days it was done in all simplicity. In Victor Hugo's *Notre Dame de Paris* an edifying and gratuitous spectacle was provided for the people in the Hotel de Ville of Paris in the reign of Louis XI in honour of the birth of the dauphin.[1] It was called *Le bon jugement de la tres sainte et gracieuse Vierge Marie,*[2] and she appears herself on the stage and pronounces her *bon jugement*. Similar plays, chiefly from the Old Testament, were occasionally performed in Moscow too, up to the times of Peter the Great.

"But besides plays there were all sorts of legends and ballads scattered about the world, in which the saints and angels and all the powers of Heaven took part when required. In our monasteries the monks busied themselves in translating, copying, and even composing such poems – and even under the Tatars. There is, for instance, one such poem (of course, from the Greek), *The Wanderings of Our Lady through Hell*, with descriptions as bold as Dante's. Our Lady visits hell, and the Archangel Michael leads her through the torments. She sees the sinners and their punishment. There she sees among others one noteworthy set of sinners in a burning lake; some of them sink to the bottom of the lake so that they can't swim out, and 'these God forgets' – an expression of extraordinary depth and force. And so Our Lady, shocked and weeping, falls before the throne of God and begs for mercy for all in hell – for all she has seen there, indiscriminately. Her conversation with God is immensely interesting. She beseeches Him, she will not desist, and when God points to the hands and feet of her Son, nailed to the Cross, and asks, 'How can I forgive His tormentors?' she bids all the saints, all the martyrs, all the angels and archangels to fall down with her and pray for mercy on all without distinction. It ends by her winning from God a respite of suffering every year from Good Friday until Trinity Day, and the sinners at once raise a cry of thankfulness from hell, chanting, 'Thou art just, O Lord, in this judgment.'

"Well, my poem would have been of that kind if it had appeared at that time. He comes on the scene in my poem, but He says nothing, only appears and passes on. Fifteen centuries have passed since He promised to come in His glory, fifteen centuries since His prophet wrote, 'Behold, I come quickly'; 'Of that day and that hour knoweth no man, neither the Son, but the Father,' as He

---

[1] Dauphin. Literally "dolphin," but more directly the heir to the throne of France.
[2] *Le bon...Marie.* The good judgment of the most blessed and graceful Virgin Mary.

Himself predicted on earth. But humanity awaits him with the same faith and with the same love. Oh, with greater faith, for it is fifteen centuries since man has ceased to see signs from heaven.

> No signs from heaven come today
> To add to what the heart doth say.

There was nothing left but faith in what the heart doth say. It is true there were many miracles in those days. There were saints who performed miraculous cures; some holy people, according to their biographies, were visited by the Queen of Heaven herself. But the devil did not slumber, and doubts were already arising among men of the truth of these miracles. And just then there appeared in the north of Germany a terrible new heresy. 'A huge star like to a torch' (that is, to a church) 'fell on the sources of the waters and they became bitter.' These heretics began blasphemously denying miracles. But those who remained faithful were all the more ardent in their faith. The tears of humanity rose up to Him as before, awaited His coming, loved Him, hoped for Him, yearned to suffer and die for Him as before. And so many ages mankind had prayed with faith and fervor, 'O Lord our God, hasten Thy coming'; so many ages called upon Him, that in His infinite mercy He deigned to come down to His servants. Before that day He had come down, He had visited some holy men, martyrs, and hermits, as is written in their lives. Among us, Tyutchev, with absolute faith in the truth of his words, bore witness that

> Bearing the Cross, in slavish dress,
> Weary and worn, the Heavenly King
> Our mother, Russia, came to bless,
> And through our land went wandering.

And that certainly was so, I assure you.

"And behold, He deigned to appear for a moment to the people, to the tortured, suffering people, sunk in iniquity, but loving Him like children. My story is laid in Spain, in Seville, in the most terrible time of the Inquisition, when fires were lighted every day to the glory of God, and 'in the splendid *auto da fe*[1] the wicked heretics were burnt.' Oh, of course, this was not the coming in which He will appear, according to His promise, at the end of time in all His heavenly glory, and which will be sudden 'as lightning flashing from east to west.' No, He visited His children only for a moment, and there where the flames were crackling round the heretics. In His infinite mercy He came once more among men in that human shape in which He walked among men for thirty-three years fifteen centuries ago. He came down to the 'hot pavements' of the southern town in which on the day before almost a hundred heretics had, *ad majorem gloriam Dei,*[2] been burnt by the cardinal, the Grand Inquisitor, in a magnificent *auto da fe*, in the presence of the king, the court, the knights, the cardinals, the most charming ladies of the court, and the whole population of Seville.

"He came softly, unobserved, and yet, strange to say, everyone recognized Him. That might be one of the best passages in the poem. I mean, why they rec-

---

[1] Auto da fe. Literally, an act of faith, but in practice the execution of heretics.
[2] *Ad majorem gloriam Dei.* To the greater glory of God.

ognized Him. The people are irresistibly drawn to Him, they surround Him, they flock about Him, follow Him. He moves silently in their midst with a gentle smile of infinite compassion. The sun of love burns in His heart, and power shine from His eyes, and their radiance, shed on the people, stirs their hearts with responsive love. He holds out His hands to them, blesses them, and a healing virtue comes from contact with Him, even with His garments. An old man in the crowd, blind from childhood, cries out, 'O Lord, heal me and I shall see Thee!' and, as it were, scales fall from his eyes and the blind man sees Him. The crowd weeps and kisses the earth under His feet. Children throw flowers before Him, sing, and cry Hosannah. 'It is He – it is He!' repeat. 'It must be He, it can be no one but Him!' He stops at the steps of the Seville cathedral at the moment when the weeping mourners are bringing in a little open white coffin. In it lies a child of seven, the only daughter of a prominent citizen. The dead child lies hidden in flowers. 'He will raise your child,' the crowd shouts to the weeping mother. The priest, coming to meet the coffin, looks perplexed, and frowns, but the mother of the dead child throws herself at His feet with a wail. 'If it is Thou, raise my child!' she cries, holding out her hands to Him. The procession halts, the coffin is laid on the steps at His feet. He looks with compassion, and His lips once more softly pronounce, 'Maiden, arise!' and the maiden arises. The little girl sits up in the coffin and looks round, smiling with wide-open wondering eyes, holding a bunch of white roses they had put in her hand.

"There are cries, sobs, confusion among the people, and at that moment the cardinal himself, the Grand Inquisitor, passes by the cathedral. He is an old man, almost ninety, tall and erect, with a withered face and sunken eyes, in which there is still a gleam of light. He is not dressed in his gorgeous cardinal's robes, as he was the day before, when he was burning the enemies of the Roman Church – at this moment he is wearing his coarse, old, monk's cassock. At a distance behind him come his gloomy assistants and slaves and the 'holy guard.' He stops at the sight of the crowd and watches it from a distance. He sees everything; he sees them set the coffin down at His feet, sees the child rise up, and his face darkens. He knits his thick grey brows and his eyes gleam with a sinister fire. He holds out his finger and bids the guards take Him. And such is his power, so completely are the people cowed into submission and trembling obedience to him, that the crowd immediately makes way for the guards, and in the midst of deathlike silence they lay hands on Him and lead him away. The crowd instantly bows down to the earth, like one man, before the old Inquisitor. He blesses the people in silence and passes on' The guards lead their prisoner to the close, gloomy vaulted prison – in the ancient palace of the Holy, inquisition and shut him in it. The day passes and is followed by the dark, burning, 'breathless' night of Seville. The air is 'fragrant with laurel and lemon.' In the pitch darkness the iron door of the prison is suddenly opened and the Grand Inquisitor himself comes in with a light in his hand. He is alone; the door is closed at once behind him. He stands in the doorway and for a minute or two gazes into His face. At last he goes up slowly, sets the light on the table and speaks.

"'Is it Thou? Thou?' but receiving no answer, he adds at once. 'Don't answer, be silent. What canst Thou say, indeed? I know too well what Thou wouldst say. And Thou hast no right to add anything to what Thou hadst said of old. Why, then, art Thou come to hinder us? For Thou hast come to hinder us, and Thou knowest that. But dost thou know what will be tomorrow? I know not who Thou art and care not to know whether it is Thou or only a semblance of Him, but tomorrow I shall condemn Thee and burn Thee at the stake as the worst of heretics. And the very people who have today kissed Thy feet, tomorrow at the faintest sign from me will rush to heap up the embers of Thy fire. Knowest Thou that? Yes, maybe Thou knowest it,' he added with thoughtful penetration, never for a moment taking his eyes off the Prisoner."

"I don't quite understand, Ivan. What does it mean?" Alyosha, who had been listening in silence, said with a smile. "Is it simply a wild fantasy, or a mistake on the part of the old man – some impossible *quid pro quo?*"[1]

"Take it as the last," said Ivan, laughing, "if you are so corrupted by modern realism and can't stand anything fantastic. If you like it to be a case of mistaken identity, let it be so. It is true," he went on, laughing, "the old man was ninety, and he might well be crazy over his set idea. He might have been struck by the appearance of the Prisoner. It might, in fact, be simply his ravings, the delusion of an old man of ninety, over-excited by the *auto da fe* of a hundred heretics the day before. But does it matter to us after all whether it was a mistake of identity or a wild fantasy? All that matters is that the old man should speak out, that he should speak openly of what he has thought in silence for ninety years."

"And the Prisoner too is silent? Does He look at him and not say a word?"

"That's inevitable in any case," Ivan laughed again. "The old man has told Him He hasn't the right to add anything to what He has said of old. One may say it is the most fundamental feature of Roman Catholicism, in my opinion at least. 'All has been given by Thee to the Pope,' they say, 'and all, therefore, is still in the Pope's hands, and there is no need for Thee to come now at all. Thou must not meddle for the time, at least.' That's how they speak and write too – the Jesuits, at any rate. I have read it myself in the works of their theologians. 'Hast Thou the right to reveal to us one of the mysteries of that world from which Thou hast come?' my old man asks Him, and answers the question for Him. 'No, Thou hast not; that Thou mayest not add to what has been said of old, and mayest not take from men the freedom which Thou didst exalt when Thou wast on earth. Whatsoever Thou revealest anew will encroach on men's freedom of faith; for it will be manifest as a miracle, and the freedom of their faith was dearer to Thee than anything in those days fifteen hundred years ago. Didst Thou not often say then, "I will make you free"? But now Thou hast seen these "free" men,' the old man adds suddenly, with a pensive smile. 'Yes, we've paid dearly for it,' he goes on, looking sternly at Him, 'but at last we have completed that work in Thy name. For fifteen centuries we have been wrestling with Thy freedom, but now it is ended and over for good. Dost Thou not believe that it's over for good? Thou lookest meekly at me and deignest not even to be wroth with me. But let me tell Thee that now, today, people are more persuaded than

---

[1] *Quid pro quo.* One favor exchanged for another.

ever that they have perfect freedom, yet they have brought their freedom to us and laid it humbly at our feet. But that has been our doing. Was this what Thou didst? Was this Thy freedom?'"

"I don't understand again." Alyosha broke in. "Is he ironical, is he jesting?"

"Not a bit of it! He claims it as a merit for himself and his Church that at last they have vanquished freedom and have done so to make men happy. 'For now' (he is speaking of the Inquisition, of course) 'for the first time it has become possible to think of the happiness of men. Man was created a rebel; and how can rebels be happy? Thou wast warned,' he says to Him. 'Thou hast had no lack of admonitions and warnings, but Thou didst not listen to those warnings; Thou didst reject the only way by which men might be made happy. But, fortunately, departing Thou didst hand on the work to us. Thou hast promised, Thou hast established by Thy word, Thou hast given to us the right to bind and to unbind, and now, of course, Thou canst not think of taking it away. Why, then, hast Thou come to hinder us?'"

"And what's the meaning of 'no lack of admonitions and warnings'?" asked Alyosha.

"Why, that's the chief part of what the old man must say.

"'The wise and dread spirit, the spirit of self-destruction and non-existence,' the old man goes on, great spirit talked with Thee in the wilderness, and we are told in the books that he "tempted" Thee. Is that so? And could anything truer be said than what he revealed to Thee in three questions and what Thou didst reject, and what in the books is called "the temptation"? And yet if there has ever been on earth a real stupendous miracle, it took place on that day, on the day of the three temptations. The statement of those three questions was itself the miracle. If it were possible to imagine simply for the sake of argument that those three questions of the dread spirit had perished utterly from the books, and that we had to restore them and to invent them anew, and to do so had gathered together all the wise men of the earth – rulers, chief priests, learned men, philosophers, poets – and had set them the task to invent three questions, such as would not only fit the occasion, but express in three words, three human phrases, the whole future history of the world and of humanity – dost Thou believe that all the wisdom of the earth united could have invented anything in depth and force equal to the three questions which were actually put to Thee then by the wise and mighty spirit in the wilderness? From those questions alone, from the miracle of their statement, we can see that we have here to do not with the fleeting human intelligence, but with the absolute and eternal. For in those three questions the whole subsequent history of mankind is, as it were, brought together into one whole, and foretold, and in them are united all the unsolved historical contradictions of human nature. At the time it could not be so clear, since the future was unknown; but now that fifteen hundred years have passed, we see that everything in those three questions was so justly divined and foretold, and has been so truly fulfilled, that nothing can be added to them or taken from them.

"Judge Thyself who was right – Thou or he who questioned Thee then?

Remember the first question; its meaning, in other words, was this: 'Thou wouldst go into the world, and art going with empty hands, with some promise of freedom which men in their simplicity and their natural unruliness cannot even understand, which they fear and dread- for nothing has ever been more insupportable for a man and a human society than freedom. But seest Thou these stones in this parched and barren wilderness? Turn them into bread, and mankind will run after Thee like a flock of sheep, grateful and obedient, though for ever trembling, lest Thou withdraw Thy hand and deny them Thy bread.' But Thou wouldst not deprive man of freedom and didst reject the offer, thinking, what is that freedom worth if obedience is bought with bread?

"Thou didst reply that man lives not by bread alone. But dost Thou know that for the sake of that earthly bread the spirit of the earth will rise up against Thee and will strive with Thee and overcome Thee, and all will follow him, crying, "Who can compare with this beast? He has given us fire from heaven!" Dost Thou know that the ages will pass, and humanity will proclaim by the lips of their sages that there is no crime, and therefore no sin; there is only hunger? "Feed men, and then ask of them virtue!" that's what they'll write on the banner, which they will raise against Thee, and with which they will destroy Thy temple. Where Thy temple stood will rise a new building; the terrible tower of Babel will be built again, and though, like the one of old, it will not be finished, yet Thou mightest have prevented that new tower and have cut short the sufferings of men for a thousand years; for they will come back to us after a thousand years of agony with their tower. They will seek us again, hidden underground in the catacombs, for we shall be again persecuted and tortured. They will find us and cry to us, "Feed us, for those who have promised us fire from heaven haven't given it!" And then we shall finish building their tower, for he finishes the building who feeds them. And we alone shall feed them in Thy name, declaring falsely that it is in Thy name. Oh, never, never can they feed themselves without us! No science will give them bread so long as they remain free.

"In the end they will lay their freedom at our feet, and say to us, 'Make us your slaves, but feed us.' They will understand themselves, at last, that freedom and bread enough for all are inconceivable together, for never, never will they be able to share between them! They will be convinced, too, that they can never be free, for they are weak, vicious, worthless, and rebellious. Thou didst promise them the bread of Heaven, but, I repeat again, can it compare with earthly bread in the eyes of the weak, ever sinful and ignoble race of man? And if for the sake of the bread of Heaven thousands shall follow Thee, what is to become of the millions and tens of thousands of millions of creatures who will not have the strength to forego the earthly bread for the sake of the heavenly? Or dost Thou care only for the tens of thousands of the great and strong, while the millions, numerous as the sands of the sea, who are weak but love Thee, must exist only for the sake of the great and strong? No, we care for the weak too. They are sinful and rebellious, but in the end they too will become obedient. They will marvel at us and look on us as gods, because we are ready to endure the freedom which they have found so dreadful and to rule over them – so awful it will seem to them to be free. But we shall tell them that we are Thy servants and rule them in Thy name. We shall deceive them again, for we will not let Thee come to us again. That deception will be our suffering, for we shall be forced to lie.

"'This is the significance of the first question in the wilderness, and this is what Thou hast rejected for the sake of that freedom which Thou hast exalted above everything. Yet in this question lies hid the great secret of this world. Choosing "bread," Thou wouldst have satisfied the universal and everlasting craving of humanity – to find someone to worship. So long as man remains free he strives for nothing so incessantly and so painfully as to find someone to worship. But man seeks to worship what is established beyond dispute, so that all men would agree at once to worship it. For these pitiful creatures are concerned not only to find what one or the other can worship, but to find community of worship is the chief misery of every man individually and of all humanity from the beginning of time. For the sake of common worship they've slain each other with the sword. They have set up gods and challenged one another, "Put away your gods and come and worship ours, or we will kill you and your gods!" And so it will be to the end of the world, even when gods disappear from the earth; they will fall down before idols just the same. Thou didst know, Thou couldst not but have known, this fundamental secret of human nature, but Thou didst reject the one infallible banner which was offered Thee to make all men bow down to Thee alone – the banner of earthly bread; and Thou hast rejected it for the sake of freedom and the bread of Heaven. Behold what Thou didst further. And all again in the name of freedom! I tell Thee that man is tormented by no greater anxiety than to find someone quickly to whom he can hand over that gift of freedom with which the ill-fated creature is born. But only one who can appease their conscience can take over their freedom. In bread there was offered Thee an invincible banner; give bread, and man will worship thee, for nothing is more certain than bread. But if someone else gains possession of his conscience – Oh! then he will cast away Thy bread and follow after him who has ensnared his conscience. In that Thou wast right. For the secret of man's being is not only to live but to have something to live for. Without a stable conception of the object of life, man would not consent to go on living, and would rather destroy himself than remain on earth, though he had bread in abundance. That is true. But what happened? Instead of taking men's freedom from them, Thou didst make it greater than ever! Didst Thou forget that man prefers peace, and even death, to freedom of choice in the knowledge of good and evil? Nothing is more seductive for man than his freedom of conscience, but nothing is a greater cause of suffering. And behold, instead of giving a firm foundation for setting the conscience of man at rest for ever, Thou didst choose all that is exceptional, vague and enigmatic; Thou didst choose what was utterly beyond the strength of men, acting as though Thou didst not love them at all – Thou who didst come to give Thy life for them! Instead of taking possession of men's freedom, Thou didst increase it, and burdened the spiritual kingdom of mankind with its sufferings for ever. Thou didst desire man's free love, that he should follow Thee freely, enticed and taken captive by Thee. In place of the rigid ancient law, man must hereafter with free heart decide for himself what is good and what is evil, having only Thy image before him as his guide. But didst Thou not know that he would at last reject even Thy image and Thy truth, if he is weighed down with the fearful burden of free choice? They will cry aloud at last that the truth is not in Thee, for they could not have been left in greater confusion and suffering than Thou hast caused, laying upon them so many cares and unanswerable problems.

"'So that, in truth, Thou didst Thyself lay the foundation for the destruction of Thy kingdom, and no one is more to blame for it. Yet what was offered Thee? There are three powers, three powers alone, able to conquer and to hold captive for ever the conscience of these impotent rebels for their happiness those forces are miracle, mystery and authority. Thou hast rejected all three and hast set the example for doing so. When the wise and dread spirit set Thee on the pinnacle of the temple and said to Thee, "If Thou wouldst know whether Thou art the Son of God then cast Thyself down, for it is written: the angels shall hold him up lest he fall and bruise himself, and Thou shalt know then whether Thou art the Son of God and shalt prove then how great is Thy faith in Thy Father." But Thou didst refuse and wouldst not cast Thyself down.

"Oh, of course, Thou didst proudly and well, like God; but the weak, unruly race of men, are they gods? Oh, Thou didst know then that in taking one step, in making one movement to cast Thyself down, Thou wouldst be tempting God and have lost all Thy faith in Him, and wouldst have been dashed to pieces against that earth which Thou didst come to save. And the wise spirit that tempted Thee would have rejoiced. But I ask again, are there many like Thee? And couldst Thou believe for one moment that men, too, could face such a temptation? Is the nature of men such, that they can reject miracle, and at the great moments of their life, the moments of their deepest, most agonizing spiritual difficulties, cling only to the free verdict of the heart? Oh, Thou didst know that Thy deed would be recorded in books, would be handed down to remote times and the utmost ends of the earth, and Thou didst hope that man, following Thee, would cling to God and not ask for a miracle. But Thou didst not know that when man rejects miracle he rejects God too; for man seeks not so much God as the miraculous. And as man cannot bear to be without the miraculous, he will create new miracles of his own for himself, and will worship deeds of sorcery and witchcraft, though he might be a hundred times over a rebel, heretic and infidel.

"Thou didst not come down from the Cross when they shouted to Thee, mocking and reviling Thee, "Come down from the cross and we will believe that Thou art He." Thou didst not come down, for again Thou wouldst not enslave man by a miracle, and didst crave faith given freely, not based on miracle. Thou didst crave for free love and not the base raptures of the slave before the might that has overawed him for ever. But Thou didst think too highly of men therein, for they are slaves, of course, though rebellious by nature. Look round and judge; fifteen centuries have passed, look upon them. Whom hast Thou raised up to Thyself? I swear, man is weaker and baser by nature than Thou hast believed him! Can he, can he do what Thou didst? By showing him so much respect, Thou didst, as it were, cease to feel for him, for Thou didst ask far too much from him – Thou who hast loved him more than Thyself! Respecting him less,

Thou wouldst have asked less of him. That would have been more like love, for his burden would have been lighter. He is weak and vile. What though he is everywhere now rebelling against our power, and proud of his rebellion? It is the pride of a child and a schoolboy. They are little children rioting and barring out the teacher at school. But their childish delight will end; it will cost them dear.

"Mankind as a whole has always striven to organize a universal state. There have been many great nations with great histories, but the more highly they were developed the more unhappy they were, for they felt more acutely than other people the craving for world-wide union. The great conquerors, Timours and Ghenghis-Khans, whirled like hurricanes over the face of the earth striving to subdue its people, and they too were but the unconscious expression of the same craving for universal unity. Hadst Thou taken the world and Caesar's purple, Thou wouldst have founded the universal state and have given universal peace. For who can rule men if not he who holds their conscience and their bread in his hands? We have taken the sword of Caesar, and in taking it, of course, have rejected Thee and followed him. Oh, ages are yet to come of the confusion of free thought, of their science and cannibalism. For having begun to build their tower of Babel without us, they will end, of course, with cannibalism. But then the beast will crawl to us and lick our feet and spatter them with tears of blood. And we shall sit upon the beast and raise the cup, and on it will be written, "Mystery." But then, and only then, the reign of peace and happiness will come for men. Thou art proud of Thine elect, but Thou hast only the elect, while we give rest to all. And besides, how many of those elect, those mighty ones who could become elect, have grown weary waiting for Thee, and have transferred and will transfer the powers of their spirit and the warmth of their heart to the other camp, and end by raising their free banner against Thee.

"Thou didst Thyself lift up that banner. But with us all will be happy and will no more rebel nor destroy one another as under Thy freedom. Oh, we shall persuade them that they will only become free when they renounce their freedom to us and submit to us. And shall we be right or shall we be lying? They will be convinced that we are right, for they will remember the horrors of slavery and confusion to which Thy freedom brought them. Freedom, free thought, and science will lead them into such straits and will bring them face to face with such marvels and insoluble mysteries, that some of them, the fierce and rebellious, will destroy themselves, others, rebellious but weak, will destroy one another, while the rest, weak and unhappy, will crawl fawning to our feet and whine to us: "Yes, you were right, you alone possess His mystery, and we come back to you, save us from ourselves!"

"'Receiving bread from us, they will see clearly that we take the bread made by their hands from them, to give it to them, without any miracle. They will see that we do not change the stones to bread, but in truth they will be more thankful for taking it from our hands than for the bread itself! For they will remember only too well that in old days, without our help, even the bread they made turned to stones in their hands, while since they have come back to us, the very stones have turned to bread in their hands. Too, too well will they know the value of complete submission! And until men know that, they will be unhappy.

subdue his flesh to make himself free and perfect. But yet all his life he loved humanity, and suddenly his eyes were opened, and he saw that it is no great moral blessedness to attain perfection and freedom, if at the same time one gains the conviction that millions of God's creatures have been created as a mockery, that they will never be capable of using their freedom, that these poor rebels can never turn into giants to complete the tower, that it was not for such geese that the great idealist dreamt his dream of harmony. Seeing all that he turned back and joined – the clever people. Surely that could have happened?"

"Joined whom, what clever people?" cried Alyosha, completely carried away. "They have no such great cleverness and no mysteries and secrets....Perhaps nothing but Atheism, that's all their secret. Your Inquisitor does not believe in God, that's his secret!"

"What if it is so! At last you have guessed it. It's perfectly true, it's true that that's the whole secret, but isn't that suffering, at least for a man like that, who has wasted his whole life in the desert and yet could not shake off his incurable love of humanity? In his old age he reached the clear conviction that nothing but the advice of the great dread spirit could build up any tolerable sort of life for the feeble, unruly, 'incomplete, empirical creatures created in jest.' And so, convinced of this, he sees that he must follow the counsel of the wise spirit, the dread spirit of death and destruction, and therefore accept lying and deception, and lead men consciously to death and destruction, and yet deceive them all the way so that they may not notice where they are being led, that the poor blind creatures may at least on the way think themselves happy. And note, the deception is in the name of Him in Whose ideal the old man had so fervently believed all his life long. Is not that tragic? And if only one such stood at the head of the whole army 'filled with the lust of power only for the sake of filthy gain' – would not one such be enough to make a tragedy? More than that, one such standing at the head is enough to create the actual leading idea of the Roman Church with all its armies and Jesuits, its highest idea. I tell you frankly that I firmly believe that there has always been such a man among those who stood at the head of the movement. Who knows, there may have been some such even among the Roman Popes. Who knows, perhaps the spirit of that accursed old man who loves mankind so obstinately in his own way, is to be found even now in a whole multitude of such old men, existing not by chance but by agreement, as a secret league formed long ago for the guarding of the mystery, to guard it from the weak and the unhappy, so as to make them happy. No doubt it is so, and so it must be indeed. I fancy that even among the Masons there's something of the same mystery at the bottom, and that that's why the Catholics so detest the Masons as their rivals breaking up the unity of the idea, while it is so essential that there should be one flock and one shepherd....But from the way I defend my idea I might be an author impatient of your criticism. Enough of it."

"You are perhaps a Mason yourself!" broke suddenly from Alyosha. "You don't believe in God," he added, speaking this time very sorrowfully. He fancied besides that his brother was looking at him ironically. "How does your poem end?" he asked, suddenly looking down. "Or was it the end?"

"I meant to end it like this. When the Inquisitor ceased speaking he waited some time for his Prisoner to answer him. His silence weighed down upon him. He saw that the Prisoner had listened intently all the time, looking gently in his face and evidently not wishing to reply. The old man longed for him to say something, however bitter and terrible. But He suddenly approached the old man in silence and softly kissed him on his bloodless aged lips. That was all his answer. The old man shuddered. His lips moved. He went to the door, opened it, and said to Him: 'Go, and come no more...come not at all, never, never!' And he let Him out into the dark alleys of the town. The Prisoner went away."

"And the old man?"

"The kiss glows in his heart, but the old man adheres to his idea."

"And you with him, you too?" cried Alyosha, mournfully.

Ivan laughed.

"Why, it's all nonsense, Alyosha. It's only a senseless poem of a senseless student, who could never write two lines of verse. Why do you take it so seriously? Surely you don't suppose I am going straight off to the Jesuits, to join the men who are correcting His work? Good Lord, it's no business of mine. I told you, all I want is to live on to thirty, and then...dash the cup to the ground!"

"But the little sticky leaves, and the precious tombs, and the blue sky, and the woman you love! How will you live, how will you love them?" Alyosha cried sorrowfully. "With such a hell in your heart and your head, how can you? No, that's just what you are going away for, to join them...if not, you will kill yourself, you can't endure it!"

"There is a strength to endure everything," Ivan said with a cold smile.

"The strength of the Karamazovs – the strength of the Karamazov baseness."

"To sink into debauchery, to stifle your soul with corruption, yes?"

"Possibly even that...only perhaps until I am thirty I shall escape it, and then –"

"How will you escape it? By what will you escape it? That's impossible with your ideas."

"In the Karamazov way, again."

"'Everything is lawful,' you mean? Everything is lawful, is that it?"

Ivan scowled, and all at once turned strangely pale.

"Ah, you've caught up yesterday's phrase, which so offended Muisov – and which Dmitri pounced upon so naively and paraphrased!" he smiled queerly. "Yes, if you like, 'everything is lawful' since the word has been said, I won't deny it. And Mitya's version isn't bad."

Alyosha looked at him in silence.

"I thought that going away from here I have you at least," Ivan said suddenly, with unexpected feeling; "but now I see that there is no place for me even in your heart, my dear hermit. The formula, 'all is lawful,' I won't renounce – will you renounce me for that, yes?"

Alyosha got up, went to him and softly kissed him on the lips.

"That's plagiarism," cried Ivan, highly delighted. "You stole that from my poem. Thank you though. Get up, Alyosha, it's time we were going, both of us."

They went out, but stopped when they reached the entrance of the restaurant.

"Listen, Alyosha," Ivan began in a resolute voice, "if I am really able to care for the sticky little leaves I shall only love them, remembering you. It's enough for me that you are somewhere here, and I shan't lose my desire for life yet. Is that enough for you? Take it as a declaration of love if you like. And now you go to the right and I to the left. And it's enough, do you hear, enough. I mean even if I don't go away tomorrow (I think I certainly shall go) and we meet again, don't say a word more on these subjects. I beg that particularly. And about Dmitri too, I ask you specially, never speak to me again," he added, with sudden irritation; "it's all exhausted, it has all been said over and over again, hasn't it? And I'll make you one promise in return for it. When at thirty, I want to 'dash the cup to the ground,' wherever I may be I'll come to have one more talk with you, even though it were from America, you may be sure of that. I'll come on purpose. It will be very interesting to have a look at you, to see what you'll be by that time. It's rather a solemn promise, you see. And we really may be parting for seven years or ten. Come, go now to your Pater Seraphicus,[1] he is dying. If he dies without you, you will be angry with me for having kept you. Good-bye, kiss me once more; that's right, now go."

Ivan turned suddenly and went his way without looking back. It was just as Dmitri had left Alyosha the day before, though the parting had been very differ-ent. The strange resemblance flashed like an arrow through Alyosha's mind in the distress and dejection of that moment. He waited a little, looking after his brother. He suddenly noticed that Ivan swayed as he walked and that his right shoulder looked lower than his left. He had never noticed it before. But all at once he turned too, and almost ran to the monastery. It was nearly dark, and he felt almost frightened; something new was growing up in him for which he could not account. The wind had risen again as on the previous evening, and the ancient pines murmured gloomily about him when he entered the hermitage copse. He almost ran. "Pater Seraphicus – he got that name from somewhere – where from?" Alyosha wondered. "Ivan, poor Ivan, and when shall I see you again?...Here is the hermitage. Yes, yes, that he is, Pater Seraphicus, he will save me – from him and for ever!"

Several times afterwards he wondered how he could, on leaving Ivan, so completely forget his brother Dmitri, though he had that morning, only a few hours before, so firmly resolved to find him and not to give up doing so, even should he be unable to return to the monastery that night.

---

[1] Pater Seraphicus. An epithet for St. Francis of Assisi, used here to refer to Alyosha's spiritual guide Zosima. See also Goethe's *Faust*, Part 2, Act 5.

Friedrich Nietzsche
1844-1900

The German philosopher Friedrich Nietzsche is one of the most influential thinkers of the twenty-first century. Though his approach was unconventional and his interests were broad, three of his concepts are controversial over a century after his death: the will to power, the Super-human, and the death of God. He believed that the central operating principle of humans was not, as Schopenhauer had argued, the "will to live" (to procreate and avoid death), but the "will to power," as seen in our struggles to achieve the highest possible goals. The Super-human (the "*Ubermensch*") according to Nietzsche is the "ultimate realization of the Will to Power, but not necessarily over others...[but] over himself." This idealized and futuristic figure (one misused by the Nazis forty years after Nietzsche's death) will be able to create new values at a time when there is an absence of other values. Such a time Nietzsche believed was upon the human race, as both science and religion itself had effectively killed any meaningful belief in God, without which the world will be plunged into nihilism, the belief that nothing, including life itself, is of real importance.

Major Works
The Birth of Tragedy (1872)
Thus Spoke Zarathustra (1883-85)
Beyond Good and Evil (1886)
On the Genealogy of Morals (1887)

CʒBꝹ
The Madman
From The Cheerful Science
Friedrich Nietzsche, 1882
TRANSLATED BY THOMAS COMMON

Have you ever heard of the madman who on a bright morning lighted a lantern and ran to the market-place calling out unceasingly: "I seek God! I seek God!"

As there were many people standing about who did not believe in God, he caused a great deal of amusement. "Why? Is he lost?" said one. "Has he strayed away like a child?" said another. "Or does he keep himself hidden? Is he afraid of us? Has he taken a sea-voyage? Has he emigrated?" the people cried out laughingly, all in a hubbub. The insane man jumped into their midst and transfixed them with his glances.

"Where is God gone?" he called out. "I mean to tell you! We have killed him – you and I! We are all his murderers! But how have we done it? How were we able to drink up the sea? Who gave us the sponge to wipe away the whole horizon? What did we do when we loosened this earth from its sun? Whither does it now move? Whither do we move? Away from all suns? Do we not dash on un¬ceasingly? Back-wards, sideways, forwards, in all directions? Is there still an above and below? Do we not stray, as through infinite nothingness? Does not empty space breathe upon us? Has it not become colder? Does not night come on continually, darker and darker? Shall we not have to light lanterns in the morning? Do we not hear the noise of the grave-diggers who are burying God? Do we not smell the divine putrefaction? For even Gods putrefy! God is dead! God remains dead! And we have killed him! How shall we console ourselves, the most murderous of all murderers? The holiest and the mightiest that the world has hitherto possessed, has bled to death under our knife – who will wipe the blood from us? With what water could we cleanse ourselves? What lustrums, what sacred games shall we have to devise? Is not the magnitude of this deed too great for us? Shall we not ourselves have to become Gods, merely to seem worthy of it? There never was a greater event – and on account of it, all who are born after us belong to a higher history than any history hitherto!"

Here the madman was silent and looked again at his hearers; they also were silent and looked at him in surprise. At last he threw his lantern on the ground, so that it broke in pieces and was extinguished. "I come too early," he then said, "I am not yet at the right time. This prodigious event is still on its way, and is traveling – it has not yet reached men's ears. Lightning and thunder need time, the light of the stars needs time, deeds need time, even after they are done, to be seen and heard. This deed is as yet further from them than the furthest star – and yet they have done it!"

It is further stated that the madman made his way into different churches on the same day, and there intoned his *Requiem aeternam deo*[1]. When led out and called to account, he always gave the reply: "What are these churches now, if they are not the tombs and monuments of God?"

---

[1] Requiem aeternam deo. [Give them] eternal rest. Lord.

Guy de Maupassant
1850-1893

In his relatively short life, Guy de Maupassant produced over 300 short stories, six novels, and over 200 sketches for newspapers and magazines, as well as essays on travel and dramatic adaptations. Born to middle-class parents in Rouen, Normandy, de Maupassant studied law and served as a soldier in the Franco-Prussian War from 1870 to 1871. In Paris, he supported himself by writing for newspapers and working as a government bureaucrat in the Ministries of the Navy and Education while he tried to write plays; eventually he discovered that his true form was the short story and was encouraged by Gustave Flaubert (his godfather) and Emile Zola. While in Paris, de Maupassant contracted syphilis, and his health deteriorated until his untimely death at forty-two.

Major Works
Une Vie (1883)
Bel-Ami (1885)
Contes du jour et de la nuit (1885)

ᘓᘔᘓ
The Necklace
Guy de Maupassant, 1884
TRANSLATED BY JONATHAN STURGES

She was one of those pretty and charming girls born, as though fate had blundered over her, into a family of artisans. She had no marriage portion, no expectations, no means of getting known, understood, loved, and wedded by a man of wealth and distinction; and she let herself be married off to a little clerk in the Ministry of Education. Her tastes were simple because she had never been able to afford any other, but she was as unhappy as though she had married beneath her; for women have no caste or class, their beauty, grace, and charm serving them for birth or family. their natural delicacy, their instinctive elegance, their nimbleness of wit, are their only mark of rank, and put the slum girl on a level with the highest lady in the land.

She suffered endlessly, feeling herself born for every delicacy and luxury.

She suffered from the poorness of her house, from its mean walls, worn chairs, and ugly curtains. All these things, of which other women of her class would not even have been aware, tormented and insulted her. The sight of the little Breton girl who came to do the work in her little house aroused heart-broken regrets and hopeless dreams in her mind. She imagined silent antechambers, heavy with Oriental tapestries, lit by torches in lofty bronze sockets, with two tall footmen in knee-breeches sleeping in large arm-chairs, overcome by the heavy warmth of the stove. She imagined vast saloons hung with antique silks, exquisite pieces of furniture supporting priceless ornaments, and small, charming, perfumed rooms, created just for little parties of intimate friends, men who were famous and sought after, whose homage roused every other woman's envious longings.

When she sat down for dinner at the round table covered with a three-days-old cloth, opposite her husband, who took the cover off the soup-tureen, exclaiming delightedly: "Aha! Scotch broth! What could be better?" she imagined delicate meals, gleaming silver, tapestries peopling the walls with folk of a past age and strange birds in fairy forests; she imagined delicate food served in marvelous dishes, murmured gallantries, listened to with an inscrutable smile as one trifled with the rosy flesh of trout or wings of asparagus chicken.

She had no clothes, no jewels, nothing. And these were the only things she loved; she felt that she was made for them. She had longed so eagerly to charm, to be desired, to be wildly attractive and sought after.

She had a rich friend, an old school friend whom she refused to visit, because she suffered so keenly when she returned home. She would weep whole days, with grief, regret, despair, and misery.

* * *

One evening her husband came home with an exultant air, holding a large envelope in his hand.

" Here's something for you," he said.

Swiftly she tore the paper and drew out a printed card on which were these words:

"The Minister of Education and Madame Ramponneau request the pleasure of the company of Monsieur and Madame Loisel at the Ministry on the evening of Monday, January the 18th."

Instead of being delighted, as her-husband hoped, she flung the invitation petulantly across the table, murmuring:

"What do you want me to do with this?"

"Why, darling, I thought you'd be pleased. You never go out, and this is a great occasion. I had tremendous trouble to get it. Every one wants one; it's very select, and very few go to the clerks. You'll see all the really big people there."

She looked at him out of furious eyes, and said impatiently: "And what do you suppose I am to wear at such an affair?"

He had not thought about it; he stammered:

"Why, the dress you go to the theatre in. It looks very nice, to me...."

He stopped, stupefied and utterly at a loss when he saw that his wife was beginning to cry. Two large tears ran slowly down from the corners of her eyes towards the corners of her mouth.

"What's the matter with you? What's the matter with you?" he faltered.

But with a violent effort she overcame her grief and replied in a calm voice, wiping her wet cheeks:

"Nothing. Only I haven't a dress and so I can't go to this party. Give your invitation to some friend of yours whose wife will be turned out better than I shall."

He was heart-broken.

"Look here, Mathilde," he persisted. "What would be the cost of a suitable dress, which you could use on other occasions as well, something very simple?"

She thought for several seconds, reckoning up prices and also wondering for how large a sum she could ask without bringing upon herself an immediate refusal and an exclamation of horror from the careful-minded clerk.

At last she replied with some hesitation:

"I don't know exactly, but I think I could do it on four hundred francs."

He grew slightly pale, for this was exactly the amount he had been saving for a gun, intending to get a little shooting next summer on the plain of Nanterre with some friends who went lark-shooting there on Sundays.

Nevertheless he said: "Very well. I'll give you four hundred francs. But try and get a really nice dress with the money."

The day of the party drew near, and Madame Loisel seemed sad, uneasy and anxious. Her dress was ready, however. One evening her husband said to her:

"What's the matter with you? You've been very odd for the last three days."

"I'm utterly miserable at not having any jewels, not a single stone, to wear," she replied. "I shall look absolutely no one. I would almost rather not go to the party."

"Wear flowers," he said. "They're very smart at this time of the year. For ten francs you could get two or three gorgeous roses."

She was not convinced.

"No . . . there's nothing so humiliating as looking poor in the middle of a lot of rich women."

"How stupid you are!" exclaimed her husband. "Go and see Madame Forestier and ask her to lend you some jewels. You know her quite well enough for that."

She uttered a cry of delight.

"That's true. I never thought of it."

Next day she went to see her friend and told her her trouble.

Madame Forestier went to her dressing-table, took up a large box, brought it to Madame Loisel, opened it, and said:

"Choose, my dear."

First she saw some bracelets, then a pearl necklace, then a Venetian cross in gold and gems, of exquisite workmanship. She tried the effect of the jewels before the mirror, hesitating, unable to make up her mind to leave them, to give them up. She kept on asking:

"Haven't you anything else?"

"Yes. Look for yourself. I don't know what you would like best."

Suddenly she discovered, in a black satin case, a superb diamond necklace; her heart began to beat covetously. Her hands trembled as she lifted it. She fastened it round her neck, upon her high dress, and remained in ecstasy at sight of herself.

Then, with hesitation, she asked in anguish:

"Could you lend me this, just this alone?"

"Yes, of course."

She flung herself on her friend's breast, embraced her frenziedly, and went away with her treasure. The day of the party arrived. Madame Loisel was a success. She was the prettiest woman present, elegant, graceful, smiling, and quite above herself with happiness. All the men stared at her, inquired her name, and asked to be introduced to her. All the Under-Secretaries of State were eager to waltz with her. The Minister noticed her.

She danced madly, ecstatically, drunk with pleasure, with no thought for anything, in the triumph of her beauty, in the pride of her success, in a cloud of happiness made up of this universal homage and admiration, of the desires she had aroused, of the completeness of a victory so dear to her feminine heart.

She left about four o'clock in the morning. Since midnight her husband had been dozing in a deserted little room, in company with three other men whose wives were having a good time. He threw over her shoulders the garments he had brought for them to go home in, modest everyday clothes, whose poverty clashed with the beauty of the ball-dress. She was conscious of this and was anxious to hurry away, so that she should not be noticed by the other women putting on their costly furs.

Loisel restrained her.

"Wait a little. You'll catch cold in the open. I'm going to fetch a cab."

But she did not listen to him and rapidly descended-the staircase. When they were out in the street they could not find a cab; they began to look for one, shouting at the drivers whom they saw passing in the distance.

They walked down towards the Seine, desperate and shivering. At last they found on the quay one of those old night-prowling carriages which are only to be seen in Paris after dark, as though they were ashamed of their shabbiness in the daylight.

It brought them to their door in the Rue des Martyrs, and sadly they walked up to their own apartment. It was the end, for her. As for him, he was thinking that he must be at the office at ten.

She took off the garments in which she had wrapped her shoulders, so as to see herself in all her glory before the mirror. But suddenly she uttered a cry. The necklace was no longer round her neck!

"What's the matter with you?" asked her husband, already half undressed.

She turned towards him in the utmost distress.

"I . . . I . . . I've no longer got Madame Forestier's necklace. . . ."

He started with astonishment.

"What! . . . Impossible!"

They searched in the folds of her dress, in the folds of the coat, in the pockets, everywhere. They could not find it.

"Are you sure that you still had it on when you came away from the ball?" he asked.

"Yes, I touched it in the hall at the Ministry."

"But if you had lost it in the street, we should have heard it fall."

"Yes. Probably we should. Did you take the number of the cab?"

"No. You didn't notice it, did you?"

"No."

They stared at one another, dumbfounded. At last Loisel put on his clothes again.

"I'll go over all the ground we walked," he said, "and see if I can't find it."

And he went out. She remained in her evening clothes, lacking strength to get into bed, huddled on a chair, without volition or power of thought.

Her husband returned about seven. He had found nothing.

He went to the police station, to the newspapers, to offer a reward, to the cab companies, everywhere that a ray of hope impelled him.

She waited all day long, in the same state of bewilderment at this fearful catastrophe.

Loisel came home at night, his face lined and pale; he had discovered nothing.

"You must write to your friend," he said, "and tell her that you've broken the clasp of her necklace and are getting it mended. That will give us time to look about us."

She wrote at his dictation.

* * *

By the end of a week they had lost all hope.

Loisel, who had aged five years, declared:

"We must see about replacing the diamonds."

Next day they took the box which had held the necklace and went to the jewelers whose name was inside. He consulted his books.

"It was not I who sold this necklace, Madame; I must have merely supplied the clasp."

Then they went from jeweler to jeweler, searching for another necklace like the first, consulting their memories, both ill with remorse and anguish of mind.

In a shop at the Palais-Royal they found a string of diamonds which seemed to them exactly like the one they were looking for. It was worth forty thousand francs. They were allowed to have it for thirty-six thousand.

They begged the jeweler not to sell it for three days. And they arranged matters on the understanding that it would be taken back for thirty-four thousand francs, if the first one were found before the end of February.

Loisel possessed eighteen thousand francs left to him by his father. He intended to borrow the rest.

He did borrow it, getting a thousand from one man, five hundred from another, five louis here, three louis there. He gave notes of hand, entered into ruinous agreements, did business with usurers and the whole tribe of money-lenders.

He mortgaged the whole remaining years of his existence, risked his signature without even knowing it he could honour it, and, appalled at the agonizing face of the future, at the black misery about to fall upon him, at the prospect of every possible physical privation and moral torture, he went to get the new necklace and put down upon the jeweler's counter thirty-six thousand francs.

When Madame Loisel took back the necklace to Madame Forestier, the latter said to her in a chilly voice:

"You ought to have brought it back sooner; I might have needed it."

She did not, as her friend had feared, open the case. If she had noticed the substitution, what would she have thought? What would she have said? Would she not have taken her for a thief?

* * *

Madame Loisel came to know the ghastly life of abject poverty. From the very first she played her part heroically. This fearful debt must be paid off. She would pay it. The servant was dismissed. They changed their flat; they took a garret under the roof.

She came to know the heavy work of the house, the hateful duties of the kitchen. She washed the plates, wearing out her pink nails on the coarse pottery and the bottoms of pans. She washed the dirty linen, the shirts and dish-cloths, and hung them out to dry on a string; every morning she took the dustbin down into the street and carried up the water, stopping on each landing to get her breath. And, clad like a poor woman, she went to the fruiterer, to the grocer, to the butcher, a basket on her arm, haggling, insulted, fighting for every wretched halfpenny of her money.

Every month notes had to be paid off, others renewed, time gained.

Her husband worked in the evenings at putting straight a merchant's accounts, and often at night he did copying at twopence-halfpenny a page.

And this life lasted ten years.

At the end of ten years everything was paid off, everything, the usurer's charges and the accumulation of superimposed interest.

Madame Loisel looked old now. She had become like all the other strong, hard, coarse women of poor households. Her hair was badly done, her skirts were awry, her hands were red. She spoke in a shrill voice, and the water slopped all over the floor when she scrubbed it. But sometimes, when her husband was at the office, she sat down by the window and thought of that evening long ago, of the ball at which she had been so beautiful and so much admired.

What would have happened if she had never lost those jewels. Who knows? Who knows? How strange life is, how fickle! How little is needed to ruin or to save!

One Sunday, as she had gone for a walk along the Champs-Élysées to freshen herself after the labours of the week, she caught sight suddenly of a woman who was taking a child out for a walk. It was Madame Forestier, still young, still beautiful, still attractive.

Madame Loisel was conscious of some emotion. Should she speak to her? Yes, certainly. And now that she had paid, she would tell her all. Why not?

She went up to her.

"Good morning, Jeanne."

The other did not recognize her, and was surprised at being thus familiarly addressed by a poor woman.

"But . . . Madame . . ." she stammered. "I don't know . . . you must be making a mistake."

"No . . . I am Mathilde Loisel."

Her friend uttered a cry.

"Oh! . . . my poor Mathilde, how you have changed! . . ."

"Yes, I've had some hard times since I saw you last; and many sorrows . . . and all on your account."

"On my account! . . . How was that?"

"You remember the diamond necklace you lent me for the ball at the Ministry?"

"Yes. Well?"

"Well, I lost it."

"How could you? Why, you brought it back."

"I brought you another one just like it. And for the last ten years we have been paying for it. You realize it wasn't easy for us; we had no money. . . . Well, it's paid for at last, and I'm glad indeed."

Madame Forestier had halted.

"You say you bought a diamond necklace to replace mine?"

"Yes. You hadn't noticed it? They were very much alike."

And she smiled in proud and innocent happiness.

Madame Forestier, deeply moved, took her two hands.

"Oh, my poor Mathilde! But mine was imitation. It was worth at the very most five hundred francs!"

Sigmund Freud
1856-1939

Sigmund Freud, Austrian neurologist, cultural philosopher, and the founder of psychoanalysis, like Nietzsche, Marx, and Darwin, is one of the most influential thinkers of this century. Though many of the specifics of his work have been superseded, his underlying ideas on the unconscious mind, the interpretation of dreams, psycho-sexual development, and the human psyche (the id, ego, and super-ego) have shaped the way that we see ourselves as humans.

The selection below outlines some fundamental elements of psychotherapy. As treatment for mental illnesses, especially neurosis and hysteria, Freud posited that the patient could be treated through a dialogue between the patient and the psychotherapist, in which the latter attempts to uncover the working of the unconscious mind, especially the patient's repressed memories of childhood.

Major Works
The Interpretation of Dreams (1899)
Civilization and Its Discontents (1930)
An Outline of Psycho-Analysis (1940)

☙☼❧

Lecture on the General Theory of Neuroses (A Selection)
Sigmund Freud, 1920
TRANSLATED BY G. STANLEY HALL

Now I shall present to you the psychoanalytic conception of neurotic manifestations. The natural thing for me to do is to connect them to the phenomena we have previously treated, for the sake of their analogy as well as their contrast. I will select as symptomatic an act of frequent occurrence in my office hour.

Of course, the analyst cannot do much for those who seek him in his medical capacity, and lay the woes of a lifetime before him in fifteen minutes. His deeper knowledge makes it difficult for him to deliver a snap decision as do other physicians – "There is nothing wrong with you" – and to give the advice, "Go to a watering-place for a while." One of our colleagues, in answer to the question as to what he did with his office patients, said, shrugging his shoulders, that he simply "fines them so many kronen for their mischief-making." So it will not surprise you to hear that even in the case of very busy analysts, the hours for consultation are not very crowded. I have had the ordinary door between my waiting room and my office doubled and strengthened by a covering of felt.

The purpose of this little arrangement cannot be doubted. Now it happens over and over again that people who are admitted from my waiting room omit to close the door behind them; in fact, they almost always leave both doors open. As soon as I have noticed this I insist rather gruffly that he or she go back in order to rectify the omission, even though it be an elegant gentleman or a lady in all her finery. This gives an impression of misapplied pedantry. I have, in fact, occasionally discredited myself by such a demand, since the individual concerned was one of those who cannot touch even a door knob, and prefer as well to have their attendants spared this contact. But most frequently I was right, for he who conducts himself in this way, and leaves the door from the waiting room into the physician's consultation room open, belongs to the rabble and deserves to be received inhospitably.

Do not, I beg you, defend him until you have heard what follows. For the fact is that this negligence of the patient's only occurs when he has been alone in the waiting room and so leaves an empty room behind him, never when others, strangers, have been waiting with him. If that latter is the case, he knows very well that it is in his interest not to be listened to while he is talking to the physician, and never omits to close both the doors with care.

This omission of the patient's is so predetermined that it becomes neither accidental nor meaningless, indeed, not even unimportant, for, as we shall see, it throws light upon the relation of this patient to the physician. He is one of the great number of those who seek authority, who want to be dazzled, intimidated. Perhaps he had inquired by telephone as to what time he had best call, he had prepared himself to come on a crowd of suppliants somewhat like those in front of a branch milk station. He now enters an empty waiting room which is, moreover, most modestly furnished, and he is disappointed. He must demand reparation from the physician for the wasted respect that he had tendered him, and so he omits to close the door between the reception room and the office. By this, he means to say to the physician: "Oh, well, there is no one here anyway, and probably no one will come as long as I am here." He would also be quite unmannerly and supercilious during the consultation if his presumption were not at once restrained by a sharp reminder.

You will find nothing in the analysis of this little symptomatic act which was not previously known to you. That is to say, it asserts that this act is not accidental, but has a motive, a meaning, a purpose, that it has its assignable connections psychologically, and that it serves as a small indication of a more important psychological process. But above all it implies that the process thus intimated is not known to the consciousness of the individual in whom it takes place, for none of the patients who left the two doors open would have admitted that they meant by this omission to show me their contempt. Some could probably recall a slight sense of disappointment at entering an empty waiting room, but the connection between this impression and the symptomatic act which followed – of these, his consciousness was surely not aware.

Charlotte Perkins Gilman
1860-1935

Charlotte Perkins Gilman wrote novels, studies, stories, and poems, and in the service of women's rights gave many lectures. Drawn from her own experience of post-partum depression, her most famous story, "The Yellow Wallpaper" is about a woman who suffers from a mental breakdown due to the birth of her child. The "rest cure" treatment she describes was indeed prescribed for Gilman by Dr. Silas Weir Mitchell, to whom she sent a copy of the story after its publication. After her recovery she rearranged her life in unconventional terms and began a prolific career as a writer and speaker.

Major Works
Herland (1915)
With Her in Ourland (1916)
Women and Economics (1898)
Concerning Children (1900)
The Home: Its Work and Influence (1903)
The Man-Made World (1911)
His Religion and Hers (1923)
Our Changing Morality (1930)

ଔଞ

The Yellow Wall-Paper
Charlotte Perkins Gilman, 1892

It is very seldom that mere ordinary people like John and myself secure ancestral halls for the summer.

A colonial mansion, a hereditary estate, I would say a haunted house, and reach the height of romantic felicity – but that would be asking too much of fate!

Still I will proudly declare that there is something queer about it.

Else, why should it be let so cheaply? And why have stood so long untenanted?

John laughs at me, of course, but one expects that in marriage.

John is practical in the extreme. He has no patience with faith, an intense horror of superstition, and he scoffs openly at any talk of things not to be felt and seen and put down in figures.

John is a physician, and *perhaps* – (I would not say it to a living soul, of course, but this is dead paper and a great relief to my mind –) *perhaps* that is one reason I do not get well faster.

You see he does not believe I am sick!

And what can one do?

If a physician of high standing, and one's own husband, assures friends and relatives that there is really nothing the matter with one but temporary nervous depression – a slight hysterical tendency – what is one to do?

My brother is also a physician, and also of high standing, and he says the same thing.

So I take phosphates or phosphites – whichever it is, and tonics, and journeys, and air, and exercise, and am absolutely forbidden to "work" until I am well again.

Personally, I disagree with their ideas.

Personally, I believe that congenial work, with excitement and change, would do me good.

But what is one to do?

I did write for a while in spite of them; but it *does* exhaust me a good deal-having to be so sly about it, or else meet with heavy opposition.

I sometimes fancy that in my condition if I had less opposition and more society and stimulus – but John says the very worst thing I can do is to think about my condition, and I confess it always makes me feel bad.

So I will let it alone and talk about the house.

The most beautiful place! It is quite alone, standing well back from the road, quite three miles from the village. It makes me think of English places that you read about, for there are hedges and walls and gates that lock, and lots of separate little houses for the gardeners and people.

There is a delicious garden! I never saw such a garden – large and shady, full of box-bordered paths and lined with long grape-covered arbors with seats under them.

There were greenhouses, too, but they are all broken now.

There was some legal trouble, I believe, something about the heirs and co-heirs; anyhow, the place has been empty for years.

That spoils my ghostliness, I am afraid, but I don't care – there is something strange about the house – I can feel it.

I even said so to John one moonlight evening, but he said what I felt was a draught, and shut the window.

I get unreasonably angry with John sometimes. I'm sure I never used to be so sensitive. I think it is due to this nervous condition.

But John says if I feel so, I shall neglect proper self-control; so I take pains to control myself – before him, at least, and that makes me very tired.

I don't like our room a bit. I wanted one downstairs that opened on the piazza and had roses all over the window, and such pretty old-fashioned chintz hangings! but John would not hear of it.

He said there was only one window and not room for two beds, and no near room for him if he took another.

He is very careful and loving, and hardly lets me stir without special direction.

I have a scheduled prescription for each hour in the day; he takes all care from me, and so I feel basely ungrateful not to value it more.

He said we came here solely on my account, that I was to have perfect rest and all the air I could get. "Your exercise depends on your strength, my dear," said he, "and your food somewhat on your appetite; but air you can absorb all the time." So we took the nursery at the top of the house.

It is a big, airy room, the whole floor nearly, with windows that look all ways, and air and sunshine galore. It was nursery first and then playroom and gymnasium, I should judge; for the windows are barred for little children, and there are rings and things in the walls.

The paint and paper look as if a boys' school had used it. It is stripped off – the paper – in great patches all around the head of my bed, about as far as I can reach, and in a great place on the other side of the room low down. I never saw a worse paper in my life.

One of those sprawling flamboyant patterns committing every artistic sin.

It is dull enough to confuse the eye in following, pronounced enough to constantly irritate and provoke study, and when you follow the lame uncertain curves for a little distance they suddenly commit suicide – plunge off at outrageous angles, destroy themselves in unheard of contradictions.

The color is repellent, almost revolting; a smouldering unclean, yellow, strangely faded by the slow-turning sunlight.

It is a dull yet lurid orange in some places, a sickly sulphur tint in others.

No wonder the children hated it! I should hate it myself if I had to live in this room long.

There comes John, and I must put this away – he hates to have me write a word.

* * *

We have been here two weeks, and I haven't felt like writing before, since that first day.

I am sitting by the window now, up in this atrocious nursery, and there is nothing to hinder my writing as much as I please, save lack of strength.

John is away all day, and even some nights when his cases are serious.

I am glad my case is not serious!

But these nervous troubles are dreadfully depressing.

John does not know how much I really suffer. He knows there is no reason to suffer, and that satisfies him.

Of course it is only nervousness. It does weigh on me so not to do my duty in any way!

I meant to be such a help to John, such a real rest and comfort, and here I am a comparative burden already!

Nobody would believe what an effort it is to do what little I am able, – to dress and entertain, and order things.

It is fortunate Mary is so good with the baby. Such a dear baby!

And yet I cannot be with him, it makes me so nervous.

I suppose John never was nervous in his life. He laughs at me so about this wall-paper!

At first he meant to repaper the room, but afterwards he said that I was letting it get the better of me, and that nothing was worse for a nervous patient than to give way to such fancies.

He said that after the wall-paper was changed it would be the heavy bedstead, and then the barred windows, and then that gate at the head of the stairs, and so on.

"You know the place is doing you good," he said, "and really, dear, I don't care to renovate the house just for a three months' rental."

"Then do let us go downstairs," I said, "there are such pretty rooms there."

Then he took me in his arms and called me, a blessed little goose, and said he would go down cellar, if I wished, and have it whitewashed into the bargain.

But he is right enough about the beds and windows and things.

It is an airy and comfortable room as any one need wish, and, of course, I would not be so silly as to make him uncomfortable just for a whim.

I'm really getting quite fond of the big room, all but that horrid paper.

Out of one window I can see the garden, those mysterious deep-shaded arbors, the riotous old-fashioned flowers, and bushes and gnarly trees.

Out of another I get a lovely view of the bay and a little private wharf belonging to the estate. There is a beautiful shaded lane that runs down there from the house. I always fancy I see people walking in these numerous paths and arbors, but John has cautioned me not to give way to fancy in the least. He says that with my imaginative power and habit of story-making, a nervous weakness like mine is sure to lead to all manner of excited fancies, and that I ought to use my will and good sense to check the tendency. So I try.

I think sometimes that if I were only well enough to write a little it would relieve the press of ideas and rest me.

But I find I get pretty tired when I try.

It is so discouraging not to have any advice and companionship about my work. When I get really well, John says we will ask Cousin Henry and Julia down for a long visit; but he says he would as soon put fireworks in my pillow-case as to let me have those stimulating people about now.

I wish I could get well faster.

But I must not think about that. This paper looks to me as if it knew what a vicious influence it had!

There is a recurrent spot where the pattern lolls like a broken neck and two bulbous eyes stare at you upside down.

I get positively angry with the impertinence of it and the everlastingness. Up and down and sideways they crawl, and those absurd, unblinking eyes are everywhere. There is one place where two breadths didn't match, and the eyes go all up and down the line, one a little higher than the other.

I never saw so much expression in an inanimate thing before, and we all know how much expression they have! I used to lie awake as a child and get more entertainment and terror out of blank walls and plain furniture than most children could find in a toystore.

I remember what a kindly wink the knobs of our big, old bureau used to have, and there was one chair that always seemed like a strong friend.

I used to feel that if any of the other things looked too fierce I could always hop into that chair and be safe.

The furniture in this room is no worse than inharmonious, however, for we had to bring it all from downstairs. I suppose when this was used as a playroom they had to take the nursery things out, and no wonder! I never saw such ravages as the children have made here.

The wall-paper, as I said before, is torn off in spots, and it sticketh closer than a brother – they must have had perseverance as well as hatred.

Then the floor is scratched and gouged and splintered, the plaster itself is dug out here and there, and this great heavy bed which is all we found in the room, looks as if it had been through the wars.

But I don't mind it a bit – only the paper.

There comes John's sister. Such a dear girl as she is, and so careful of me! I must not let her find me writing.

She is a perfect and enthusiastic housekeeper, and hopes for no better profession. I verily believe she thinks it is the writing which made me sick!

But I can write when she is out, and see her a long way off from these windows.

There is one that commands the road, a lovely shaded winding road, and one that just looks off over the country. A lovely country, too, full of great elms and velvet meadows.

This wall-paper has a kind of sub-pattern in a different shade, a particularly irritating one, for you can only see it in certain lights, and not clearly then.

But in the places where it isn't faded and where the sun is just so – I can see a strange, provoking, formless sort of figure, that seems to skulk about behind that silly and conspicuous front design. There's sister on the stairs!

* * *

Well, the Fourth of July is over! The people are all gone and I am tired out. John thought it might do me good to see a little company so we just had mother and Nellie and the children down for a week.

Of course I didn't do a thing. Jennie sees to everything now.

But it tired me all the same.

John says if I don't pick up faster he shall send me to Weir Mitchell in the fall.

But I don't want to go there at all. I had a friend who was in his hands once, and she says he is just like John and my brother, only more so!

Besides, it is such an undertaking to go so far.

I don't feel as if it was worth while to turn my hand over for anything, and I'm getting dreadfully fretful and querulous.

I cry at nothing, and cry most of the time.

Of course I don't when John is here, or anybody else, but when I am alone.

And I am alone a good deal just now. John is kept in town very often by serious cases and Jennie is good and lets me alone when I want her to.

So I walk a little in the garden or down that lovely lane, sit on the porch under the roses, and lie down up here a good deal.

I'm getting really fond of the room in spite of the wall-paper. Perhaps because of the wall-paper.

It dwells in my mind so!

I lie here on this great immovable bed – it is nailed down, I believe – and follow that pattern about by the hour. It is as good as gymnastics, I assure you. I start, we'll say, at the bottom, down in the corner over there where it has not been touched, and I determine for the thousandth time that I will follow that pointless pattern to some sort of a conclusion.

I know a little of the principle of design, and I know this thing was not arranged on any laws of radiation, or alternation, or repetition, or symmetry, or anything else that I ever heard of.

It is repeated, of course, by the breadths, but not otherwise.

Looked at in one way each breadth stands alone, the bloated curves and flourishes – a kind of "debased Romanesque" with delirium tremens go waddling up and down in isolated columns of fatuity.

But, on the other hand, they connect diagonally, and the sprawling outlines run off in great slanting waves of optic horror, like a lot of wallowing seaweeds in full chase.

The whole thing goes horizontally, too, at least it seems so, and I exhaust myself in trying to distinguish the order of its going in that direction.

They have used a horizontal breadth for a frieze, and that adds wonderfully to the confusion. There is one end of the room where it is almost intact, and there, when the crosslights fade and the low sun shines directly upon it, I can almost fancy radiation after all, – the interminable grotesques seems to form around a common centre and rush off in headlong plunges of equal distraction. It makes me tired to follow it. I will take a nap I guess.

* * *

I don't know why I should write this.

I don't want to.

I don't feel able.

And I know John would think it absurd. But I must say what I feel and think in some way – it is such a relief!

But the effort is getting to be greater than the relief.

Half the time now I am awfully lazy, and lie down ever so much.

John says I mustn't lose my strength, and has me take cod liver oil and lots of tonics and things, to say nothing of ale and wine and rare meat.

Dear John! He loves me very dearly, and hates to have me sick. I tried to have a real earnest reasonable talk with him the other day, and tell him how I wish he would let me go and make a visit to Cousin Henry and Julia.

But he said I wasn't able to go, nor able to stand it after I got there; and I did not make out a very good case for myself, for I was crying before I had finished.

It is getting to be a great effort for me to think straight. Just this nervous weakness I suppose.

And dear John gathered me up in his arms, and just carried me upstairs and laid me on the bed, and sat by me and read to me till it tired my head.

He said I was his darling and his comfort and all he had, and that I must take care of myself for his sake, and keep well.

He says no one but myself can help me out of it, that I must use my will and self-control and not let any silly fancies run away with me.

There's one comfort, the baby is well and happy, and does not have to occupy this nursery with the horrid wall-paper.

If we had not used it, that blessed child would have! What a fortunate escape! Why, I wouldn't have a child of mine, an impressionable little thing, live in such a room for worlds.

I never thought of it before, but it is lucky that John kept me here after all, I can stand it so much easier than a baby, you see.

Of course I never mention it to them any more – I am too wise, – but I keep watch of it all the same.

There are things in that paper that nobody knows but me, or ever will.

Behind that outside pattern the dim shapes get clearer every day.

It is always the same shape, only very numerous.

And it is like a woman stooping down and creeping about behind that pattern. I don't like it a bit. I wonder – I begin to think – I wish John would take me away from here!

It is so hard to talk with John about my case, because he is so wise, and because he loves me so.

But I tried it last night.

It was moonlight. The moon shines in all around just as the sun does.

I hate to see it sometimes, it creeps so slowly, and always comes in by one window or another.

John was asleep and I hated to waken him, so I kept still and watched the moonlight on that undulating wall-paper till I felt creepy.

The faint figure behind seemed to shake the pattern, just as if she wanted to get out.

I got up softly and went to feel and see if the paper did move, and when I came back John was awake.

"What is it, little girl?" he said. "Don't go walking about like that – you'll get cold."

I thought it was a good time to talk, so I told him that I really was not gaining here, and that I wished he would take me away.

"Why, darling!" said he, "our lease will be up in three weeks, and I can't see how to leave before.

"The repairs are not done at home, and I cannot possibly leave town just now. Of course if you were in any danger, I could and would, but you really are better, dear, whether you can see it or not. I am a doctor, dear, and I know. You are gaining flesh and color, your appetite is better, I feel really much easier about you."

"I don't weigh a bit more," said I, "nor as much; and my appetite may be better in the evening when you are here, but it is worse in the morning when you are away!"

"Bless her little heart!" said he with a big hug, "she shall be as sick as she pleases! But now let's improve the shining hours by going to sleep, and talk about it in the morning!"

"And you won t go away?" I asked gloomily.

"Why, how can I, dear? It is only three weeks more and then we will take a nice little trip of a few days while Jennie is getting the house ready. Really dear you are better!"

Better in body perhaps –" I began, and stopped short, for he sat up straight and looked at me with such a stern, reproachful look that I could not say another word.

"My darling," said he, "I beg of you, for my sake and for our child's sake, as well as for your own, that you will never for one instant let that idea enter your mind! There is nothing so dangerous, so fascinating, to a temperament like yours. It is a false and foolish fancy. Can you not trust me as a physician when I tell you so?"

So of course I said no more on that score, and we went to sleep before long. He thought I was asleep first, but I wasn't, and lay there for hours trying to decide whether that front pattern and the back pattern really did move together or separately.

* * *

On a pattern like this, by daylight, there is a lack of sequence, a defiance of law, that is a constant irritant to a normal mind.

The color is hideous enough, and unreliable enough, and infuriating enough, but the pattern is torturing.

You think you have mastered it, but just as you get well underway in following, it turns a back-somersault and there you are. It slaps you in the face, knocks you down, and tramples upon you. It is like a bad dream.

The outside pattern is a florid arabesque, reminding one of a fungus. If you can imagine a toadstool in joints, an interminable string of toadstools, budding and sprouting in endless convolutions – why, that is something like it.

That is, sometimes!

There is one marked peculiarity about this paper, a thing nobody seems to notice but myself, and that is that it changes as the light changes.

When the sun shoots in through the east window – I always watch for that first long, straight ray – it changes so quickly that I never can quite believe it. That is why I watch it always.

By moonlight – the moon shines in all night when there is a moon – I wouldn't know it was the same paper.

At night in any kind of light, in twilight, candlelight, lamplight, and worst of all by moonlight, it becomes bars! The outside pattern I mean, and the woman behind it is as plain as can be.

I didn't realize for a long time what the thing was that showed behind, that dim sub-pattern, but now I am quite sure it is a woman.

By daylight she is subdued, quiet. I fancy it is the pattern that keeps her so still. It is so puzzling. It keeps me quiet by the hour.

THE ESSENTIAL HUMANITIES READER

I lie down ever so much now. John says it is good for me, and to sleep all I can.

Indeed he started the habit by making me lie down for an hour after each meal.

It is a very bad habit I am convinced, for you see I don't sleep.

And that cultivates deceit, for I don't tell them I'm awake – O no!

The fact is I am getting a little afraid of John.

He seems very queer sometimes, and even Jennie has an inexplicable look.

It strikes me occasionally, just as a scientific hypothesis, – that perhaps it is the paper!

I have watched John when he did not know I was looking, and come into the room suddenly on the most innocent excuses, and I've caught him several times looking at the paper! And Jennie too. I caught Jennie with her hand on it once.

She didn't know I was in the room, and when I asked her in a quiet, a very quiet voice, with the most restrained manner possible, what she was doing with the paper – she turned around as if she had been caught stealing, and looked quite angry – asked me why I should frighten her so!

Then she said that the paper stained everything it touched, that she had found yellow smooches on all my clothes and John's, and she wished we would be more careful!

Did not that sound innocent? But I know she was studying that pattern, and I am determined that nobody shall find it out but myself!

* * *

Life is very much more exciting now than it used to be. You see I have some-thing more to expect, to look forward to, to watch. I really do eat better, and am more quiet than I was.

John is so pleased to see me improve! He laughed a little the other day, and said I seemed to be flourishing in spite of my wall-paper.

I turned it off with a laugh. I had no intention of telling him it was because of the wall-paper – he would make fun of me. He might even want to take me away.

I don't want to leave now until I have found it out. There is a week more, and I think that will be enough.

* * *

I'm feeling ever so much better! I don't sleep much at night, for it is so inter-esting to watch developments; but I sleep a good deal in the daytime.

In the daytime it is tiresome and perplexing.

There are always new shoots on the fungus, and new shades of yellow all over it. I cannot keep count of them, though I have tried conscientiously.

It is the strangest yellow, that wall-paper! It makes me think of all the yellow things I ever saw – not beautiful ones like buttercups, but old foul, bad yellow things.

But there is something else about that paper – the smell! I noticed it the moment we came into the room, but with so much air and sun it was not bad. Now we have had a week of fog and rain, and whether the windows are open or not, the smell is here.

It creeps all over the house.

I find it hovering in the dining-room, skulking in the parlor, hiding in the hall, lying in wait for me on the stairs.

It gets into my hair.

Even when I go to ride, if I turn my head suddenly and surprise it – there is that smell!

Such a peculiar odor, too! I have spent hours in trying to analyze it, to find what it smelled like.

It is not bad – at first, and very gentle, but quite the subtlest, most enduring odor I ever met.

In this damp weather it is awful, I wake up in the night and find it hanging over me.

It used to disturb me at first. I thought seriously of burning the house – to reach the smell.

But now I am used to it. The only thing I can think of that it is like is the color of the paper! A yellow smell.

There is a very funny mark on this wall, low down, near the mopboard. A streak that runs round the room. It goes behind every piece of furniture, except the bed, a long, straight, even smooch, as if it had been rubbed over and over.

I wonder how it was done and who did it, and what they did it for. Round and round and round – round and round and round! – it makes me dizzy!

* * *

I really have discovered something at last.

Through watching so much at night when it changes so, I have finally found out.

The front pattern *does* move – and no wonder! The woman behind shakes it!

Sometimes I think there are a great many women behind, and sometimes only one, and she crawls around fast, and her crawling shakes it all over.

Then in the very bright spots she keeps still, and in the very shady spots she just takes hold of the bars and shakes them hard.

And she is all the time trying to climb through. But nobody could climb through that pattern – it strangles so; I think that is why it has so many heads.

They get through, and then the pattern strangles them off and turns them upside down, and makes their eyes white!

If those heads were covered or taken off it would not be half so bad.

* * *

I think that woman gets out in the daytime!

And I'll tell you why – privately – I've seen her!

I can see her out of every one of my windows!

It is the same woman, I know, for she is always creeping, and most women do not creep by daylight.

I see her in that long shaded lane, creeping up and down. I see her in those dark grape arbors, creeping all around the garden.

I see her on that long road under the trees, creeping along, and when a carriage comes she hides under the black-berry vines.

I don't blame her a bit. It must be very humiliating to be caught creeping by daylight!

I always lock the door when I creep by daylight. I can't do it at night for I know John would suspect something at once.

And John is so queer now, that I don't want to irritate him. I wish he would take another room! Besides, I don't want anybody to get that woman out at night but myself.

I often wonder if I could see her out of all the windows at once.

But turn as fast as I can, I can only see out of one at one time.

And though I always see her, she may be able to creep faster than I can turn!

I have watched her sometimes away off in the open country, creeping as fast as a cloud shadow in a high wind.

* * *

If only that top pattern could be gotten off from the under one! I mean to try it, little by little.

I have found out another funny thing, but I shan't tell it this time! It does not do to trust people too much.

There are only two more days to get

this paper off, and I believe John is beginning to notice. I don't like the look in his eyes.

And I heard him ask Jennie a lot of professional questions about me. She had a very good report to give.

She said I slept a good deal in the daytime.

John knows I don't sleep very well at night, for all I'm so quiet!

He asked me all sorts of questions, too, and pretended to be very loving and kind.

As if I couldn't see through him!

Still, I don't wonder he acts so, sleeping under this paper for three months.

It only interests me, but I feel sure John and Jennie are secretly affected by it.

* * *

Hurrah! This is the last day, but it is enough. John to stay in town over night, and won't be out until this evening.

Jennie wanted to sleep with me – the sly thing! but I told her I should undoubtedly rest better for a night all alone.

That was clever, for really I wasn't alone a bit! As soon as it was moonlight and that poor thing began to crawl and shake the pattern, I got up and ran to help her.

I pulled and she shook, I shook and she pulled, and before morning we had peeled off yards of that paper.

A strip about as high as my head and half around the room.

And then when the sun came and that awful pattern began to laugh at me, I declared I would finish it today!

We go away tomorrow, and they are moving all my furniture down again to leave things as they were before.

Jennie looked at the wall in amazement, but I told her merrily that I did it out of pure spite at the vicious thing.

She laughed and said she wouldn't mind doing it herself, but I must not get tired.

How she betrayed herself that time!

But I am here, and no person touches this paper but me, – not alive!

She tried to get me out of the room – It was too patent! But I said it was so quiet and empty and clean now that I believed I would lie down again and sleep all I could; and not to wake me even for dinner – I would call when I woke.

So now she is gone, and the servants are gone, and the things are gone, and there is nothing left but that great bedstead nailed down, with the canvas mattress we found on it.

We shall sleep downstairs to-night, and take the boat home tomorrow.

I quite enjoy the room, now it is bare again.

How those children did tear about here!

This bedstead is fairly gnawed!

But I must get to work.

I have locked the door and thrown the key down into the front path.

I don't want to go out, and I don't want to have anybody come in, till John comes.

I want to astonish him.

I've got a rope up here that even Jennie did not find. If that woman does get out, and tries to get away, I can tie her!

But I forgot I could not reach far without anything to stand on!

This bed will not move!

I tried to lift and push it until I was lame, and then I got so angry I bit off a little piece at one corner – but it hurt my teeth.

Then I peeled off all the paper I could reach standing on the floor. It sticks horribly and the pattern just enjoys it! All those strangled heads and bulbous eyes and waddling fungus growths just shriek with derision!

I am getting angry enough to do something desperate. To jump out of the window would be admirable exercise, but the bars are too strong even to try.

Besides I wouldn't do it. Of course not. I know well enough that a step like that is improper and might be misconstrued.

I don't like to look out of the windows even – there are so many of those creeping women, and they creep so fast.

I wonder if they all come out of that wall-paper as I did?

But I am securely fastened now by my well-hidden rope – you don't get me out in the road there!

I suppose I shall have to get back behind the pattern when it comes night, and that is hard!

It is so pleasant to be out in this great room and creep around as I please!

I don't want to go outside. I won't, even if Jennie asks me to.

For outside you have to creep on the ground, and everything is green instead of yellow.

But here I can creep smoothly on the floor, and my shoulder just fits in that long smooch around the wall, so I cannot lose my way.

Why there's John at the door!

It is no use, young man, you can't open it!

How he does call and pound!

Now he's crying for an axe.

It would be a shame to break down that beautiful door!

"John dear!" said I in the gentlest voice, "the key is down by the front steps, under a plaintain leaf!"

That silenced him for a few moments.

Then he said – very quietly indeed, "Open the door, my darling!"

"I can't," said I. "The key is down by the front door under a plantain leaf!"

And then I said it again, several times, very gently and slowly, and said it so often that he had to go and see, and he got it of course, and came in. He stopped short by the door.

"What is the matter?" he cried. "For God's sake, what are you doing!"

I kept on creeping just the same, but I looked at him over my shoulder.

"I've got out at last," said I, "in spite of you and Jane? And I've pulled off most of the paper, so you can't put me back!"

Now why should that man have fainted? But he did, and right across my path by the wall, so that I had to creep over him every time!

T. S. Eliot
1888 – 1965

Thomas Stearns Eliot, an innovative Anglo-American poet, critic, publisher, dramatist, social critic, and editor, was the most honored and imitated poet of the twentieth century. Eliot was alarmed to see that between the Metaphysical Poets (selections earlier in this volume) and his own time poets no longer brought together their minds and hearts in their work. This "dissociation of sensibilities" needed to be remedied via a "unified sensibility" if poetry were to progress. For Eliot, "the presence of some outward object...to correspond to the preexisting idea in its living power, is essential to the evolution of...the pleasurable emotion."[1] This "objective correlative," the manifestation of an idea in the physical world, led to Eliot's emphasis on stark imagery, which changed the shape of poetry to this day.

Major Works
The Waste Land (1922)
Old Possum's Book of Practical Cats (1939)
Murder in the Cathedral (1935)

ଔଞ୍ଚ

The Love Song of J. Alfred Prufrock[2]
T. S. Eliot, 1917

S'io credessi che mia risposta fosse
A persona che mai tornasse al mondo,
Questa fiamma staria senza piu scosse.
Ma per cio che giammai di questo fondo
Non torno viva alcun, s'i'odo il vereo,
Senza tema d'infamia ti rispondo.[3]

---

[1] "Hamlet and His Problems" in *The Sacred Wood*. London: Methuen, 1921.
[2] Prufrock. The title implies an ironic contrast between the romantic suggestions of "love song" and the dull prosaic name "J. Alfred Prufrock."
[3] *S'io credessi...rispondo.* "If I thought that my reply would be to one who would ever return to the world, this flame would stay without further movement; but since none has ever returned alive from this depth, if what I hear is true, I answer you without fear of

Let us go then, you and I,
When the evening is spread out against the sky
Like a patient etherized upon a table;
Let us go, through certain half-deserted streets,
5   The muttering retreats
Of restless nights in one-night cheap hotels
And sawdust restaurants with oyster-shells;
Streets that follow like a tedious argument
Of insidious intent
10 To lead you to an overwhelming question . . .
Oh, do not ask, "What is it?"
Let us go and make our visit.

In the room the women come and go
Talking of Michelangelo.

15 The yellow fog that rubs its back upon the window panes,
The yellow smoke that rubs its muzzle on the window-panes,
Licked its tongue into the corners of the evening,
Lingered upon the pools that stand in drains,
Let fall upon its back the soot that falls from chimneys,
20 Slipped by the terrace, made a sudden leap,
And seeing that it was a soft October night,
Curled once about the house, and fell asleep.

And indeed there will be time[1]
For the yellow smoke that slides along the street
25 Rubbing its back upon the window-panes;
There will be time, there will be time
To prepare a face to meet the faces that you meet;
There will be time to murder and create,
And time for all the works and days of hands[2]
30 That lift and drop a question on your plate;
Time for you and time for me,
And time yet for a hundred indecisions,
And for a hundred visions and revisions,
Before the taking of a toast and tea.

35 In the room the women come and go
Talking of Michelangelo.

---

infamy" (Dante, *Inferno* 27.61-66). Guido da Montefeltro, shut up in his flame (the punishment given to false counselors), tells the shame of his evil life to Dante because he believes Dante will never return to earth to report it.

[1] There will be time. Cf. Andrew Marvell, "To His Coy Mistress," line 1: "Had we but world enough, and time."

[2] Works...hands. *Works and Days* is a poem about the farming year by Hesiod (8th century B.C.), Greek poet. Eliot's contrast is between useful agricultural labor and the futile "works and days of hands" engaged in meaningless social gesturing.

And indeed there will be time
To wonder, "Do I dare?" and, "Do I dare?"
Time to turn back and descend the stair,
40 With a bald spot in the middle of my hair –
(They will say: "How his hair is growing thin!")
My morning coat, my collar mounting firmly to the chin,
My necktie rich and modest, but asserted by a simple pin –
(They will say: "But how his arms and legs are thin!")
45 Do I dare
Disturb the universe?
In a minute there is time
For decisions and revisions which a minute will reverse.

For I have known them all already, known them all –
50 Have known the evenings, mornings, afternoons,
I have measured out my life with coffee spoons;
I know the voices dying with a dying fall[1]
Beneath the music from a farther room,
  So how should I presume?

55 And I have known the eyes already, known them all –
The eyes that fix you in a formulated phrase,
And when I am formulated, sprawling on a pin,
When I am pinned and wriggling on the wall,
Then how should I begin?
60 To spit out all the butt-ends of my days and ways?
  And how should I presume?

And I have known the arms already, known them all –
Arms that are braceleted and white and bare
(But in the lamplight, downed with light brown hair!)
65 Is it perfume from a dress
That makes me so digress?
Arms that lie along a table, or wrap about a shawl.
  And should I then presume?
  And how should I begin?

* * * * *

70 Shall I say, I have gone at dusk through narrow streets
And watched the smoke that rises from the pipes
Of lonely men in shirt-sleeves, leaning out of windows? . . .

I should have been a pair of ragged claws
Scuttling across the floors of silent seas.[2]

---

[1] I know…fall. Ironic recollection of Orsino's speech in *Twelfth Night* 1.1.4: "That strain
again! It had a dying fall."
[2] I should…seas. I.e., he would have been better as a crab on the ocean bed. Perhaps, too,
the motion of a crab suggests futility and growing old. Cf. *Hamlet* 2.2.205-206: "for you

THE ESSENTIAL HUMANITIES READER

* * * * *

75 And the afternoon, the evening, sleeps so peacefully
Smoothed by long fingers,
Asleep . . . tired . . . or it malingers,
Stretched on the floor, here beside you and me.
Should I, after tea and cakes and ices,
80 Have the strength to force the moment to its crisis?
But though I have wept and fasted, wept and prayed,
Though I have seen my head (grown slightly bald) brought in upon a plat-
ter,[1]
I am no prophet – and here's no great matter;
I have seen the moment of my greatness flicker,
85 And I have seen the eternal Footman hold my coat, and snicker,
And in short, I was afraid.

And would it have been worth it, after all,
After the cups, the marmalade, the tea,
Among the porcelain, among some talk of you and me,
90 Would it have been worth while,
To have bitten off the matter with a smile,
To have squeezed the universe into a ball[2]
To roll it towards some overwhelming question,
To say: "I am Lazarus,[3] come from the dead,
95 Come back to tell you all, I shall tell you all" –
If one, settling a pillow by her head,
  Should say: "That is not what I meant at all,
  That is not it, at all."

And would it have been worth it, after all,
100 Would it have been worth while,
After the sunsets and the dooryards and the sprinkled streets,
After the novels, after the teacups, after the skirts that trail along the floor –
And this, and so much more? –
It is impossible to say just what I mean!
105 But as if a magic lantern threw the nerves in patterns on a screen:
Would it have been worth while
If one, settling a pillow or throwing off a shawl,
And turning toward the window, should say:
  "That is not it at all,
110 That is not what I meant, at all."

---

yourself, sir, should be old as I am, if, like a crab, you could go backward."
[1] Head...platter. Like that of John the Baptist. See Mark 6.17-28 and Matthew 14.3-11.
[2] To have...ball. Cf. Marvell, "To His Coy Mistress," lines 41-44: "Let us roll all of our strength and all / Our sweetnesses up into one ball, / And tear our pleasures with rough strife / Through the iron gates of life."
[3] Lazarus. Risen from death to life by Jesus Christ. See Luke 16.19-31 and John 11.1-44.

* * * * *

No! I am not Prince Hamlet, nor was meant to be;
Am an attendant lord, one that will do
To swell a progress,[1] start a scene or two,
Advise the prince; no doubt, an easy tool,
115 Deferential, glad to be of use,
Politic, cautious, and meticulous;
Full of high sentence,[2] but a bit obtuse;
At times, indeed, almost ridiculous –
Almost, at times, the Fool.

120 I grow old . . . I grow old . . .
I shall wear the bottoms of my trousers rolled.

Shall I part my hair behind? Do I dare to eat a peach?
I shall wear white flannel trousers, and walk upon the beach.
I have heard the mermaids singing, each to each.

125 I do not think that they will sing to me.

I have seen them riding seaward on the waves
Combing the white hair of the waves blown back
When the wind blows the water white and black.

We have lingered in the chambers of the sea
130 By sea-girls wreathed in seaweed red and brown
Till human voices wake us, and we drown.

---

[1] Swell a progress. In the Elizabethan sense of a state journey made by a royal or noble person. Elizabethan plays sometimes showed such "progresses" crossing the stage.
[2] Sentence. In its older meanings: "opinions," "sententiousness."

Wilfred Owen
1893 – 1918

Wilfred Owen, perhaps the leading poet of World War I, is remembered both as a British soldier who was awarded the Military Cross and as a writer of shocking poetry based on the horrors of his war experience. Owen, like other soldier poets, Rupert Brooke and Siegfried Sassoon, set aside the trend of writing patriotic poetry and offered a more realistic and pessimistic view of war. Owen suffered several potentially fatal injuries in the war, but each time returned to battle after his recovery. His recoveries at Craiglockhart War Hospital in Edinburgh were important to him as a poet, as he met and befriended Sassoon there, and as his doctor encouraged him to write about his war experiences as therapy. Only one week before the end of the war, Owen was shot and killed in a military maneuver. After his death, thanks to the influence of Sassoon and the controversial poet and editor Edith Sitwell, Owen's poems (among them *"Dulce et Decorum est,"* included below) were published and have been popular ever since.

ᘓৰ৪ড

Dulce et Decorum est
Wilfred Owen, 1920

Bent double, like old beggars under sacks,
Knock-kneed, coughing like hags, we cursed through sludge,
Till on the haunting flares we turned our backs
And towards our distant rest began to trudge.
5   Men marched asleep. Many had lost their boots
But limped on, blood-shod. All went lame; all blind;
Drunk with fatigue; deaf even to the hoots
Of gas-shells dropping softly behind.

Gas! GAS! Quick, boys! – An ecstasy of fumbling
10   Fitting the clumsy helmets just in time,
But someone still was yelling out and stumbling
And flound'ring like a man in fire or lime. –
Dim, through the misty panes and thick green light,

As under a green sea, I saw him drowning.

15 In all my dreams before my helpless sight
He plunges at me, guttering, choking, drowning.

If in some smothering dreams you too could pace
Behind the wagon that we flung him in,
And watch the white eyes writhing in his face,
20 His hanging face, like a devil's sick of sin,
If you could hear, at every jolt, the blood
Come gargling from the froth-corrupted lungs,
Bitter as the cud
Of vile, incurable sores on innocent tongues, –
25 My friend, you would not tell with such high zest
To children ardent for some desperate glory,
The old Lie: *Dulce et decorum est*
Pro patria mori.

Gertrude Stein
1874 – 1946

Gertrude Stein, writer, playwright, poet, and philosopher, was one of the most influential figures in the arts in the twentieth century. In her novels, poetry, and plays, which were almost always experimental, she tried to change the way that we receive language. Just as Picasso set aside conventions of perspective and volume, she set aside conventions of narrative and grammar. A native of Pittsburgh, she spent most of her life in Europe, especially Paris, where she and her lifetime companion Alice B. Toklas maintained a salon where most of the great writers, thinkers, and artists congregated and were advised by Stein.

In the passage below, excerpted from "Portrait of Three Artists," Stein attempts to replicate in words what we see in film, a series of very similar but always changing images, or in this case sentences.

Major Works
Three Lives (1905 – 1906)
Tender Buttons (1912)
Four Saints in Three Acts (1928)
The Autobiography of Alice B. Toklas (1933)

ଓଃ୫ଠ
Portrait of Picasso
Gertrude Stein, 1912

One whom some were certainly following was one who was completely charming. One whom some were certainly following was one who was charming. One whom some were following was one who was completely charming. One whom some were following was one who was certainly completely charming.

Some were certainly following and were certain that the one they were then following was one working and was one bringing out of himself then something. Some were certainly following and were certain that the one they were then following was one bringing out of himself then something that was coming to be a heavy thing, a solid thing and a complete thing.

One whom some were certainly following was one working and certainly was one bringing something out of himself then and was one who had been all his living had been one having something coming out of him.

Something had been coming out of him, certainly it had been coming out of him, certainly it was something, certainly ft had been coming out of him and it had meaning, a charming meaning, a solid meaning, a struggling meaning, a clear meaning.

One whom some were certainly following and some were certainly following him, one whom some were certainly following was one certainly working.

One whom some were certainly following was one having something coming out of him something having meaning and this one was certainly working then.

This one was working on something was coming then, something was coming out of this one then. This one was one and always there was something coming out of this one and always there had been something coming out of this one. This one had never been one not having something coming out of this one. This one was one having something coming out of this one. This one had been one whom some were following. This one was one whom some were following. This one was being one whom some were following. This one was one who was working.

This one was one who was working. This one was one being one having something being coming out of him. This one was one going on having something come out of him. This one going on working. This one was one whom some were following. This one was one who was working.

This one always had something being coming out of this one. This one was working. This one always had been working. This one was always having something that was coming out of this one that was a solid thing, a charming thing, a lovely thing, a perplexing thing, a disconcerting thing, a simple thing, a clear thing, a complicated thing, an interesting thing, a disturbing thing, a repellant thing, a very pretty thing. This one was one certainly being one having something coming out of him. This one was one whom some were following. This one was one who was working.

This one was one who was working and certainly this one was needing to be working so as to be one being working. This one was one having something coming out of him. This one would be one all his living having something coming out of him. This one was working and then this one was working and this one was needing to be working, not to be one having something coming out of him something having meaning, but was needing to be working so as to be one working.

This one was certainly working and working was something this one was certain this one would be doing and this one was doing that thing; this one was working. This one was not one completely working. This one certainly was not completely working.

This one was one having always something being coming out of him, something having completely a real meaning. This one was one whom some were following. This one was one who was working. This one was one who was working and he was one needing this thing needing to be working so as to be one having some way of being one having some way of working. This one was one who was working. This one was one having something come out of him something having meaning. This one was one always having something come out of him and this thing the thing coming out of him always had real meaning. This one was one who was working. This one was one who was almost always working. This one was not one completely working. This one was one not ever completely working. This one was not one working to have anything come out of him. He always did have something having meaning that did come out of him. He always did have something corn e out of him. He was working, he was not ever completely working. He did have. Some following. They were always following him, Some were certainly following him. He was one who was working. He was one having something coming out of him something having meaning. He was not ever completely working.

Mister Rogers
1928 – 2003

Fred Rogers, American educator, Presbyterian minister, songwriter, author, and television host, was most famous for creating and hosting *Mister Rogers' Neighborhood* on PBS. His optimism, his emphasis on feeling secure, and his hope to allow youth to grow and to enjoy their world stand in strong relief to the otherwise gloomy view of life that most twentieth-century artists offered to us.

ೞ
Quotes from Mister Rogers

"In some way just by being a human being each one of us is very very fancy."

"You're just the way you're supposed to be; you're growing just right."

"You're unique. You're the only person who is you. There has never been another person exactly like you, and there never ever will be again."

"I hope wherever you are or wherever you are going you will have a very special day."

"I feel the greatest gift we can give to anybody is the gift of our honest self."

"Of course, I get angry. Of course, I get sad. I have a full range of emotions. I also have a whole smorgasbord of ways of dealing with my feelings. That is what we should give children. Give them...ways to express their rage without hurting themselves or somebody else. That's what the world needs."

"You know, you don't have to look like everybody else to be acceptable and to feel acceptable."

"We live in a world in which we need to share responsibility. It's easy to say 'It's not my child, not my community, not my world, not my problem.' Then there are those who see the need and respond. I consider those people my heroes."

"There's a generous current in the American spirit. And if we can simply give voice to that once in a while, I think it's a good message."

"What really matters is not just our own winning but helping other people to win, too."

"I think everybody longs to be loved and longs to know that he or she is lovable and, consequently, the greatest thing that we can do is to help somebody know that they are loved and capable of loving."

"Children see television much the same way they see a refrigerator or a stove. It's something that parents provide. In a young child's mind, parents probably condone what's on the television, just like they choose what's in the refrigerator or on the stove."

"There has never been a time in our history when there have been so many changes. But we all have different gifts and different ways of saying to the world who we are. The world needs a sense of worth, and it will achieve it only by its people feeling they are worthwhile."

"I'd love to go off to heaven knowing that kids...[understand]...that their neighbor is every bit as important as they are."

"You've made this day a special day by just your being you. There's no person in the whole world like you. And I like you just the way you are."

ᘓᘔᘓ
ACKNOWLEDGEMENT OF SOURCES

TEXTS

PAGE 1. THE BIBLE. KING JAMES VERSION, 1611. ADAPTED BY GERARD P. NECASTRO, 2013.

PAGE 3. THE BIBLE. KING JAMES VERSION, 1611. ADAPTED BY GERARD P. NECASTRO, 2013.

PAGE 4. THE BIBLE. KING JAMES VERSION, 1611. ADAPTED BY GERARD P. NECASTRO, 2013.

PAGE 5. THE BIBLE. KING JAMES VERSION, 1611. ADAPTED BY GERARD P. NECASTRO, 2013.

PAGE 7. THE BIBLE. KING JAMES VERSION, 1611. ADAPTED BY GERARD P. NECASTRO, 2013.

PAGE 12. HOMER. *THE ILIAD*. TRANSLATED BY SAMUEL BUTLER. LONDON: LONGMANS, 1898.

PAGE 26. HOMER. *THE ODYSSEY*. TRANSLATED BY SAMUEL BUTLER. LONDON: A. C. FIFIELD, 1900.

PAGE 34. THUCYDIDES. *HISTORY OF THE PELOPONNESIAN WAR*. TRANSLATED BY BENJAMIN JOWETT. OXFORD: CLARENDEN PRESS, 1881.

PAGE 39. PLATO. "THE ALLEGORY OF THE CAVE." FROM *THE REPUBLIC*. TRANSLATED BY BENJAMIN JOWETT. NEW YORK: OXFORD UNIVERSITY PRESS, 1892.

PAGE 44. VERGIL. *THE AENEID*. TRANSLATED BY JOHN DRYDEN, 1697. REVISED BY GERARD P. NECASTRO, 2013.

PAGE 61. HORACE. "SNOW IS GONE." *THE ODES AND CARMEN SAECULARE OF HORACE*. JOHN CONINGTON. TRANS. LONDON. GEORGE BELL AND SONS. 1882.

PAGE 62. HORACE. "DULCE ET DECOREM EST." *THE ODES AND CARMEN SAECULARE OF HORACE*. JOHN CONINGTON. TRANS. LONDON. GEORGE BELL AND SONS. 1882.

PAGE 64. OVID. "THE STORY OF PYRAMUS AND THISBE." FROM *THE METAMORPHOSES*, 8 AD. TRANSLATED BY ARTHUR GOLDING, 1565 – 1567.

PAGE 69. THE BIBLE. AMERICAN STANDARD VERSION, 1901.

PAGE 74. THOMAS À CELANO. "*DIES IRAE*" (DAY OF WRATH). WILLIAM JOSIAH IRONS. *THE CHRISTIAN SERVANT'S BOOK*. 1849.

PAGE 77. JACOBUS DE BENEDICTIS. "*STABAT MATER*" (THE MOTHER STANDING). TRANS. D. F. MACCARTHY. "*STABAT MATER*." IN *ANNUS SANCTUS: HYMNS OF THE CHURCH FOR THE ECCLESIASTICAL YEAR*. ED. ORBY SHIPLEY. LONDON AND NEW YORK: BURNS AND OATES, 1884.

PAGE 80. ANONYMOUS. "GAUDEAMUS IGITUR." ED. BLISS CARMAN. *THE WORLD'S BEST POETRY*. 1904.

PAGE 82. DANTE ALIGHIERI. *THE DIVINE COMEDY OF DANTE ALIGHIERI*; TRANSLATED BY CHARLES ELIOT NORTON. BOSTON, NEW YORK: HOUGHTON, MIFFLIN AND COMPANY, 1891-1892. SUMMARIES BY GERARD P. NECASTRO.

PAGE 108. DANTE ALIGHIERI. *THE NEW LIFE (LA VITA NUOVA) OF DANTE ALIGHIERI*. TRANSLATED BY DANTE GABRIEL ROSSETTI. LONDON: ELLIS AND ELVEY, 1899. ABRIDGED, AMENDED, AND EDITED BY GERARD P. NECASTRO, 2013.

PAGE 118. PETRARCH. POETRY SELECTIONS. *THE SONNETS, TRIUMPHS, AND OTHER POEMS OF PETRARCH*. TRANSLATED BY MAJOR MACGREGOR. EDITED BY THOMAS CAMPBELL. LONDON: GEORGE BELL AND SONS, 1879.

PAGE 120. GEOFFREY CHAUCER. *THE CANTERBURY TALES*, C.1380. IN *THE ESSENTIAL CHAUCER*. EDITED AND TRANSLATED BY GERARD P. NECASTRO. THE PRIMAVERA

PRESS, 2013.

PAGE 123. GEOFFREY CHAUCER. *BOOK OF THE DUCHESS*, 1372-1376. IN *THE ESSENTIAL CHAUCER*. EDITED AND TRANSLATED BY GERARD P. NECASTRO. THE PRIMAVERA PRESS, 2013.

PAGE 140. GIOVANNI BOCCACCIO. "THE TALE OF GRISELDA." (DAY 10, TALE 10, OF THE DECAMERON.) TRANSLATED BY GERARD P. NECASTRO. *THE BOOK OF GRISELDA*. PRIMAVERA PRESS, 2014. BASED ON THE DECAMERON OF GIOVANNI BOCCACCIO. TRANSLATED BY J.M. RIGG. NEW YORK, E. P. DUTTON, 1903.

PAGE 148. FRNCESCO PETRARCH. "THE TALE OF GRISELDA." FROM *RERUM SENILIUM LIBRI*. IN ROBERT D. FRENCH. *A CHAUCER HANDBOOK*. NEW YORK, 1927. ADAPTED BY GERARD P. NECASTRO.

PAGE 149. GEOFFREY CHAUCER. *THE CLERK'S TALE*. IN *THE ESSENTIAL CHAUCER*. EDITED AND TRANSLATED BY GERARD P. NECASTRO. THE PRIMAVERA PRESS, 2013.

PAGE 151. PICO DELLA MIRANDOLA. "ORATION ON THE DIGNITY OF MAN." HTTP://WEB.MNSTATE.EDU/GRACYK/COURSES/WEBPUBLISHING/PICO_ORATION.HTM. (SITE MAINTAINED BY THEODORE GRACYK.) JANUARY 15, 2013. EDITED AND ABRIDGED BY GERARD P. NECASTRO.

PAGE 154. MICHEL DE MONTAIGNE. "OF REPENTANCE." *THE WORKS OF MICHAEL DE MONTAIGNE*. TRANSLATED BY CHARLES COTTON. EDITED BY WILLIAM HAZLITT. LONDON: TEMPLEMAN, 1842.

PAGE 156. MARTIN LUTHER. *"REPLY AT THE DIET OF WORMS"." IN LIBRARY OF THE WORLD'S BEST LITERATURE, ANCIENT AND MODERN*, VOLUME 16. ED. CHARLES DUDLEY WARNER, ET AL. NEW YORK: J. A. HILL & COMPANY, 1902.

PAGE 160. WILLIAM SHAKESPEARE, *ROMEO AND JULIET*, C. 1595. *THE ILLUSTRATED SHAKESPEARE*. GULIAN C. VERPLANCK, NEW YORK: HARPER AND BROTHERS, 1847.

PAGE 163. WILLIAM SHAKESPEARE, *HAMLET*, C. 1600. *THE ILLUSTRATED SHAKESPEARE*. GULIAN C. VERPLANCK, NEW YORK: HARPER AND BROTHERS, 1847.

PAGE 167. WILLIAM SHAKESPEARE, SONNETS, C. 1590-1609. *SHAKE-SPEARES SONNETS, NEVER BEFORE IMPRINTED*. LONDON: G. ELD, T.T, WILLIAM ASPLEY, 1609.

PAGE 168. *THE SONNETS OF MICHAEL ANGELO BUONARROTI AND TOMMASO CAMPANELLA, NOW FOR THE FIRST TIME TRANSLATED INTO RHYMED ENGLISH*. TRANSLATED BY JOHN ADDINGTON SYMONDS. LONDON: SMITH, ELDER, AND CO., 1878.

PAGE 170. MIGUEL DE CERVANTES SAAVEDRA. *THE INGENIOUS GENTLEMAN DON QUIXOTE OF LA MANCHA*. TRANSLATED BY JOHN ORMSBY. NEW YORK: DODD, MEAD, 1916.

PAGE 193. JOHN DONNE. "BATTER MY HEART, THREE PERSON'D GOD," "THE FLEA," AND "A VALEDICTION: FORBIDDING MOURNING," 1633. ANDREW MARVELL. TO HIS COY MISTRESS," 1681. *POEMS OF JOHN DONNE*. E. E. K. CHAMBERS, 1901.

PAGE 197. JOHN MILTON. *PARADISE LOST*, 1667. PARADISE LOST BY JOHN MILTON. ED. HENRY STEBBING. NEW YORK: APPLETON AND CO, 1850.

PAGE 201. APHRA BEHN. "LOVE ARM'D," 1684. *WORKS OF APHRA BEHN*. ED. MONTAGUE SUMMERS. LONDON: W. HEINEMANN, 1915.

PAGE 203. JANE BARKER. *LOVE INTRIGUES*, 1713. EDITED BY GERARD P. NECASTRO. THE PRIMAVERA PRESS, 2013.

PAGE 206. ALEXANDER POPE. *AN ESSAY ON MAN*, 1733 – 34. ED. MARK PATTISON. OXFORD: CLERENDON PRESS, 1879.

PAGE 214. THOMAS JEFFERSON. THE DECLARATION OF INDEPENDENCE, 1776. WIKISOURCE.

PAGE 218. WILLIAM BLAKE. "THE TYGER." FROM *SONGS OF EXPERIENCE*. 1794. *THE POEMS OF WILLIAM BLAKE: COMPRISING SONGS OF INNOCENCE AND OF EXPERIENCE*. ED. R. H. SHEPHERD. LONDON: PICKERING AND CHATTO, 1887.

PAGE 219. WILLIAM BLAKE. "AND DID THOSE FEET IN ANCIENT TIME." FROM *SONGS OF EXPERIENCE*. 1808. *THE POEMS OF WILLIAM BLAKE: COMPRISING SONGS OF INNOCENCE AND OF EXPERIENCE*. ED. R. H. SHEPHERD. LONDON: PICKERING AND CHATTO, 1887.

PAGE 219. WILLIAM BLAKE. "LONDON." FROM *SONGS OF EXPERIENCE*. 1794. *THE POEMS OF WILLIAM BLAKE: COMPRISING SONGS OF INNOCENCE AND OF EXPERIENCE*. ED. R. H. SHEPHERD. LONDON: PICKERING AND CHATTO, 1887.

PAGE 221. MARY WOLLSTONECRAFT. *A VINDICATION OF THE RIGHTS OF WOMEN*, 1792. NEW YORK: A. J. MATSELL, 1833.

PAGE 226. WILLIAM WORDSWORTH. "LINES COMPOSED A FEW MILES ABOVE TINTERN ABBEY, 1798. *LYRICAL BALLADS, WITH A FEW OTHER POEMS*. LONDON: J. & A. ARCH, 1798.

PAGE 231. PERCY BYSSHE SHELLEY. "OZYMANDIUS," 1821. THE COMPLETE POETICAL WORKS OF PERCY BYSSHE SHELLEY. ED. THOMAS HUTCHINSON. NEW YORK: OXFORD UP, 1914.

PAGE 232. PERCY BYSSHE SHELLEY. *A DEFENCE OF POETRY*, 1840. *A DEFECE OF POETRY*. PORTLAND, ME: T. B. MOSHER, 1910.

PAGE 233. JOHN KEATS. "ODE ON A GRECIAN URN," 1820. *OXFORD BOOK OF ENGLISH VERSE*. ED. ARTHUR THOMAS QUILLER-COUCH. OXFORD: CLARENDON, 1919.

PAGE 235. JOHN KEATS. "*LA BELLE DAME SANS MERCI*," 1819. *OXFORD BOOK OF ENGLISH VERSE*. ED. ARTHUR THOMAS QUILLER-COUCH. OXFORD: CLARENDON, 1919.

PAGE 237. CHARLES DARWIN. *THE ORIGIN OF THE SPECIES*, 1859. NEW YORK: COLLIER, 1909.

PAGE 241. ALFRED LORD TENNYSON. "ULYSSES." *POEMS*, 2 VOLS. BOSTON: W. D. TICKNOR, 1842.

PAGE 244. KARL MARX AND FRIEDRICH ENGELS. *COMMUNIST MANIFESTO*, 1848. TRANSLATED BY SAMUEL MOORE. CHICAGO: CHARLES, H. KERR & CO, 1910.

PAGE 249. FYODOR DOSTOYEVSKY. THE GRAND INQUISITOR, FROM *THE BROTHERS KARAMAZOV*, 1880. TRANSLATED BY CONSTANCE GARNETT. NEW YORK: LOWELL PRESS, 1911.

PAGE 264. FRIEDRICH NIETZSCHE. *THE JOYFUL WISDOM* 1882. TRANSLATED BY THOMAS COMMON. NEW YORK: THE MACMILLAN COMPANY, 1910.

PAGE 266. GUY DE MAUPASSANT. "THE NECKLACE" 1884. IN *STORIES BY FOREIGN AUTHORS*. TRANSLATED BY JONATHAN STURGES. NEW YORK: HARPER & BROTHERS. COPYRIGHT, 1889.

PAGE 273. SIGMUND FREUD. LECTURE ON THE GENERAL THEORY OF NEUROSES. FROM *A GENERAL INTRODUCTION TO PSYCHO-ANALYSIS*. TRANSLATED BY G. STANLEY HALL. NEW YORK: HARACE LIVERIGHT, INC., 1920.

PAGE 275. CHARLOTTE PERKINS GILMAN. "THE YELLOW WALLPAPER," 1892. BOSTON: SMALL, MAYNARD, & CO. 1901

PAGE 288. THOMAS STERNS ELIOT. "THE LOVE SONG OF J. ALFRED PRUFROCK," 1917. *PRUFROCK AND OTHER OBSERVATIONS*. LONDON: THE EGOIST, 1917.

PAGE 293. WILFRED OWEN. *DULCE ET DECORUM EST*, 1920. *POEMS*. LONDON: CHATTO & WINDUS, 1920.

PAGE 295. GERTRUDE STEIN. "PORTRAIT OF PICASSO." ORIGINALLY PUBLISHED IN *CAMERA WORLD,* AUGUST, 1912.

PAGE 298. FRED ROGERS. VARIOUS QUOTES. VARIOUS SOURCES.

IMAGES

Unless otherwise noted, all images are from Wikimedia.

PAGE 1. DETAIL OF MICHELANGELO'S' *CREATION OF ADAM* FRESCO ON THE SISTINE CHAPEL CEILING, 1508-12.

COVER IMAGES
TOP ROW
AUGUSTE RENOIR. *MOULIN DE LA GALETTE.*
JAN VERMEER. *THE CONCERT.*
WILLIAM BLAKE. *A MIDSUMMER NIGHT'S DREAM.*
CARAVAGGIO (MICHELANGELO MERISI). *THE CALLING OF SAINT MATTHEW.*
JAN VAN EYCK. *THE ARNOLFINI MARRIAGE.*

SECOND ROW
PARMIGIANINO (GIROLAMO MAZZOLA). *MADONNA WITH THE LONG NECK.*
JACQUES-LOUIS DAVID. *OATH OF THE HORATII.*
GIANLORENZO BERNINI. *SAINT TERESA IN ECSTASY.*
EDGAR DEGAS. *FOUR DANCERS.*
EDVARD MUNCH. *THE SCREAM.*

THIRD ROW
EUGÈNE DELACROIX. *LIBERTY LEADING THE PEOPLE.*
GEORGES SEURAT. *A SUNDAY AFTERNOON ON THE ISLAND OF LA GRANDE JATTE.*
DIEGO VELÁZQUEZ. *LAS MENINAS (THE HANDMAIDS).*
VINCENT VAN GOGH. *STARRY NIGHT.*

BOTTOM ROW
ANTOINE WATTEAU. *GERSAINT'S SIGNBOARD.*
REMBRANDT VAN RIJN. *THE SHOOTING COMPANY OF FRANS BANNING COCQ (THE NIGHT WATCH).*
CLAUDE MONET. *MADAME MONET IN A JAPANESE COSTUME,*
EL GRECO (DOMENIKOS THEOTOKÓPOULOS). *THE BURIAL OF COUNT ORGAZ.*

ABOUT THE EDITOR

Gerard NeCastro is Professor of English at The University of Maine at Machias and Visiting Professor of English at The University of Maine. He teaches courses in Humanities, Creative Writing, Theater History, World Literature, Art History, Latin, Shakespeare, and Chaucer. He is the long-term editor of *The Binnacle: The Literary Journal of Coastal Maine.*. After years of short stories, poems, academic writing, and translations, he has completed his first novel, *Columbine AS3*.

ALSO AVAILABLE FROM THE PRIMAVERA PRESS

A Rump-Sprung Chair and a One-Eyed Cat: Poems by Down East Maine's Salt
  Coast Sages
      Poems by M. Kelly Lombardi, Sharon Bray, Donald Crane, Gerald
        George, Philip Rose, and Grace Sheridan
      Edited by M. Kelly Lombardi

Book of the Duchess
      Geoffrey Chaucer
      Edited and Translated by Gerard P. NeCastro

Double Double: Tales of the Double
      Tales by Chaucer, Conrad, Dostoevsky, James, Melville, Poe, and
        Salvia
      Edited by Gerard P. NeCastro

The Essential Chaucer Reader: Selected Writings of Geoffrey Chaucer
      Edited and Translated by Gerard P. NeCastro

Jack in the Cracks, A Memoir
      Jack Dennis

King Arthur and the Knights of the Round Table
      Blanche Winder's revision of the original anonymous Stories of King
      Arthur, newly revised, updated, and edited by Gerard P. NeCastro and
      Maria T. NeCastro

Troilus and Criseyde
      Geoffrey Chaucer
      Edited and Translated by Gerard P. NeCastro

The Primavera Press invites proposals for publications by authors, especially
of certain varieties: 1. poets who have published volumes of poetry and would
like to publish e-book reprints; 2. writers of tales of or about ancient times,
especially books for young readers; and 3. authors of memoirs.

All of our titles are now available through Amazon on Kindle. Several of
them are now available in print, and all of them will be soon. For more
information on these and several other forthcoming titles, please visit us at
www.primaverapress.com.